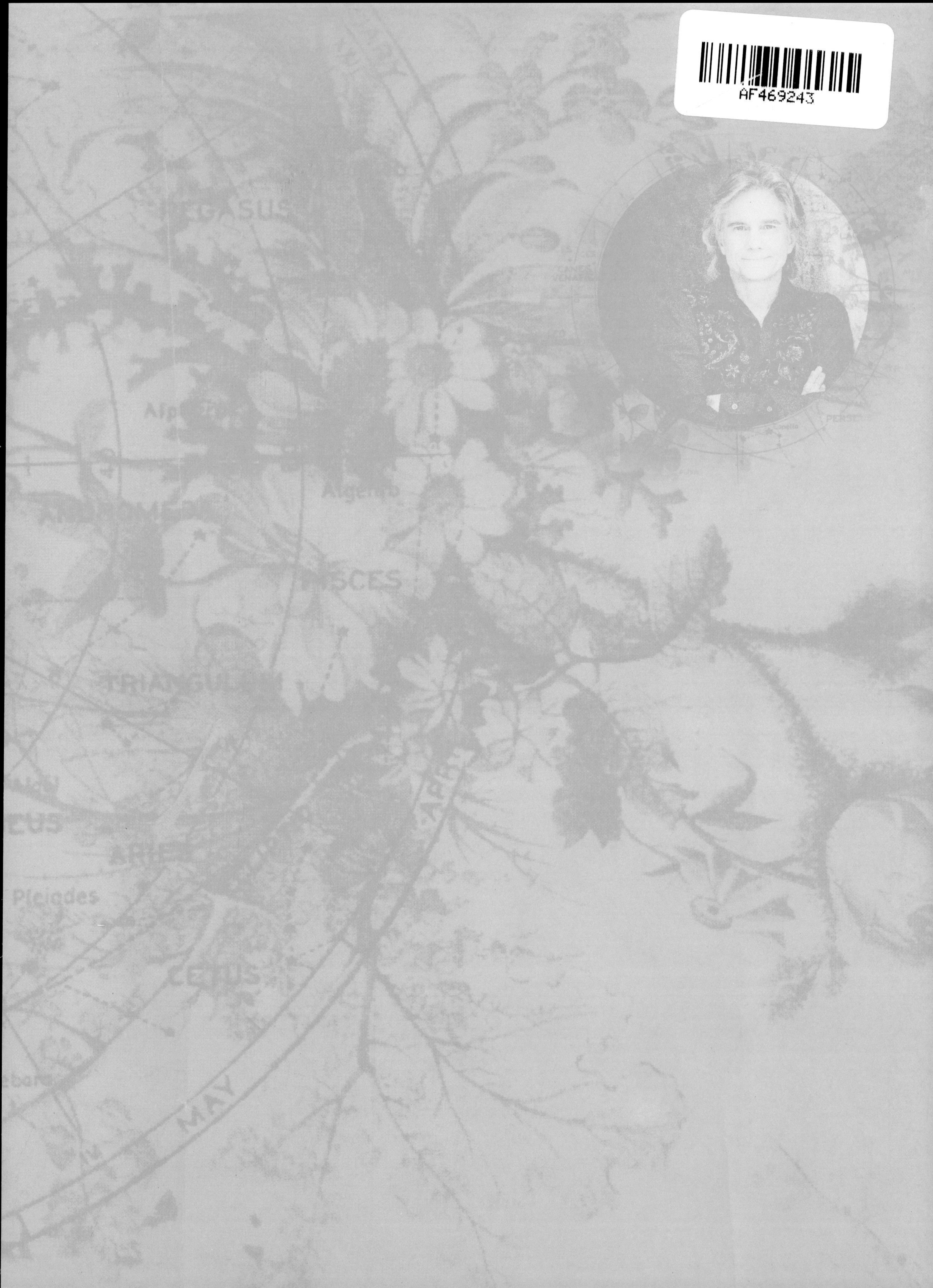
Pleiades
CETUS
MAY

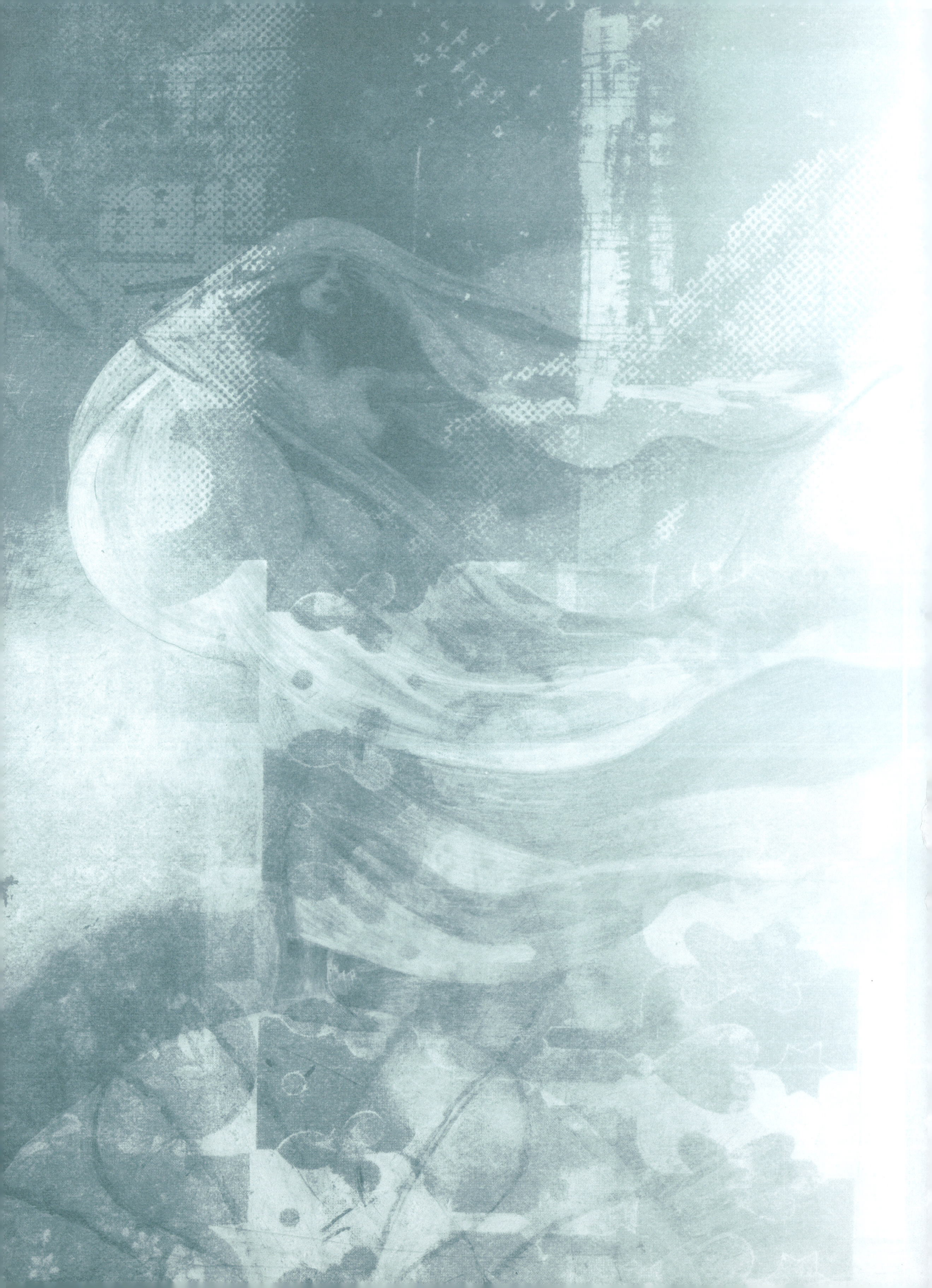

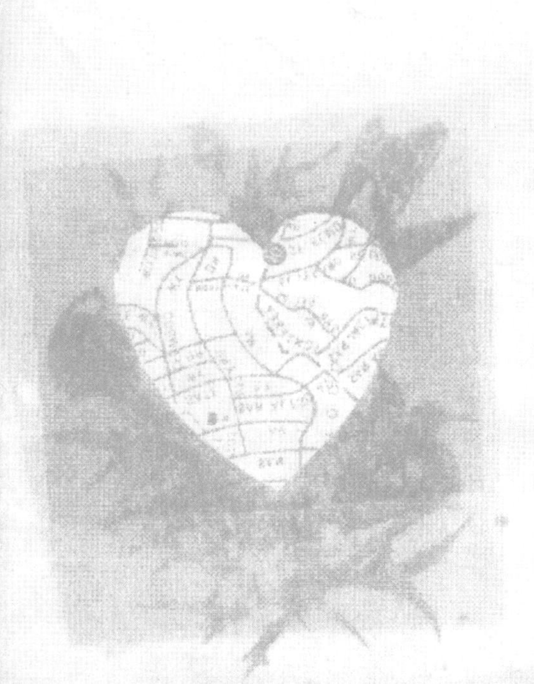

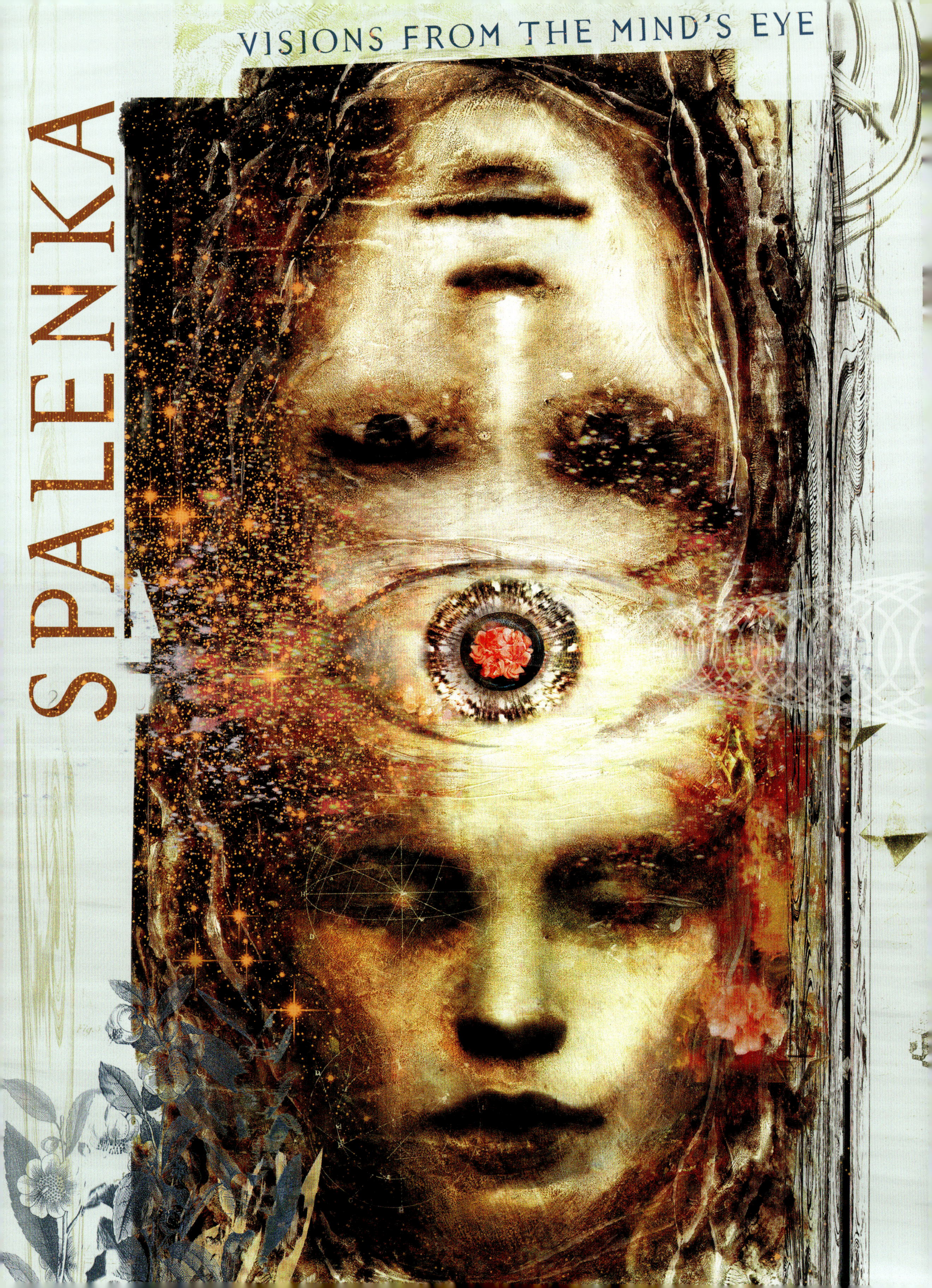
VISIONS FROM THE MIND'S EYE
SPALENKA

A heartfelt thank you goes out to my parents, family, friends and those individuals who believed in and supported my creative quest. I am blessed and sustained by everyone's love and encouragement. May I always be a pure channel of the art spirit.

table of contents

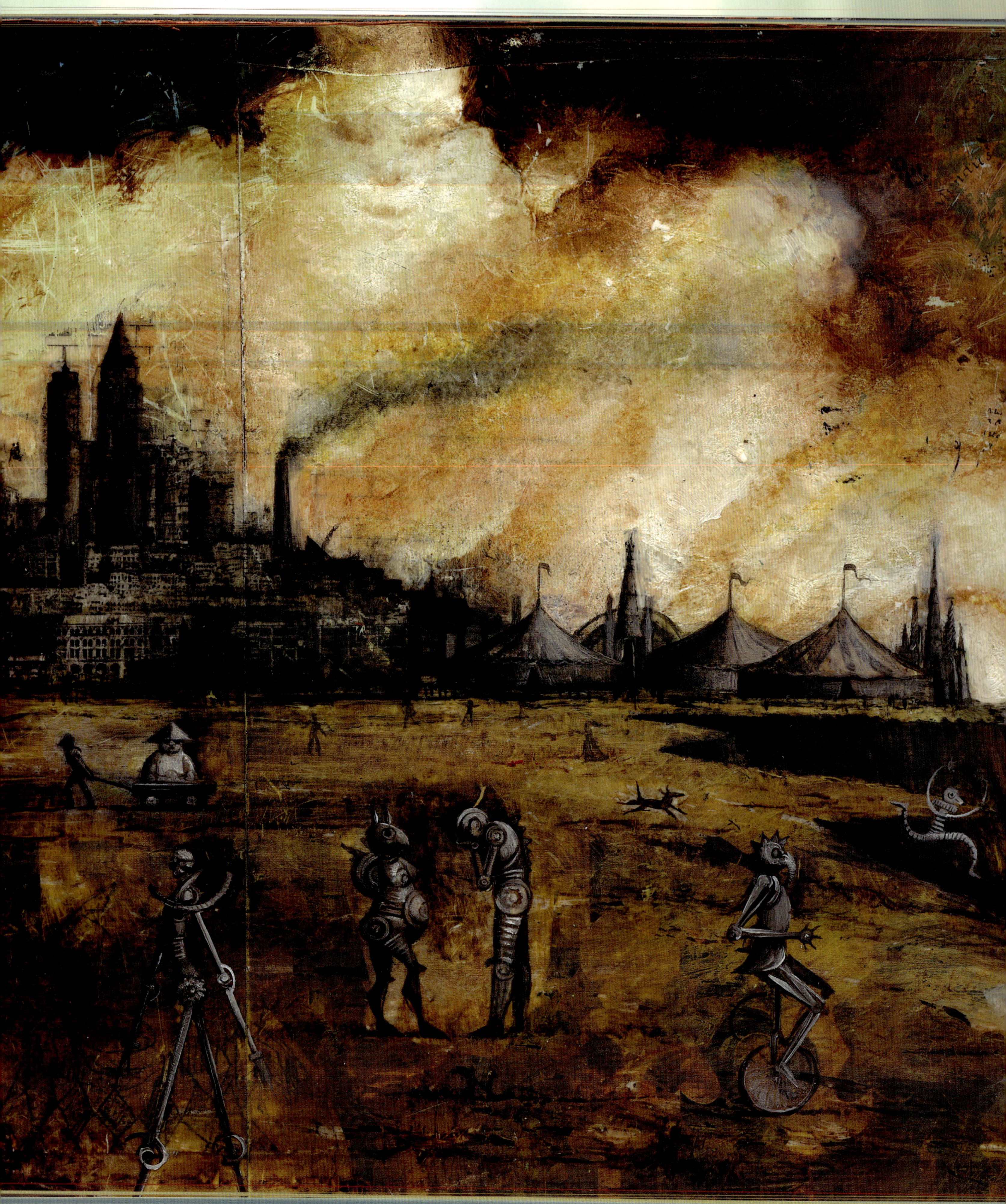

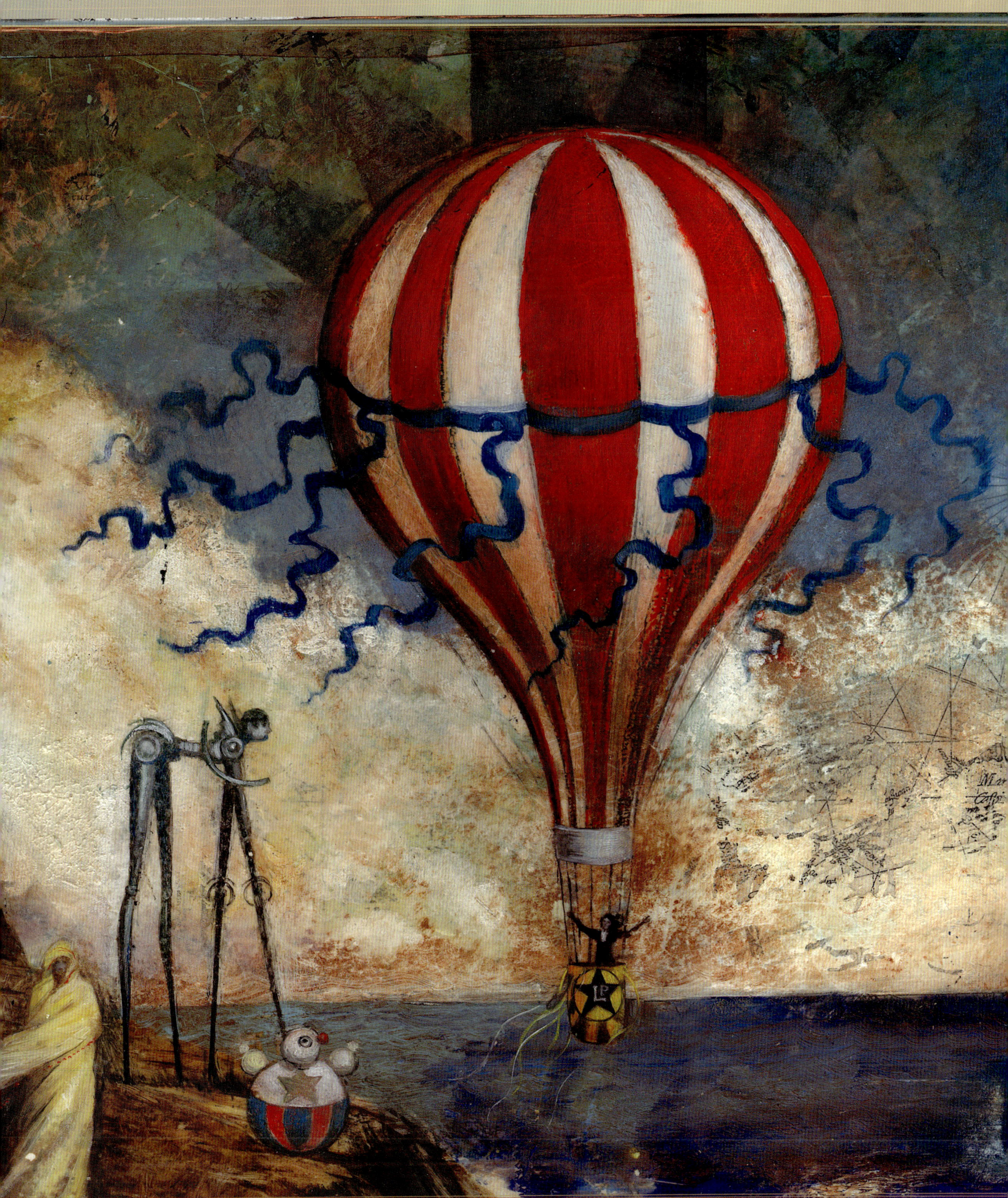

introduction

by Arnie Fenner

Andy Warhol once said, "An artist is somebody who produces things that people don't need to have." People tend to grind their teeth a bit when the quote is mentioned, but it's hard to argue that Warhol was wrong. Food, shelter, water, healthcare, security, transportation, social interaction...there's a lot of needs much higher on the list than a nice picture.

But that doesn't mean he was right, either.

Because when you stop and think about it, art – and by extension, the artist – is essential.

Art is communication; art is history; art is a record; art is an expression of thought and emotion; art is the ethereal given form. Art reflects both our virtues and our failings, our foolishness and our nobility. Art is what makes us human. Artists are our guides...and often, our conscious. They're the pathfinders and trailblazers; they're the conservators and the commentators. I've often said that artists are on a journey of discovery and we're fortunate that they take us with them on their voyages.

So I consider myself lucky to have followed Greg Spalenka along the many paths his career has taken through the decades. The tool he uses – paint, charcoal, collage, photography, and digital software – has never mattered to him as much as the creative challenges he faced. Whether he was chronicling the rise of heavyweight boxer Mike Tyson, painting portraits of contemporary artists, illustrating countless magazine articles, ad campaigns, and book covers, or designing the visual language for films, Greg has always produced work that rewards both the intellect and the soul. Perhaps the latter is one of the most unique aspects to Greg Spalenka's art: there is a spiritual subtext to his work that is deeply felt without ever devolving into dogma. If there's any preachiness to be found in his work (New Age or otherwise), it is a subtle belief in people and in nature. A belief in appreciating beauty, a belief in the import or having a sense of wonder.

Greg has been sharing his skills, his outlook, and his beliefs with students through his Artist As Brand® program in recent years rather than pursuing an already successful career as an illustrator. The concept of "giving back," not money, is paramount to him; helping artists learn how to empower themselves and master their artistic destinies is a message that resonates, particularly as markets evolve. Altruism may be a difficult concept for some to understand, but that doesn't bother him. He does what he does because he believes he should. As I said, artists take us on a journey: regardless of the destination, Greg always rewards his fellow voyagers at the end of the trip.

Yes, Andy Warhol was correct: we don't "need" art to survive.

But we definitely need art to live. And Greg Spalenka helps us, in the words of Emile Zola, to "live out loud." We couldn't ask for better.

Arnie Fenner

Arnie Fenner
Director Emeritus/Spectrum Fantastic Art

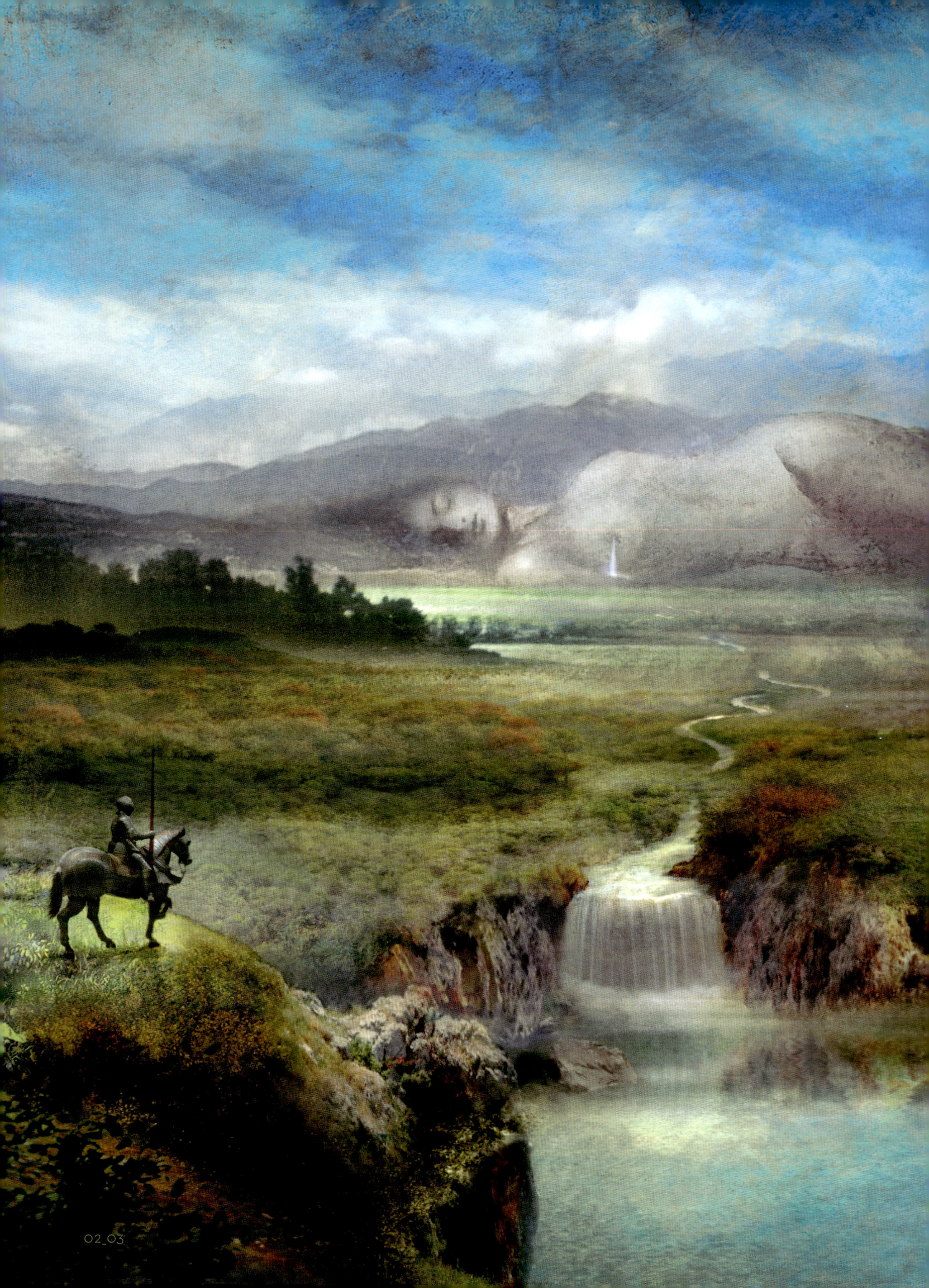

02_03

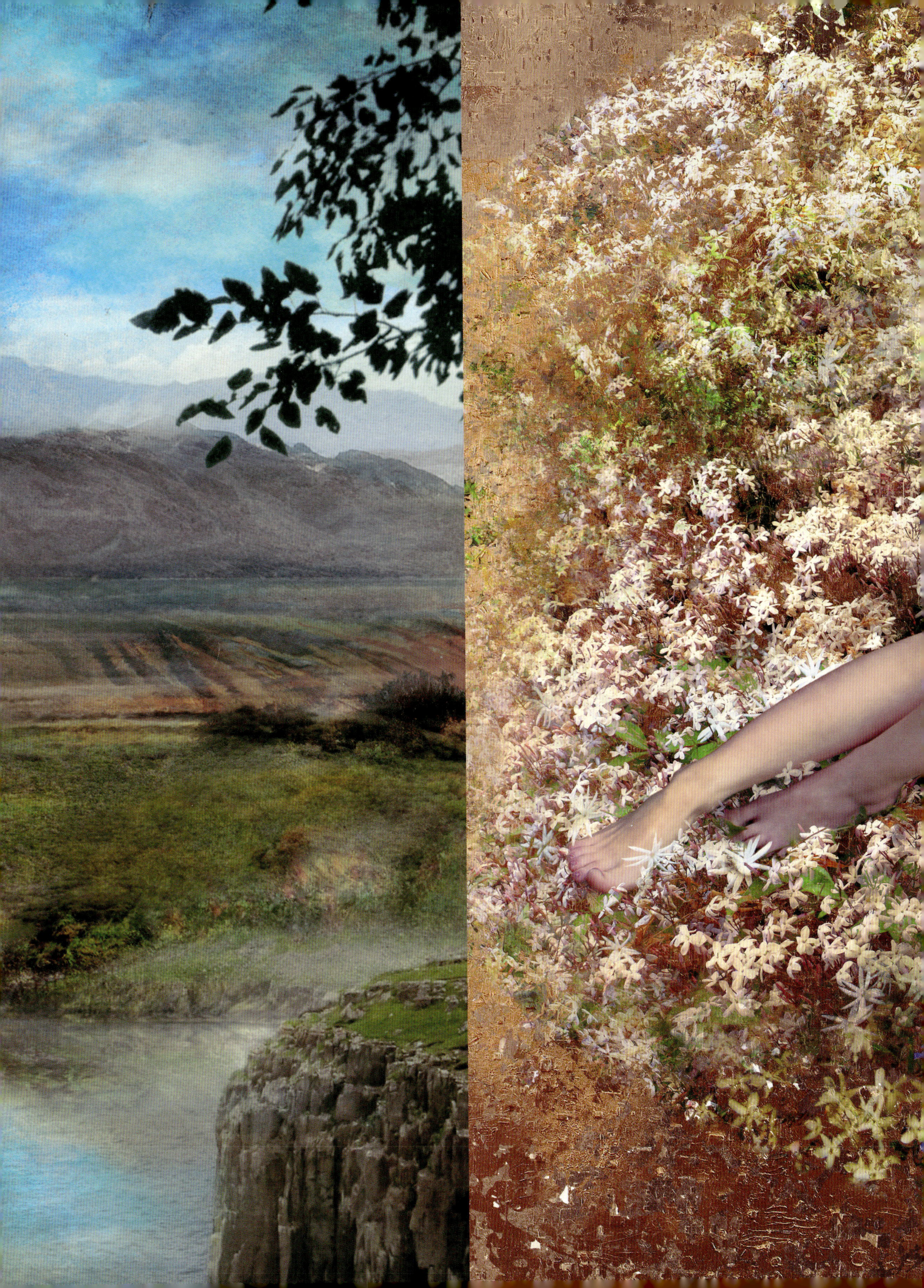

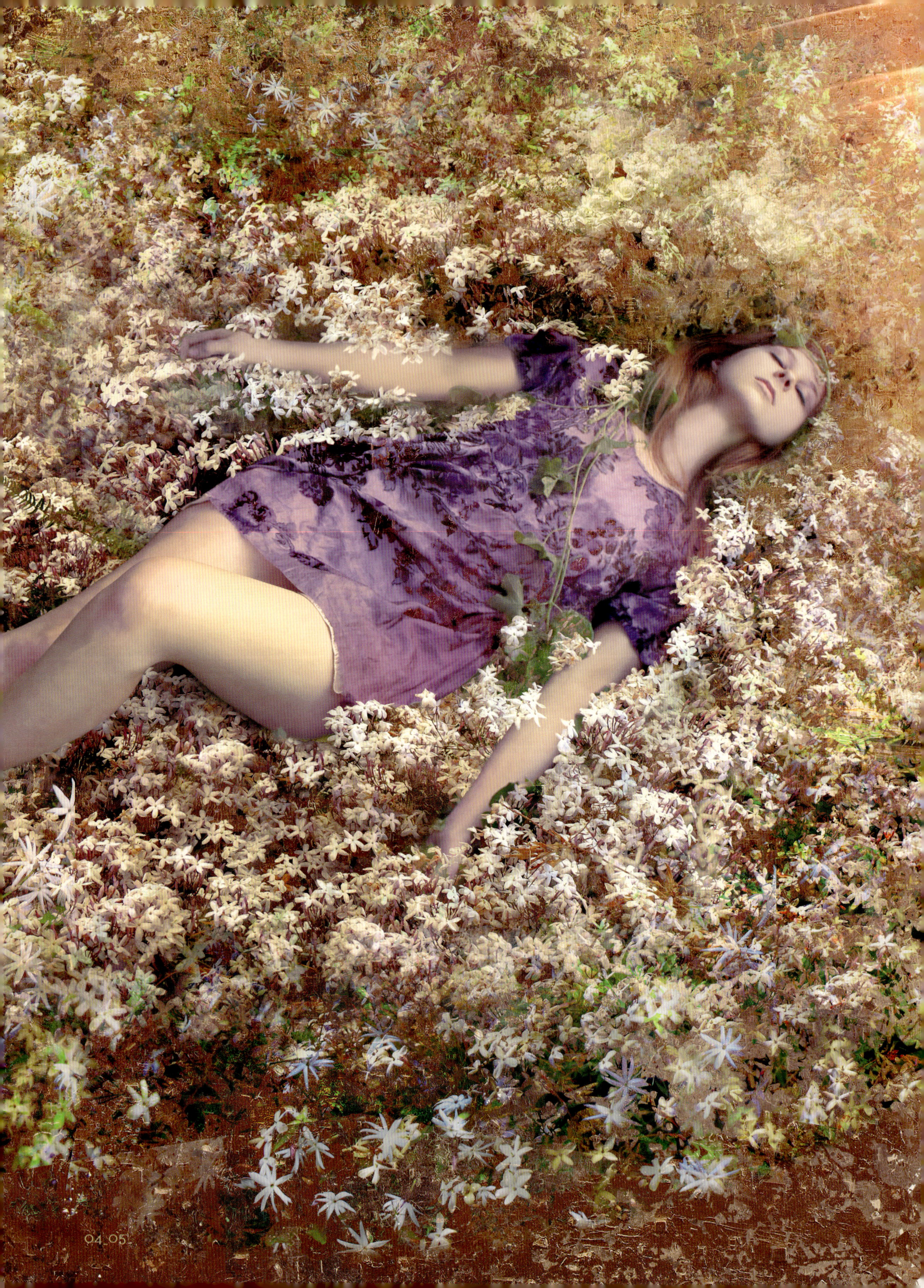

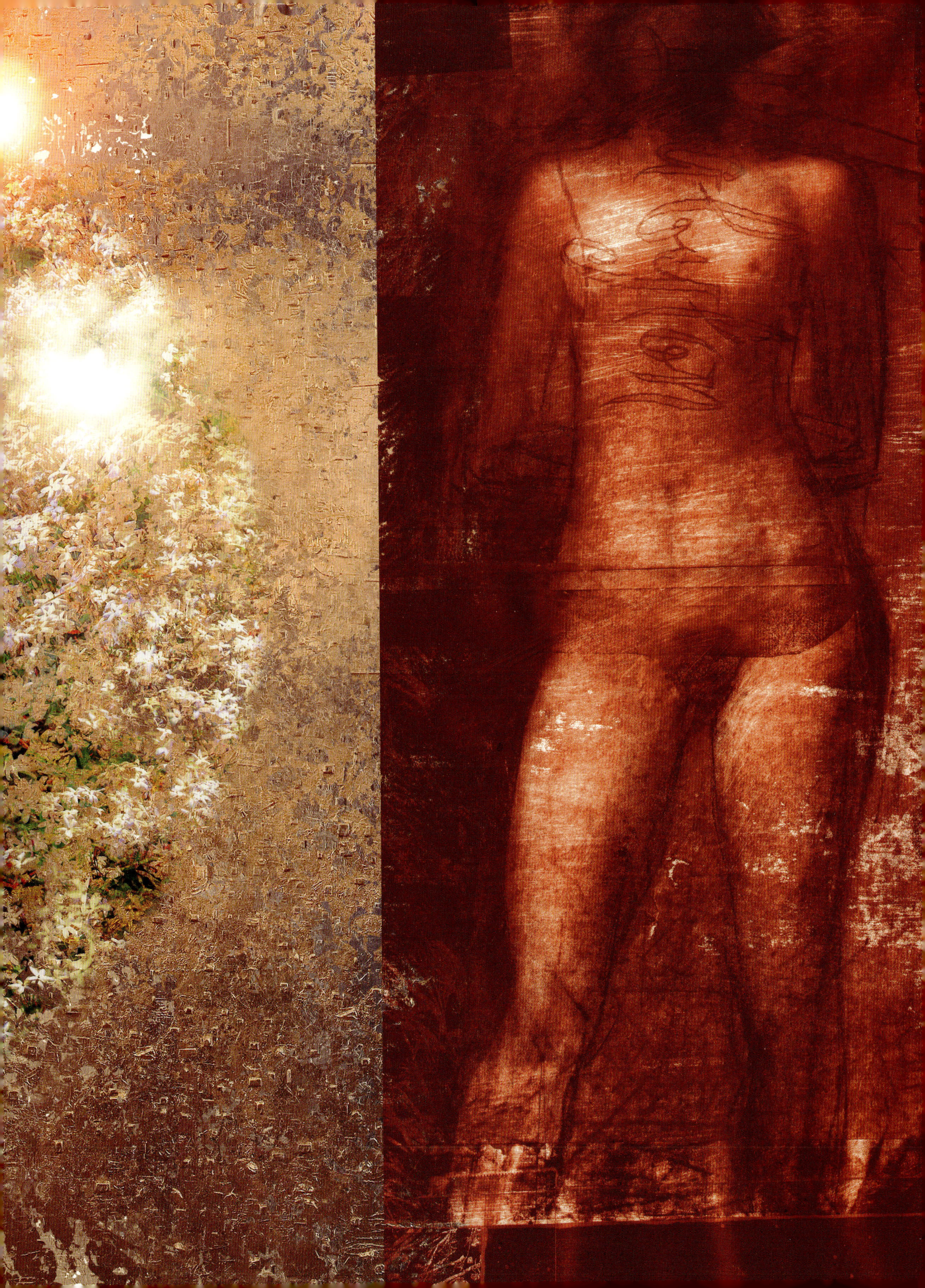

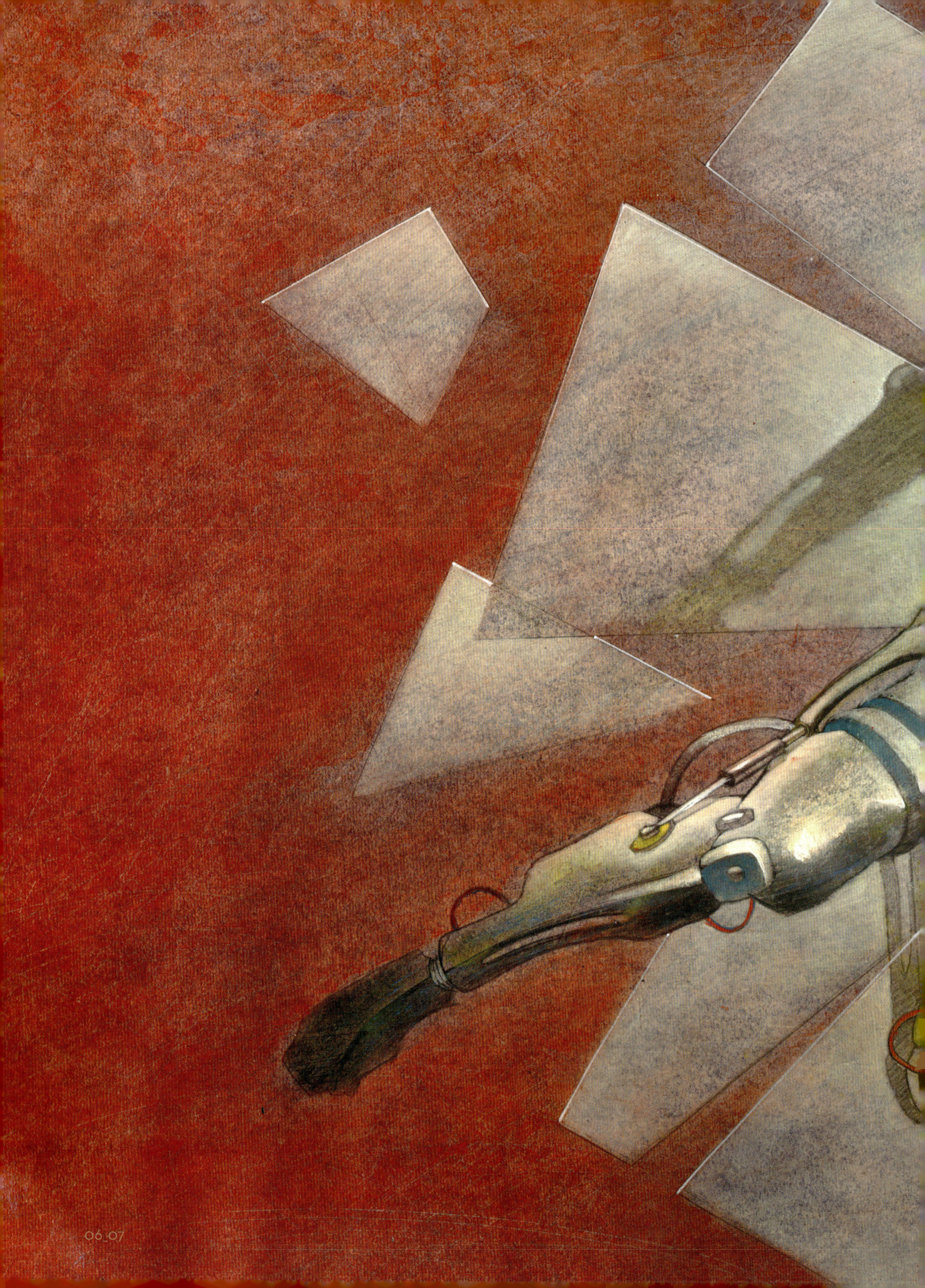

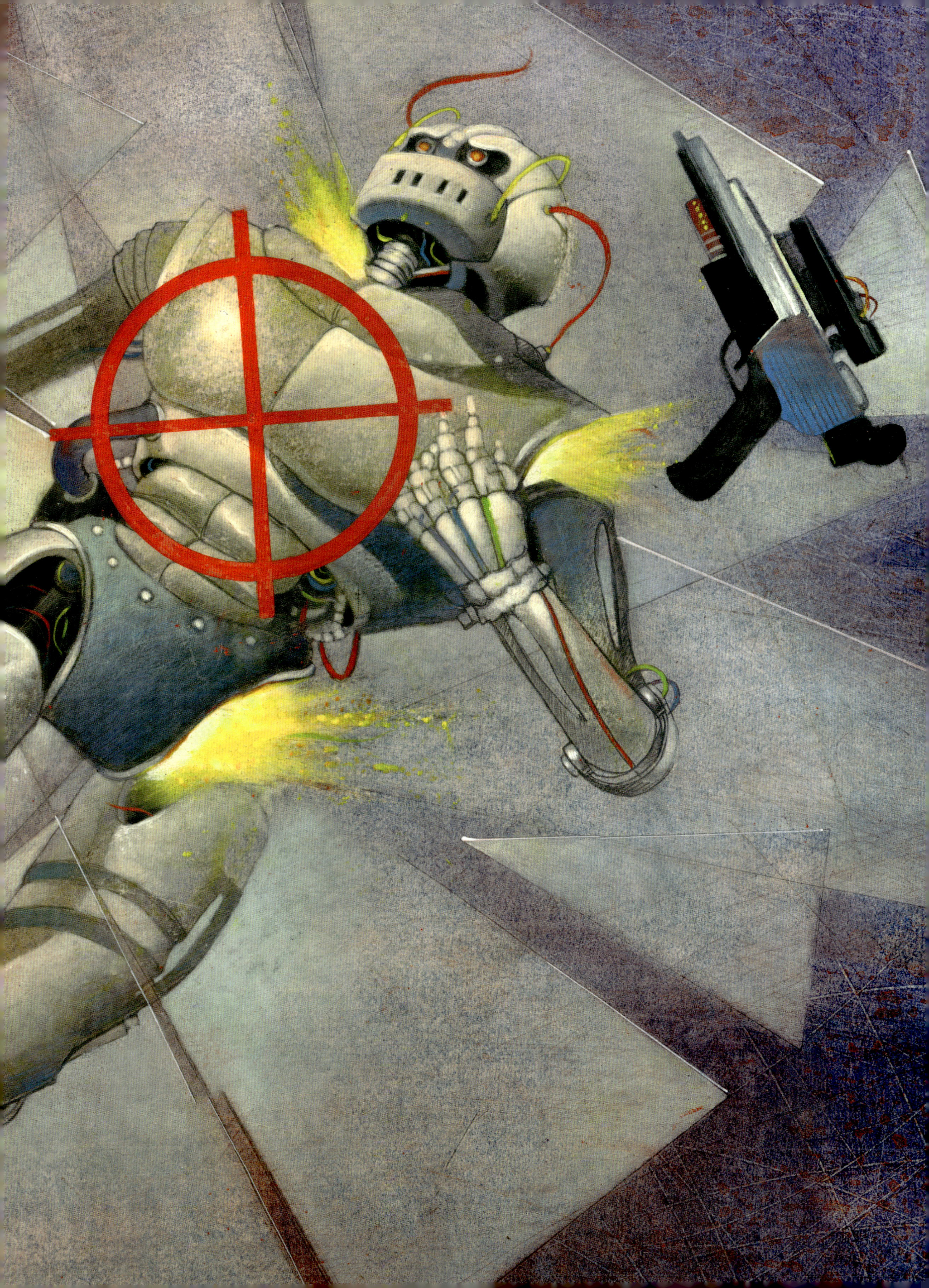

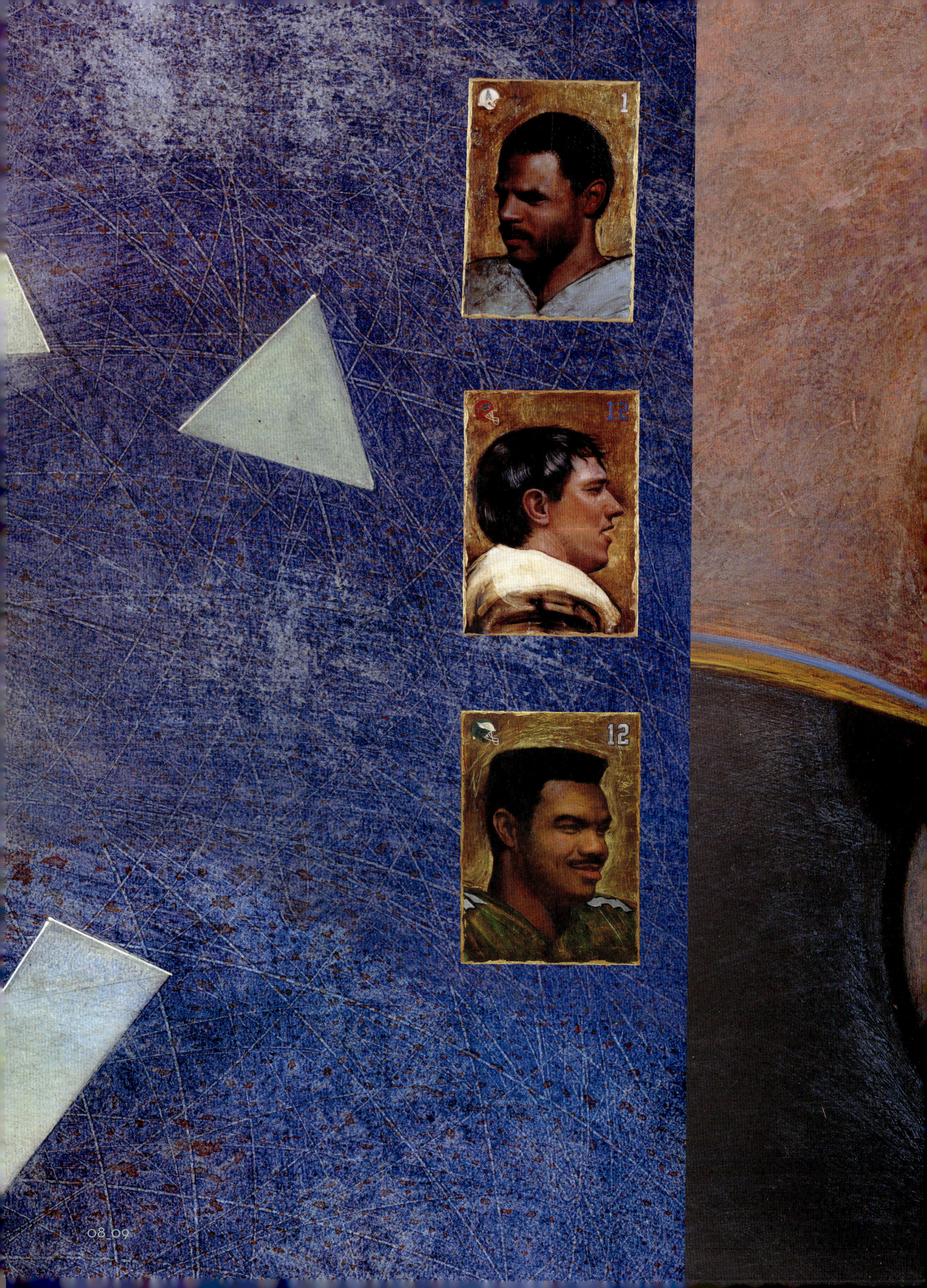
1
12
12

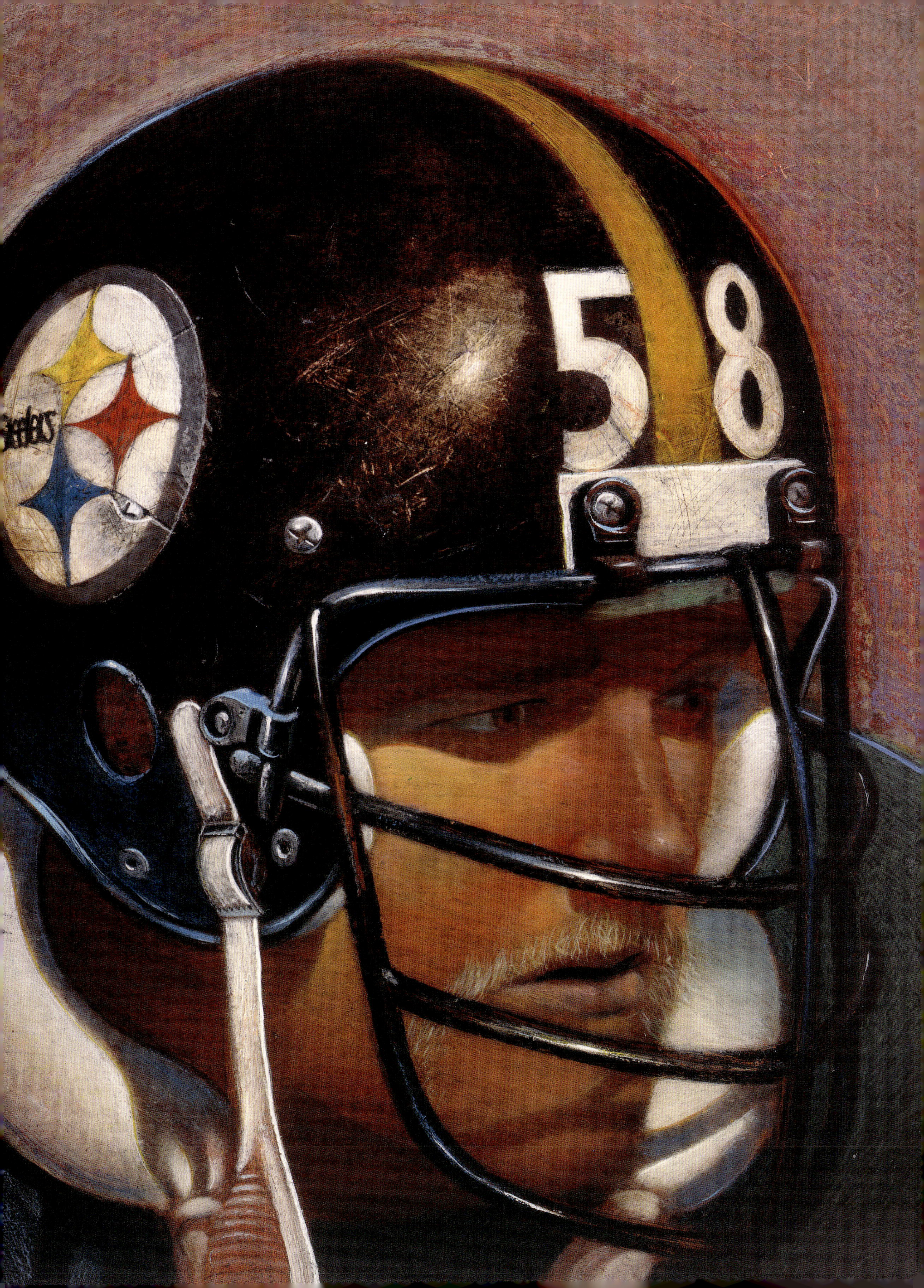
58
Steelers

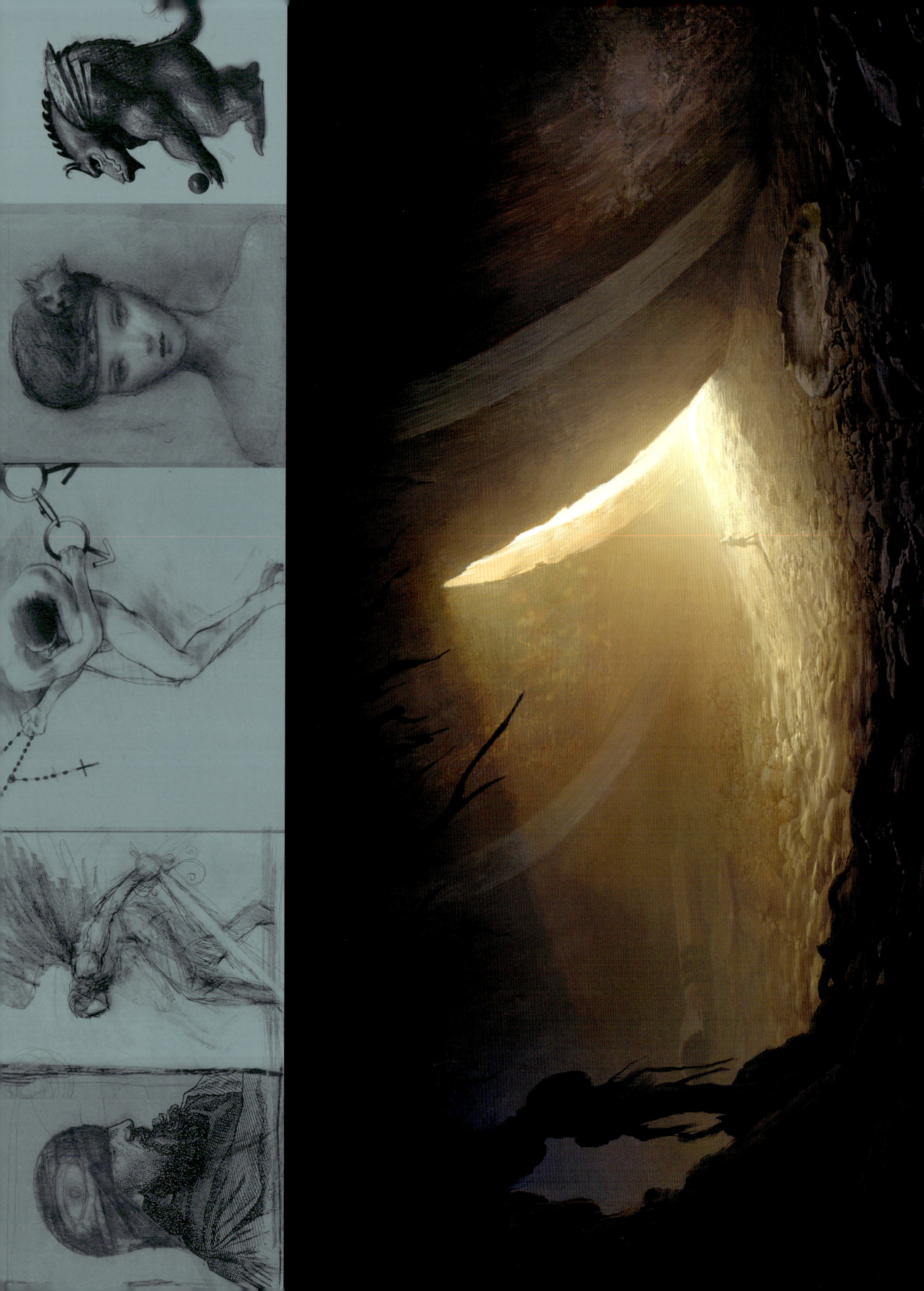

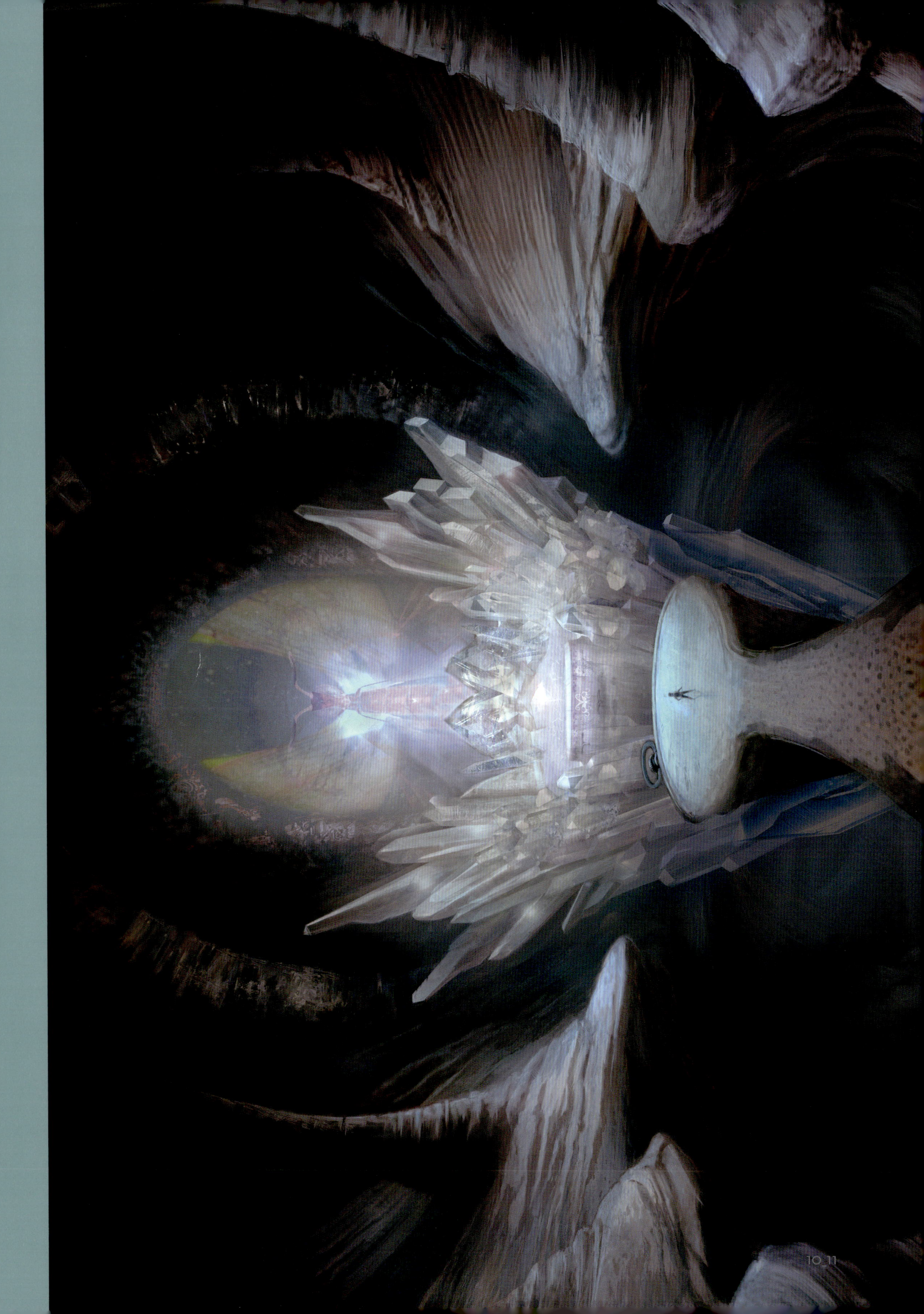

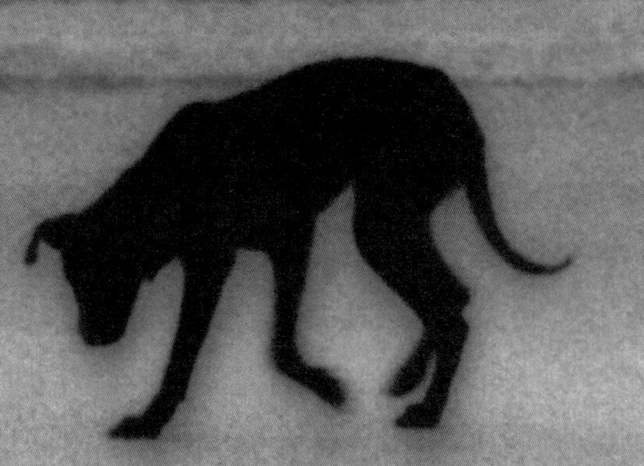

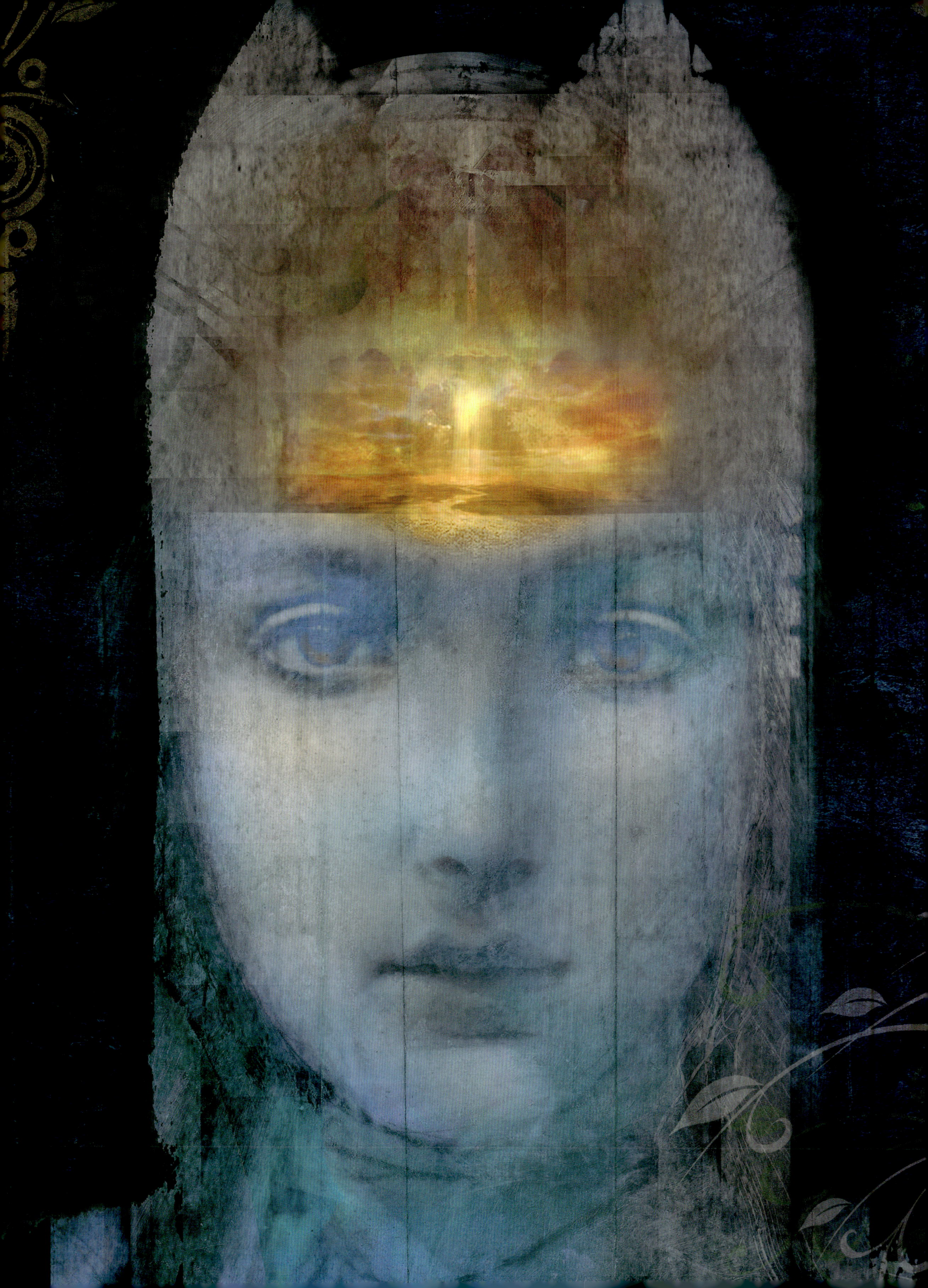

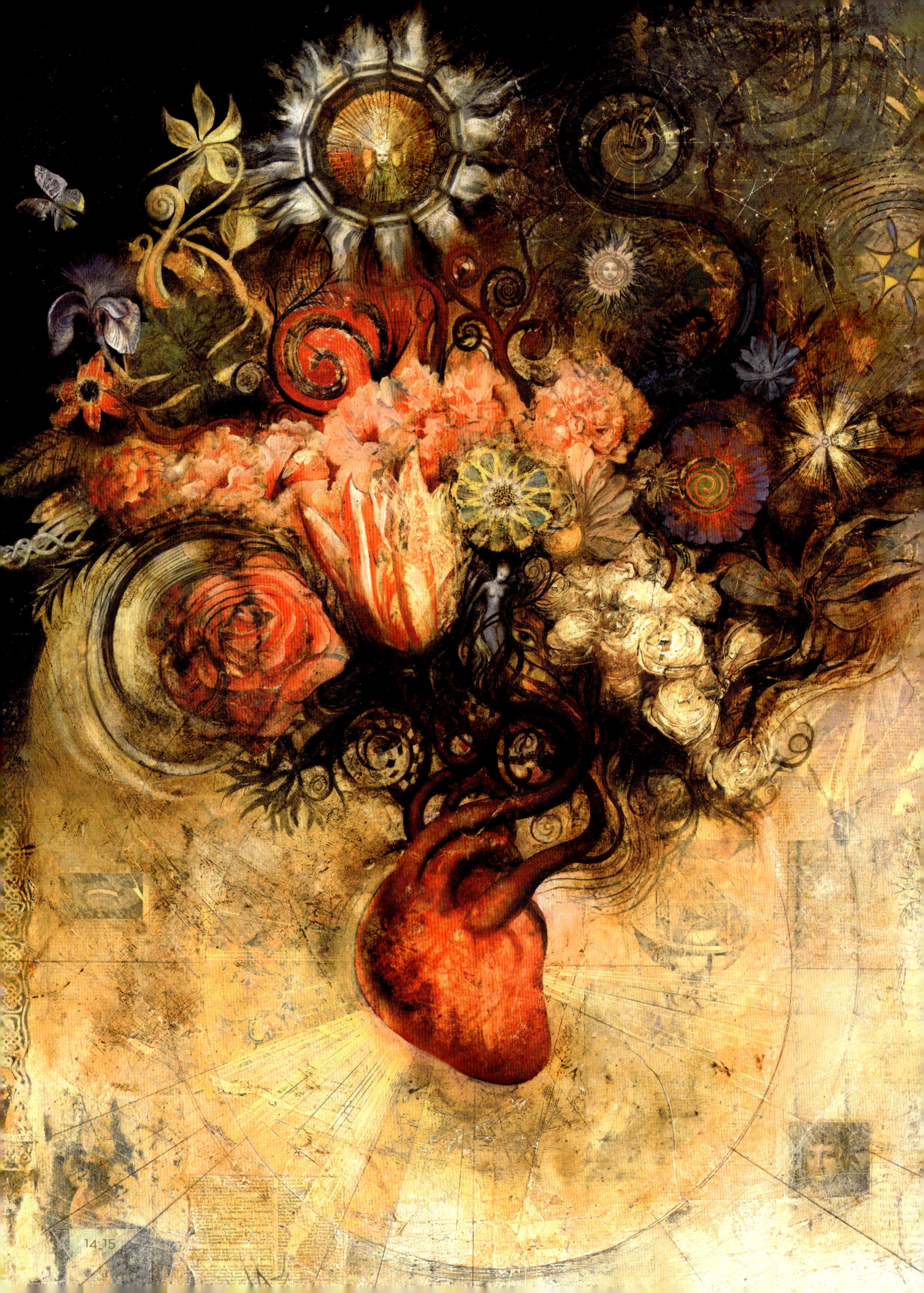

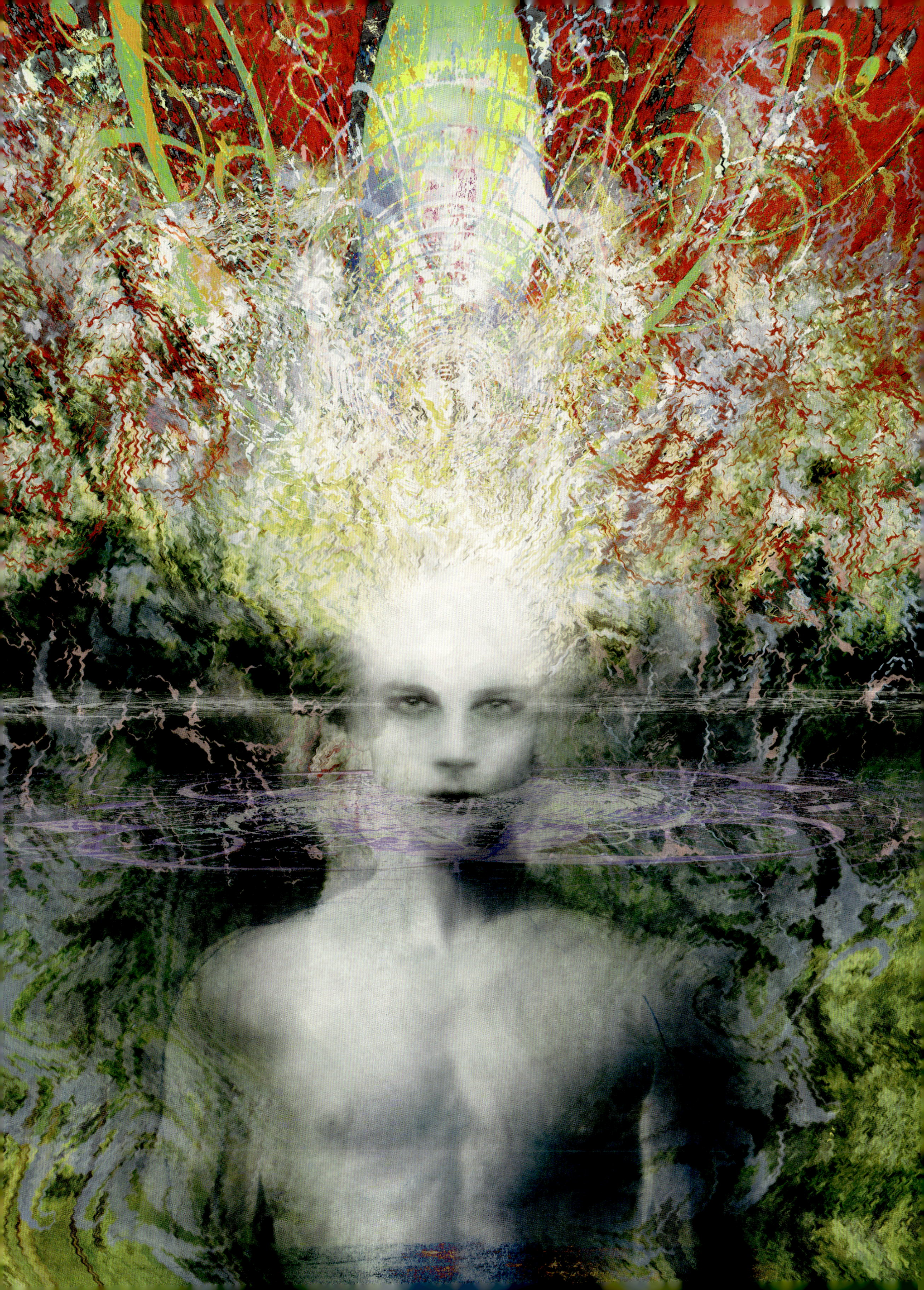

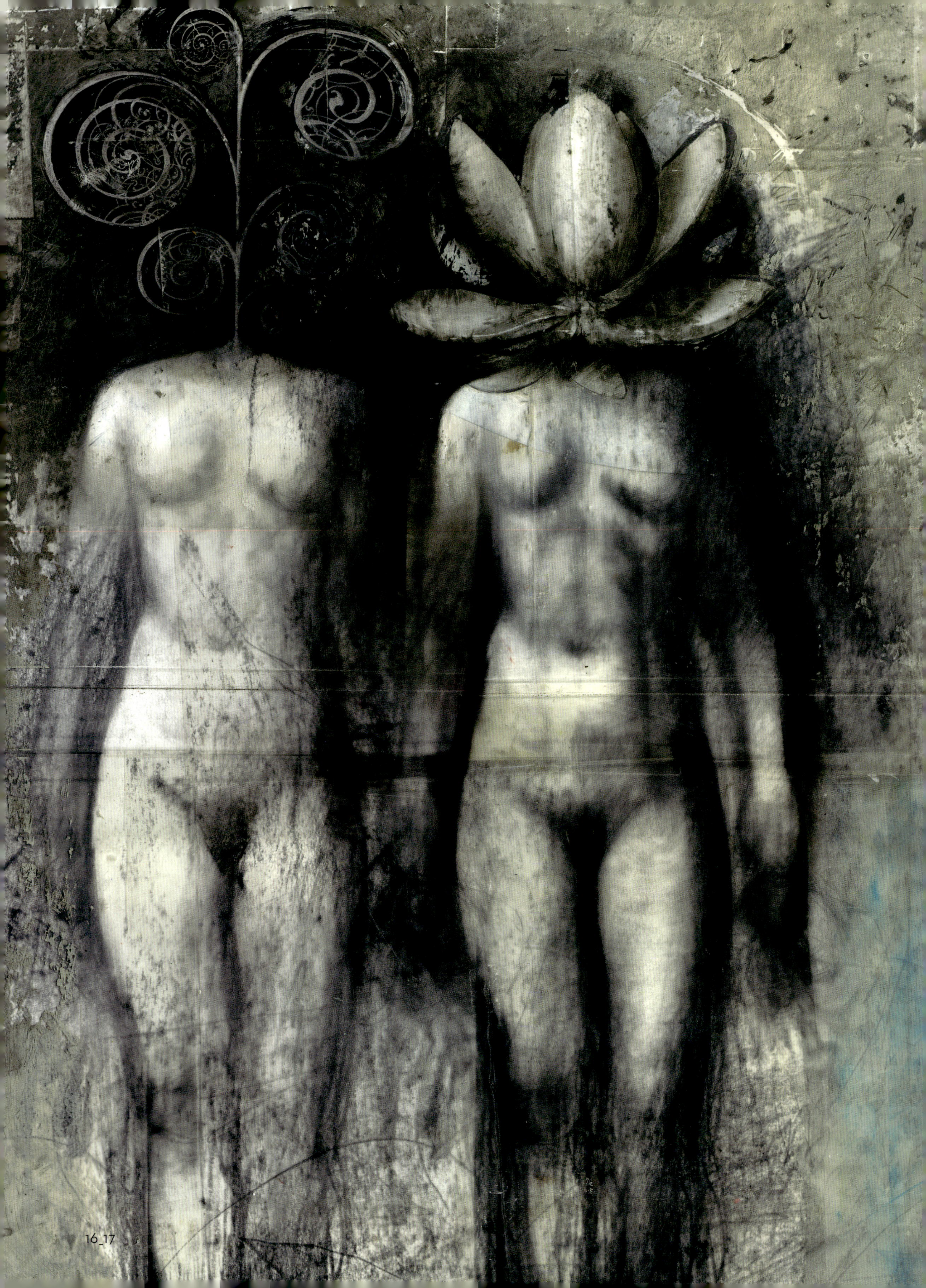

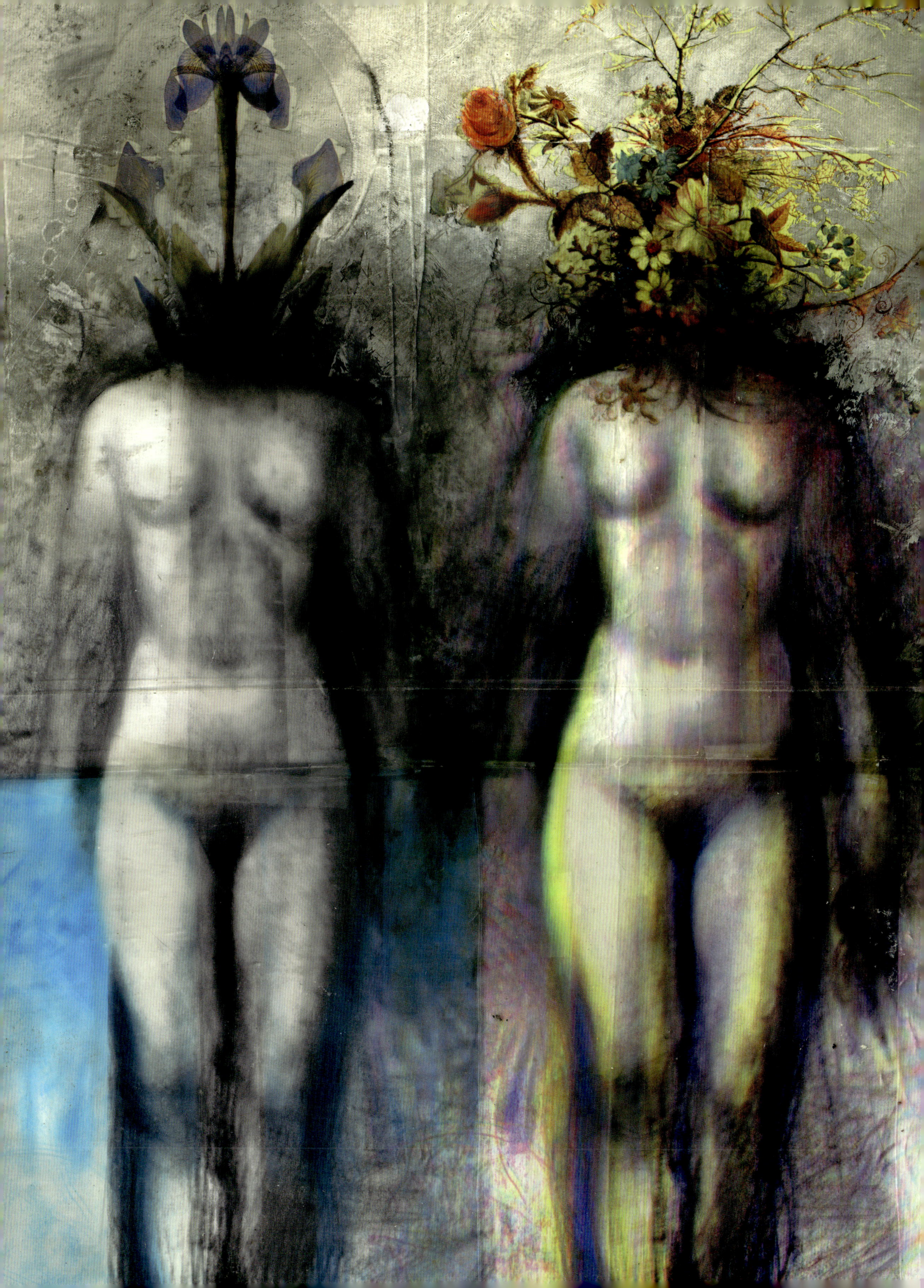

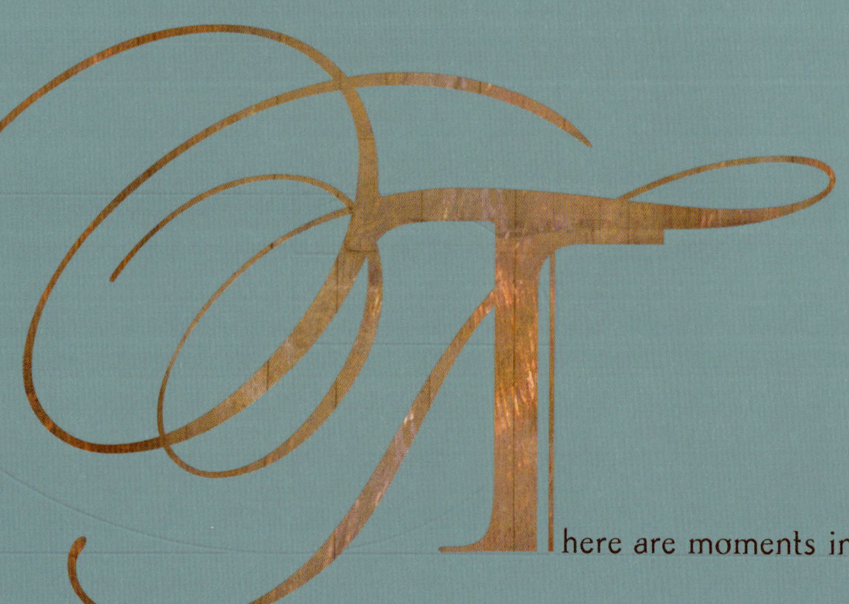

here are moments in our lives,

there are moments in a day,

when we seem to see beyond the usual.

Such are the moments of our greatest happiness.

Such are the moments of our greatest wisdom.

If one could but recall his vision by some sort of sign.

It was in this hope that the arts were invented.

Sign-posts on the way to what may be.

Sign-posts toward greater knowledge.

– ROBERT HENRI

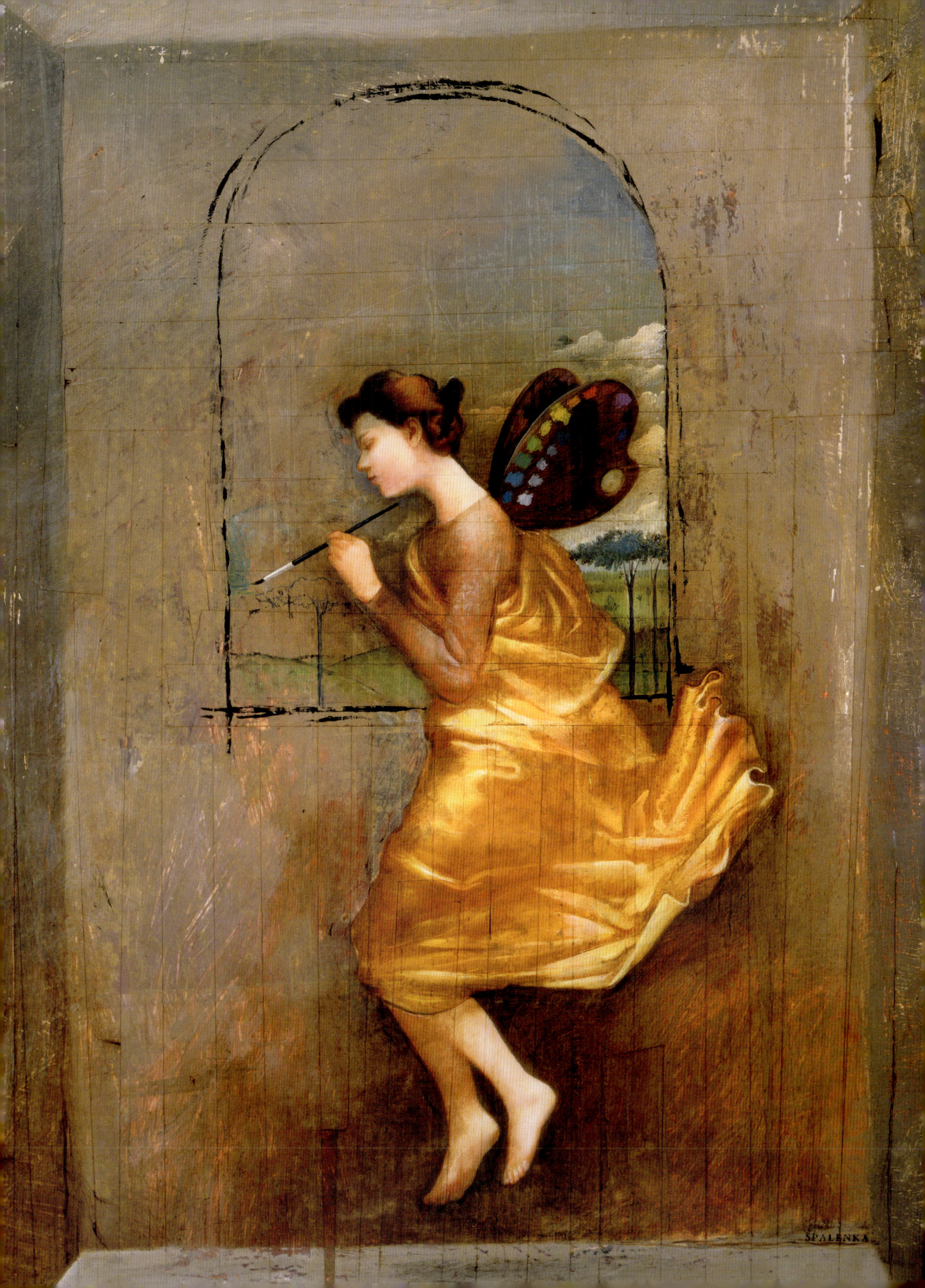
ŠPALENKA

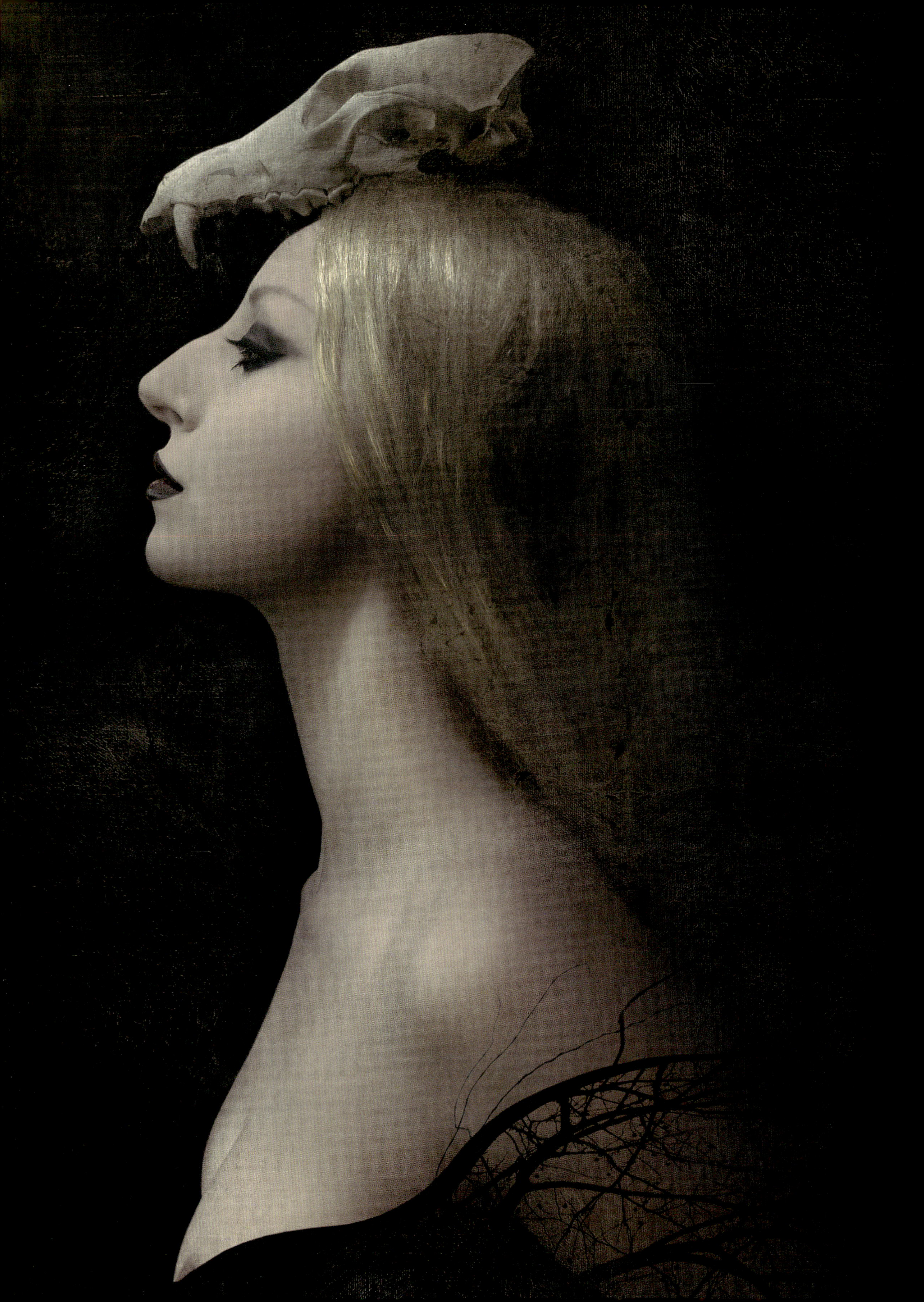

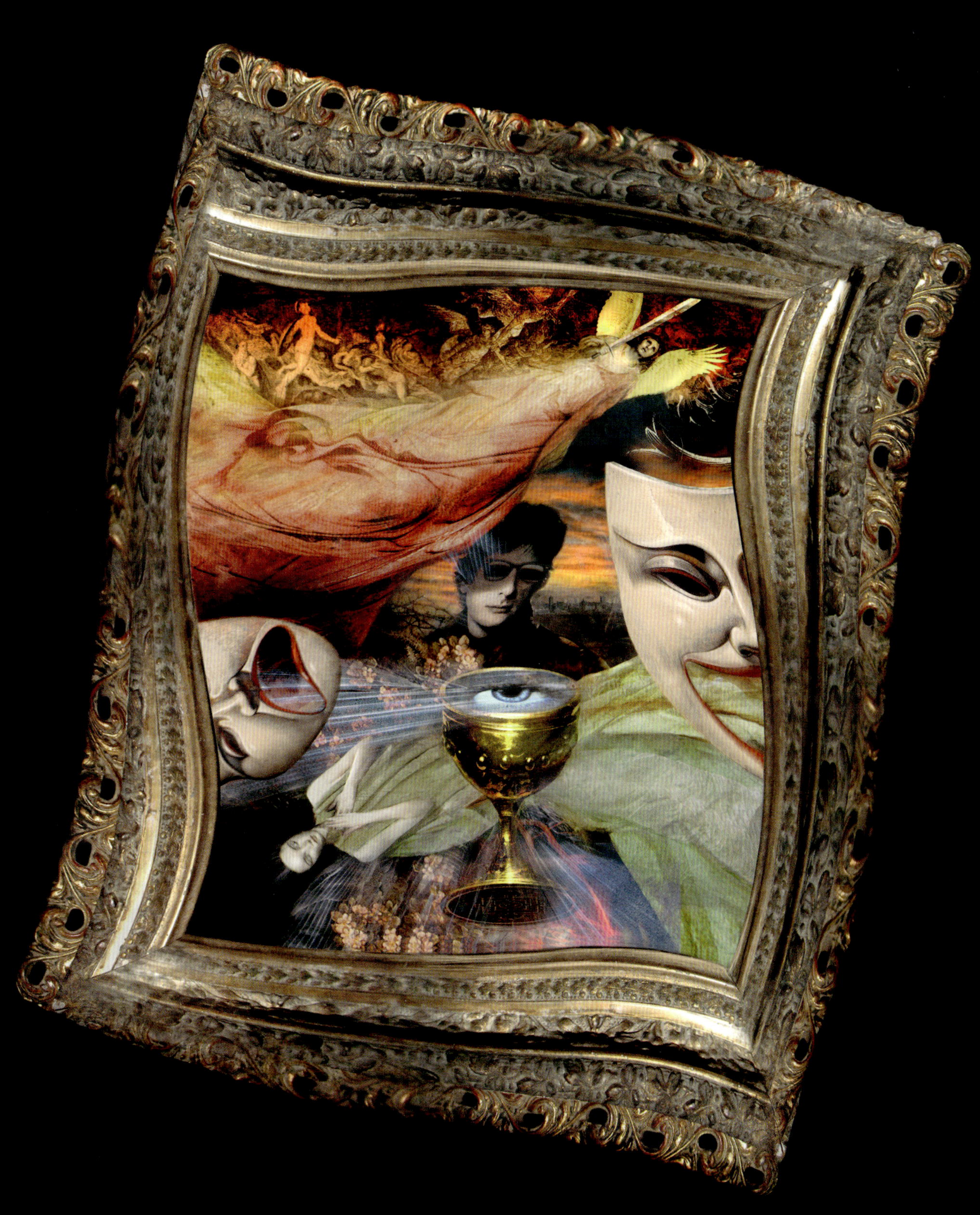

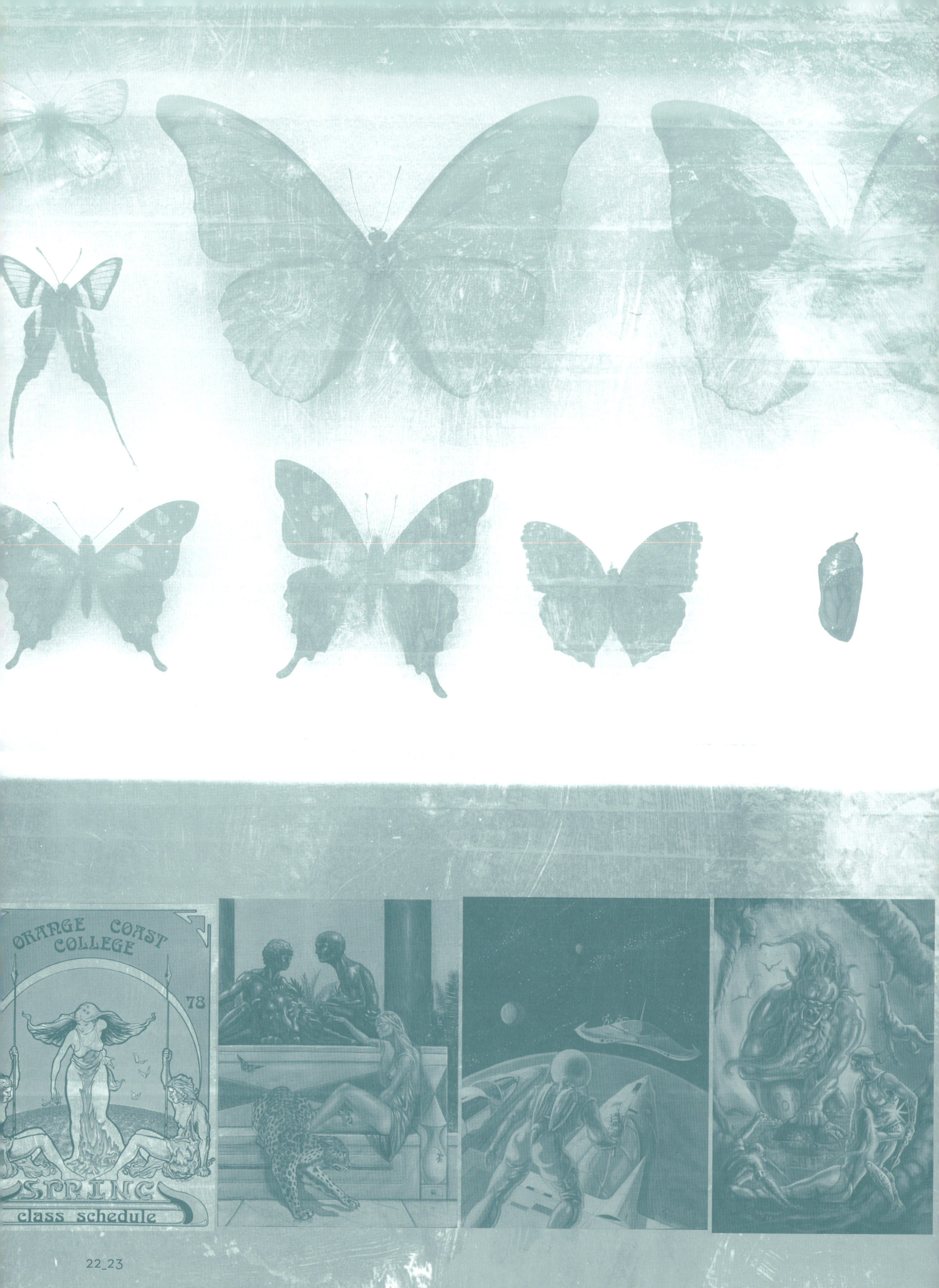
ORANGE COAST COLLEGE
78
SPRING
class schedule

the early work

emergence

the early work

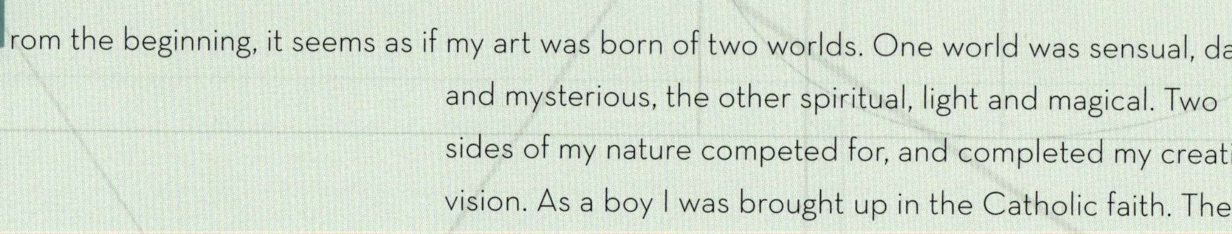

From the beginning, it seems as if my art was born of two worlds. One world was sensual, dark, and mysterious, the other spiritual, light and magical. Two sides of my nature competed for, and completed my creative vision. As a boy I was brought up in the Catholic faith. The imagery and feeling that came from standing in a large church – with statues of various saints looking over me, with candles flickering, and full of glowing stained glass windows – was hypnotizing. I was enthralled and impressed, but the glimpses I got of the cathedral inside my head were even more amazing!

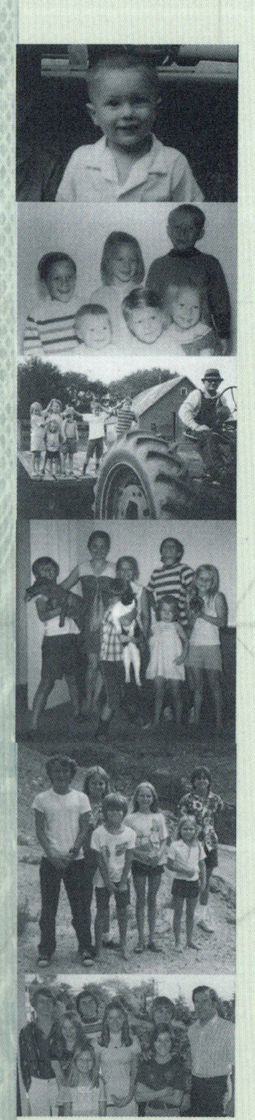

While growing up alongside five brothers and sisters (I was the oldest), space was at a premium in our small house so I used my bed as a workspace to make art on. Books on Michelangelo, da Vinci, Bernini, and other classical artists were my main inspiration via the public library, but I was usually drawing something up from my imagination. When I subscribed to the Science Fiction Book Club in fourth grade the Edgar Rice Burroughs novels (*John Carter of Mars* series) caught my interest. The stories were fun, but it was Frank Frazetta's amazing covers and inside illustrations that sparked my passion! Here was imagery imbued with vitality and sexuality. I would stare at, study and copy Frazetta's images, over and over again. What power his drawings and paintings possessed! My love for the human figure blossomed.

It was also at this time that popular art culture was really hitting the airwaves. We had characters such as Mickey Mouse, Bugs Bunny, the Flintstones, Yogi Bear, the Jetsons, Jonny Quest. Anime from Japan began to pop up – *Gigantor*, *Kimba the White Lion*, and *Speed Racer*, to name a few. From Great Britain we had *Thunderbirds* with its marionette puppetry. When *Batman* aired on ABC in 1966 it rocked my world. With its pop art stylization and costumes that accentuated the human form, I was hooked.

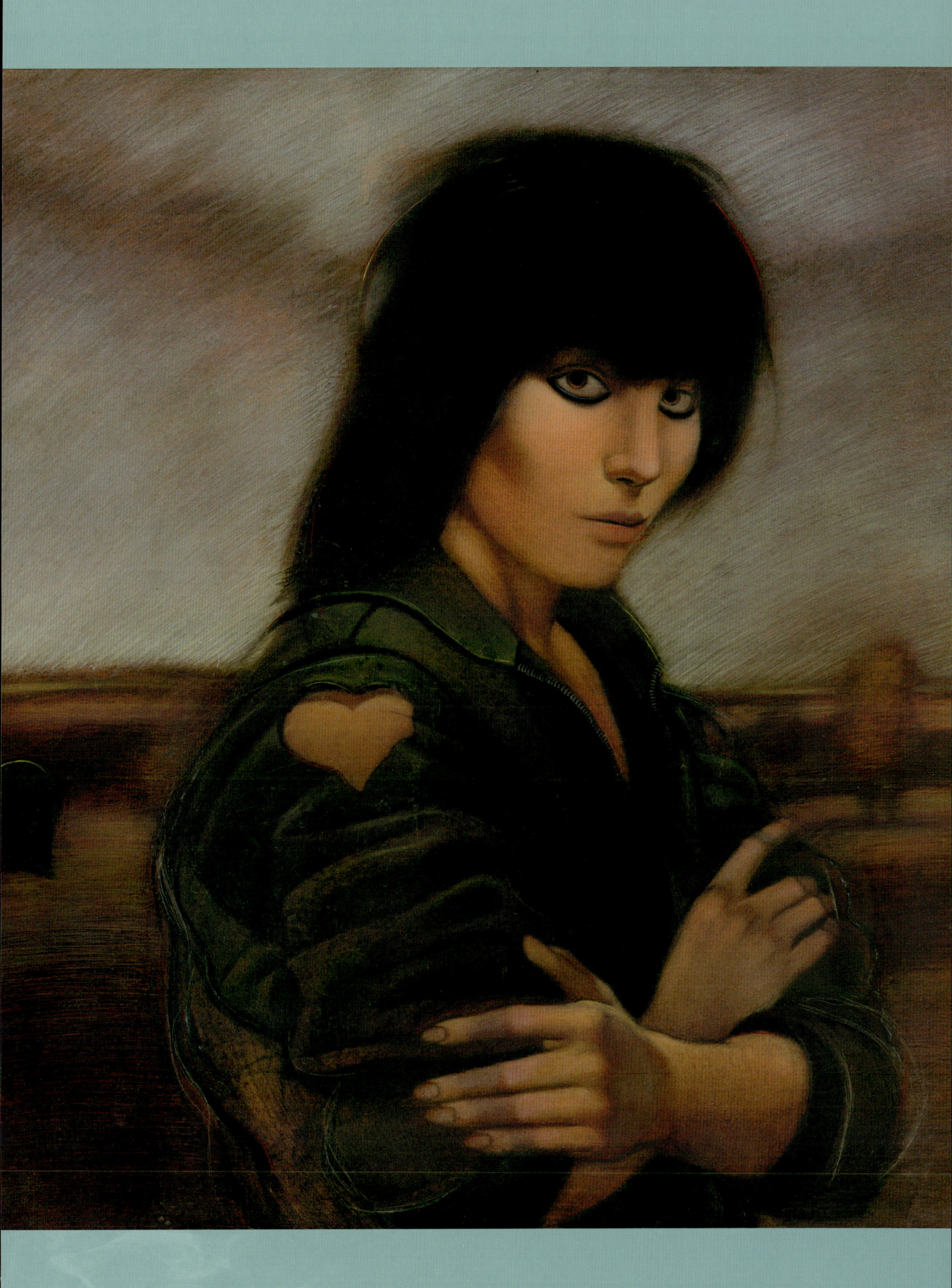

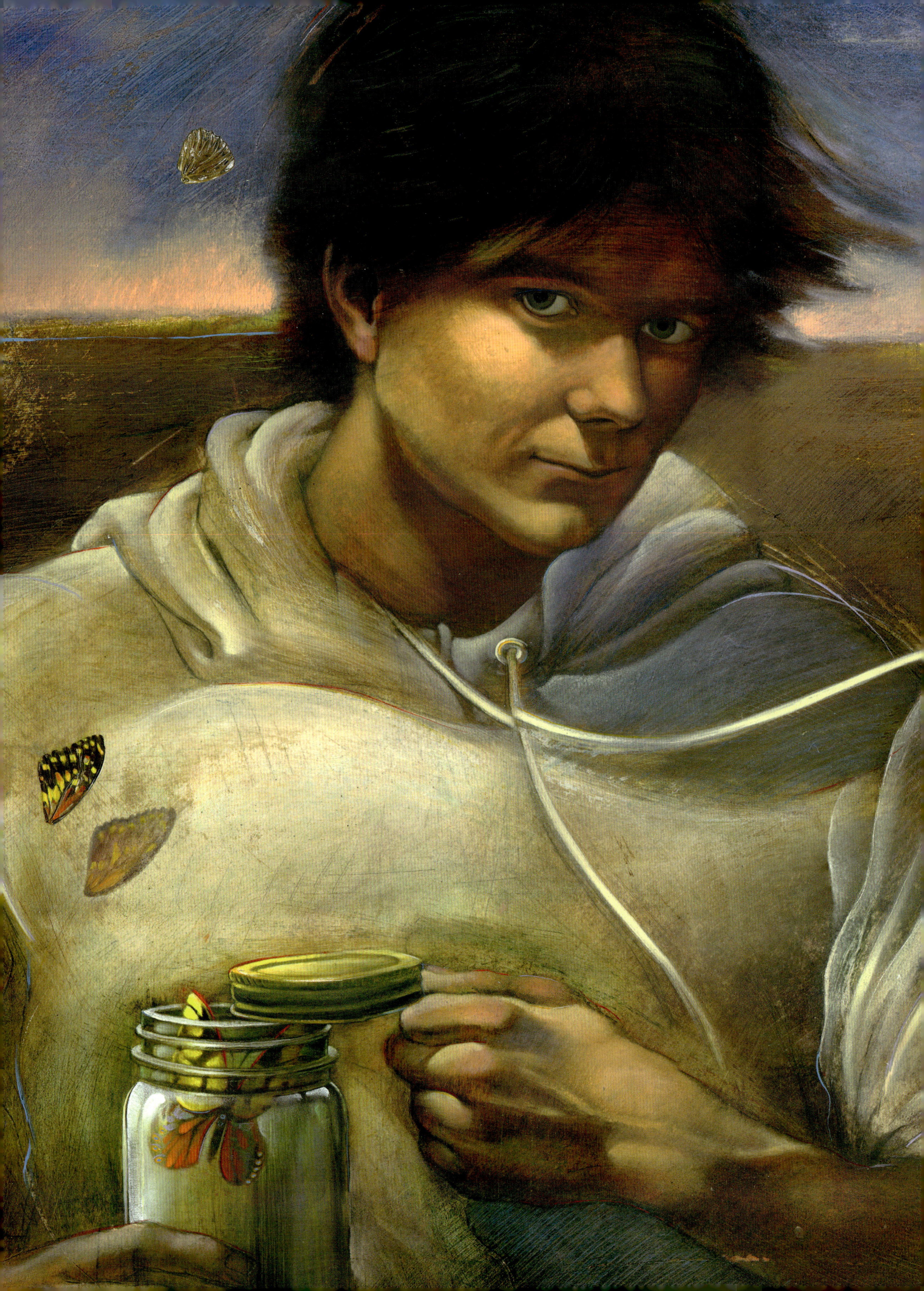

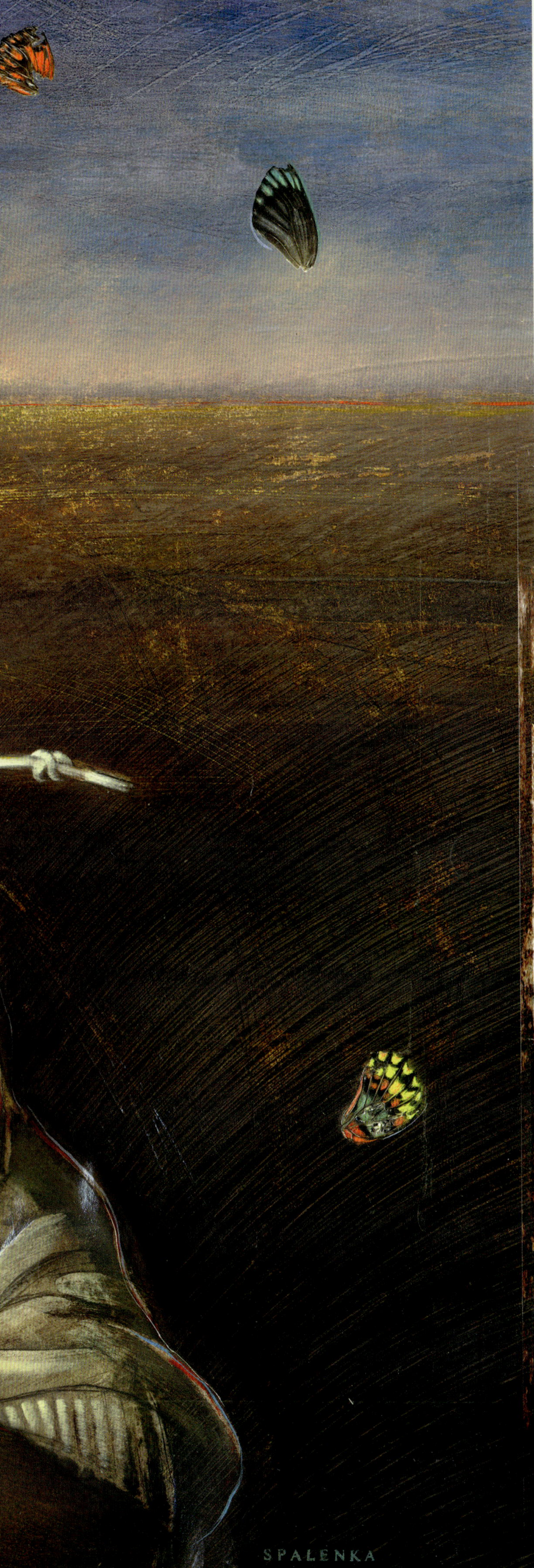

Television put a man on the moon in our family room, but also took me to other dimensions with *Lost in Space*, *Voyage to the Bottom of the Sea*, and *The Time Tunnel*. *The Outer Limits*, and Rod Serling's *The Twilight Zone* opened up the darker side of my imagination. I developed many demented and nightmarish drawings at this time, so much so that I created a walk of horrors in the garage with stuffed dummies, shadow plays, and my brother in a box-like coffin with ketchup on his face. I charged the local kids 25 cents to get in.

Soon after graduating high school I became a full-time student at Art Center College of Design in Pasadena, California. Jumping into this school was a lesson in observation. I learned as much from the students as I did from the professors.

Lane Smith, who became a successful children's book illustrator, would bring in art assignments that had pieces of garbage, or crunched up Polaroid film collaged into them. He would find this art material sweeping the streets at Disneyland. Matt Mahurin, who became a well-known illustrator, photographer, and filmmaker, created art for his classes that many times had little to do with the given assignment but showcased the power of conceptual thinking. His pieces would raise the ire of the teacher but open my eyes to what was most important in creating powerful images.

I was turned on to Gothic, Renaissance, and late 1800s art. I loved the Symbolist period with the Pre-Raphaelites (Millais, Rossetti, Burne-Jones, Hunt, eg.), the Decadents, and Art Nouveau. There was also an ethereal quality I loved in the Pictorialist photographers of those days too (Demachy, Cameron, Ortiz-Echagüe, Conklin, Holland Day, eg.).

The editorial illustrators back then, like Marshall Arisman, John Collier, Allan Cober, Ralph Steadman, Brad Holland, and others, also grabbed my attention. The social and political commentary these illustrators were making struck a chord within me.

Here was art with a purpose—communicating issues about humanity, from gun violence and racism to social welfare. These images were speaking to thousands, and in some cases, millions of people. I learned that the publishing world could be a powerful platform as well as an industry to work in.

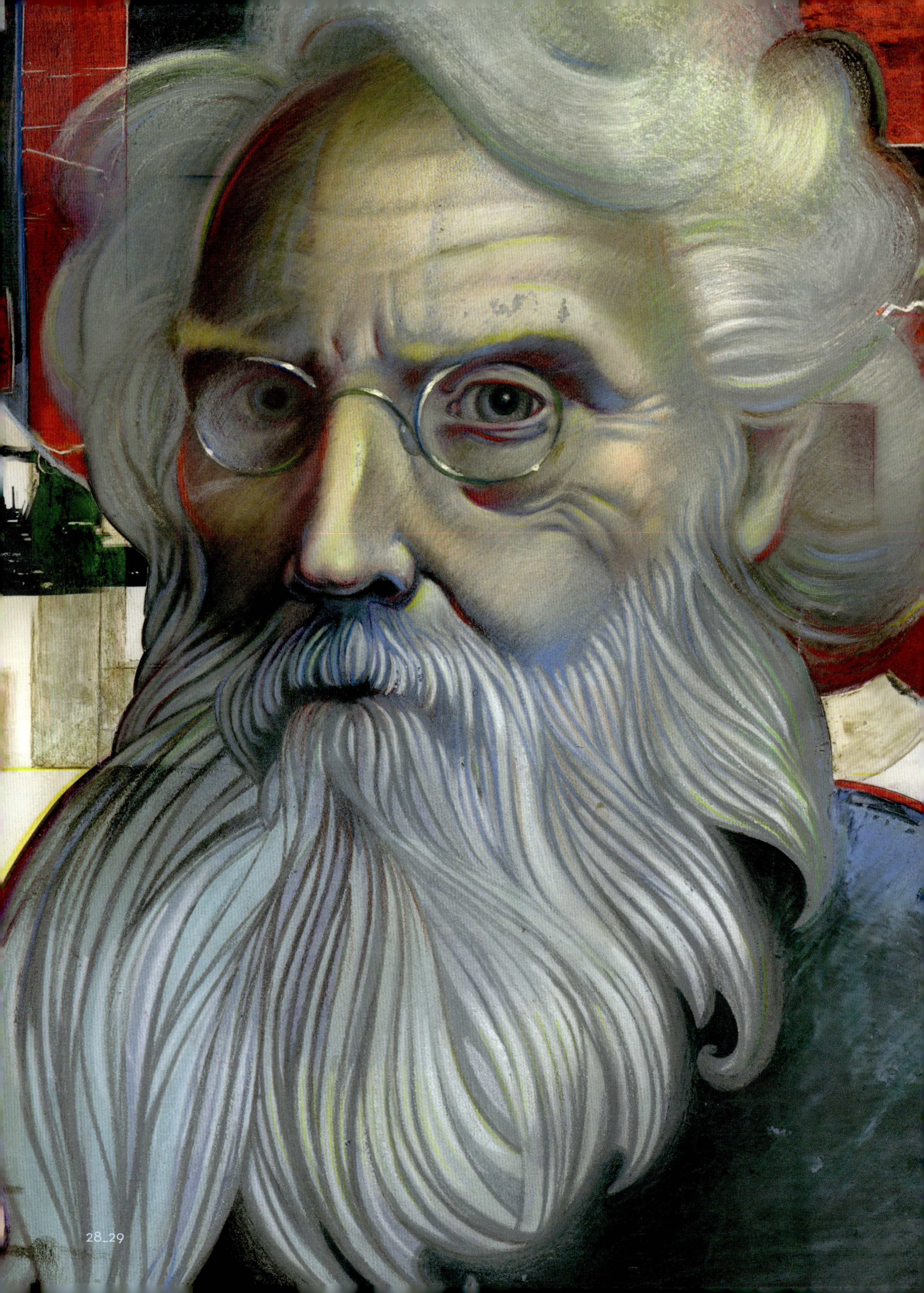

Mahurin also taught me how an individual's personal vision develops by taking risks: that all art is study, so don't get too precious with it. One day there was a class assignment I was struggling with. I asked Mahurin to come by and offer some suggestions. When he arrived at my place on the second floor of an apartment complex, he took my art outside onto the balcony, "To get a better look at it in the sun." He looked at the painting then at me, and said, **"Sometimes Spalenka, you just have to know when to let a piece go,"** then feigned throwing it out into the street. "Yeah, sure..." I said jokingly, then watched as he winged my piece into a blue California sky. It landed in the road and a car drove over it.

When I finally pulled the art from the asphalt, deep gashes now covered part of the surface, and new textures came to light. It actually improved the piece! Allowing happy accidents to play a part of my art-making process turned out to be a grand revelation.

Experimentation is good, but studying the history of your craft is also important. There are not many shortcuts to learning a skill or technique well. I can feel immense frustration during this learning process, but it is ultimately well worth the effort to master the tools, then transcend them.

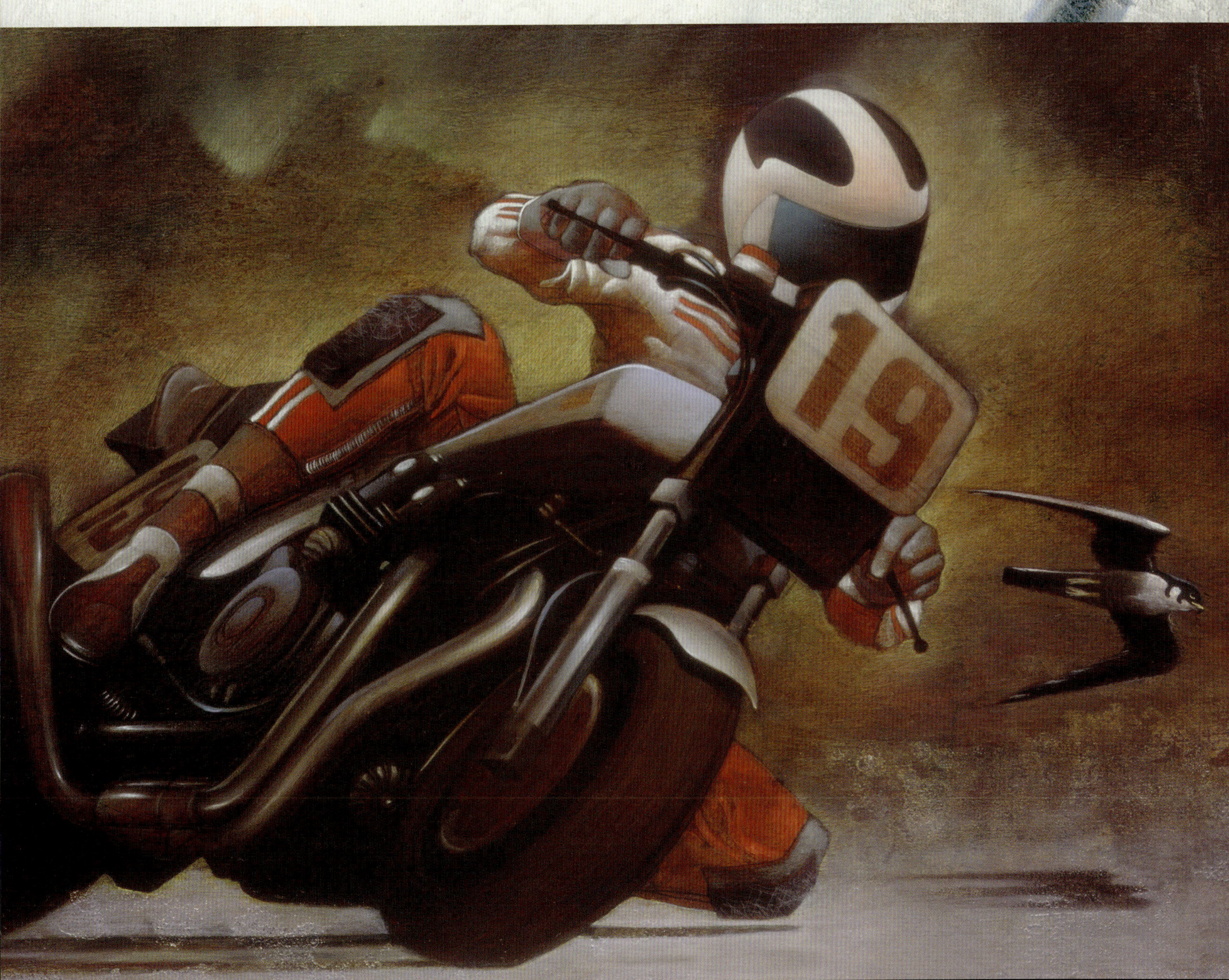

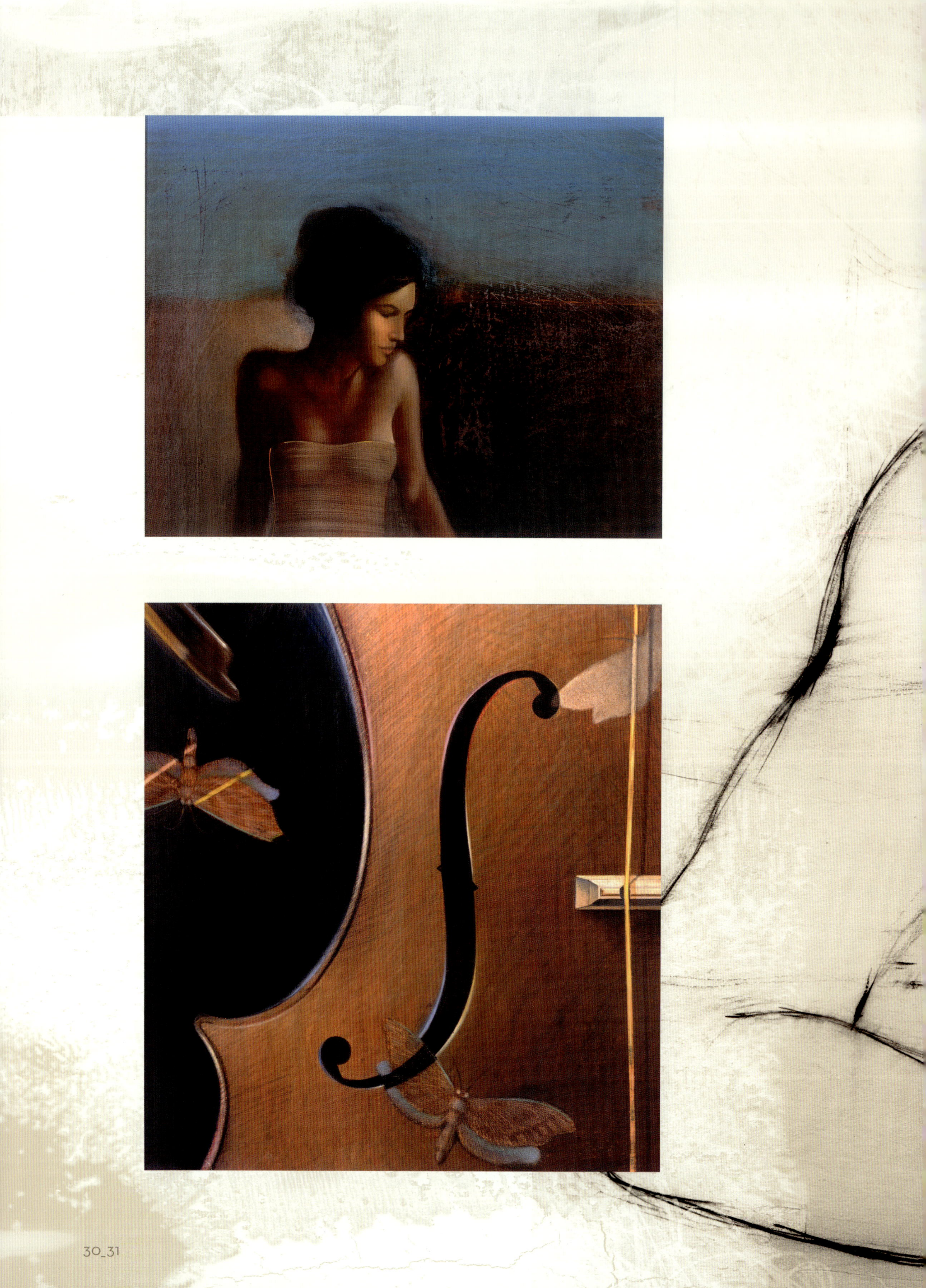

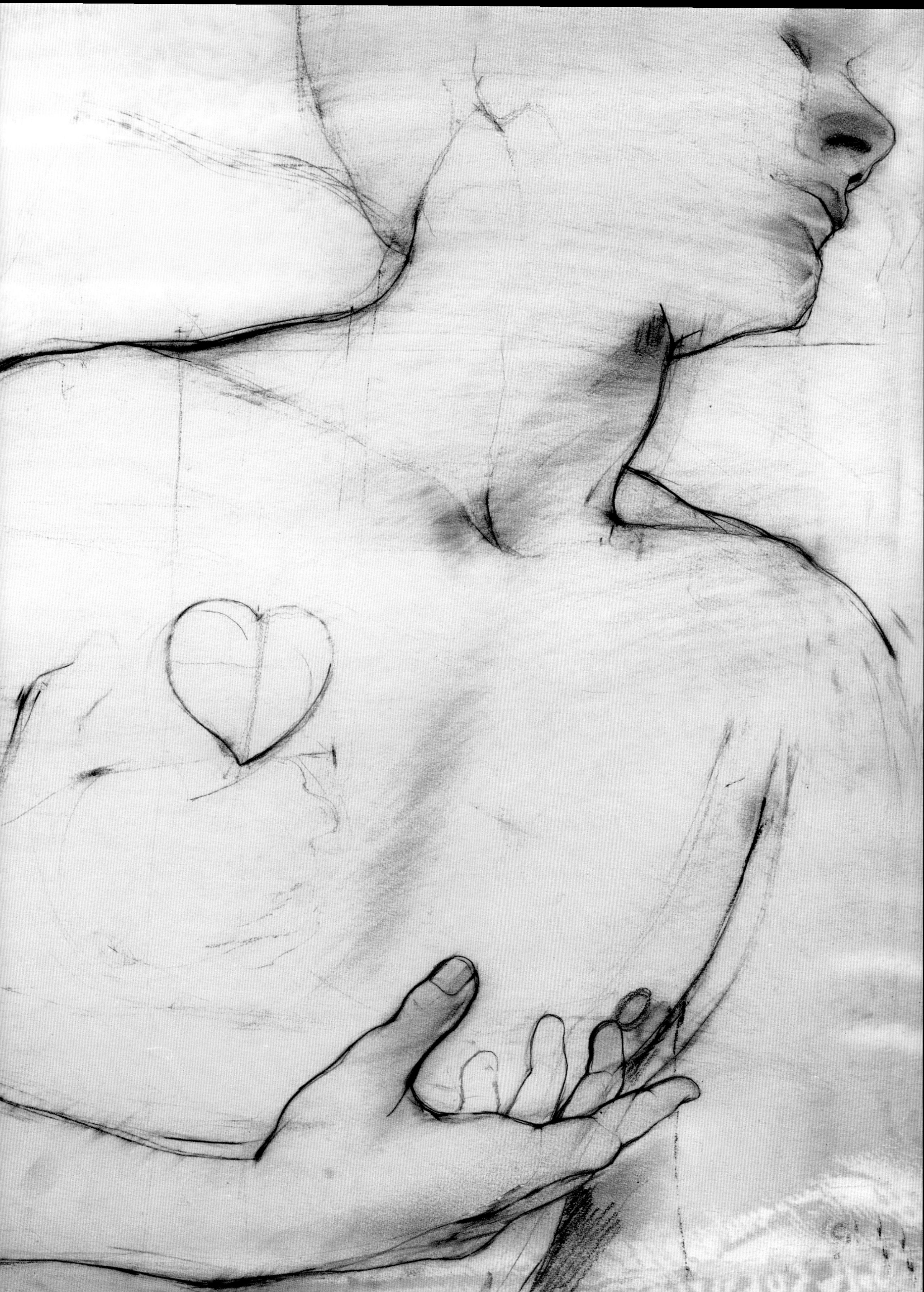

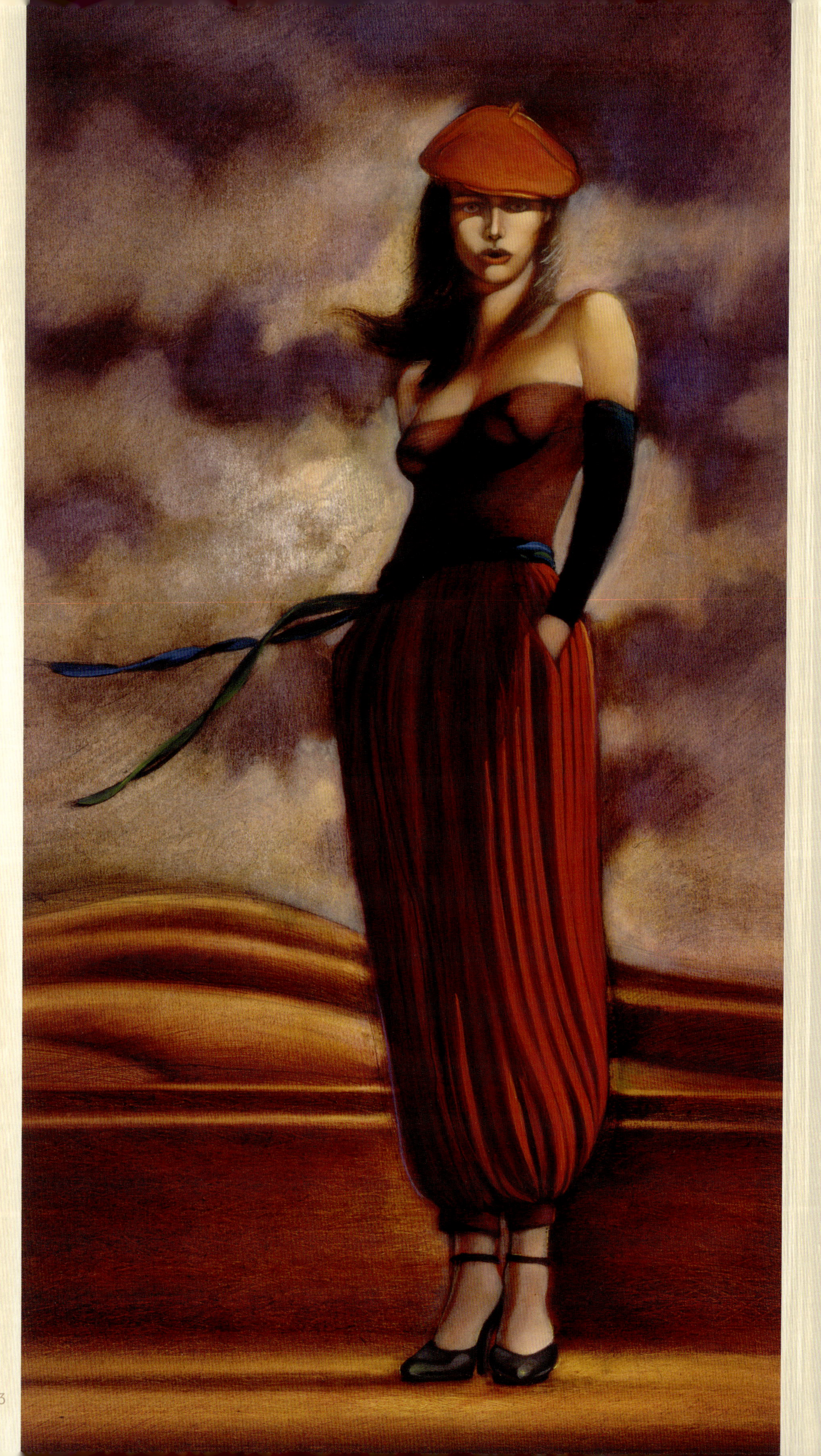

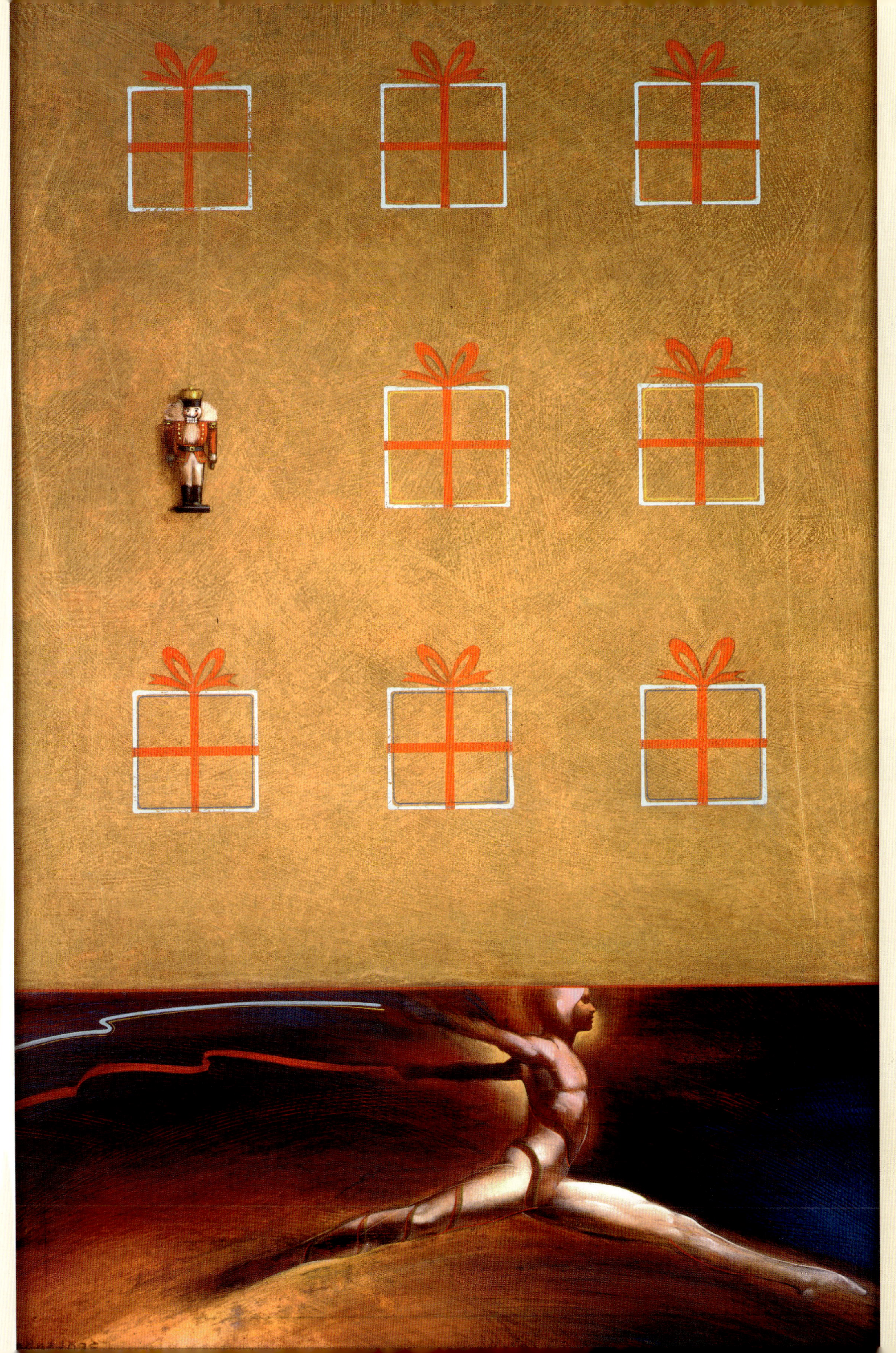

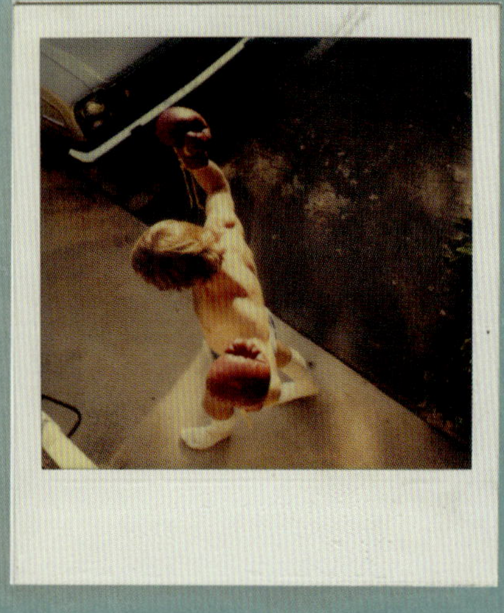
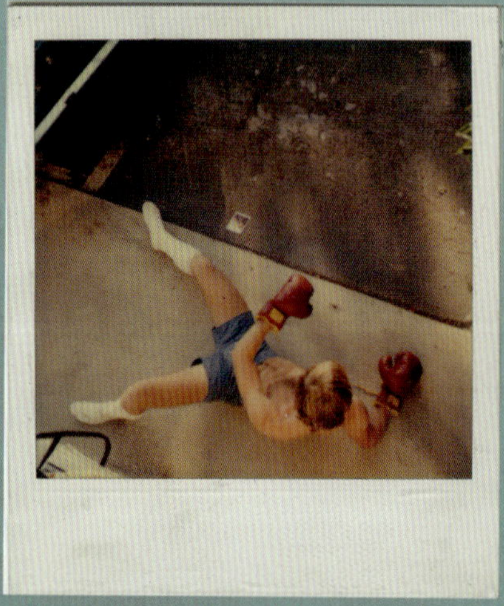
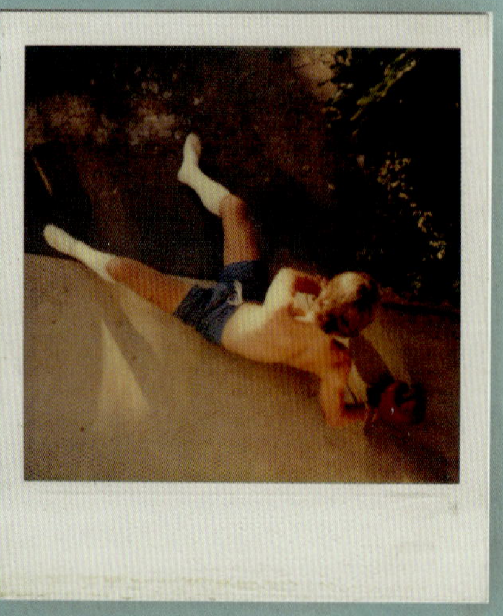
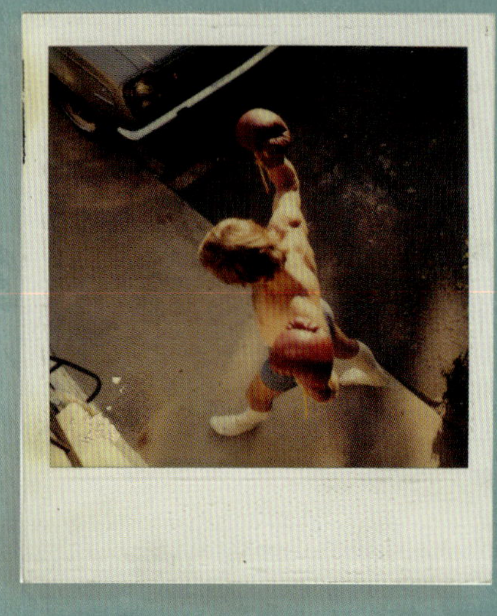
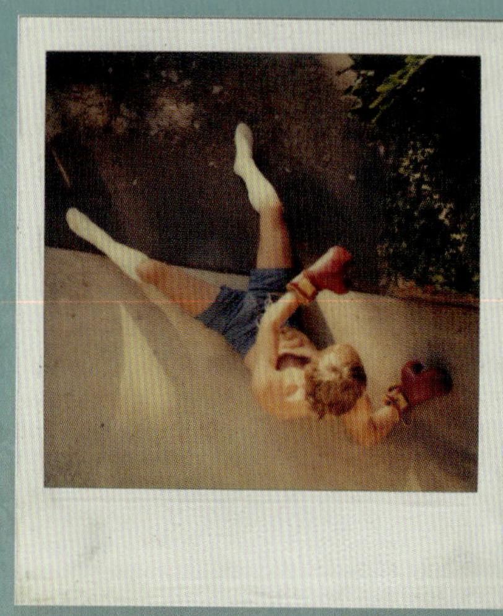
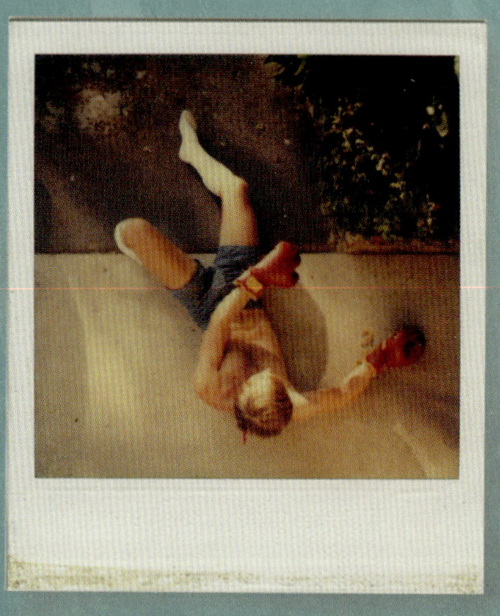
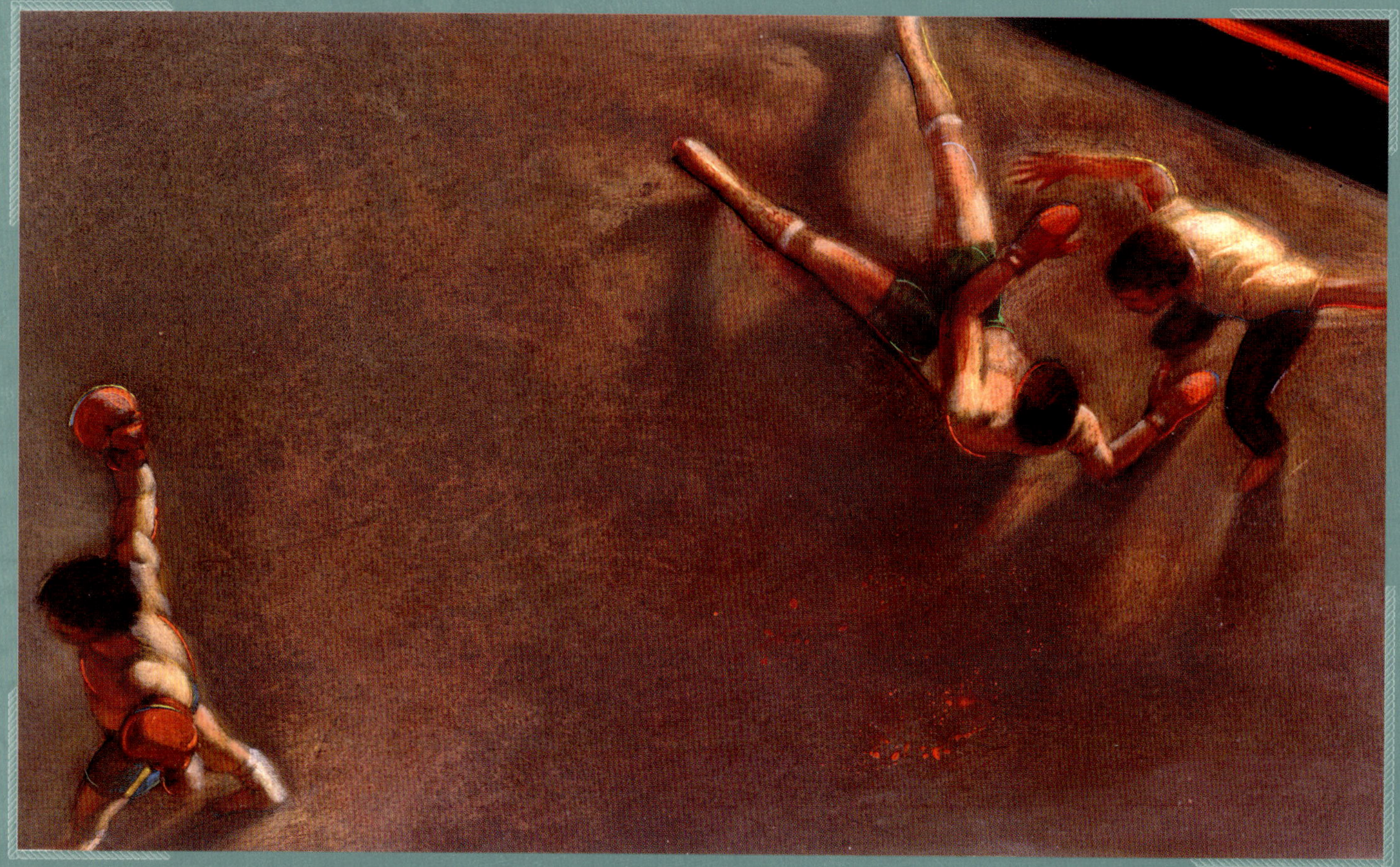

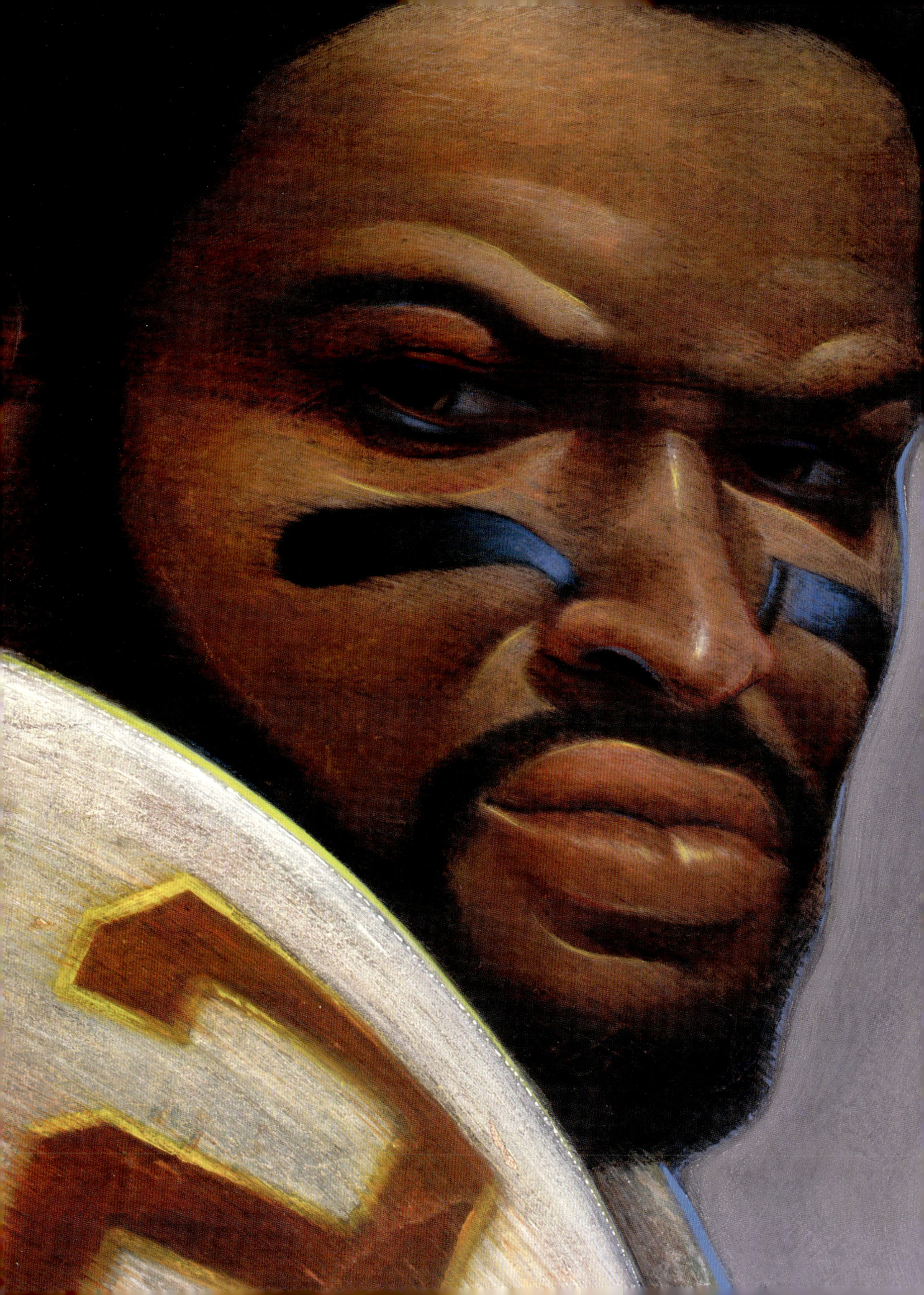

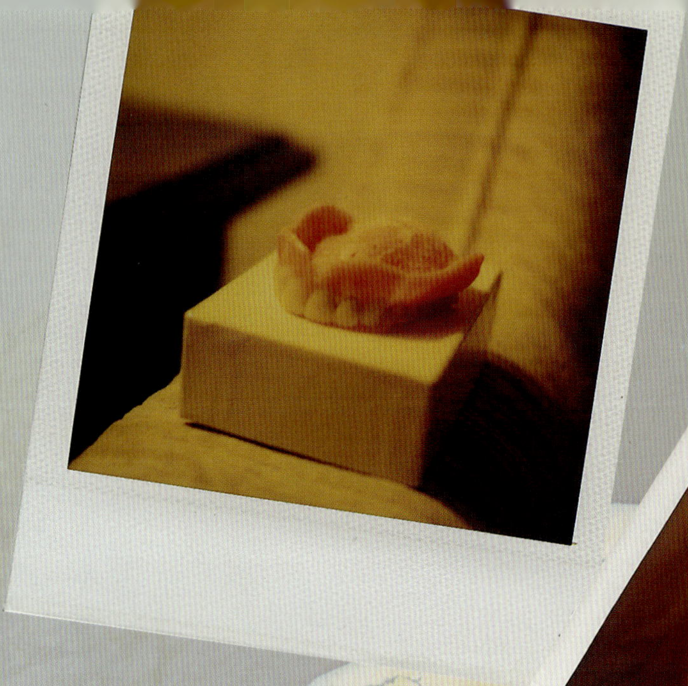

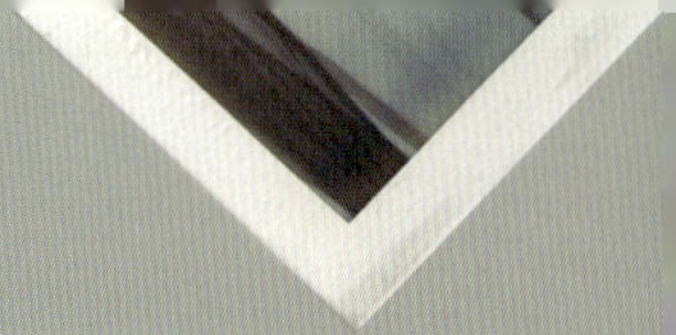

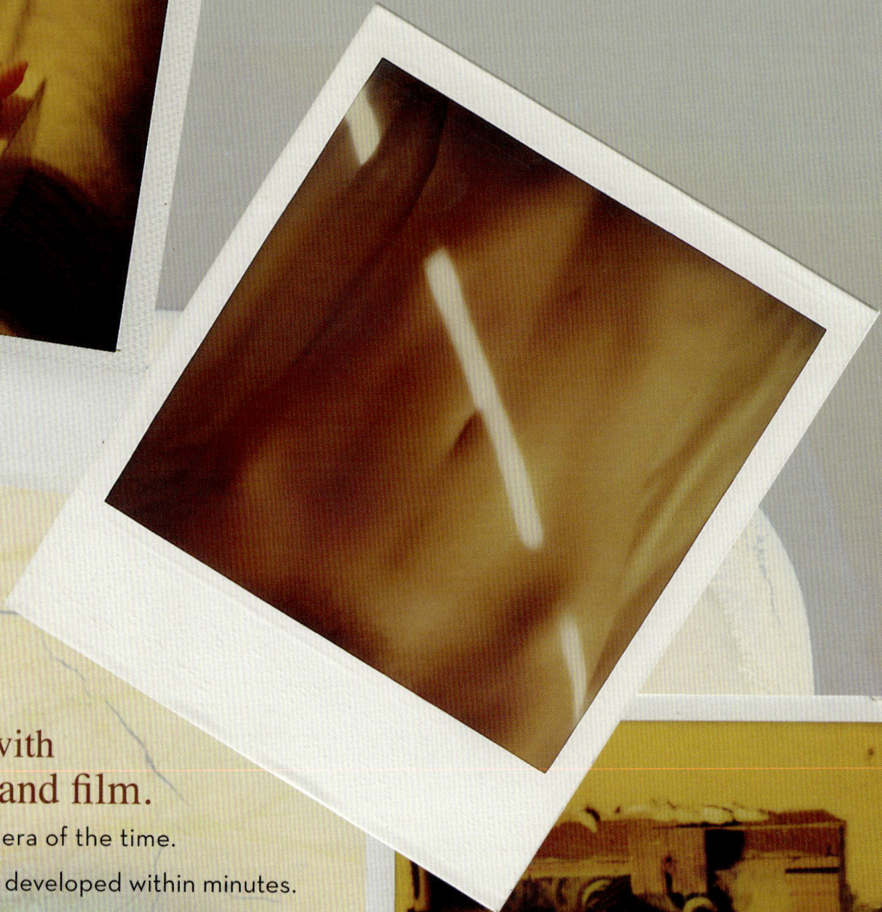

I had a love/hate relationship with the SX-70 Polaroid camera and film.

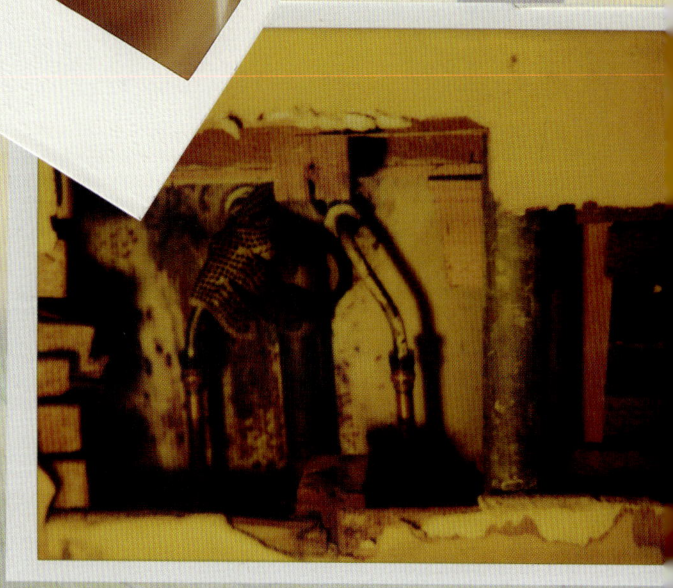

In the 70s and 80s this was the digital camera of the time. It was great for instant reference; the image developed within minutes. I used this film in different ways, sometimes cutting it up, painting on it, and integrating it into the final art. The technology was maddening because it was inconsistent. Sometimes the image would be blurry or the chemicals that were squeezed into the transparent window of the film would simply squirt out funny and leave anomalies on the image. On the flip side, occasionally a fuzzy picture would evoke a beautiful, ethereal quality or a chemical mishap could turn out to be a fascinating abstract gem. The SX-70 had "happy accident" technology built into it, because at times it could manifest real magic.

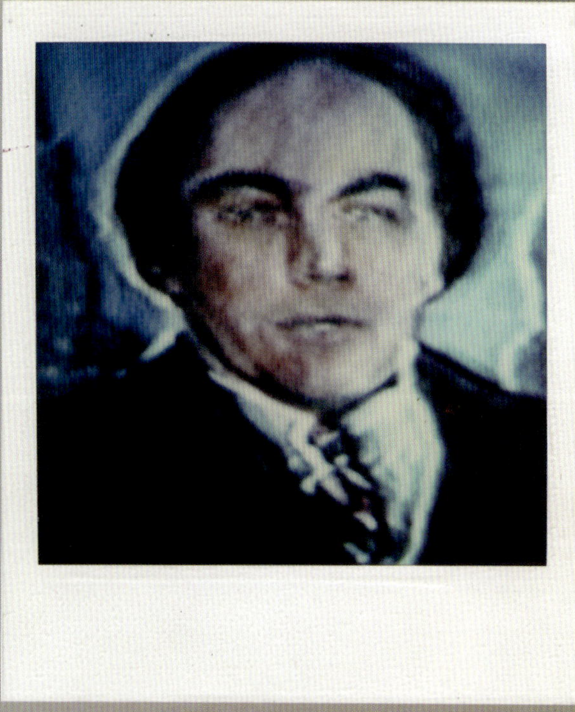

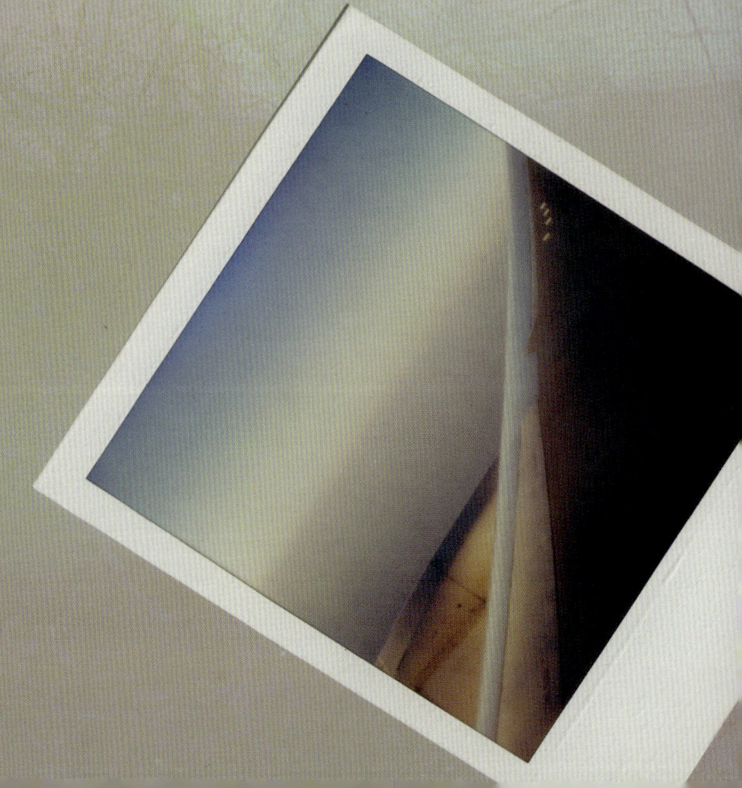

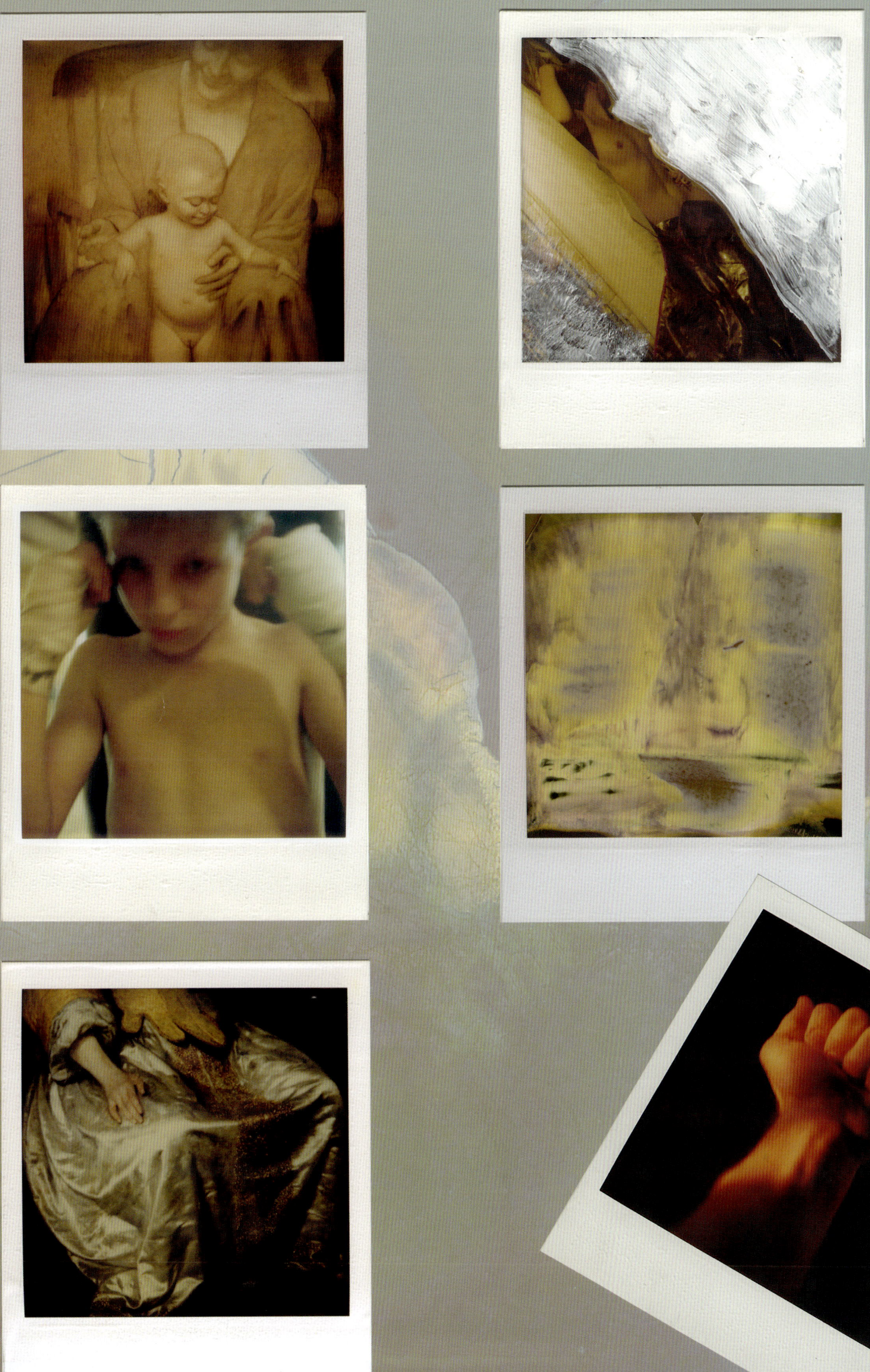

Polaroid was the Instagram of its time.

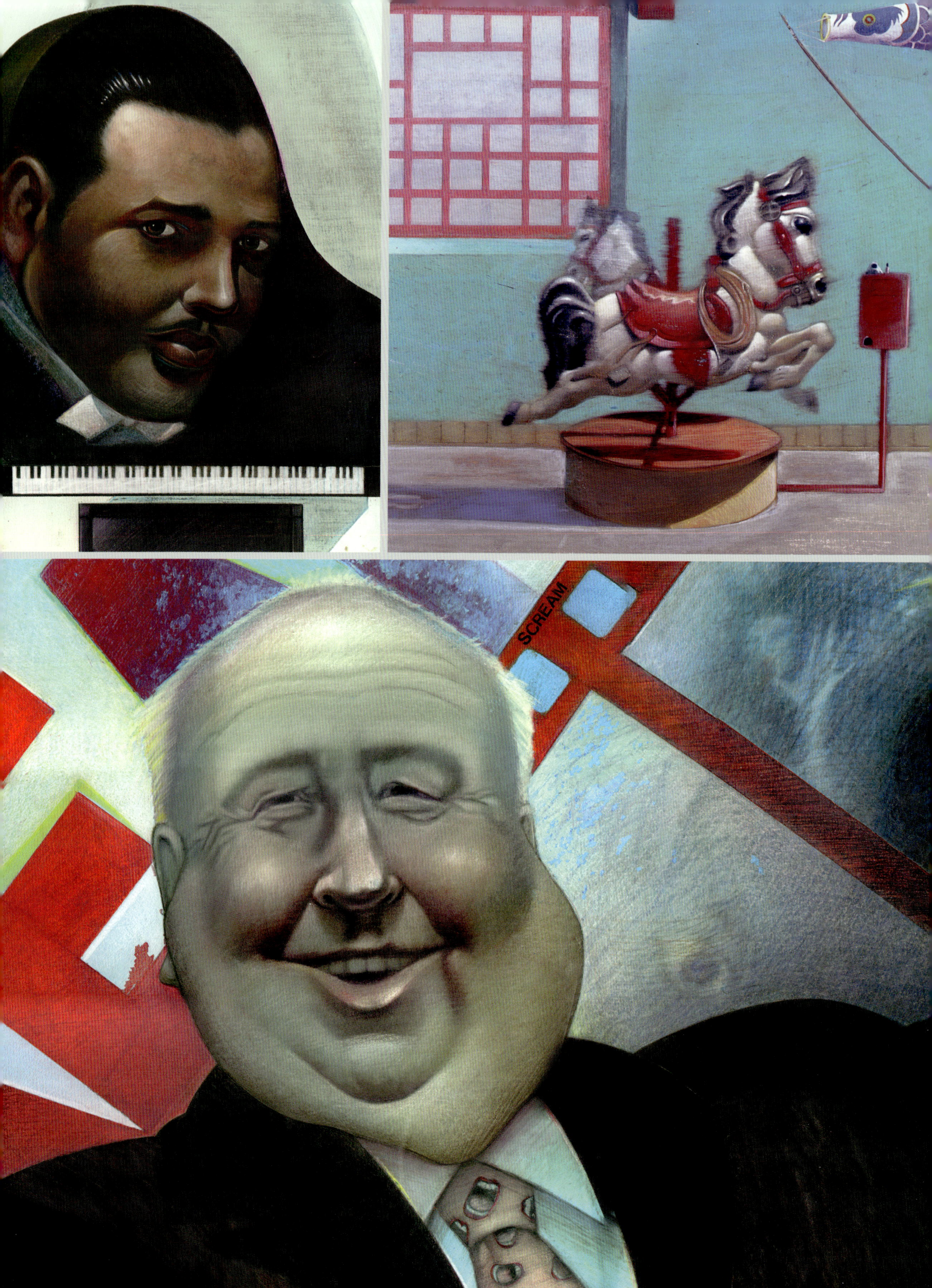
SCREAM

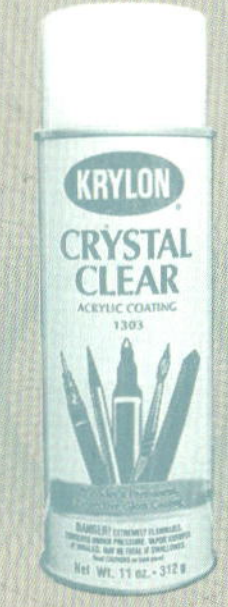

i eXperimented with different art materials

and was not afraid to mix and match. Graphite, charcoal, Prismacolor pencils, pastels, pigments, any type of paint, tar, bromo seltzer and chemicals were some of the supplies I used in the service of exploring new techniques. Mahurin and I were obsessed with the glazing techniques of the masters, especially of Rembrandt, but we were too impatient to sit around and wait for a normal oil glaze to dry. The Crystal Clear technique was born.

This involved spraying a product called Krylon Crystal Clear in massive doses over wet oil paint, essentially sealing the oil underneath a plastic layer. Layering oil paint with Crystal Clear between them (sometimes using many cans) created a deep transparent, almost stained glass window quality to the surface. It was fascinating to see what type of effect we could get when this chemical brew interacted with oil and turpentine. I was so addicted to this product I bought cases of it at a time.

A big problem was the immense toxicity. When I started getting headaches from using it I experimented with other non-toxic glazing options. Breathing in those fumes for years I am sure did us some damage. Doh! So don't try this technique at home kids, unless you are wearing a gas mask.

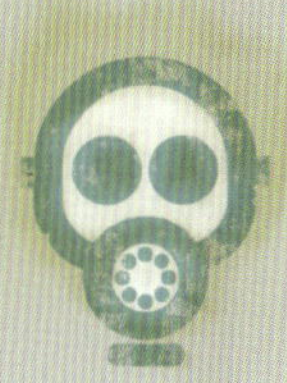

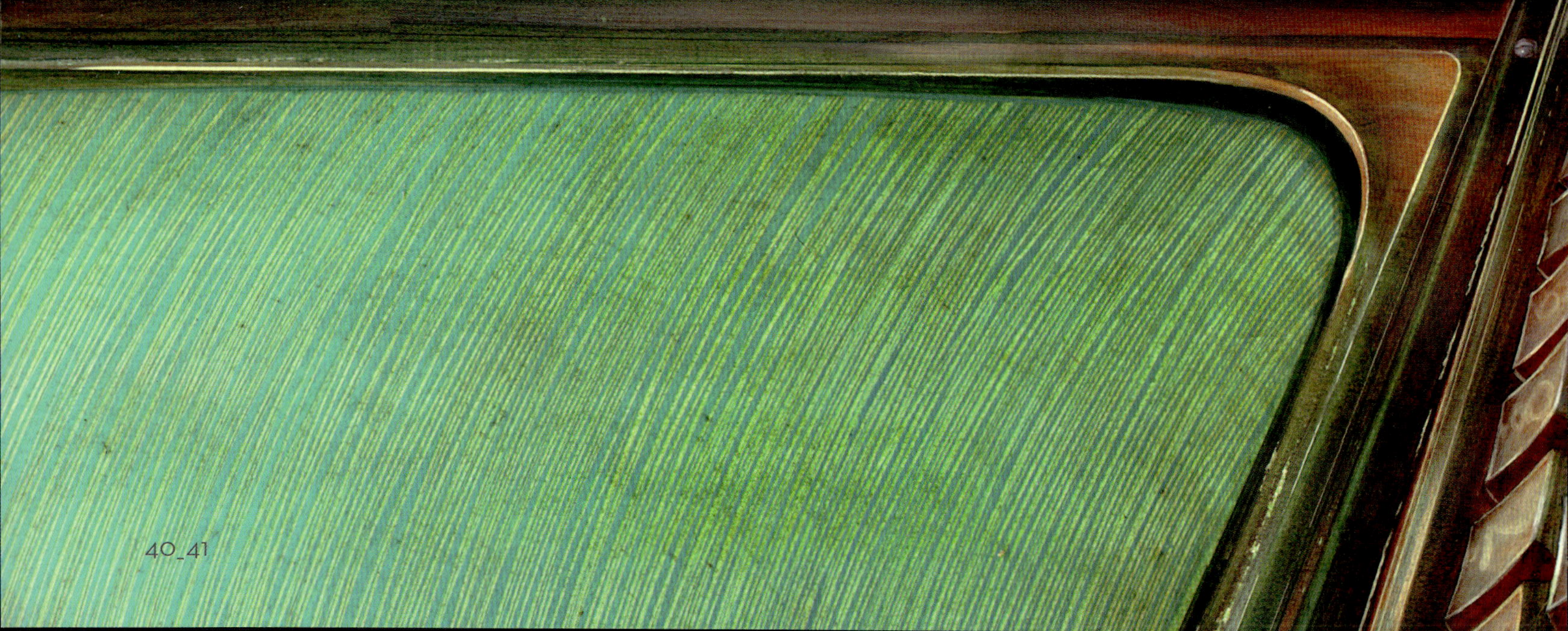

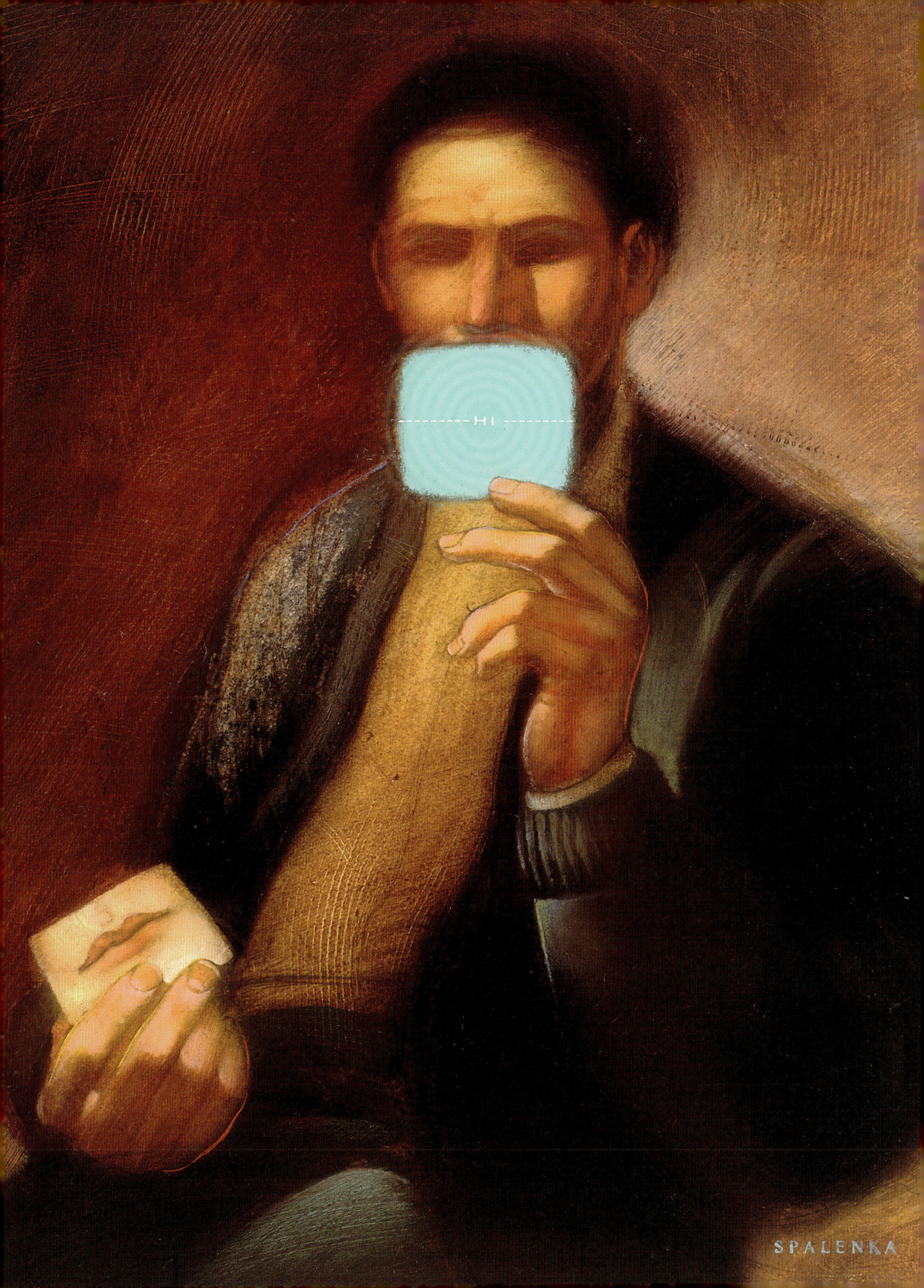
HI
SPALENKA

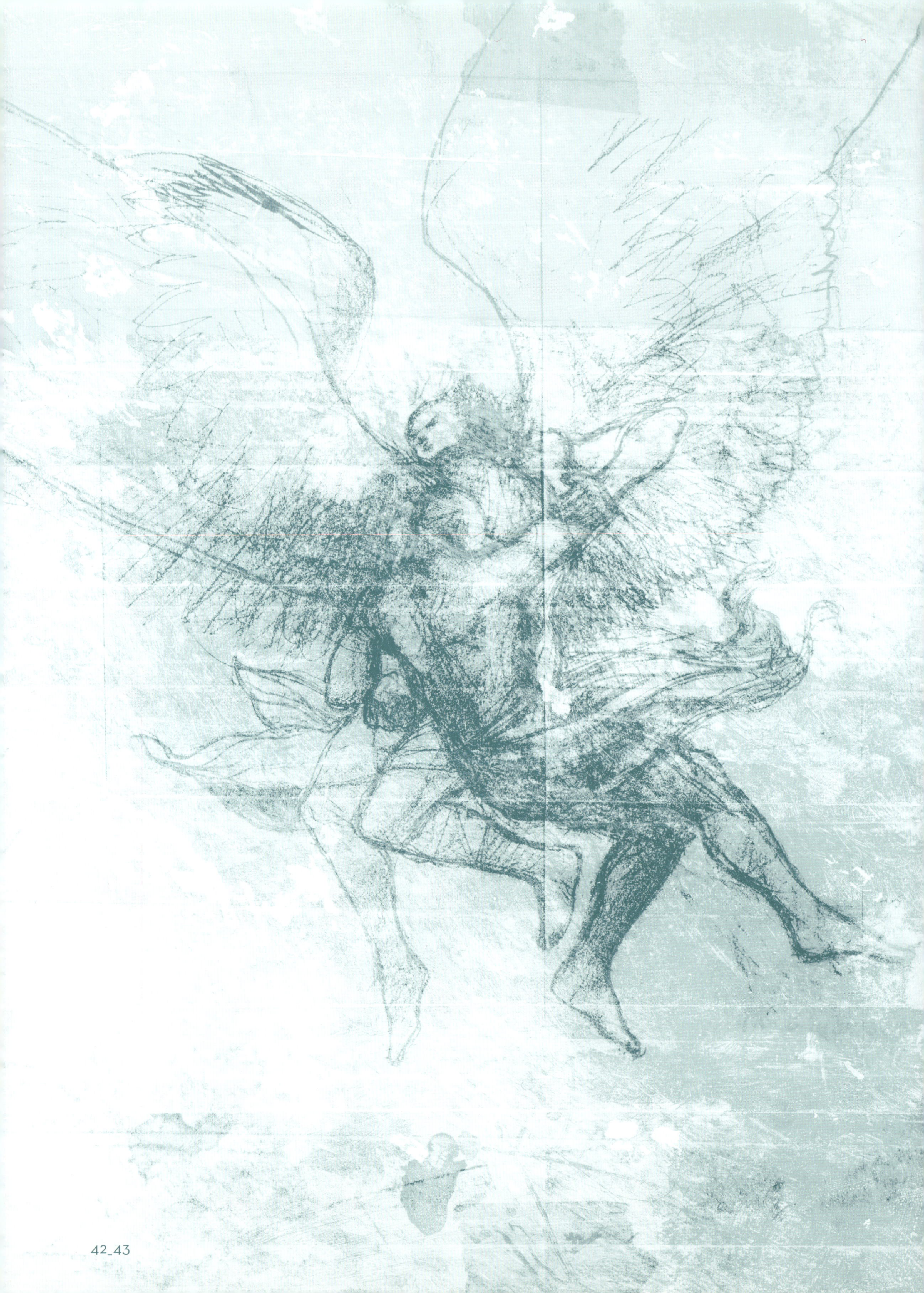

the sketch

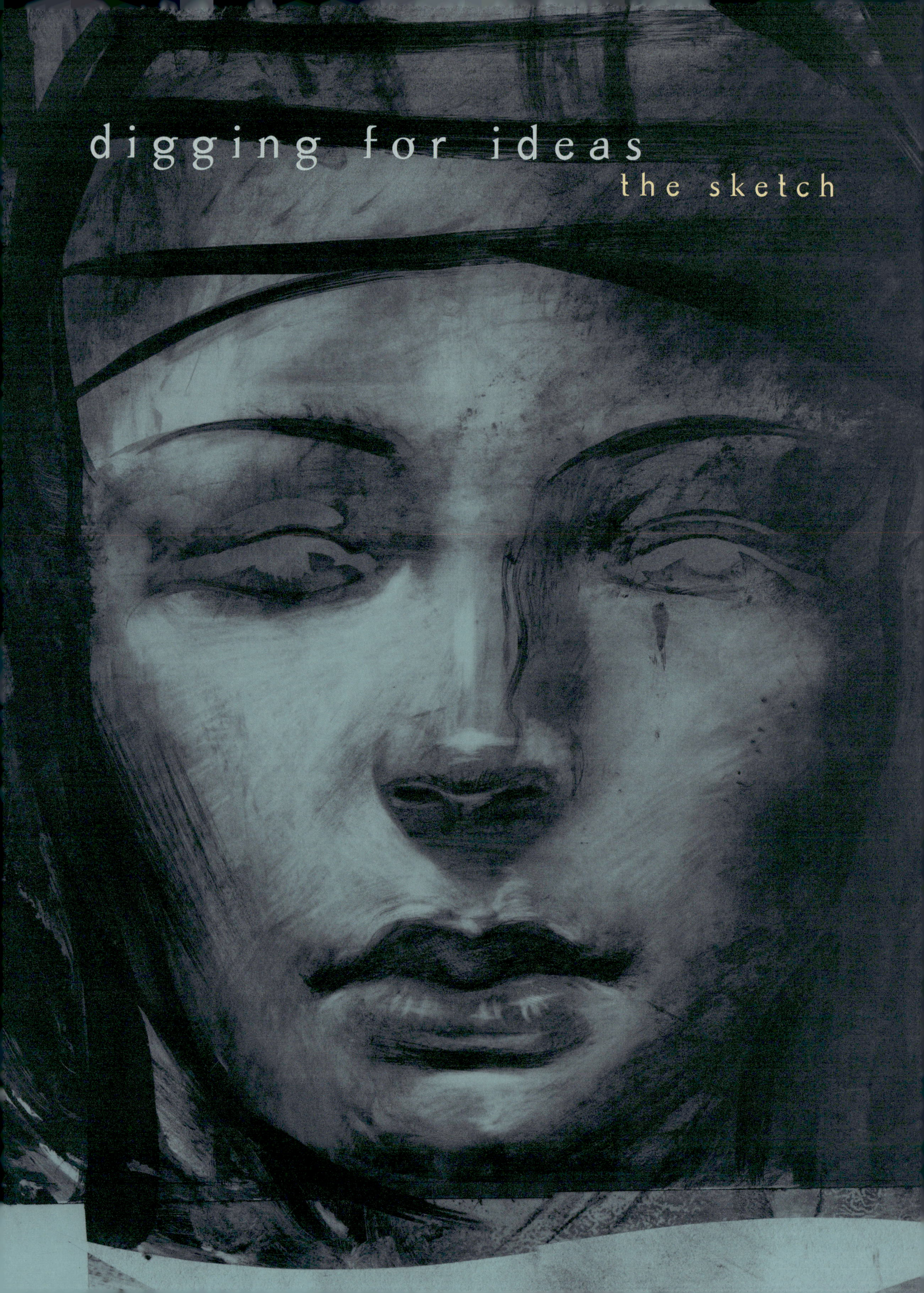
digging for ideas
the sketch

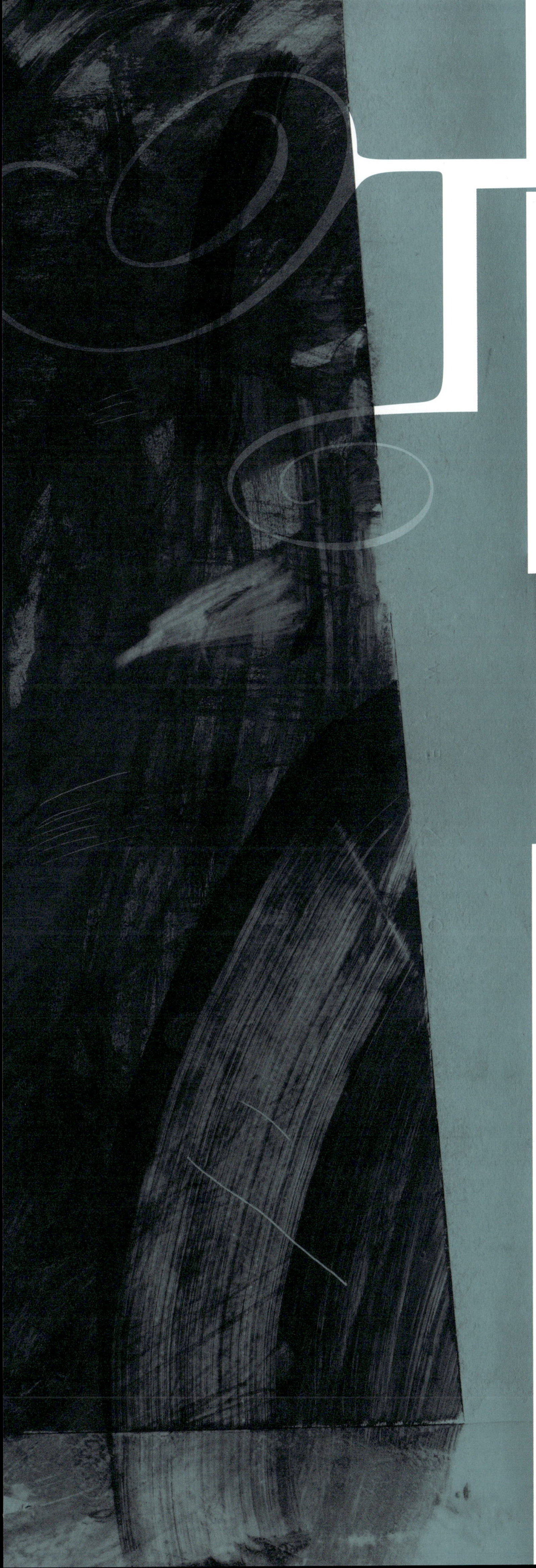

The idea is the foundation of all great art, but how to get a good one? First I think big by determining what universal themes I want to address, then I look at the details. It is the same with illustration and concept design – getting to the core of a concept then breaking it down into specifics. I create simple icons inspired by words from a story or scene then cross reference and overlay them to produce new images. Beginning as thumbnails they evolve into loose sketches.

I love the tactile quality of a pencil moving against the surface of paper. It connects me with the world of image potentiality. Many of my early sketches are indiscernible scribbles and smudged lines, yet slowly they reveal their secrets. This is usually enough information for me to get started on my final art.

Every so often I will put a sketch through a process of collage, or scan it into the computer to flesh it out more, but the initial idea is born from those primal marks on paper. My ideas flow out onto notecards, scraps of tissue, or on the back side of used printing paper. I know that artists throughout time have loved the freedom associated with the sketch, whatever material it is drawn on. It is fascinating how some roughly hewn lines can imbue a sense of wonder or explain an idea or tell a story with such vitality. This is one ancient and timeless technology that is not going away.

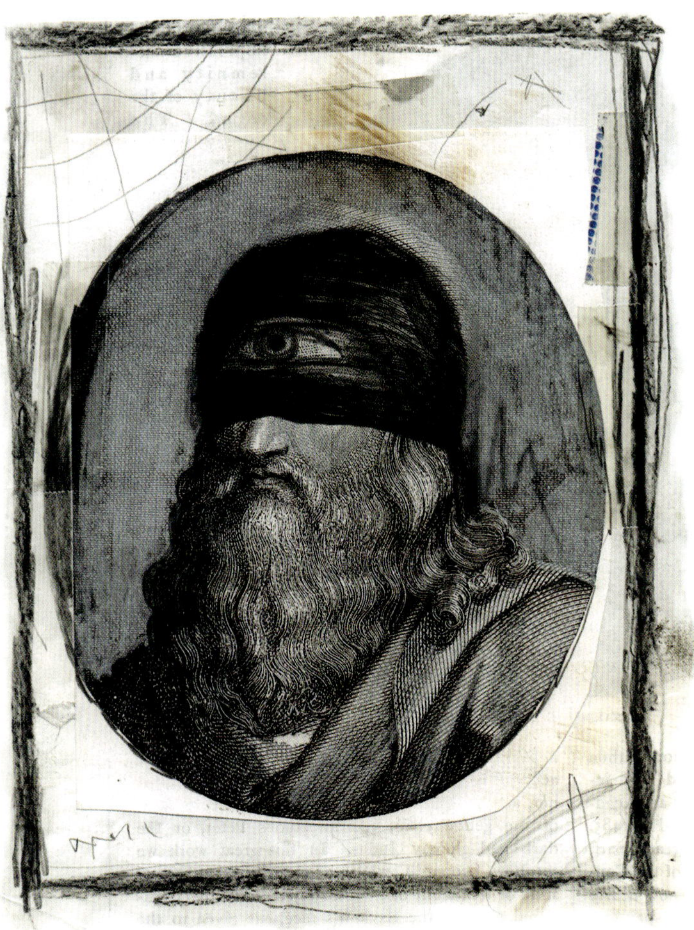

#3 This image shows a tree that is shaped like a hand growing, reaching out of the ground. Some of the branches (fingers) are cut off. New green saplings are growing out of each finger.

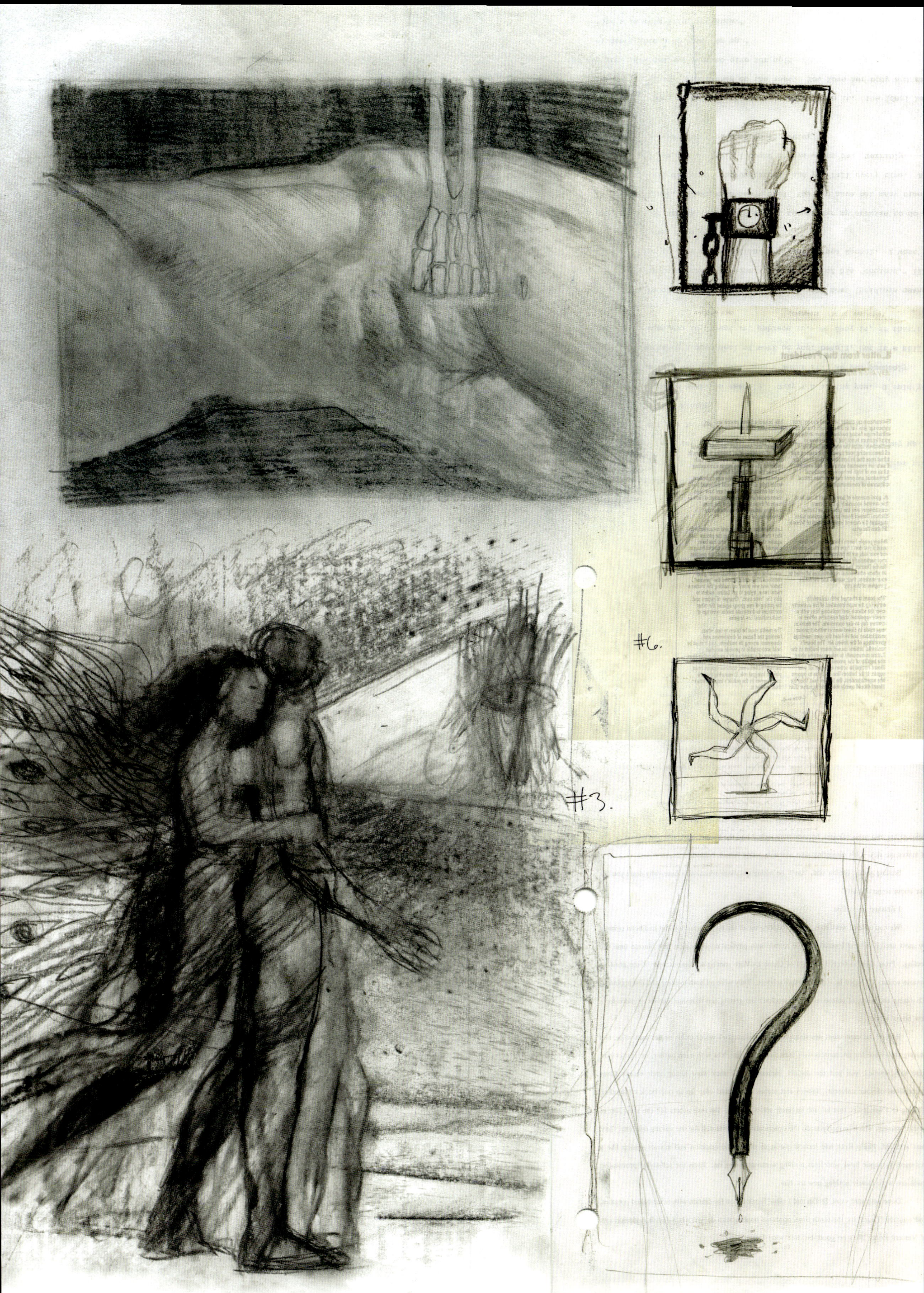
#6.
#3.

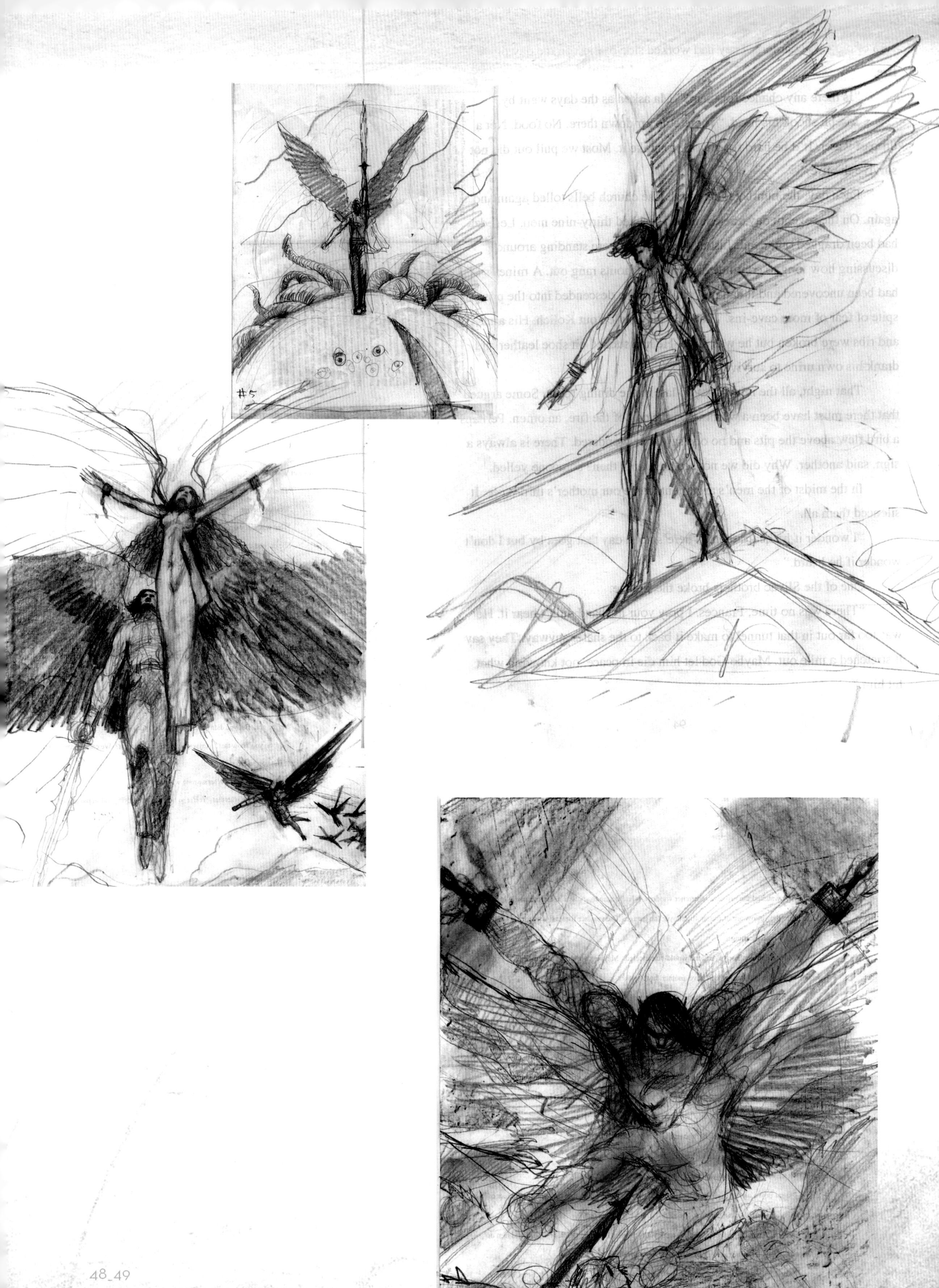
#5

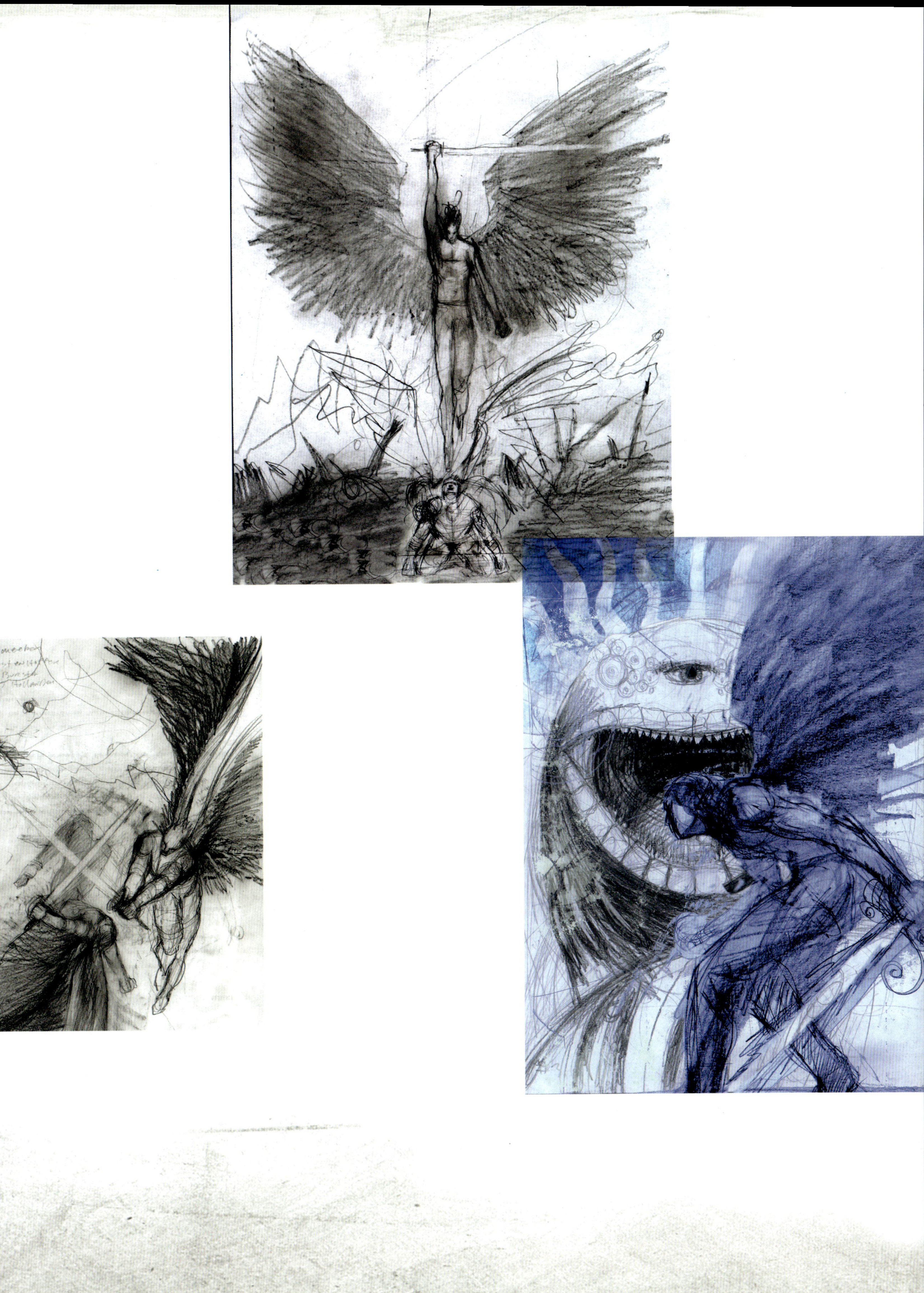

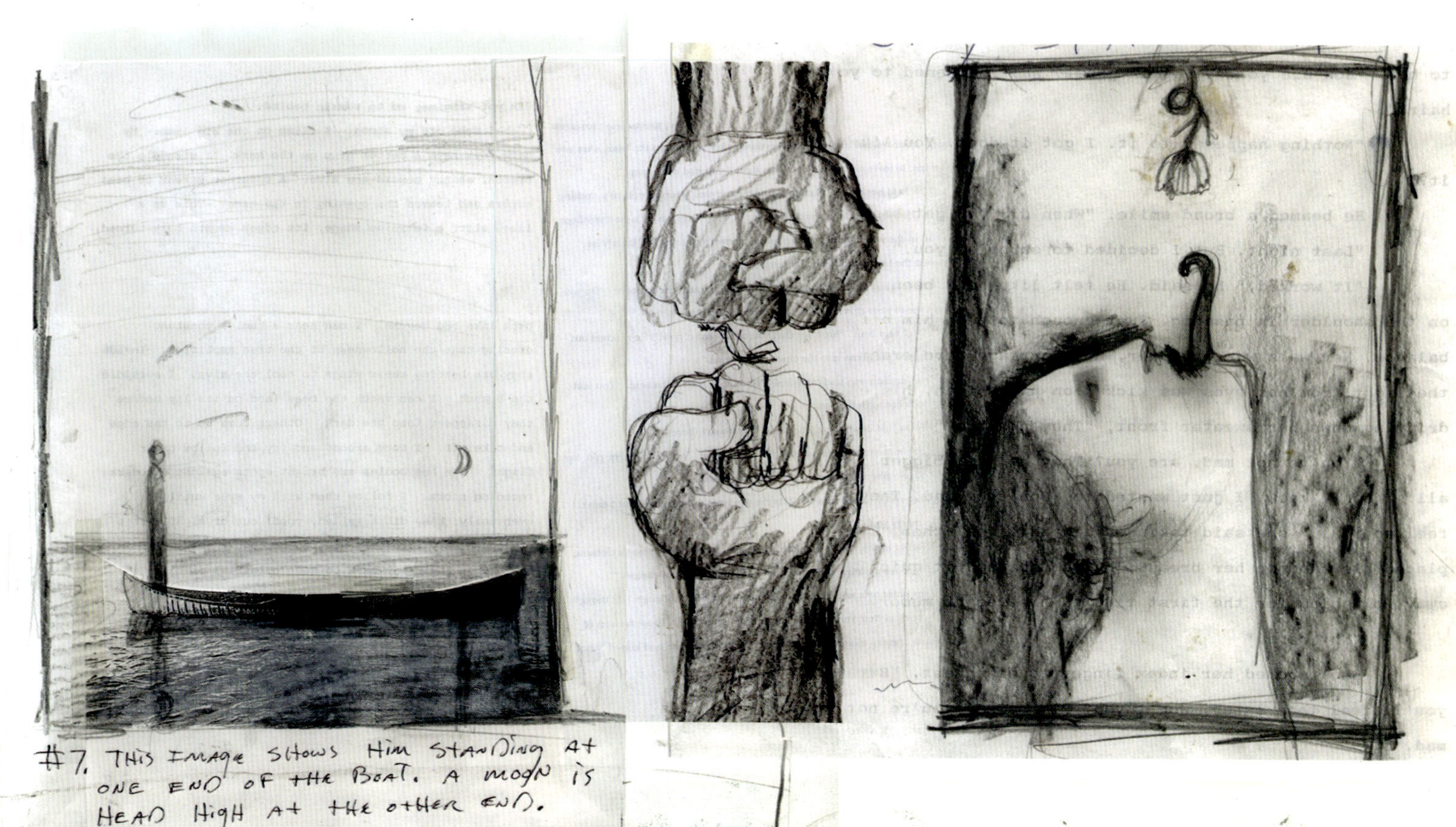

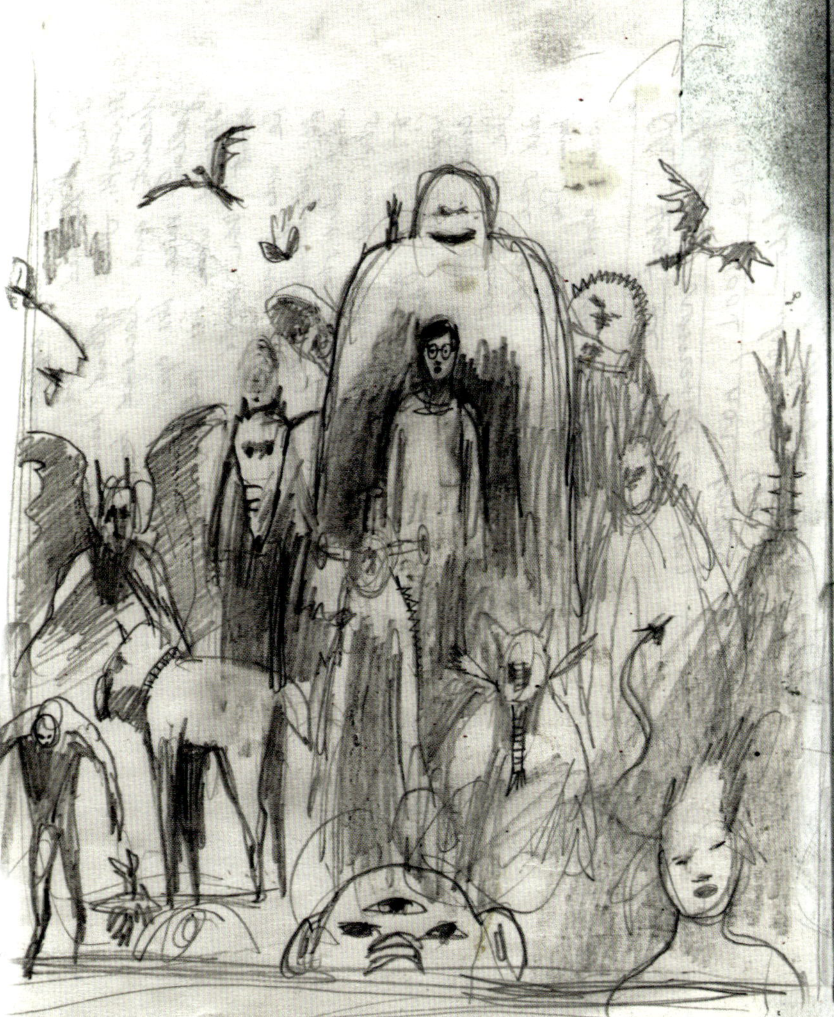

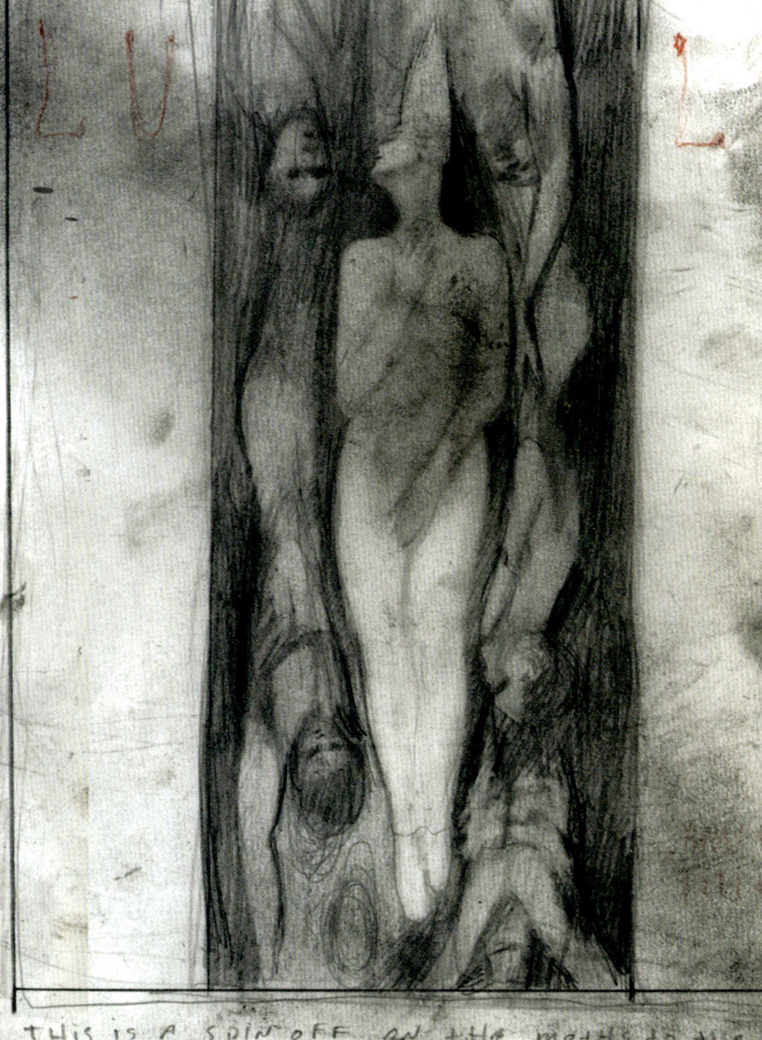

THIS IS A SPINOFF ON THE MOTHS TO THE
IDEA. LULU WHO IS IN A THIN ALMOST SEE
GOWN IS ALMOST GLOWING WHITE. HER SKIN IS LIKE
PORCELAIN. HER HEAD IS THROWN BACK IN A VAMPIS

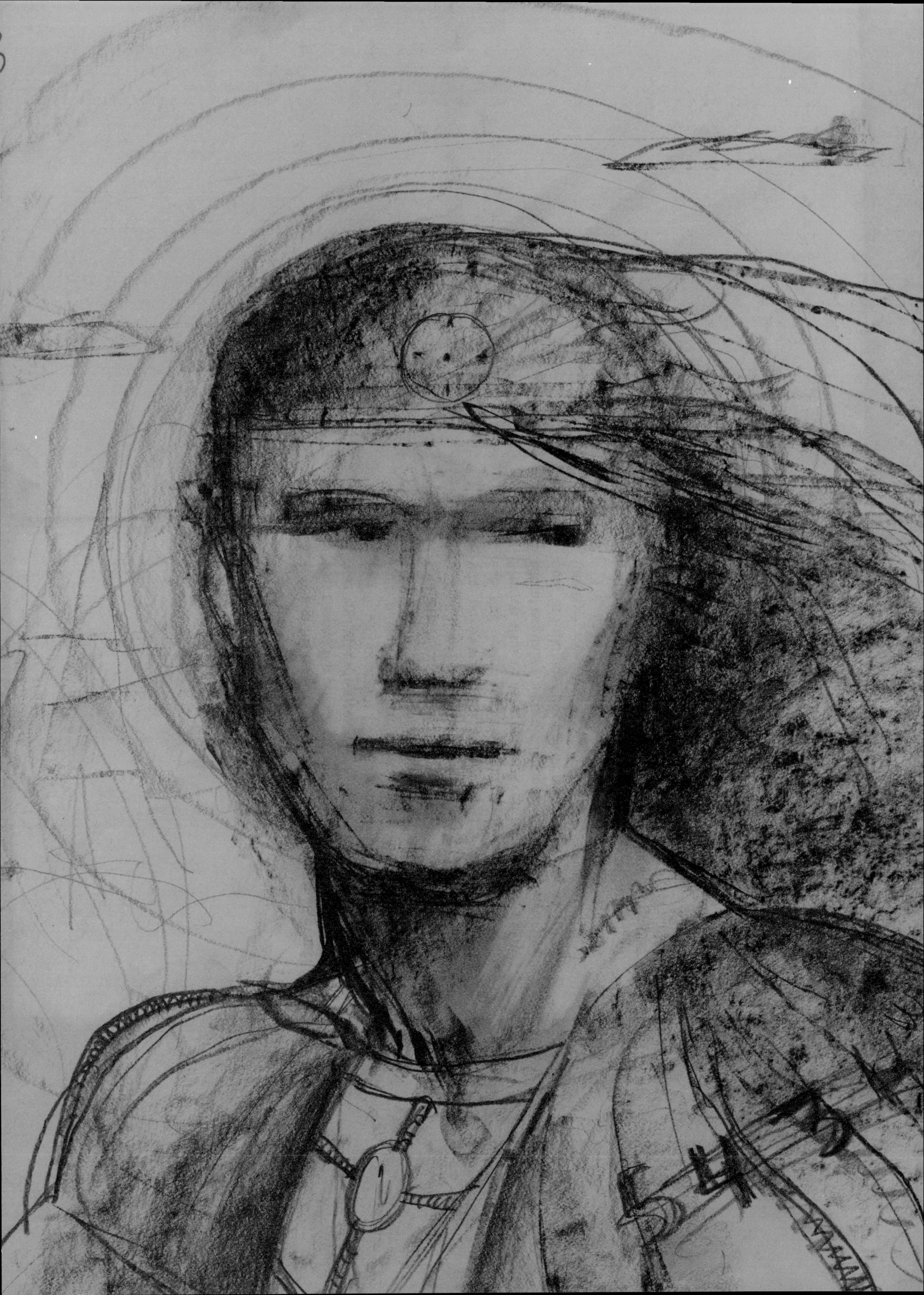

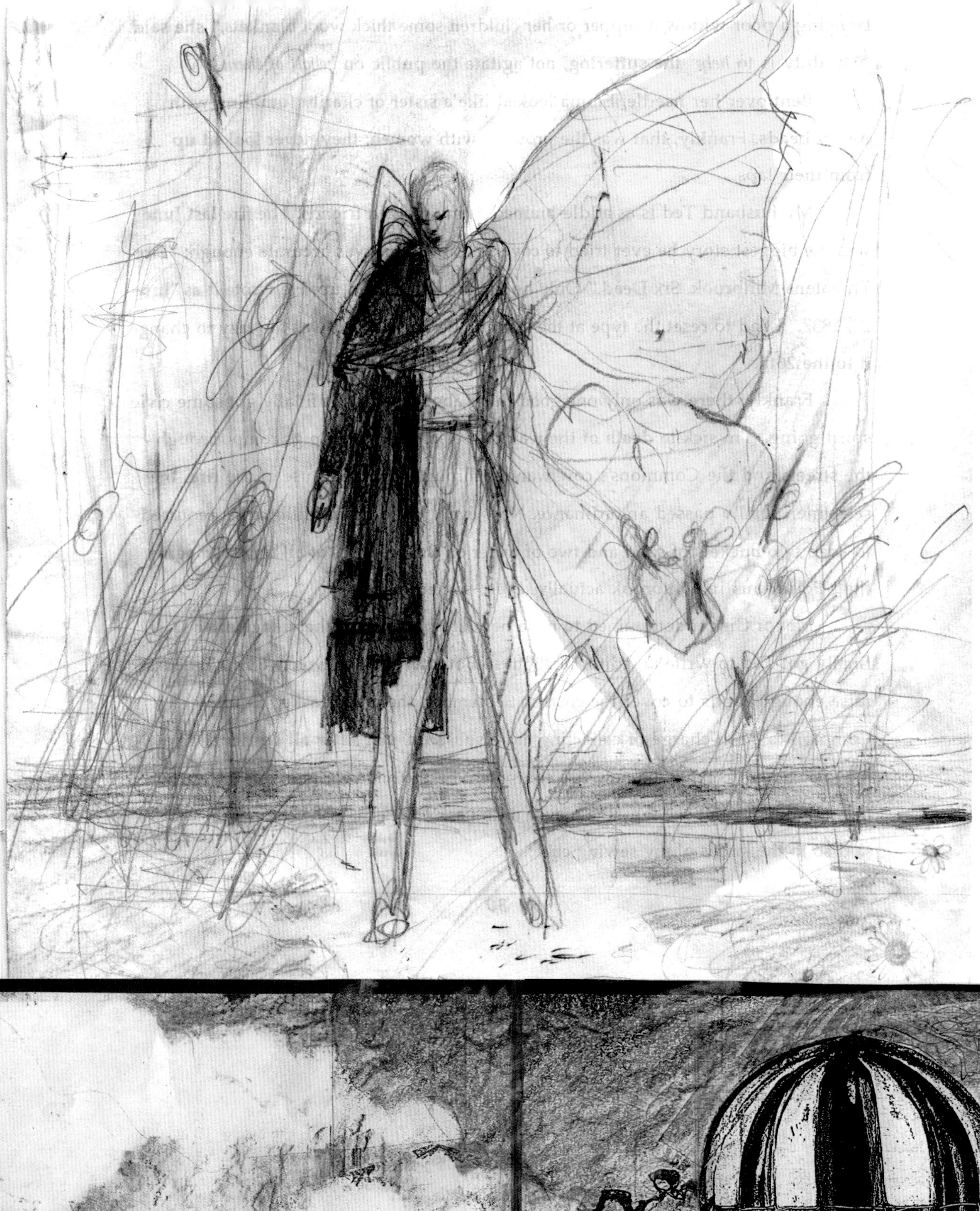

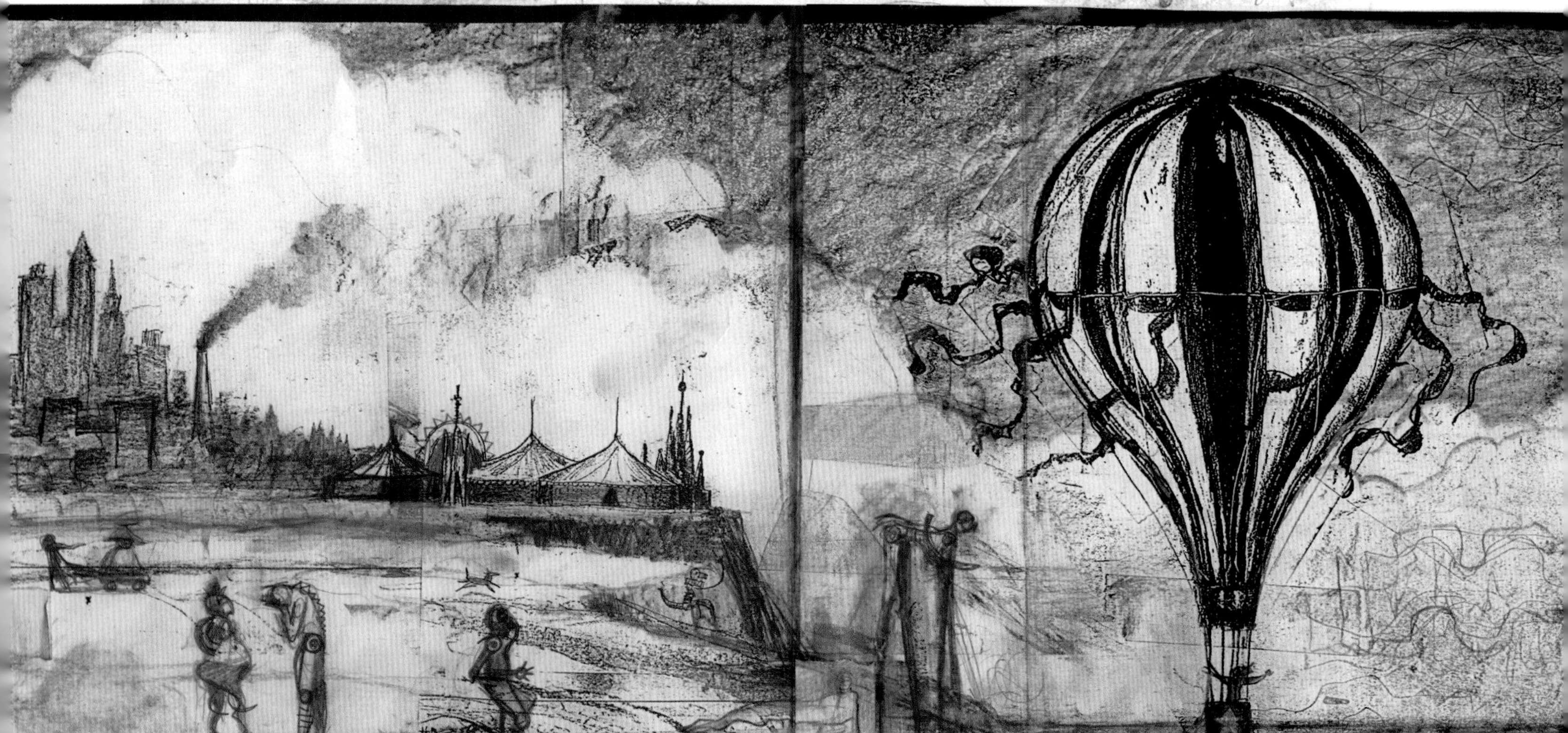

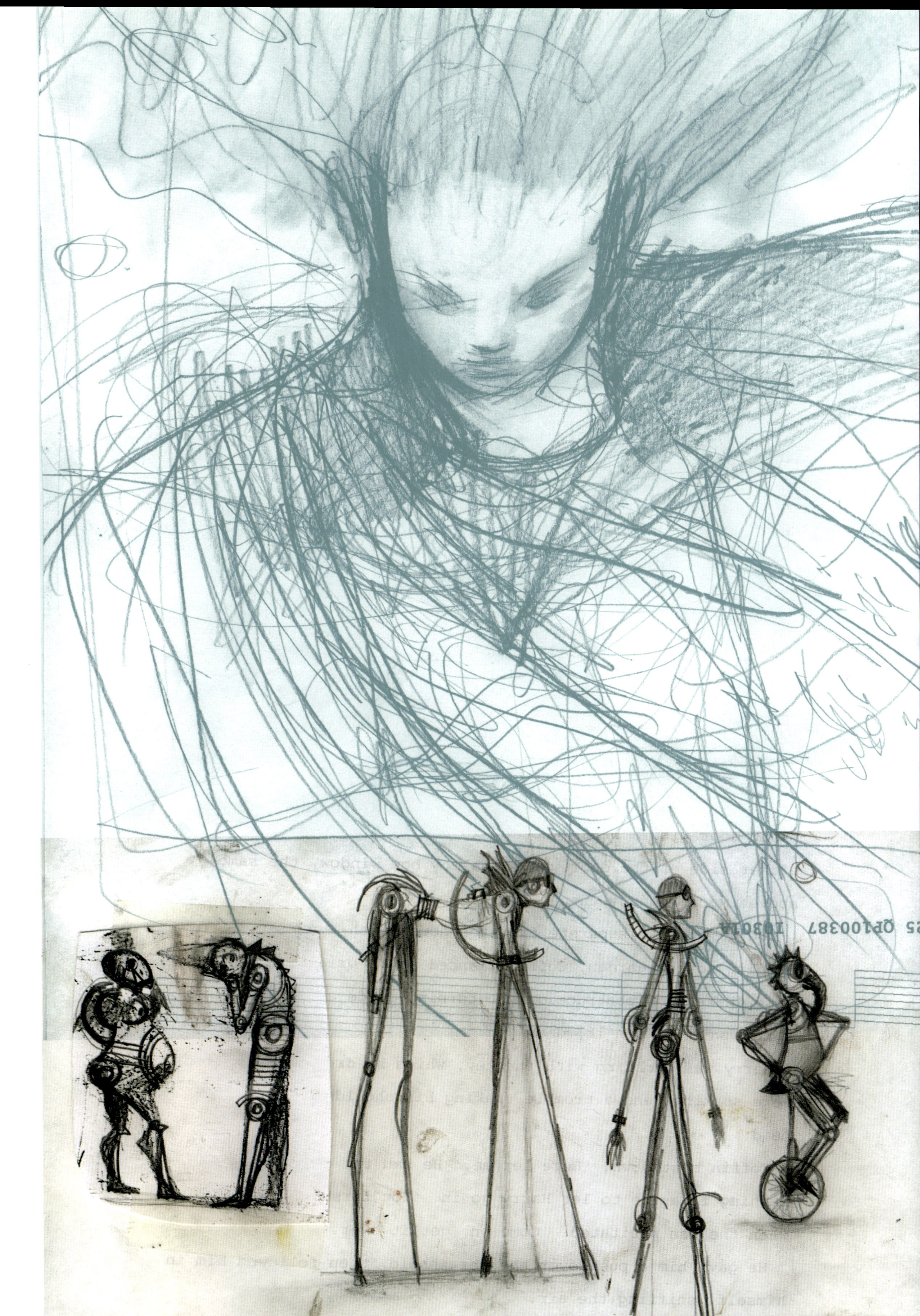

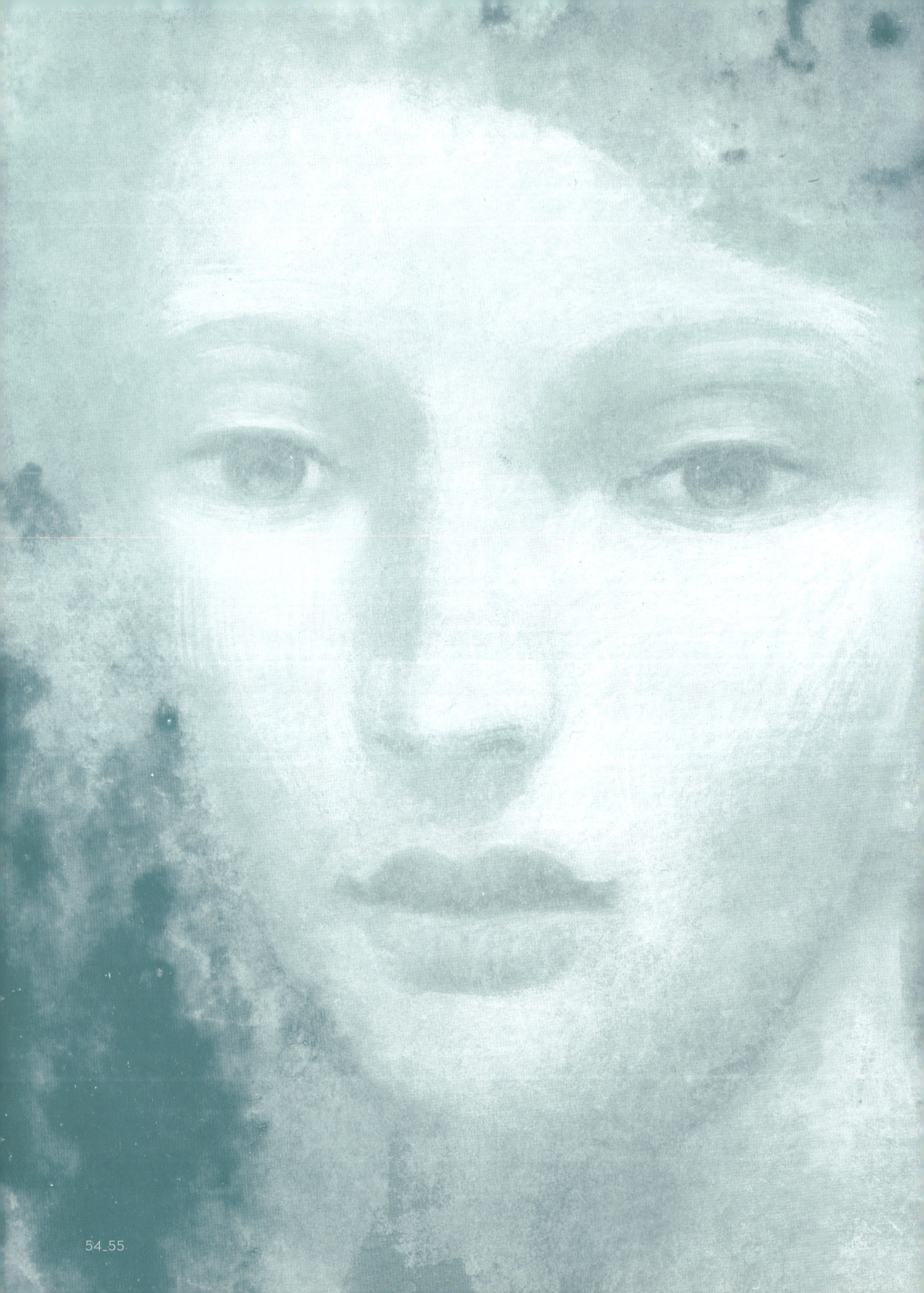

portraits

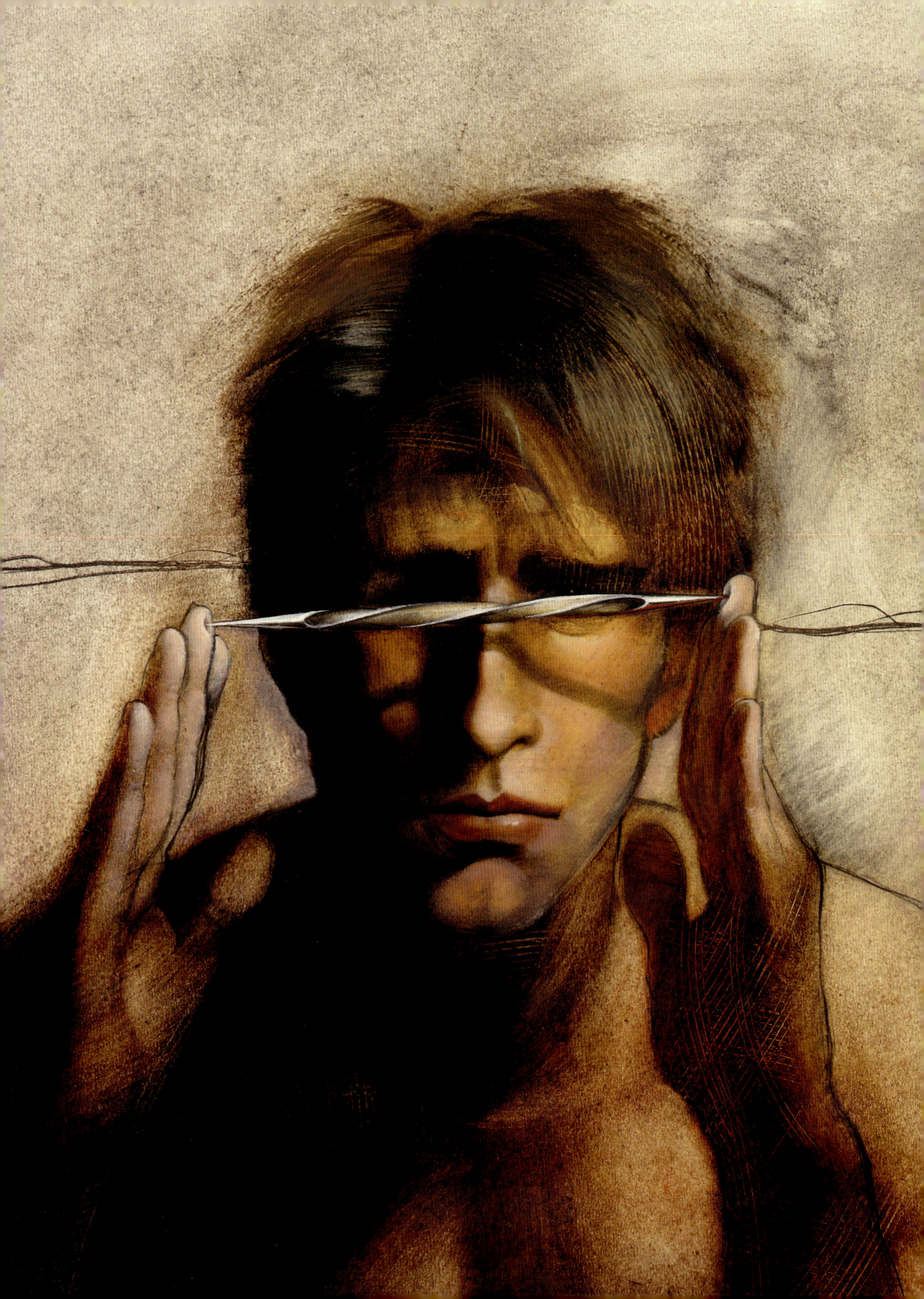

portraits

mirrored essence

The human figure had a timeless hold on my art making consciousness, and I loved drawing and painting it. Portraiture is similar to the figurative arts but translating an individual's essence into graphite and pigment is mysterious and difficult.

In the early days of living in NYC I started a series of portraits of young up and coming illustrators and devised a technique I called the visual interview, consisting of taking in as much information as I could through my fields of perception and then shooting some Polaroid pictures. I paid attention to as many details as possible – the person's movements, energy, skin color, attitude, stance, smell. My goal was to create the art as soon as possible while the individual was still vivid in my memory. *Peer Portraits* was printed in a NYC art magazine and the publishing world took notice.

One of my first portrait jobs was with *Rolling Stone* when they commissioned a painting of Elvis Costello. *The New York Times Magazine* put my portrait of a young Hemingway on its cover, but it was a series of illustrations I created for *Sports Illustrated* that finally put me on the map for this type of work. It was an article on chess champion Bobby Fischer that contained portraits and other conceptual pieces, 11 illustrations in all. I had the opportunity to visit the places and people written about in the article. This in turn inspired other illustrative journalistic projects. One of my favorites involved 10 days with soon-to-be boxing champion Mike Tyson. I created life-size drawings, paintings, and studies of Tyson, the trainers, and boxers of Cus D'Amato's gym, which were published alongside my commentary in the 1989 January issue of *Print* magazine.

Meeting people even for a short period of time allowed me to feel their likeness, bringing another dimension to the art.

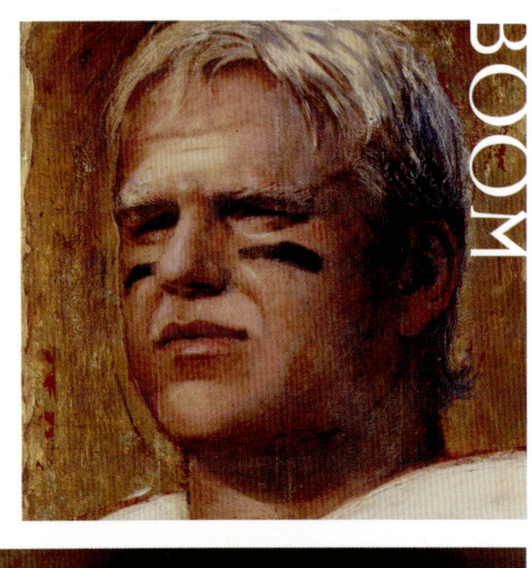
BOOM

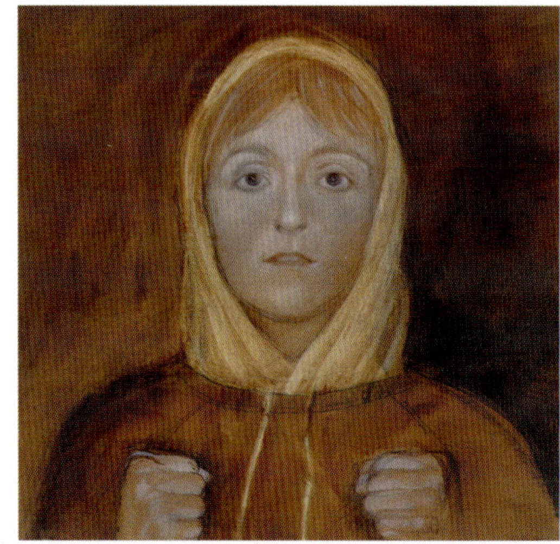

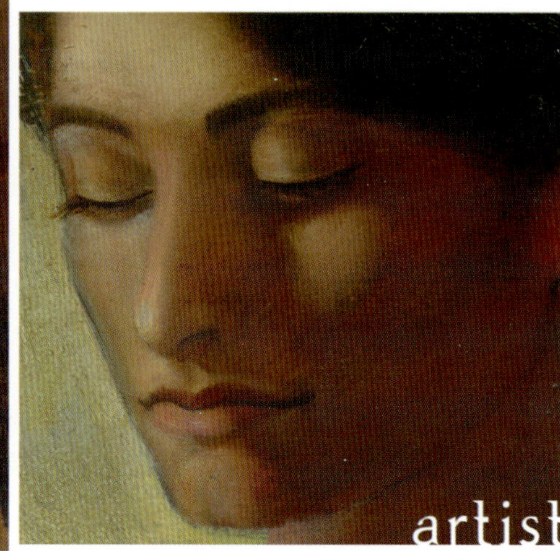
artist

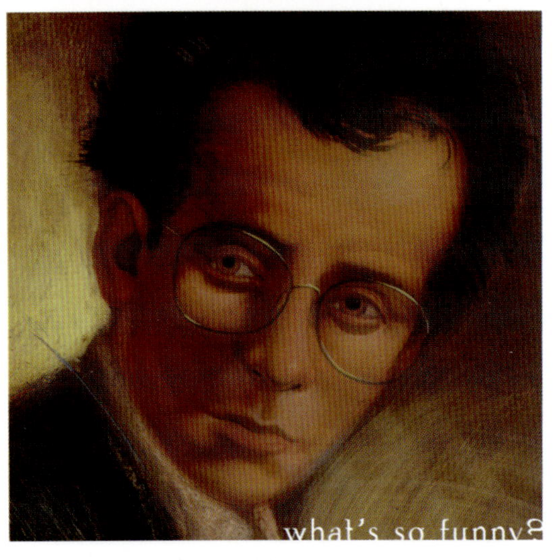
what's so funny?

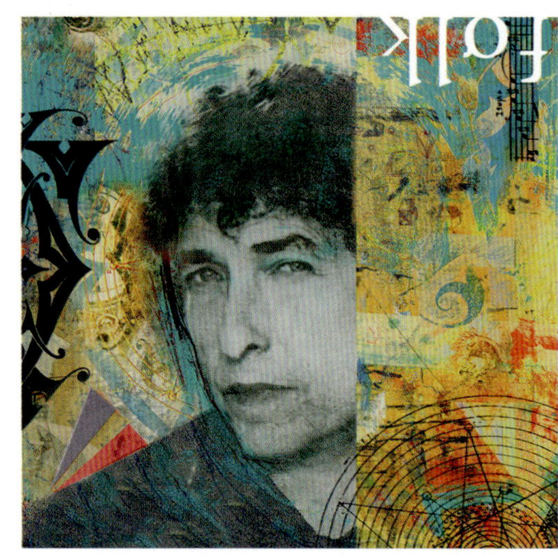
folk

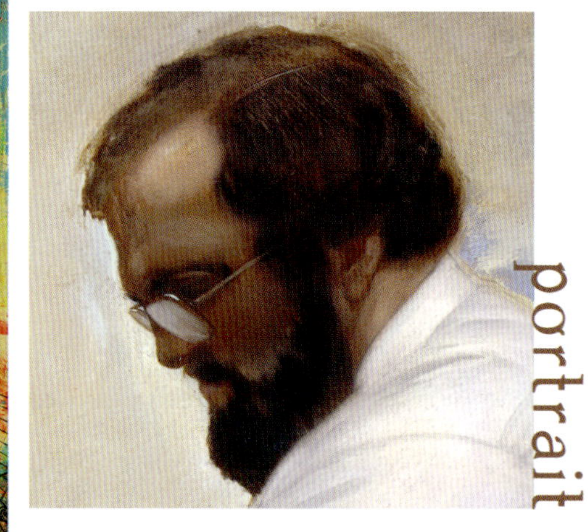
portrait

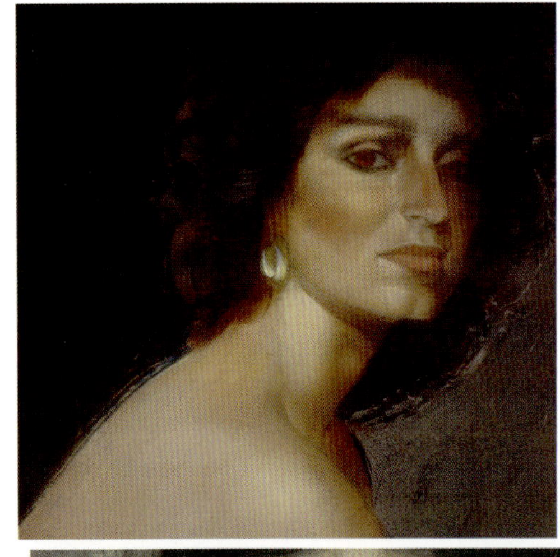

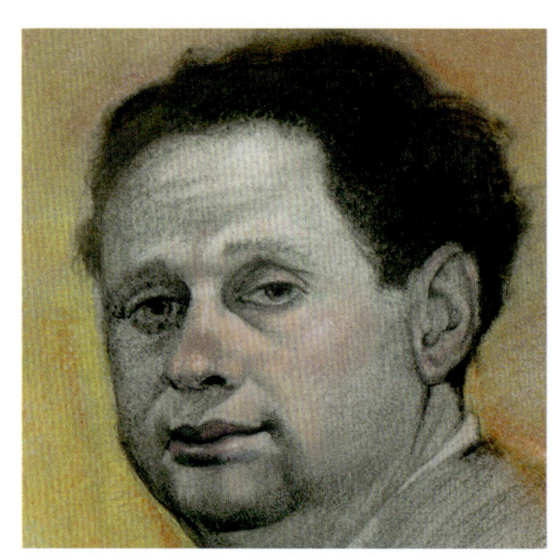

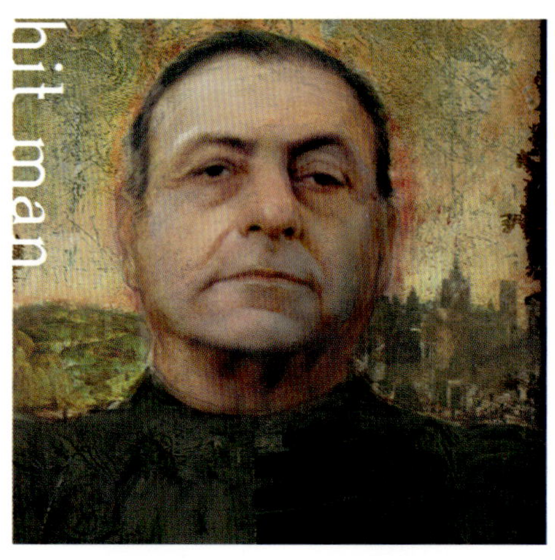
hit man

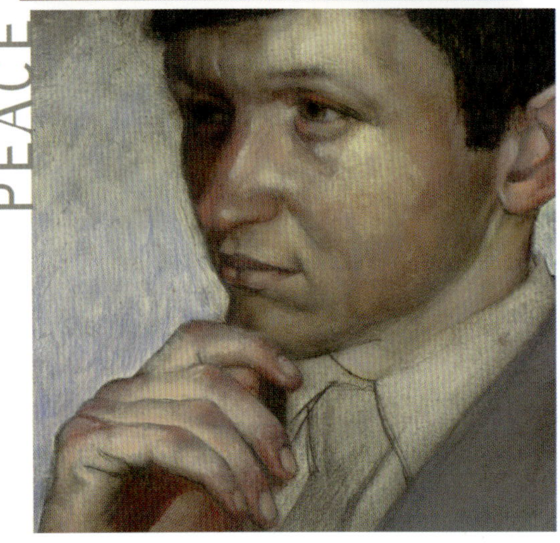
PEACE

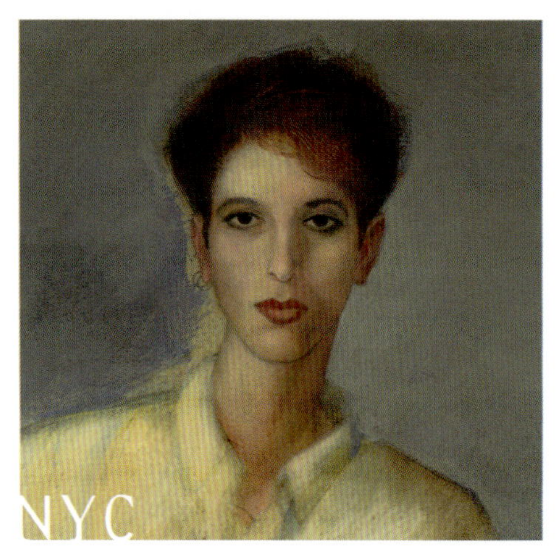
NYC

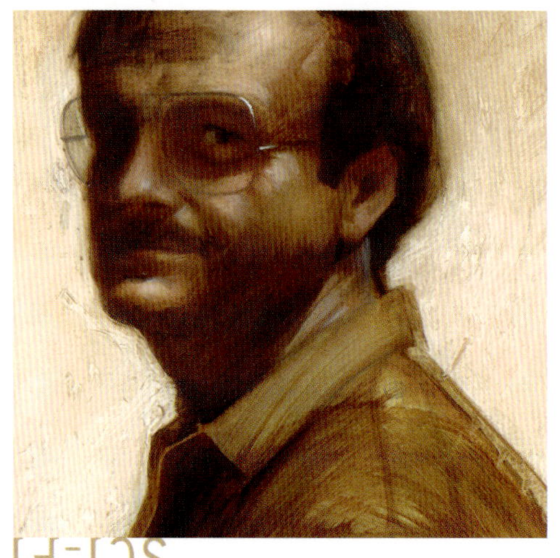
SCI-FI

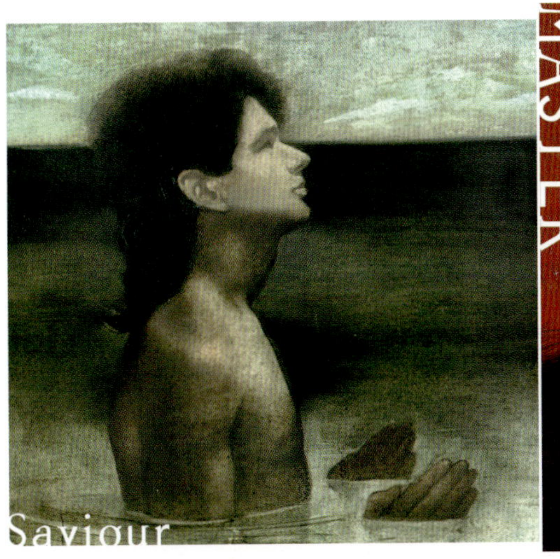
Saviour

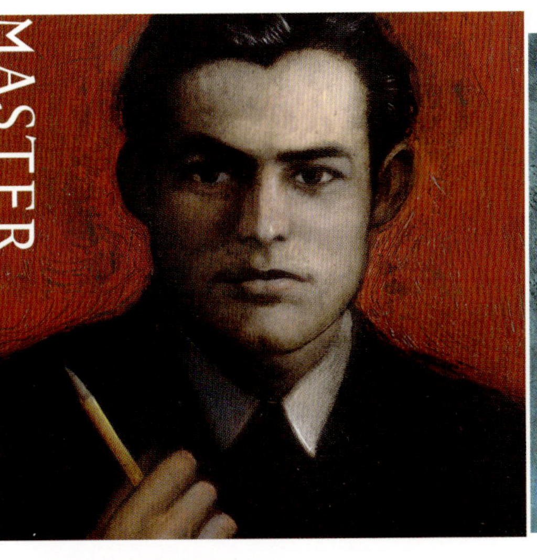
MASTER

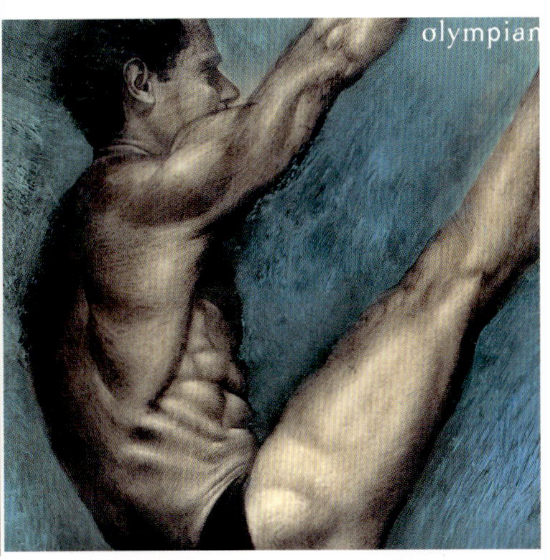
olympian

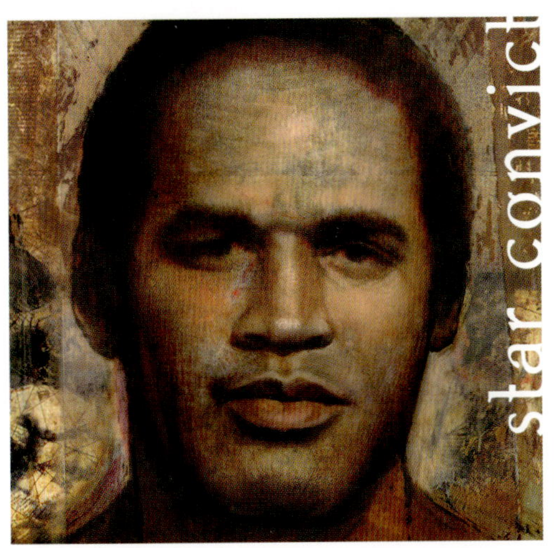
star convict

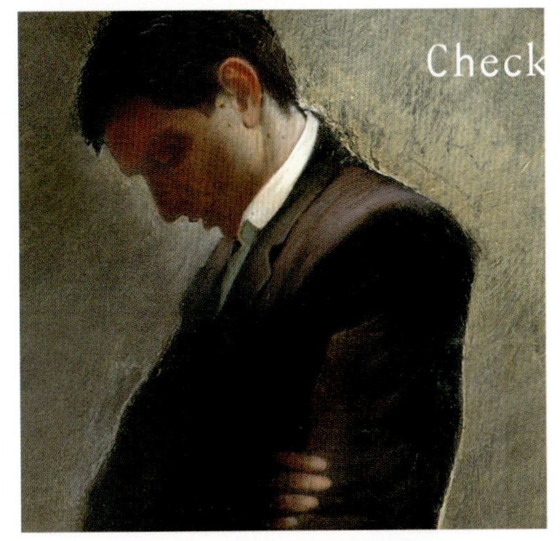
Check

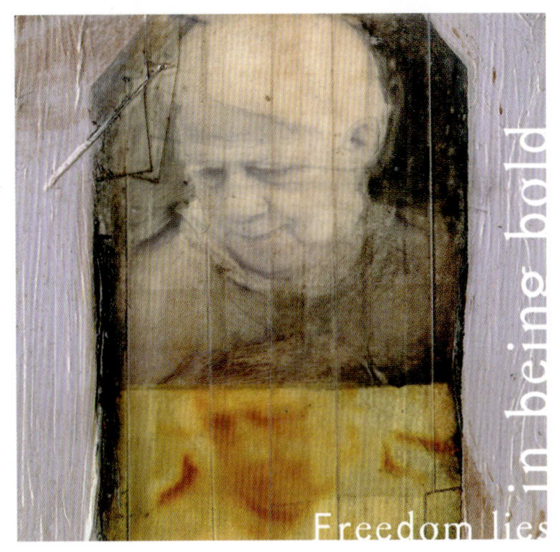
Freedom lies
in being bold

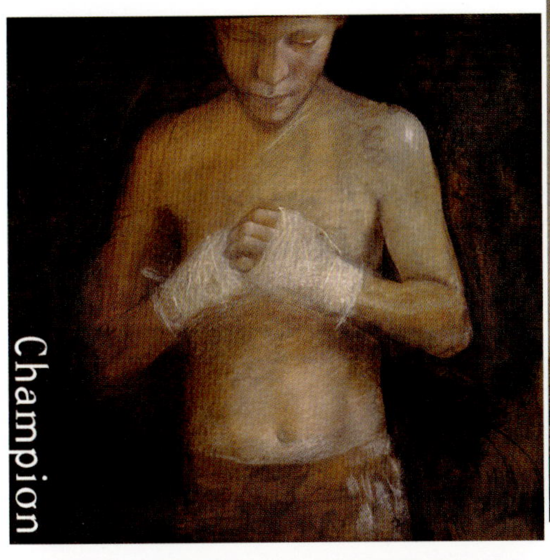
Champion

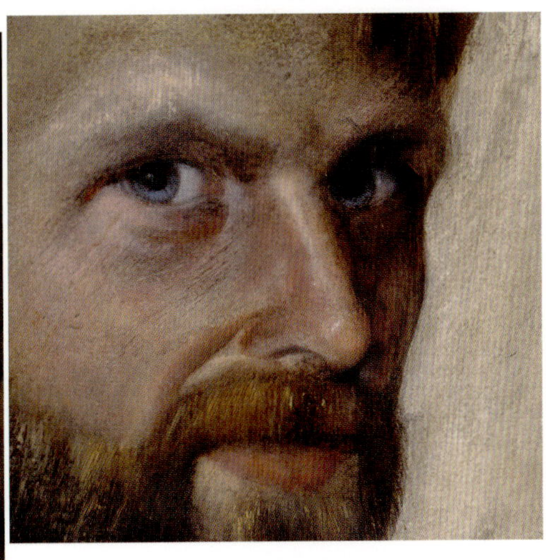

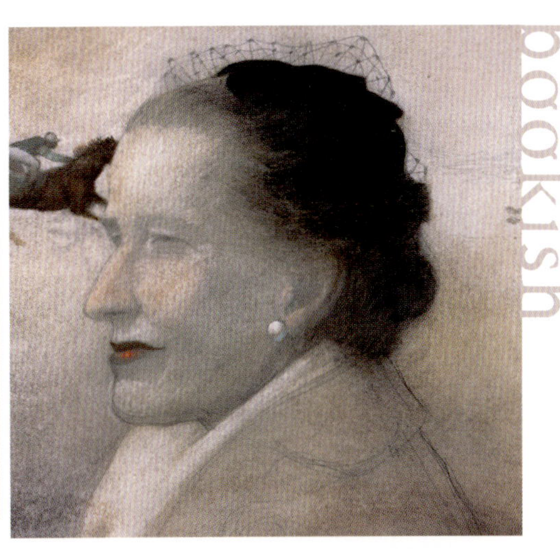
bookish

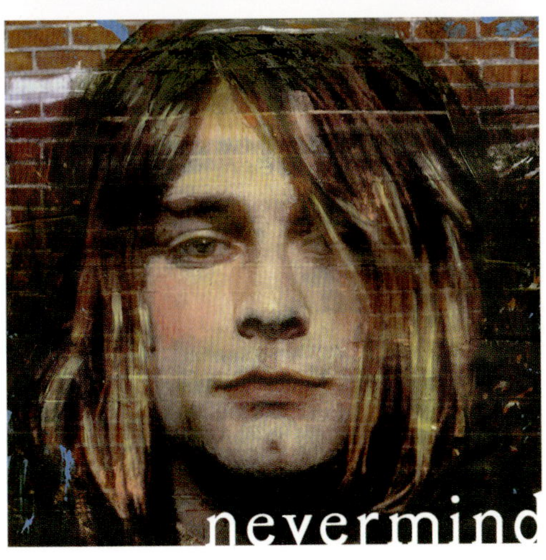
nevermind

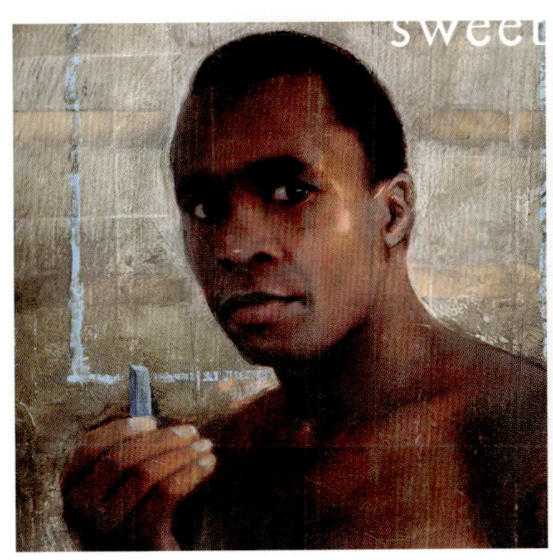
sweet

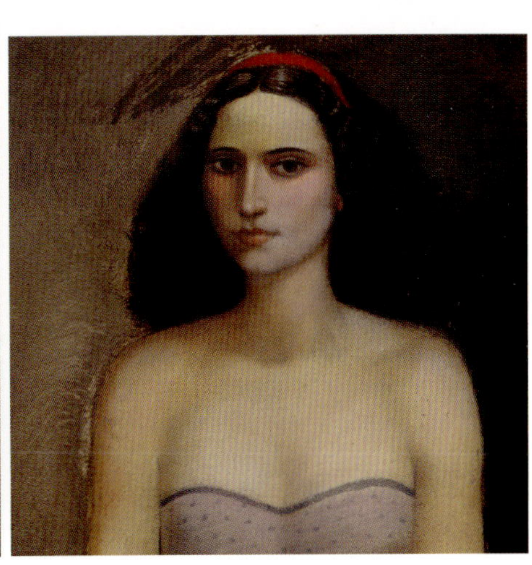

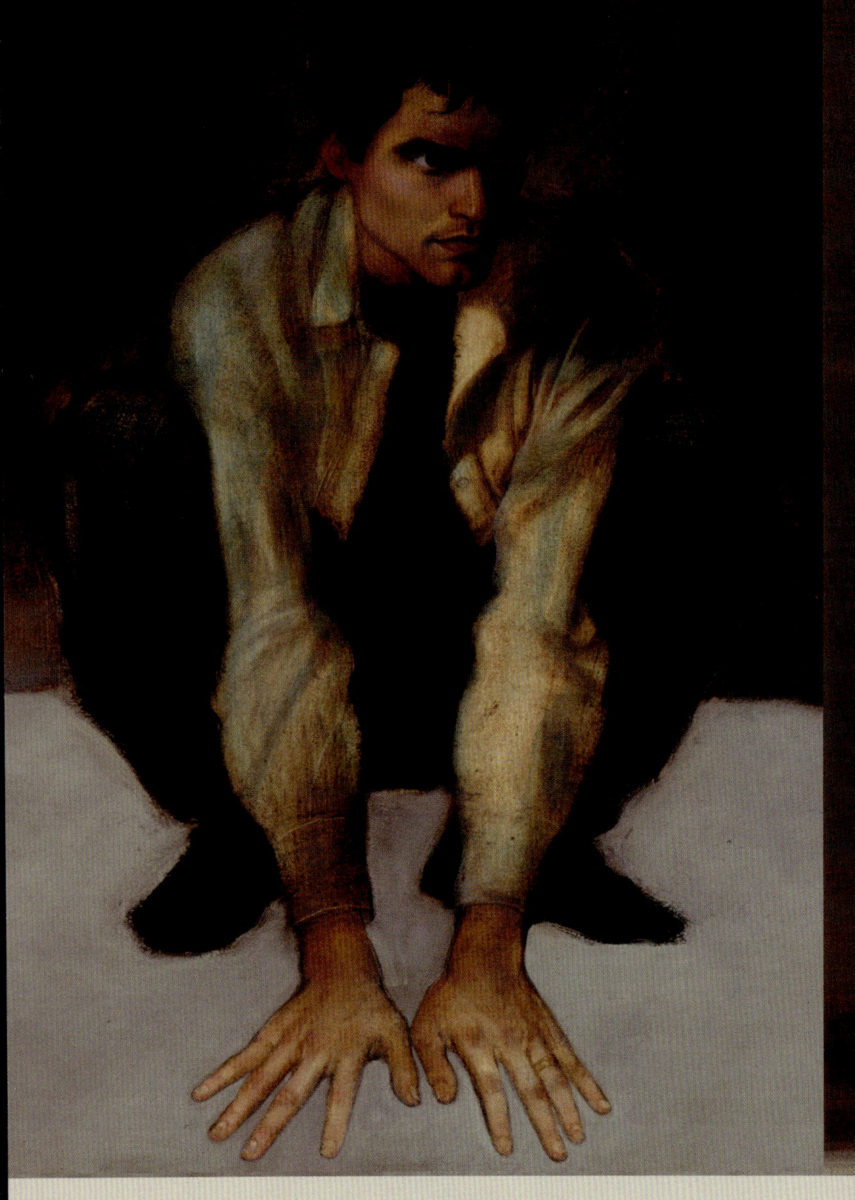

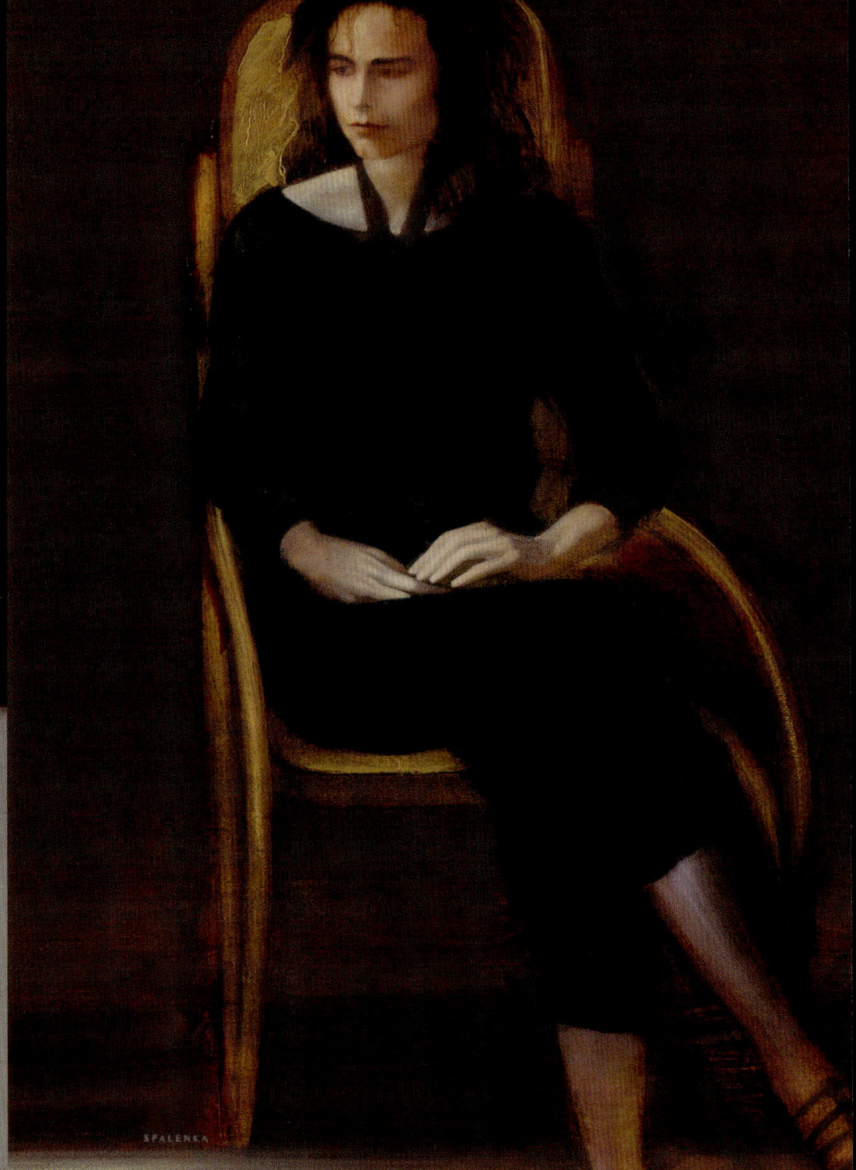
SPALENKA

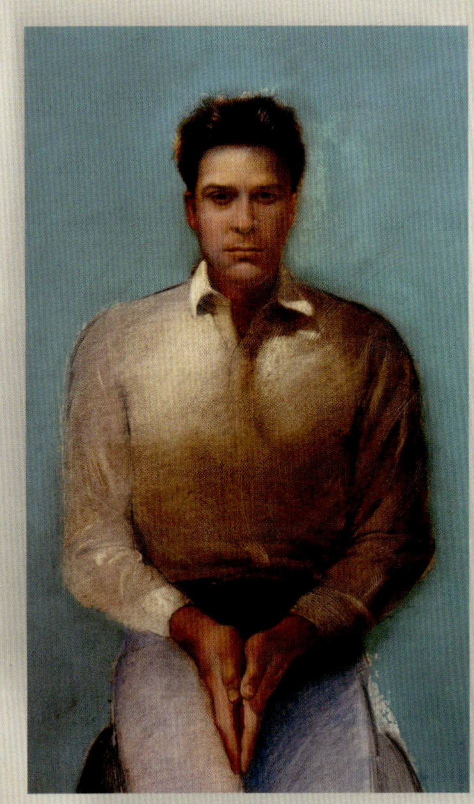

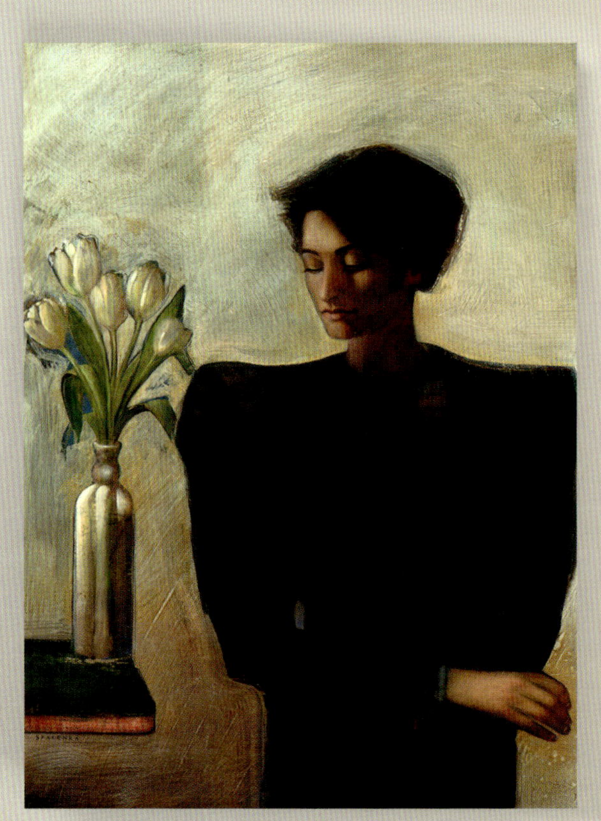

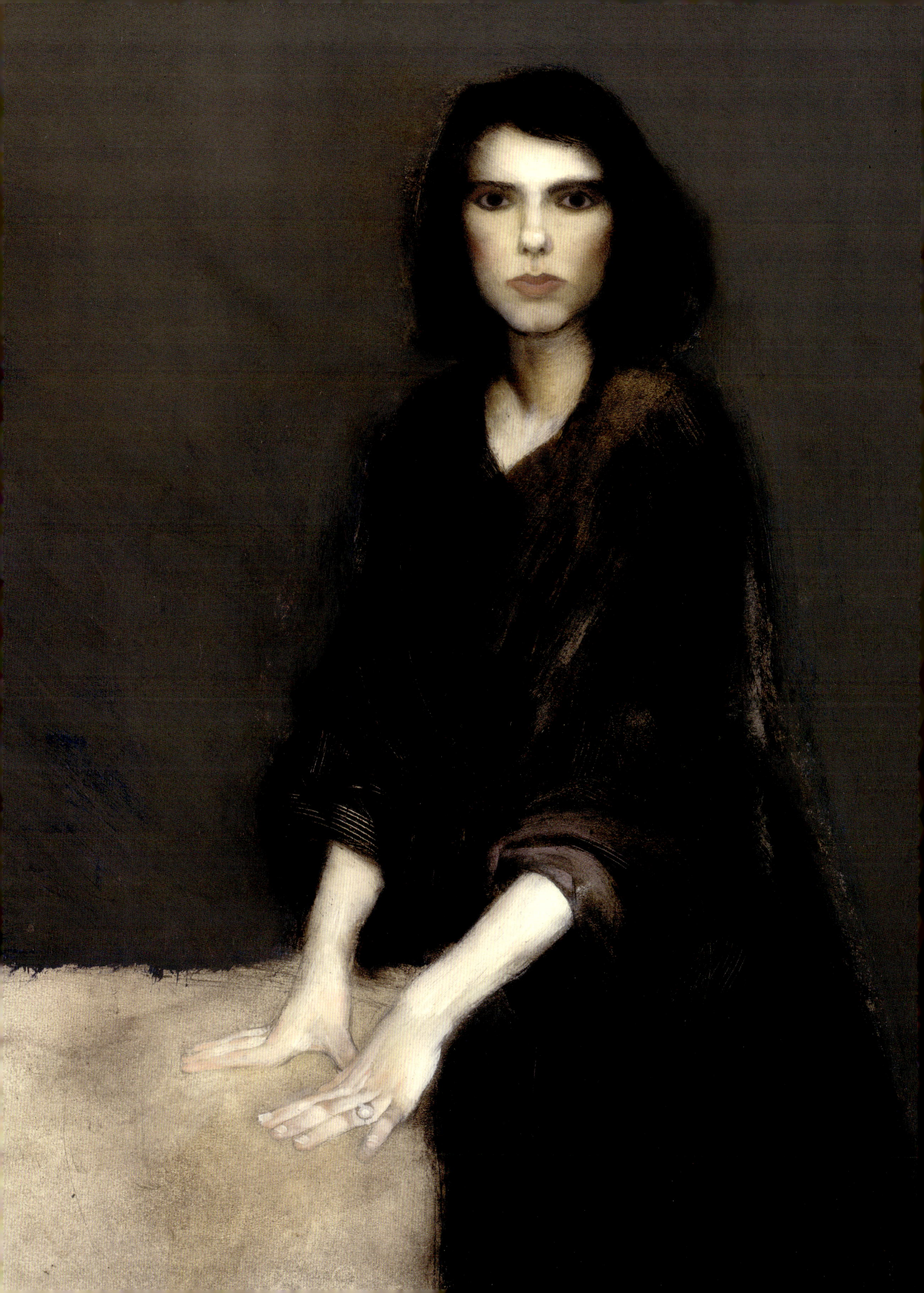

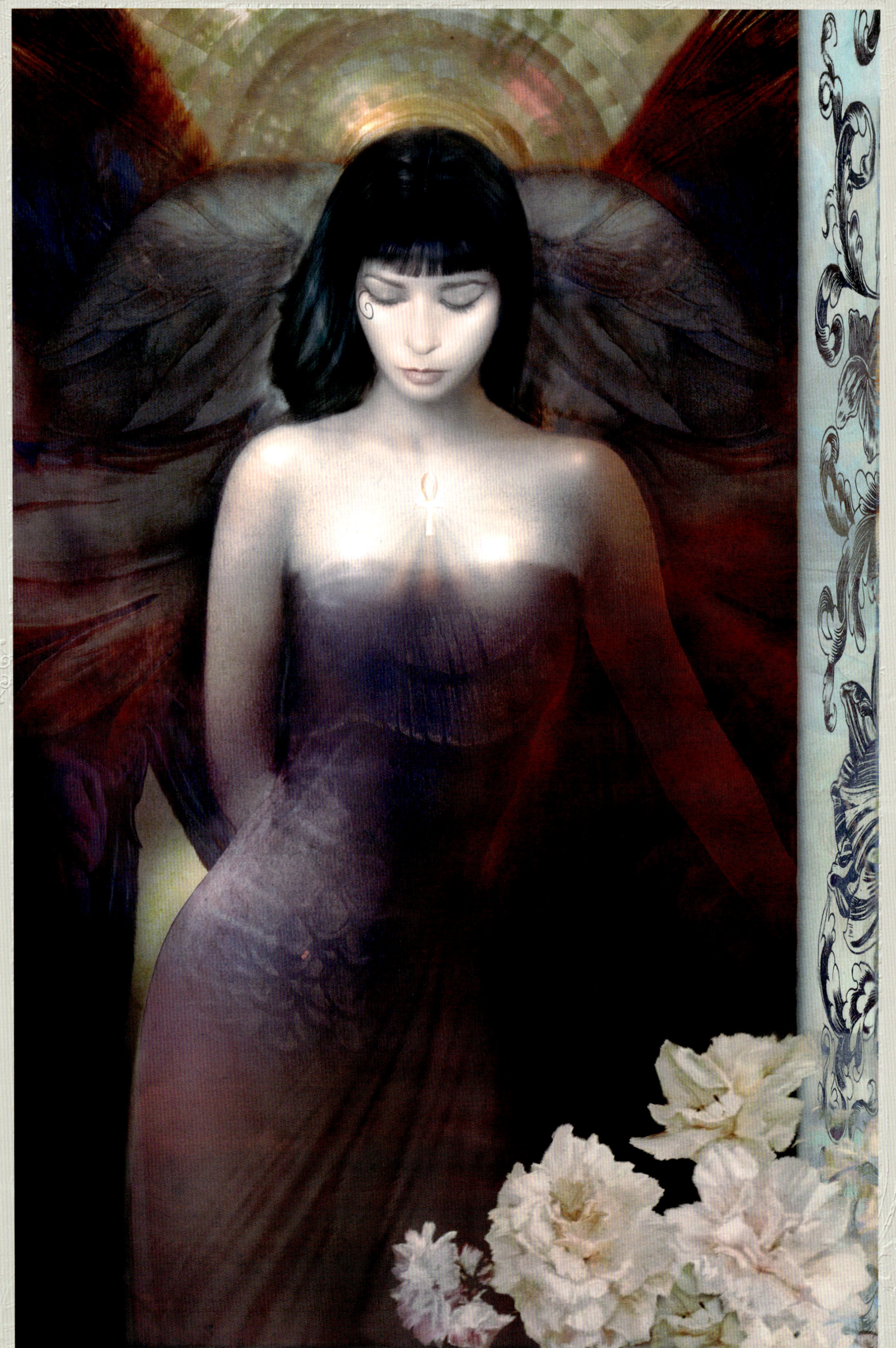

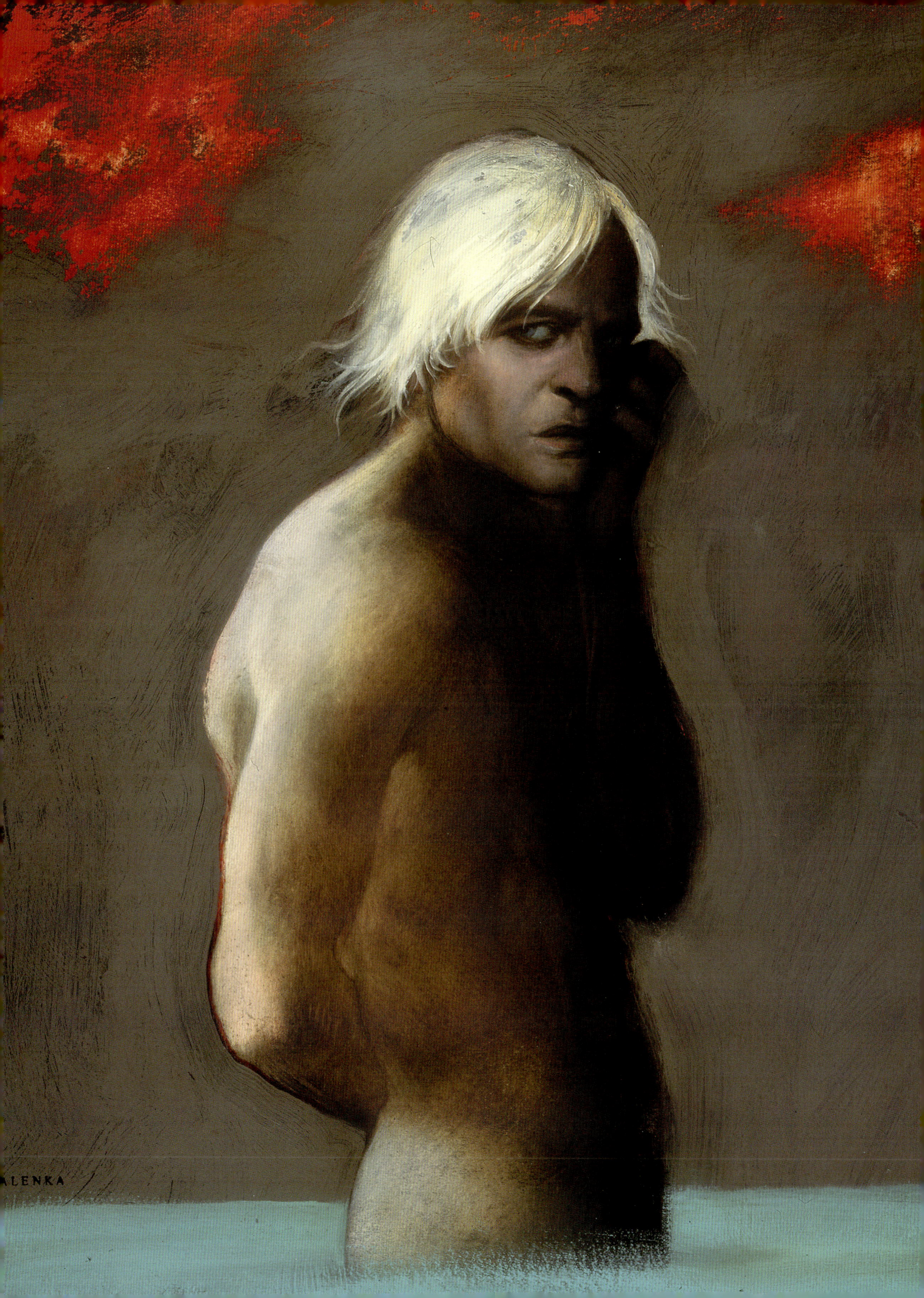
ALENKA

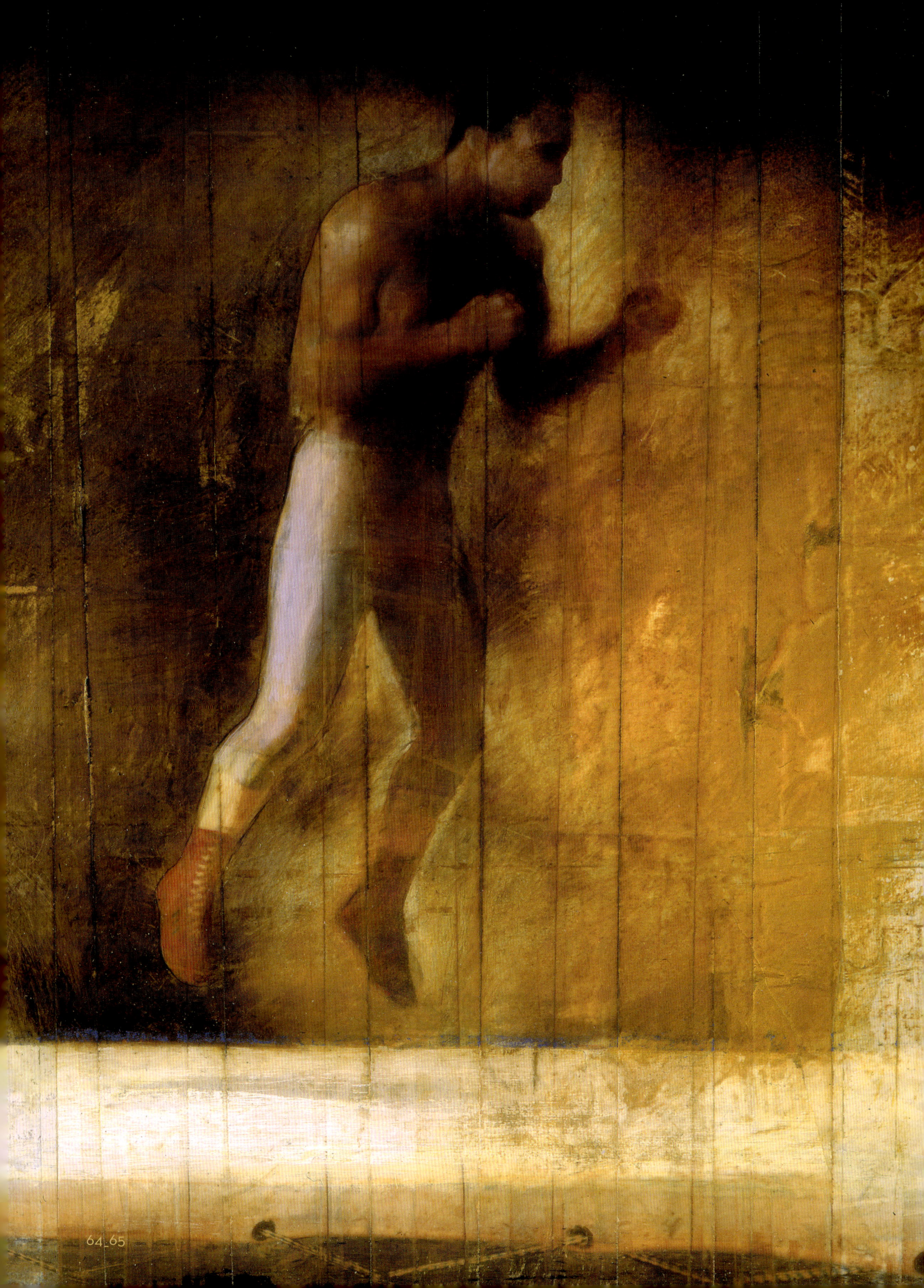

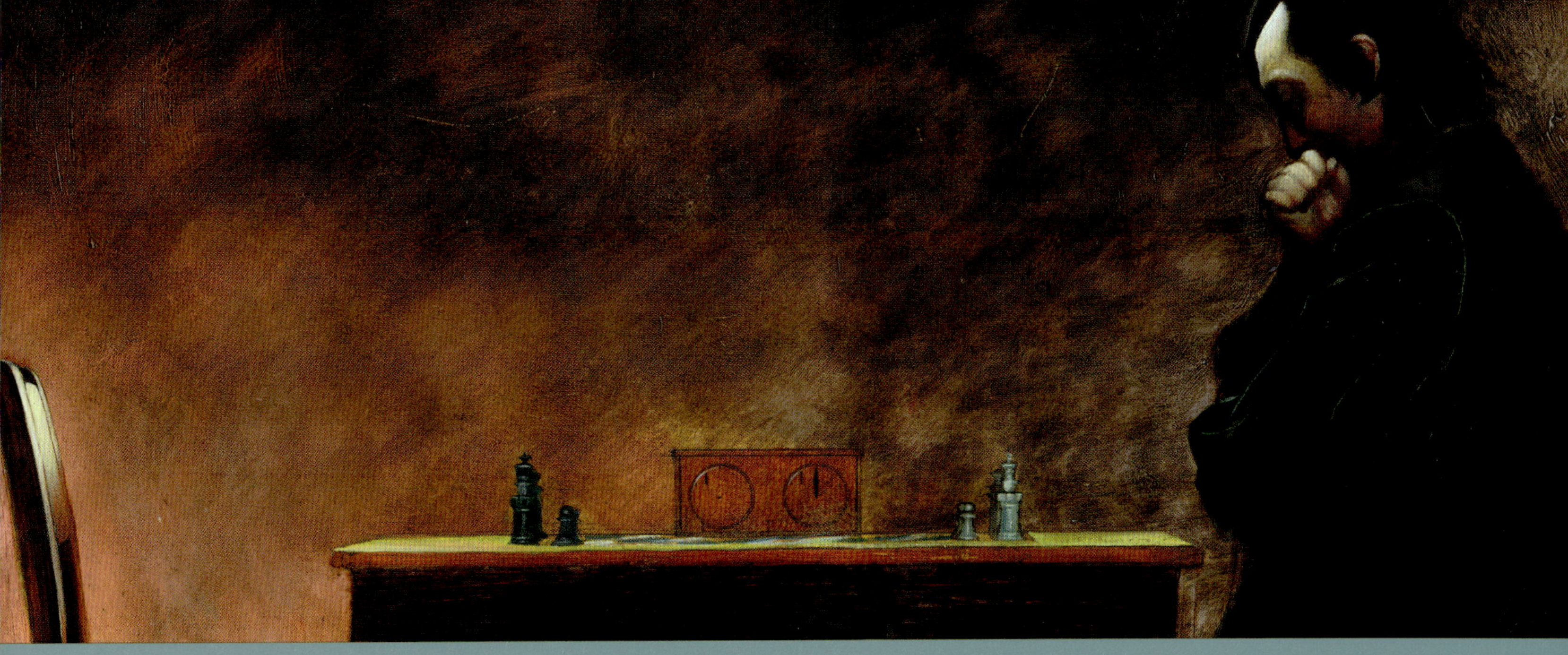

Athletic excellence and training come in many styles and this was no more apparent than in the boxers Mike Tyson and Sugar Ray Leonard. Whereas Tyson's camp was gritty, bare bones – Ray's gym, where I met him, was inside a hotel. Tyson's style was the boxer/slugger, whereas Ray floated around an opponent, striking with well-placed punches. Tyson was almost childlike in manner and speech (until he got in the ring and the monster appeared). Ray was the consummate gentleman, gracious and in control even when sparring. The one thing that was constant with athletes and other ambitious souls I met was their sacrificial devotion to achievement, conquering, and winning.

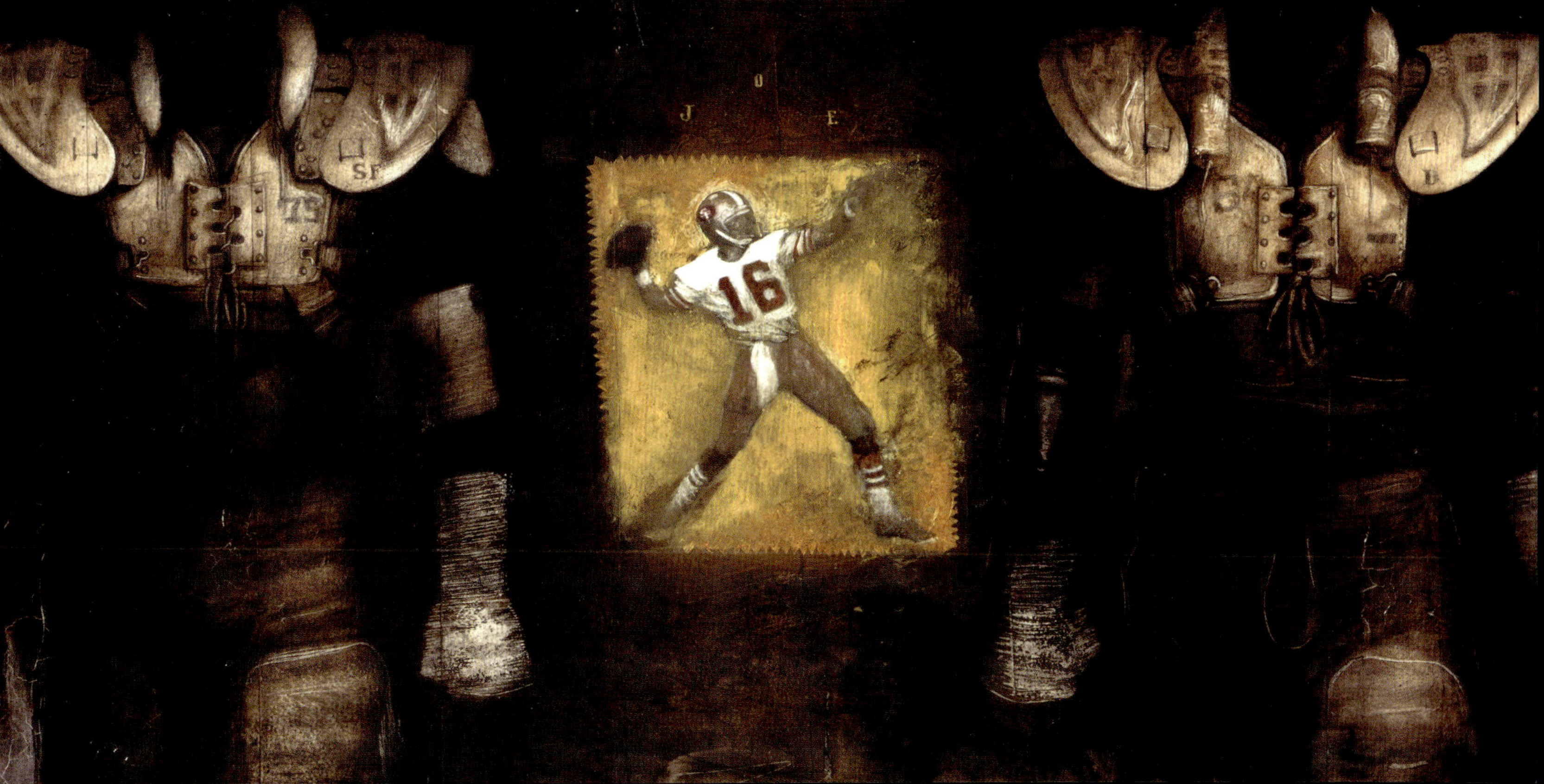

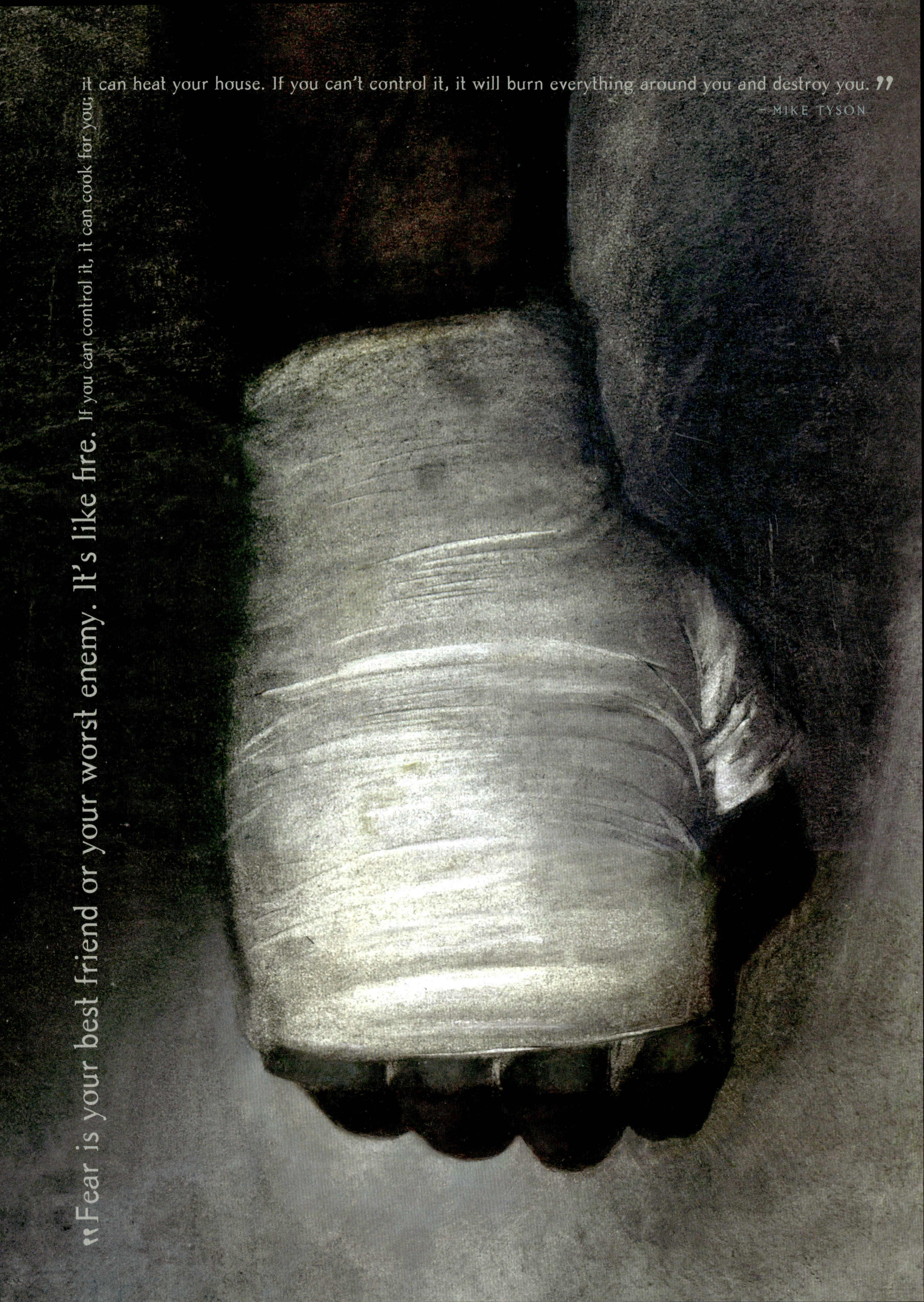

“Fear is your best friend or your worst enemy. It’s like fire. If you can control it, it can cook for you; it can heat your house. If you can’t control it, it will burn everything around you and destroy you.”

—MIKE TYSON

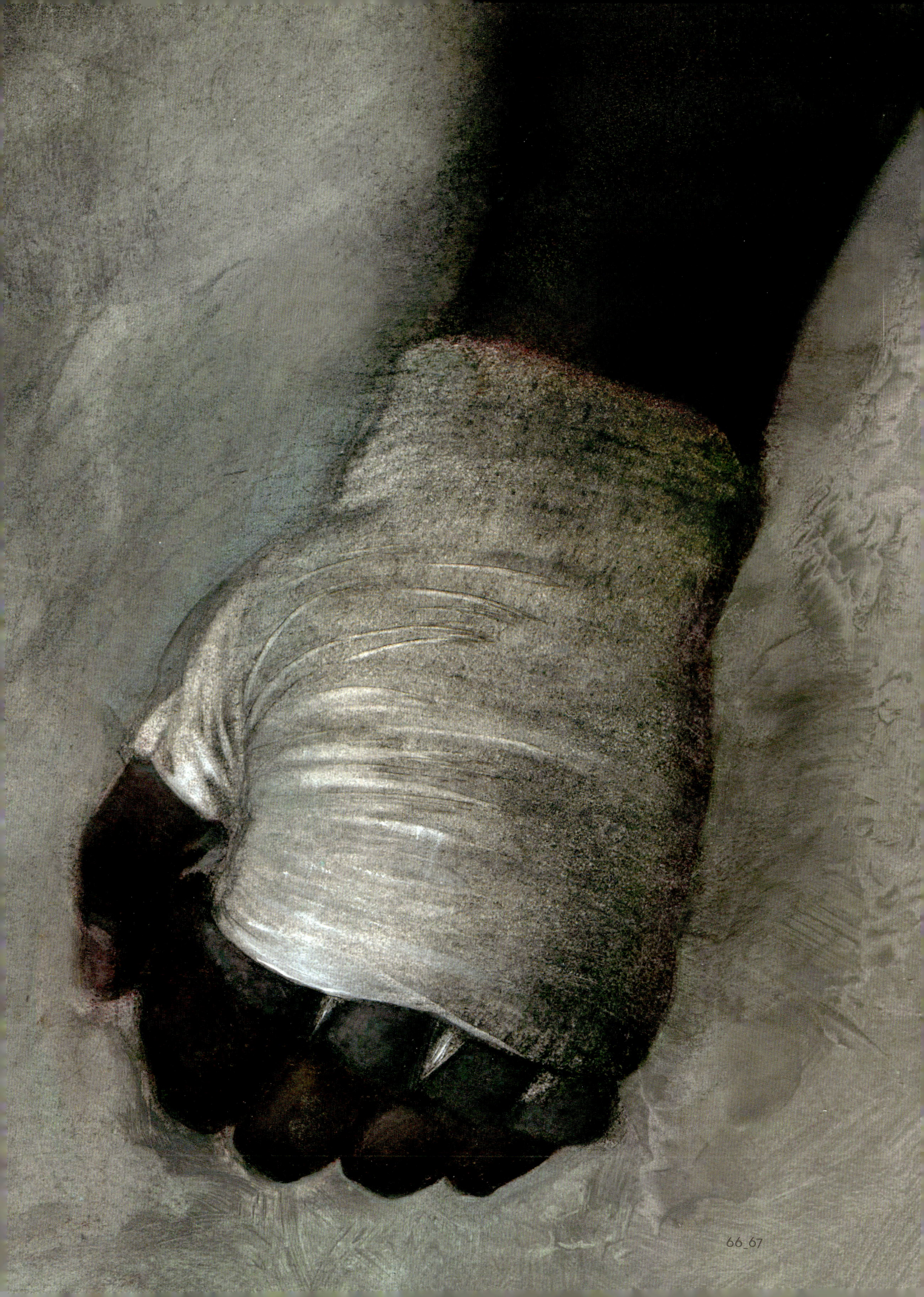

A little green light went on and a trainer yelled "Time!"

Tyson moved into his sparring partner. Rooney barked out orders: "That's a good right hand. Finish with a hook. Seven-seven, five-six, five-six, five-six. That's it!

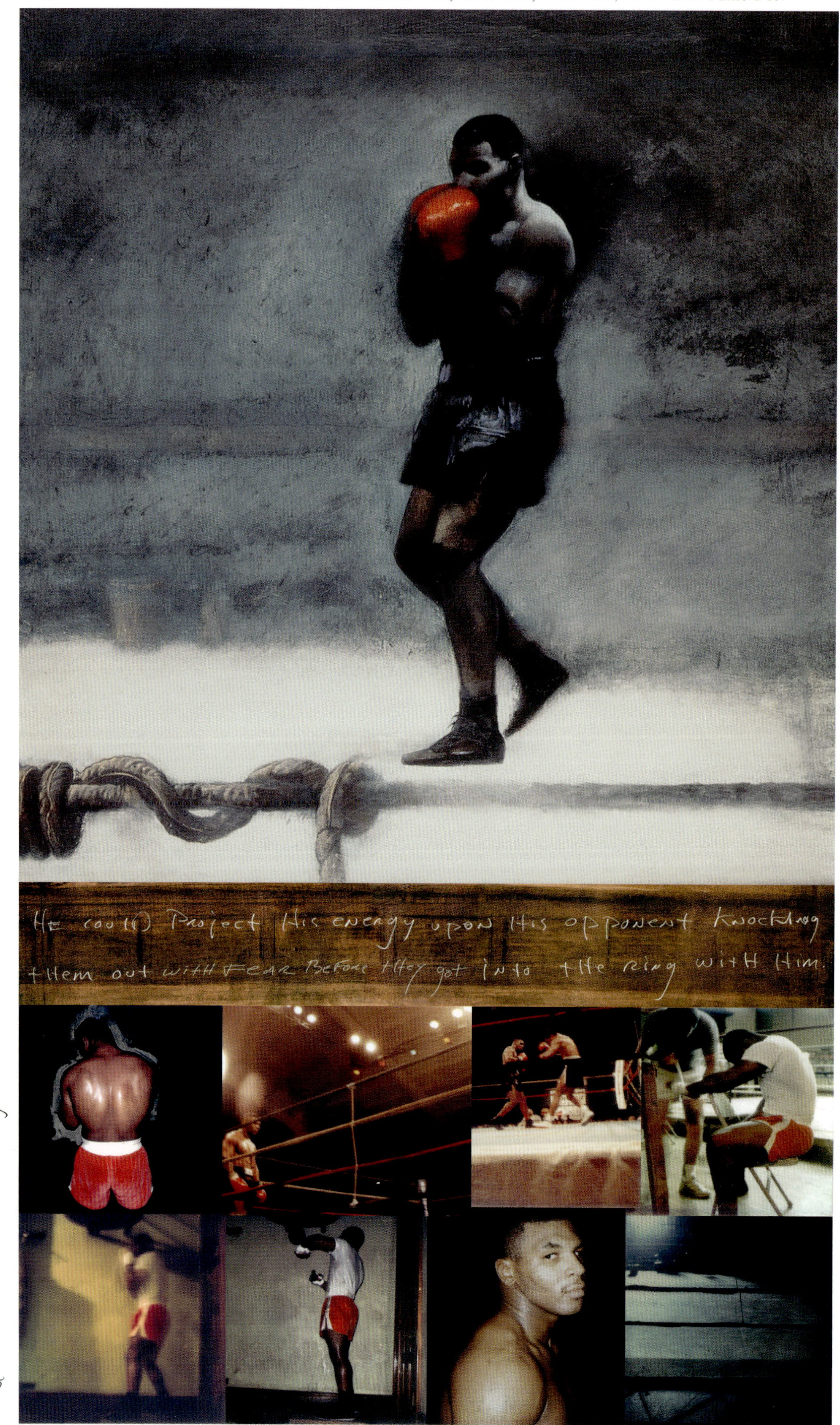

An ominous sensation flooded the gym. I experienced an adrenaline rush and identified with Tyson's opponent. I felt fear.

Watching Tyson Hit the Speed Bag was mesmerizing.

Bam! Bam! Bam!

Bam! Bam! Bam! My ears reverberated with what sounded like gunshots. These blasts were actually Tyson's blows to his sparring partner's body.

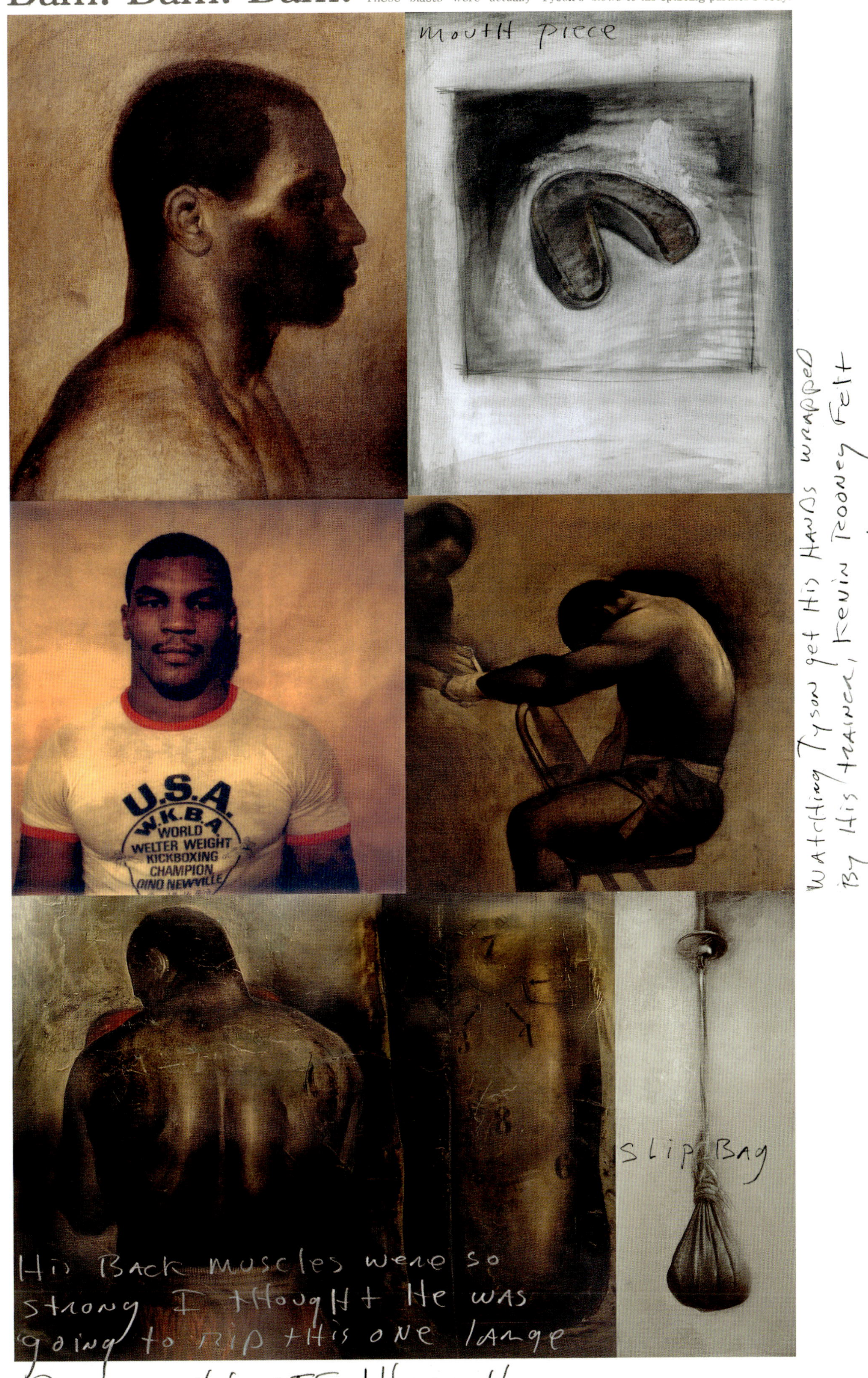

Before his opponent gets in the ring, said Tyson, "he's bigger than me and faster. But once he's in the ring, it's different. I'm so confident, it's ridiculous. I can almost predict the round I'm going to knock him out in."

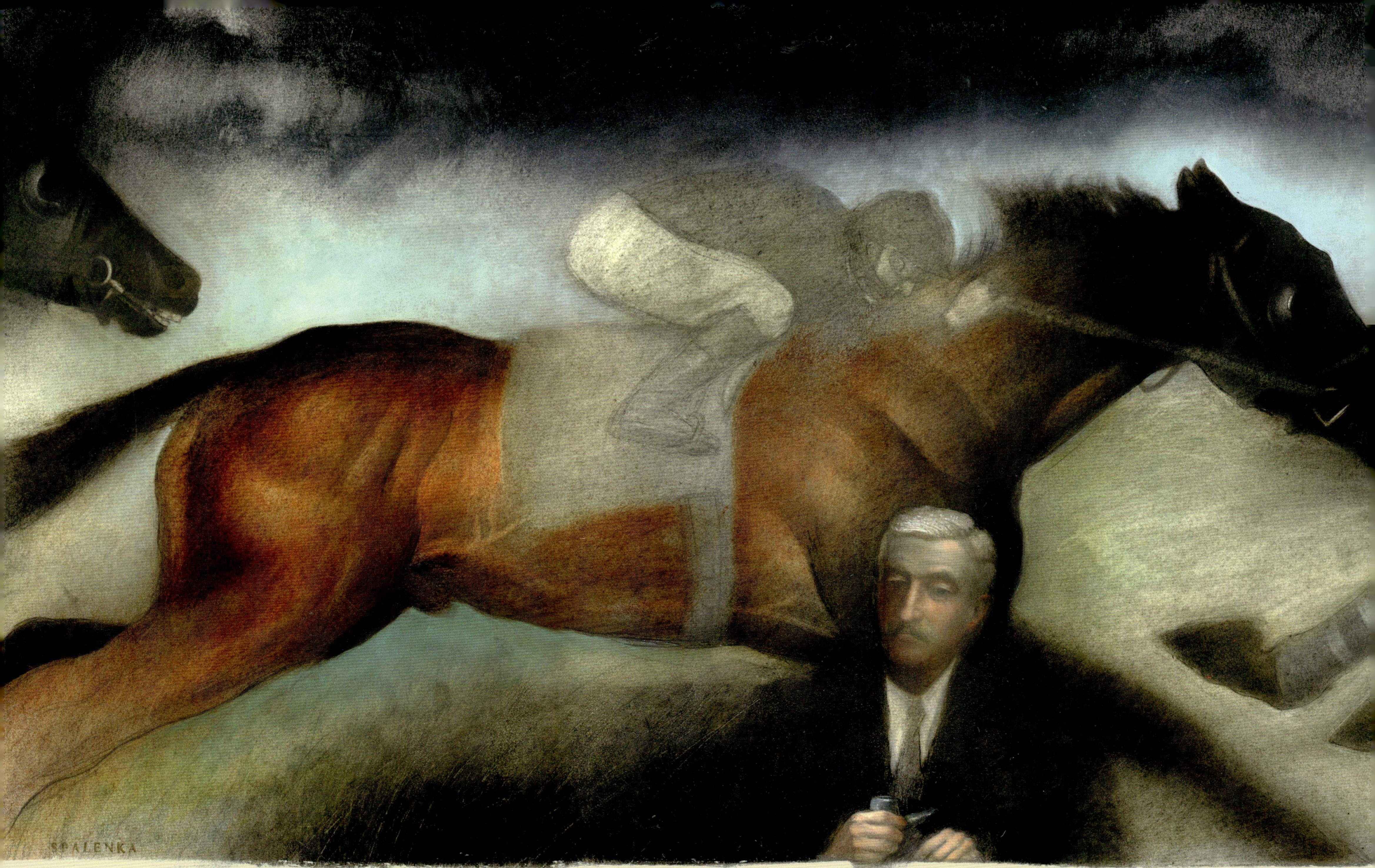

SPALENKA

"When my horse is running good, I don't stop to give him sugar."

–WILLIAM FAULKNER

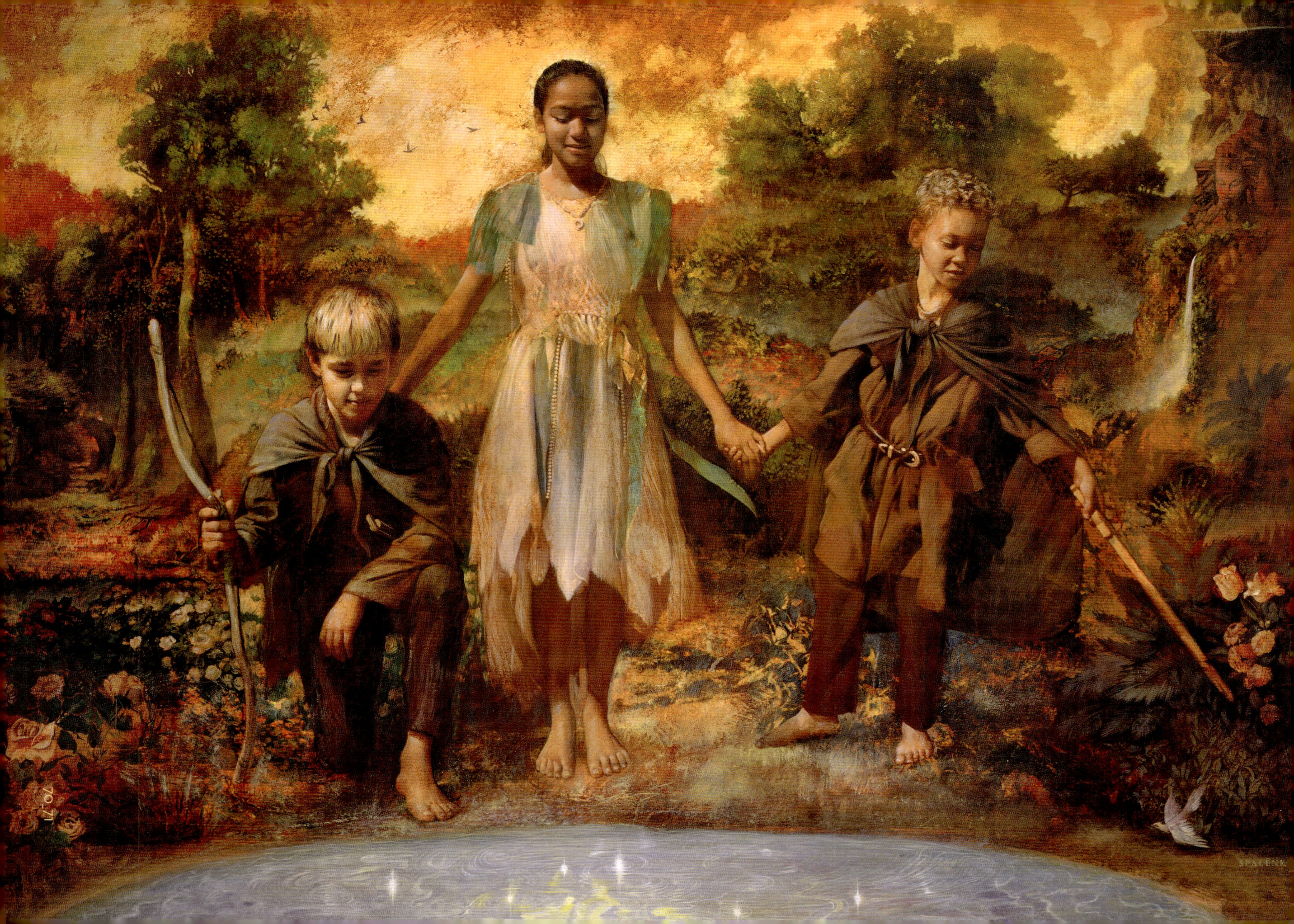

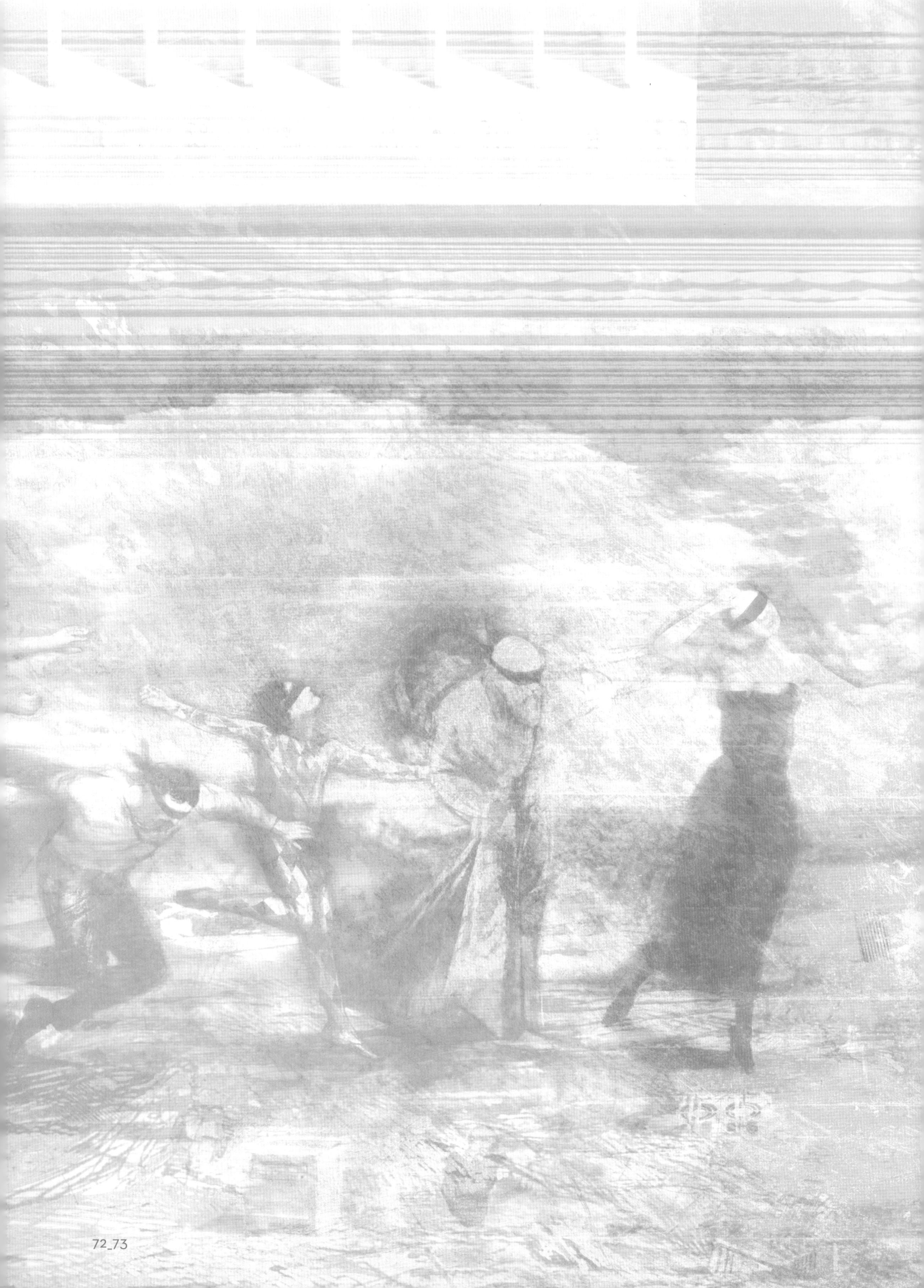

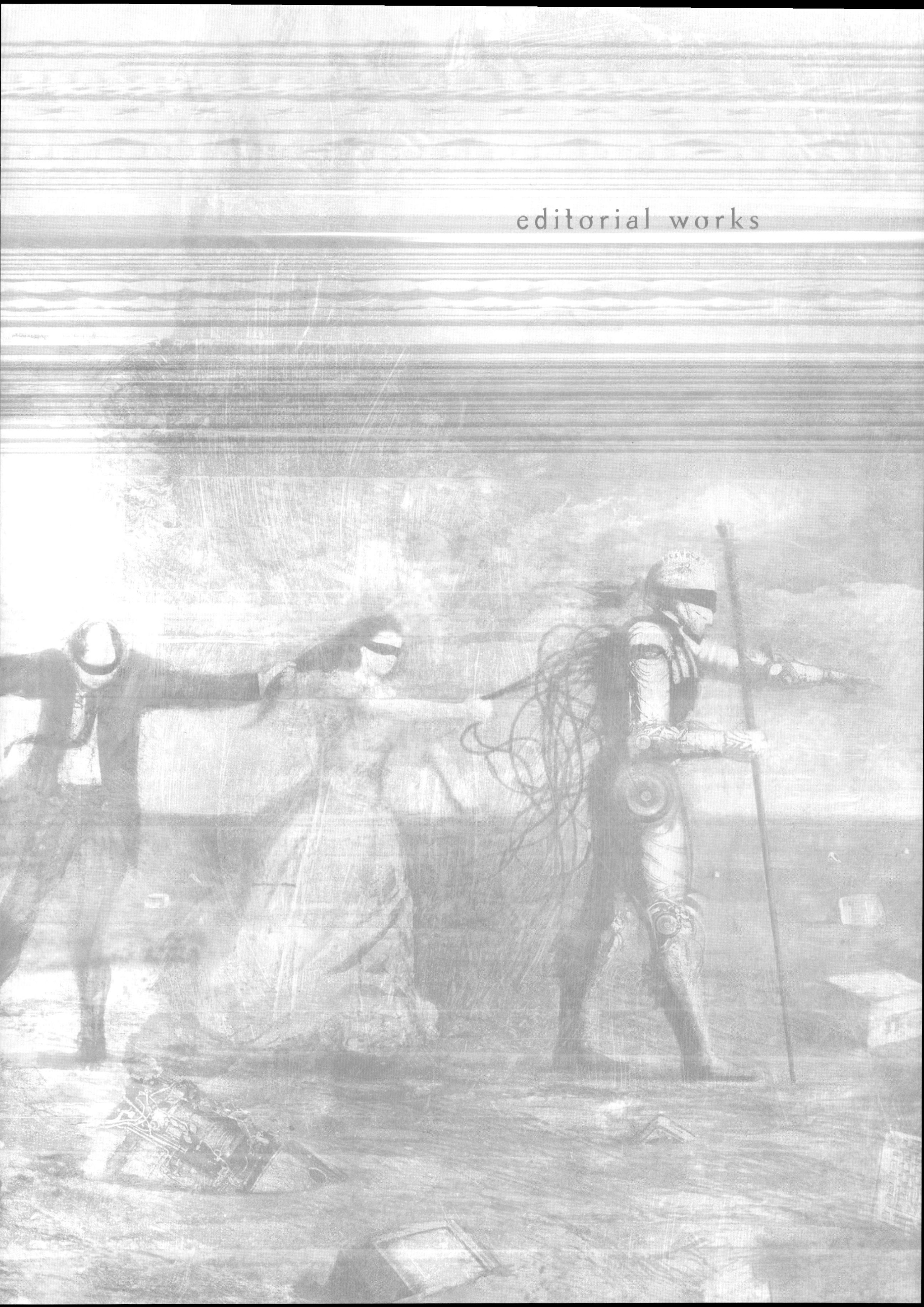

editorial works

art & purpose

During the 80s I cranked out mainly social and political illustrations for magazines and newspapers, as well as book covers. *TIME, Newsweek, U.S. News & World Report, The Atlantic, Businessweek, Mother Jones, Omni, Psychology Today, Ms., Playboy, The New York Times, Los Angeles Times, The Washington Post, The Boston Globe, The San Francisco Examiner, The Wall Street Journal, HarperCollins, Viking Penguin, Random House* were some of these clients. I say "cranked out" because most of the time the deadlines were very tight. Many times finished art was due within a day or two of being handed the assignment.

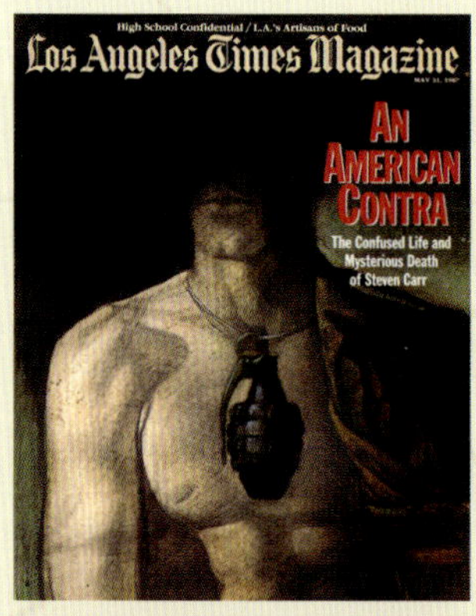

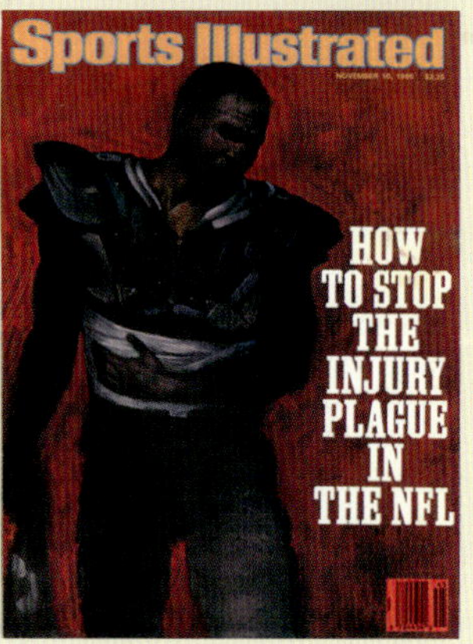

Most of the subject matter I illustrated was on the heavy side: apartheid, terrorists, war, government corruption, injustice, corporatism, pollution, murder, mafia, child abuse, psychology and the like. I got a good look at the underbelly of humanity. However, I truly believed this was art with an important purpose behind it. Recognizing the wounds of the world is the first step to healing them.

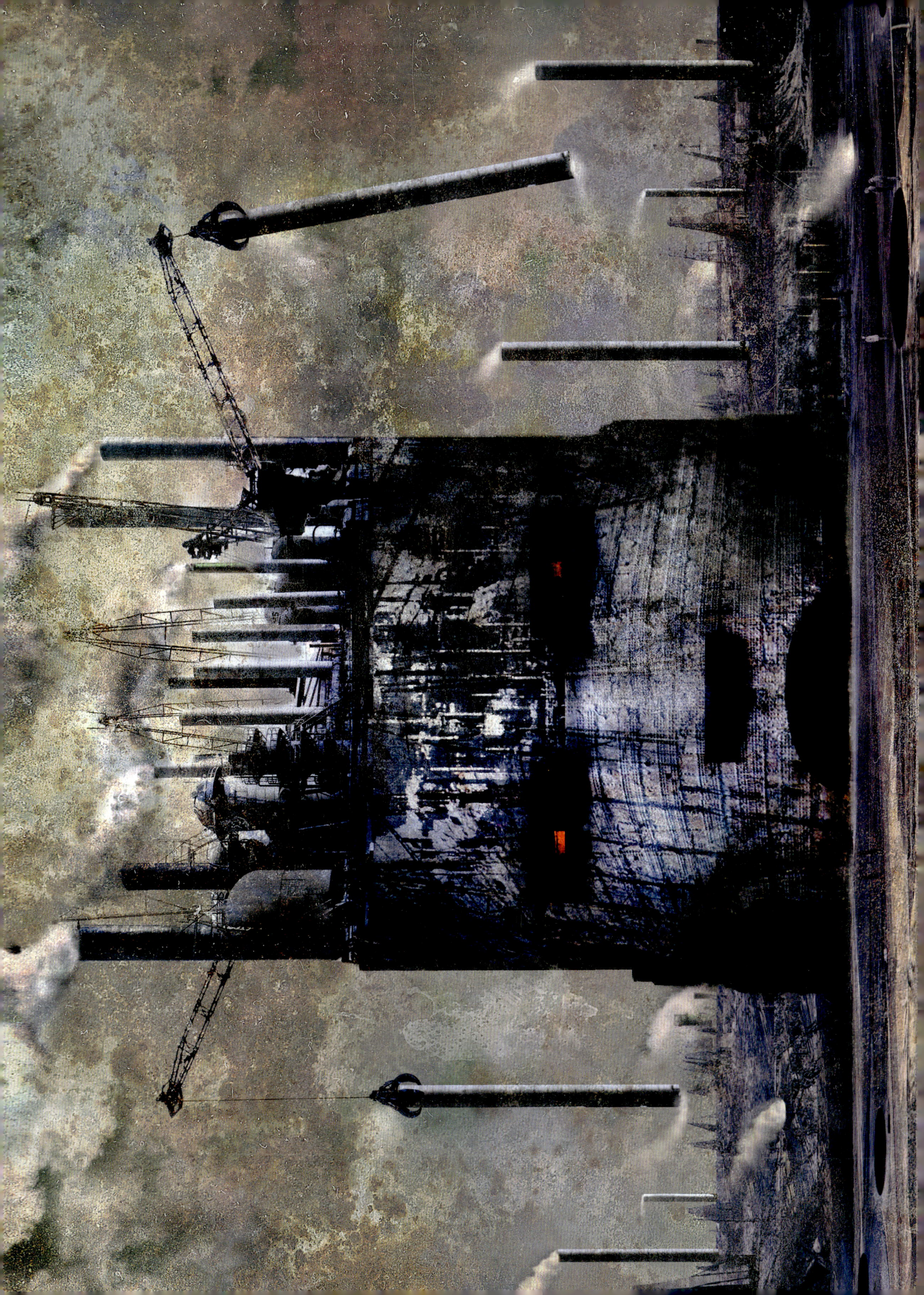

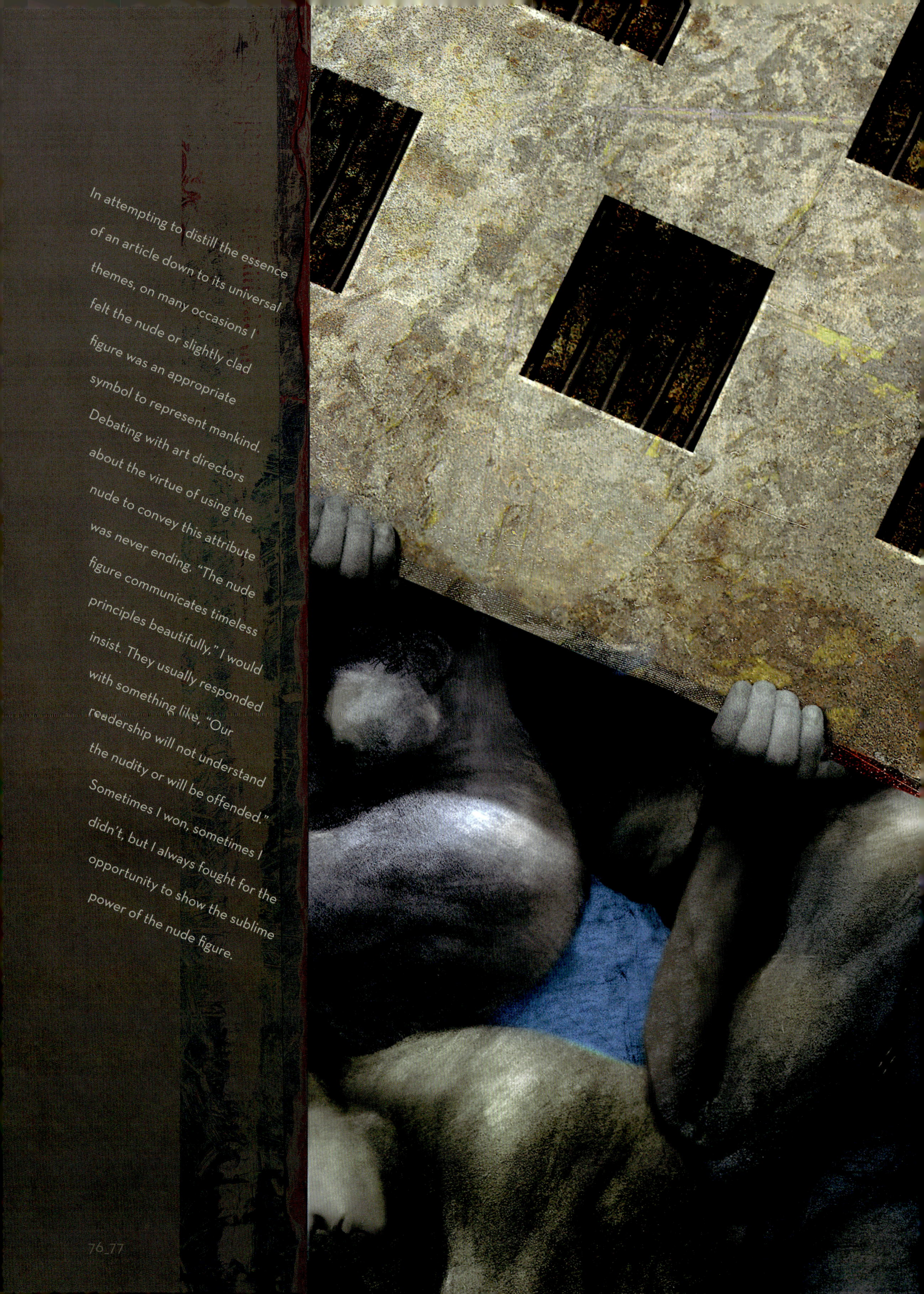

In attempting to distill the essence of an article down to its universal themes, on many occasions I felt the nude or slightly clad figure was an appropriate symbol to represent mankind. Debating with art directors about the virtue of using the nude to convey this attribute was never ending. "The nude figure communicates timeless principles beautifully," I would insist. They usually responded with something like, "Our readership will not understand the nudity or will be offended." Sometimes I won, sometimes I didn't, but I always fought for the opportunity to show the sublime power of the nude figure.

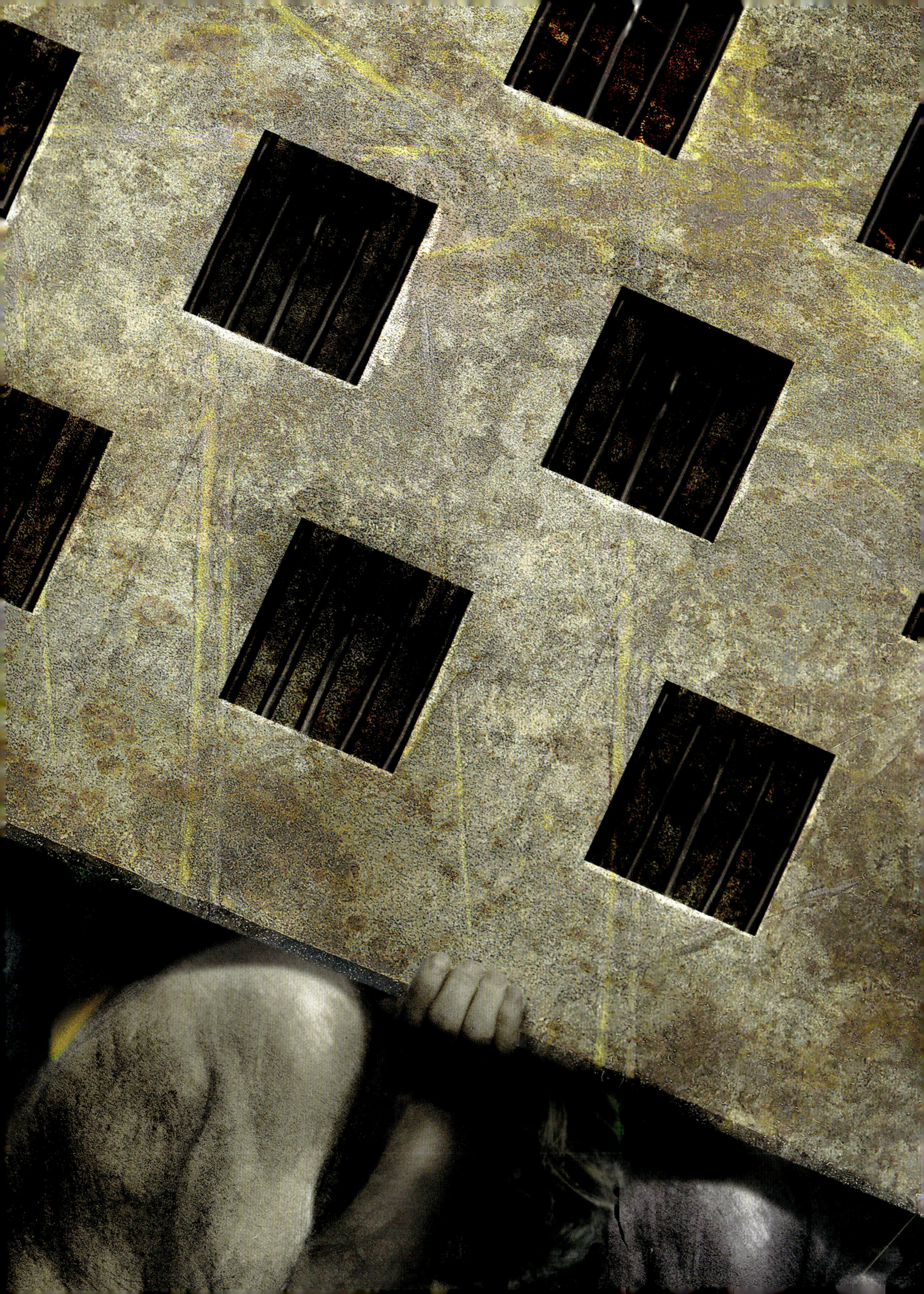

freedom to present a unique ide

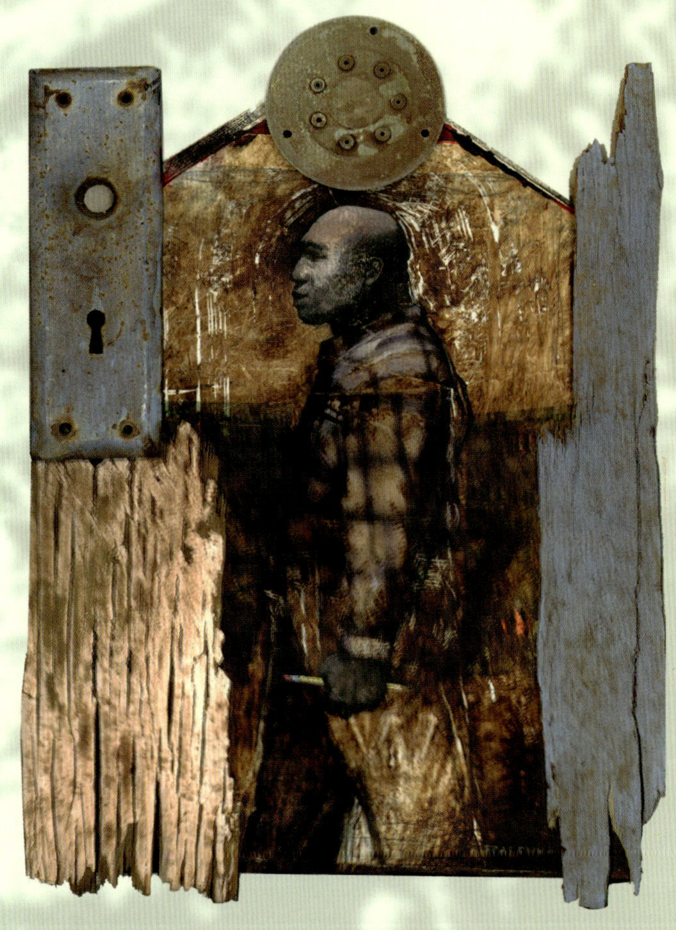

The other thing I always fought for was the freedom to present a unique idea. I worked very hard at conceptualizing new imagery. In an era of visual bombardment, which so often relies on the obvious, the literal, and the cliché, I wanted to create something different and not use so much borrowed interest. There are too many editors and marketing people beholden to corporate interests making decisions on art today.

It was fascinating to see how different publishers would run the same story and skew it (depending on their political leanings) so the reader would view it through their lens. I would be asked to create an illustration for their publication that would match their paradigm. It became clear that revealing the truth on any given subject meant looking at the same article from different publications and using my own common sense.

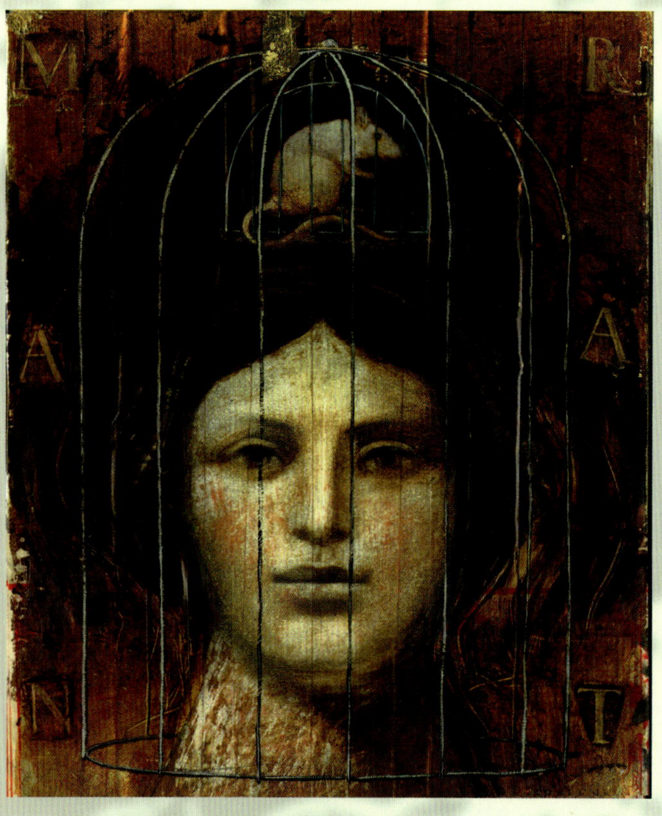

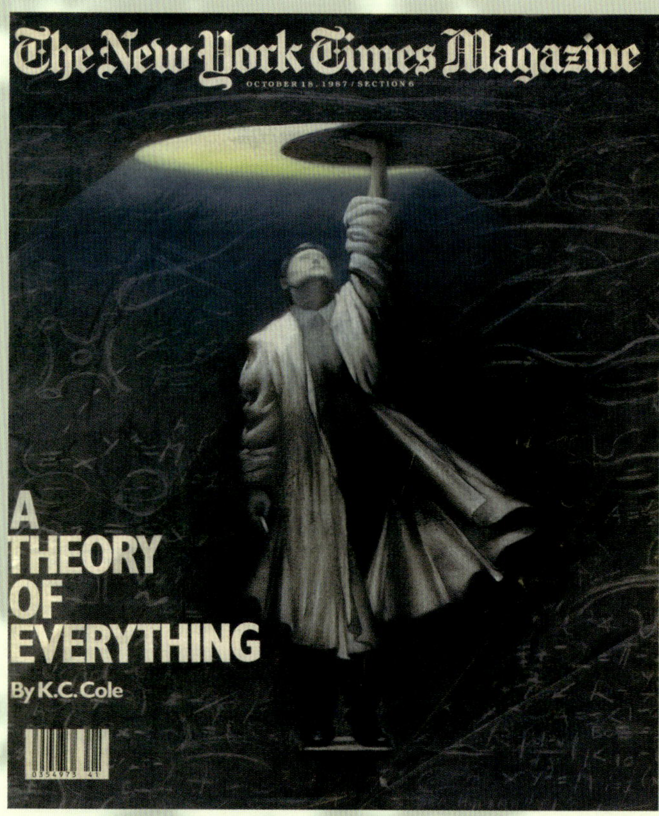

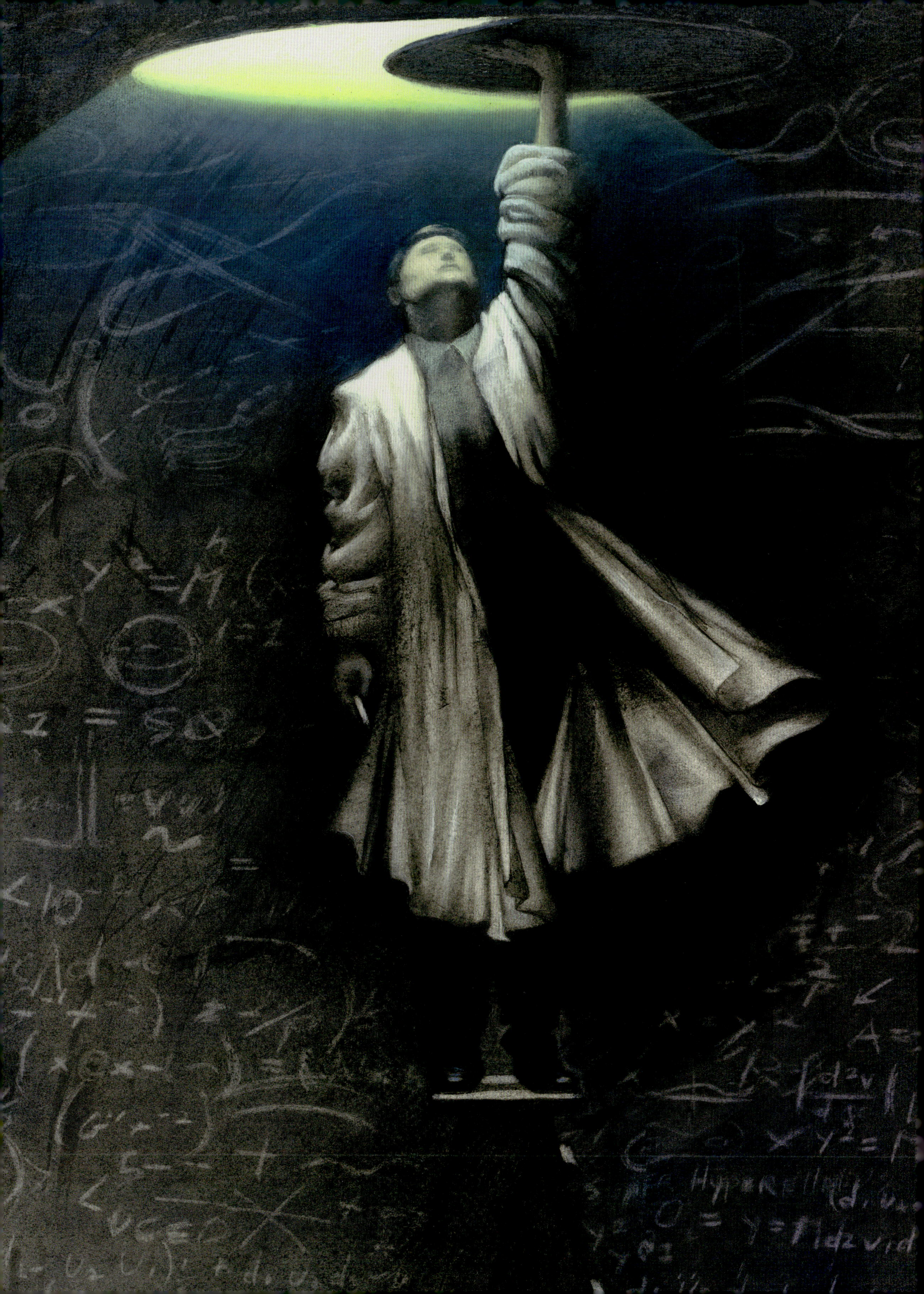

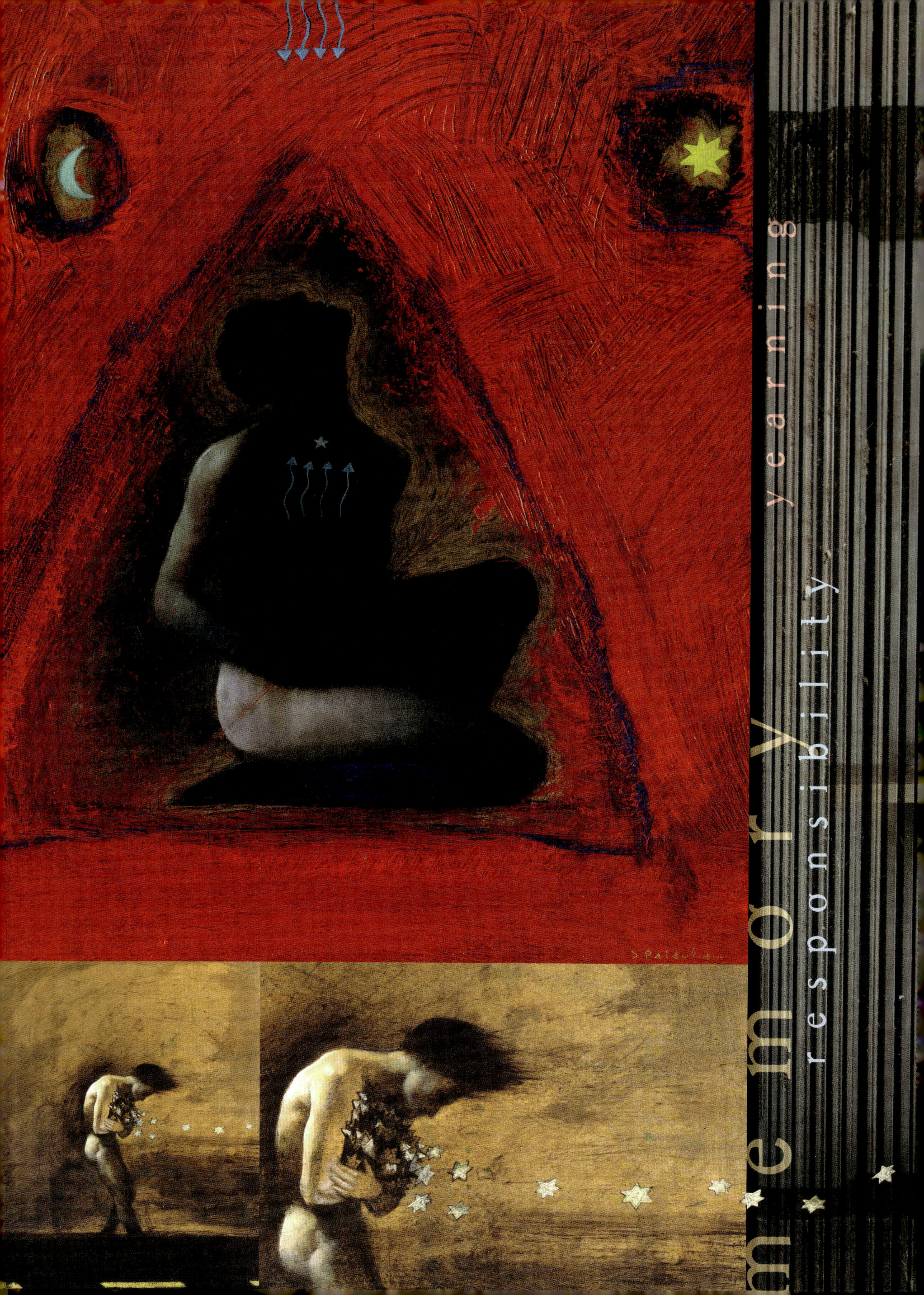
memory
yearning
responsibility

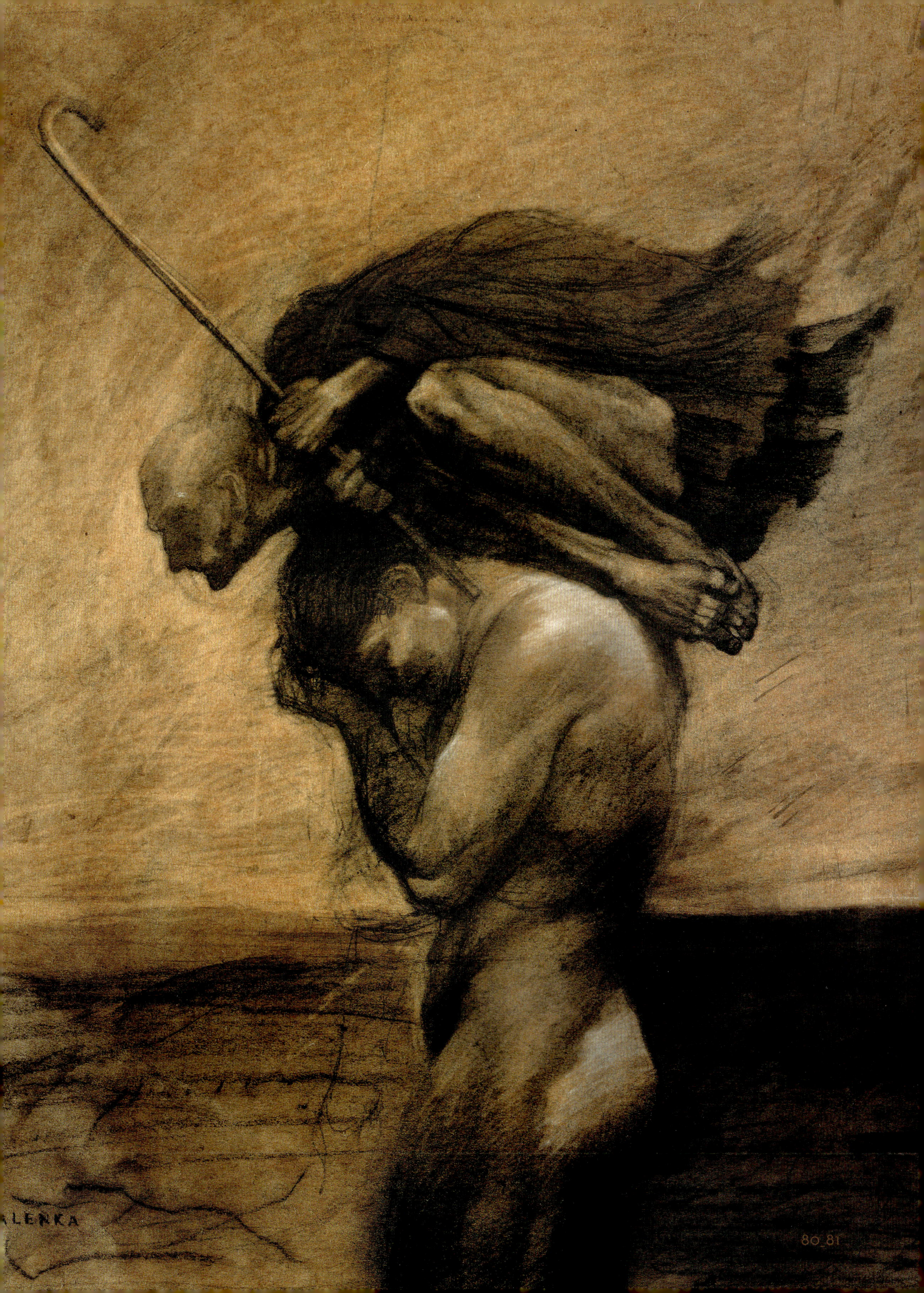

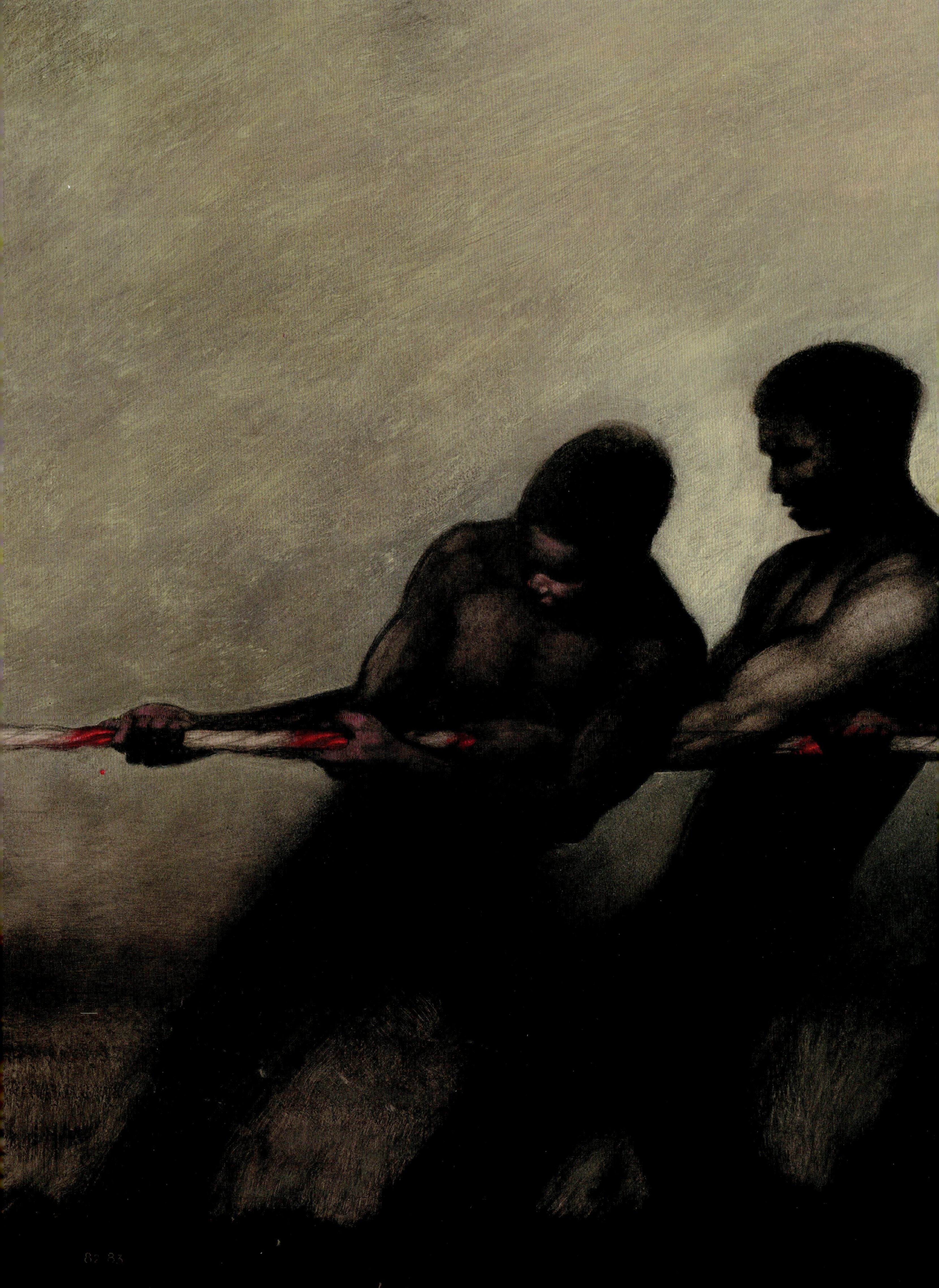

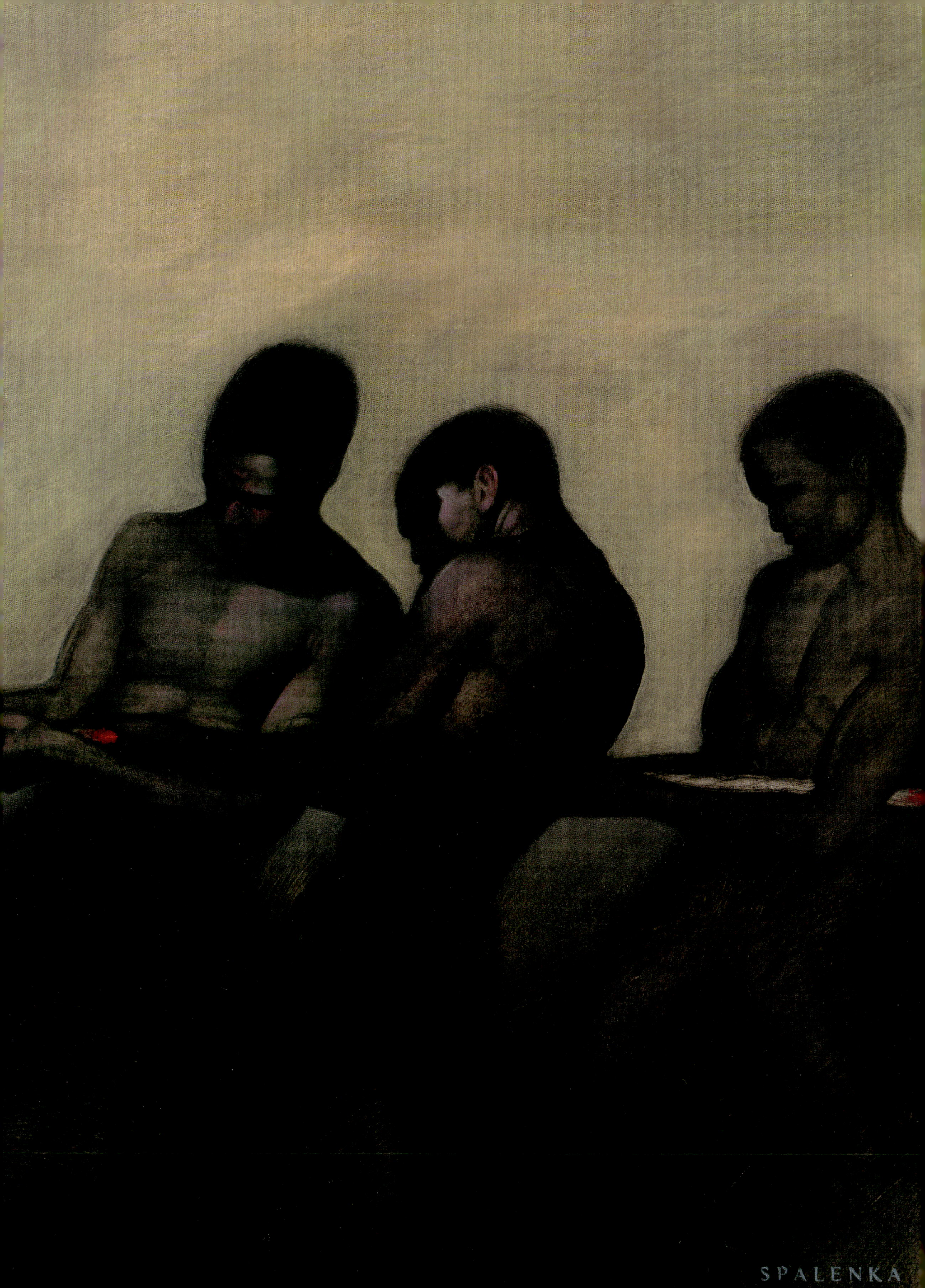
SPALENKA

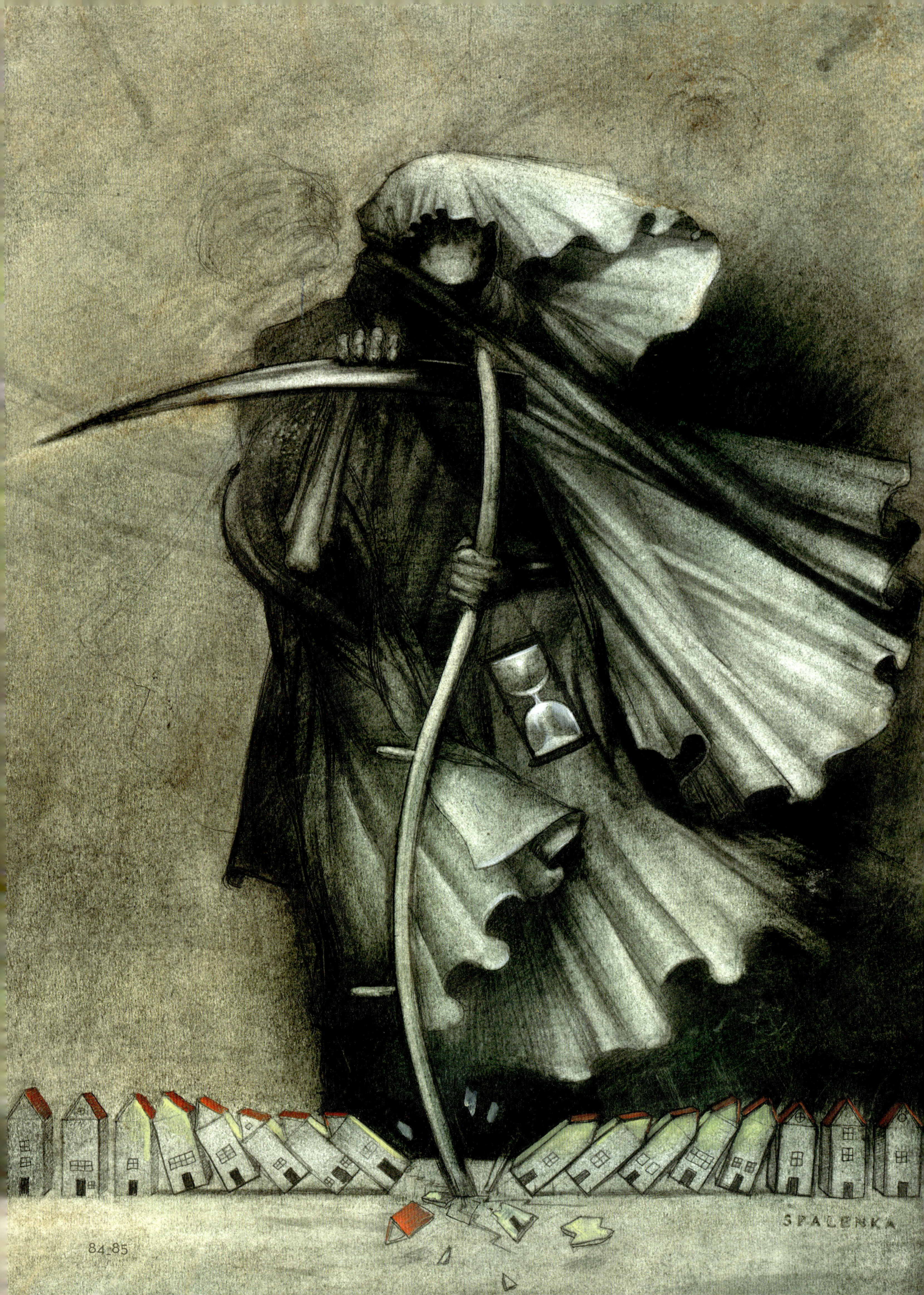
SPALENKA
84-85

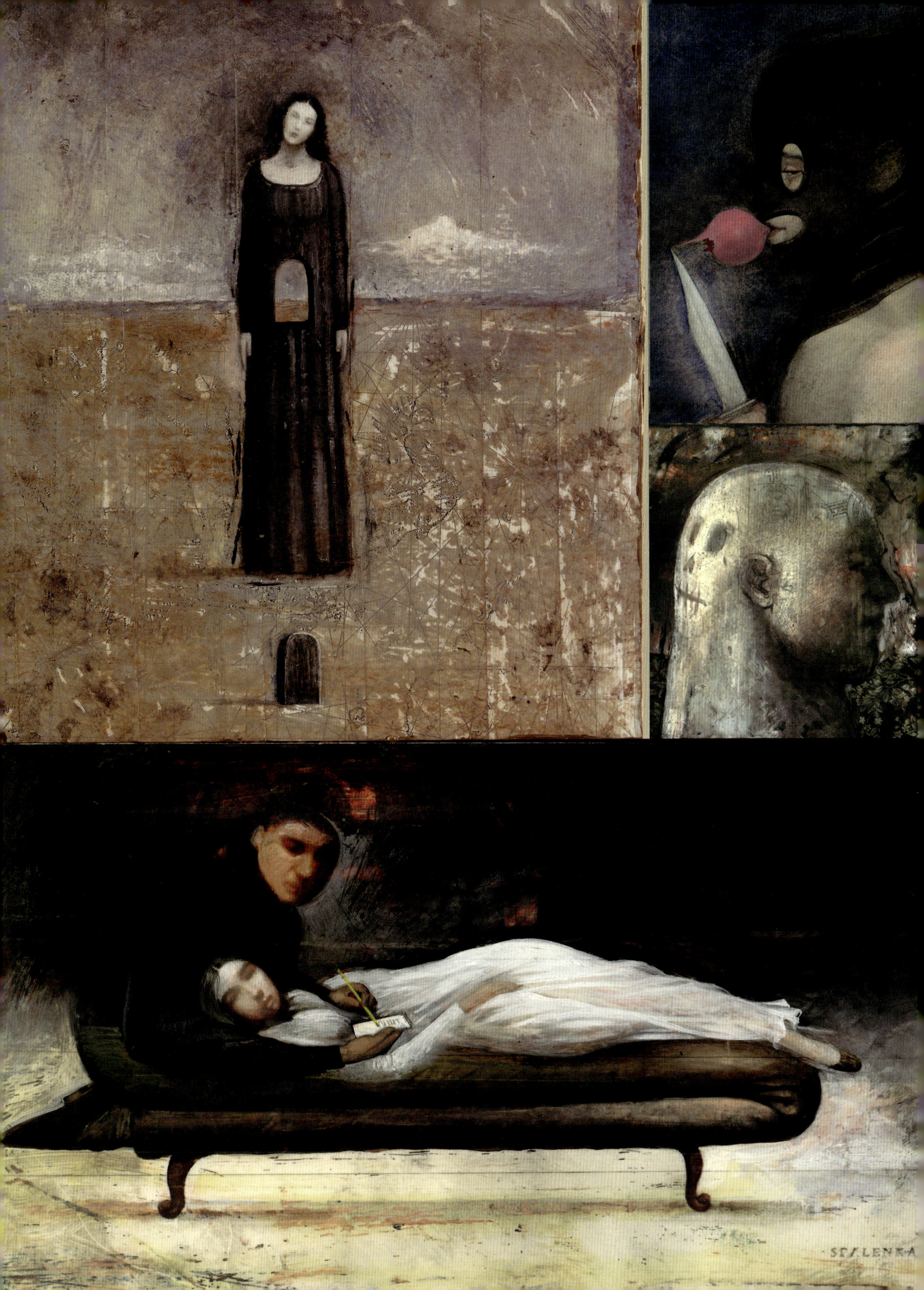
ST/LENKA

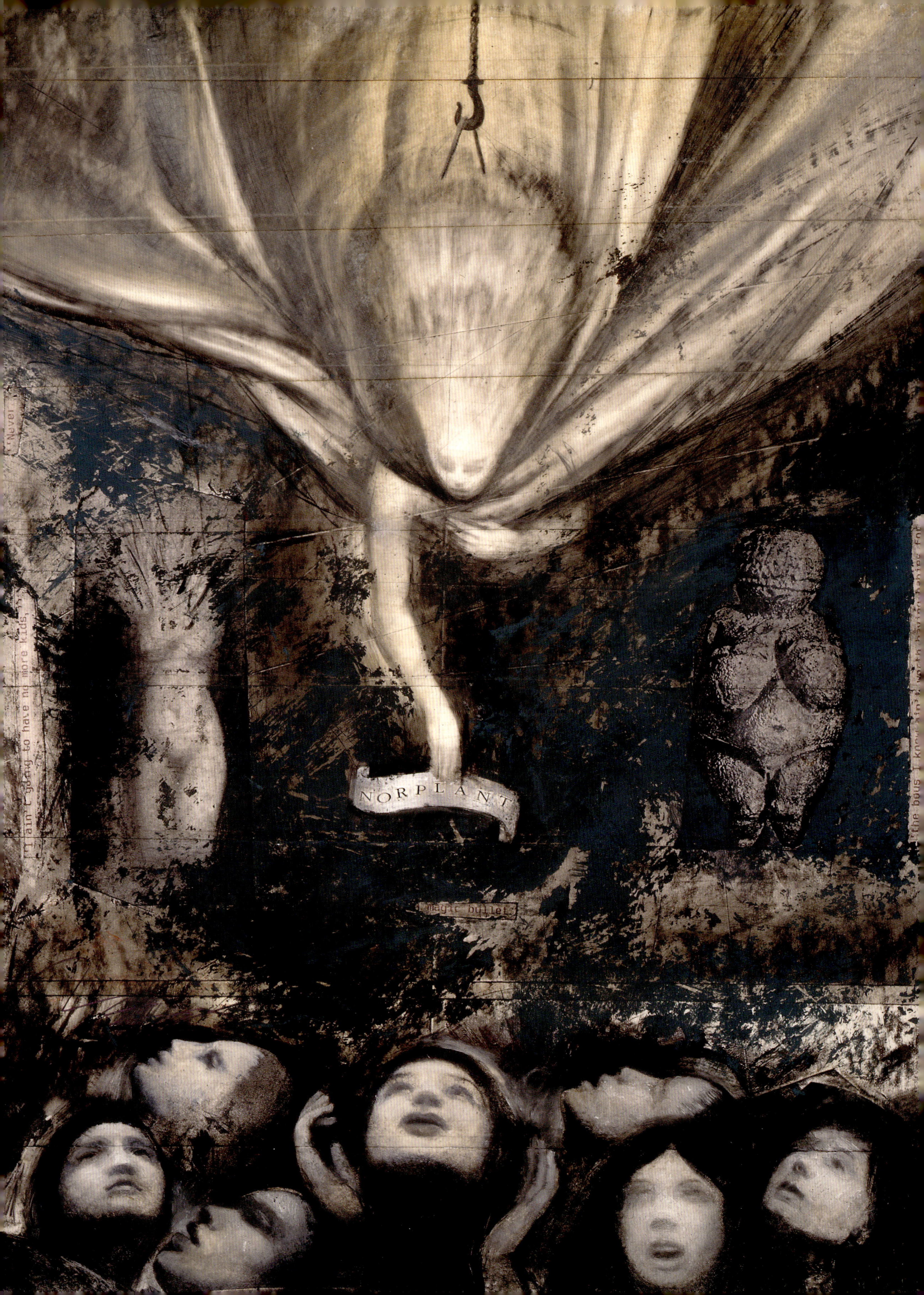
"Never
I ain't going to have no more kids,
NORPLANT
magic bullet
the boys I

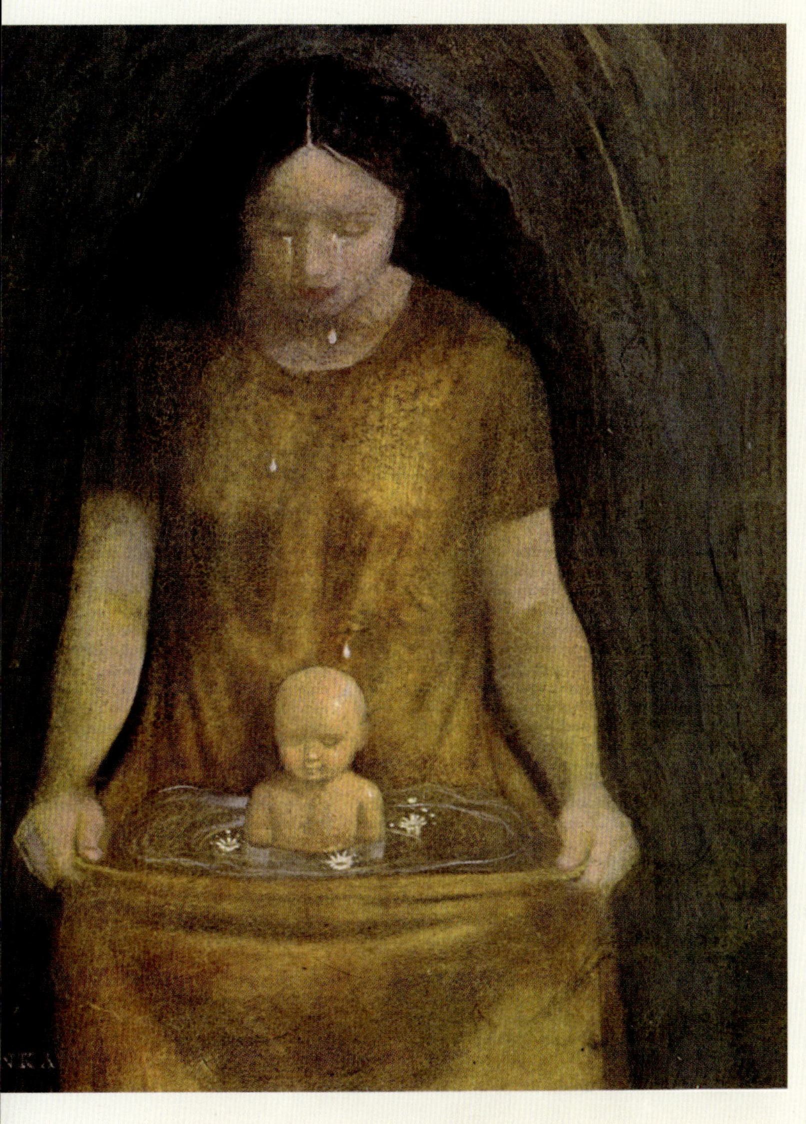

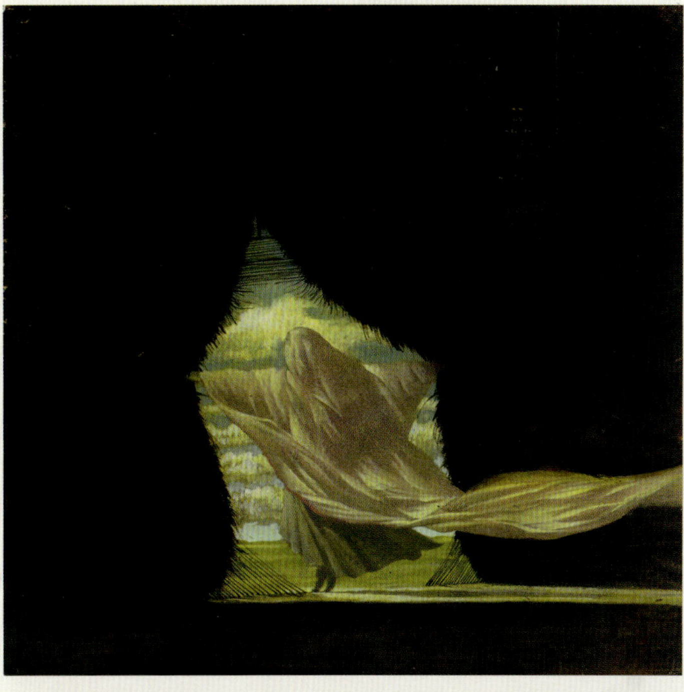

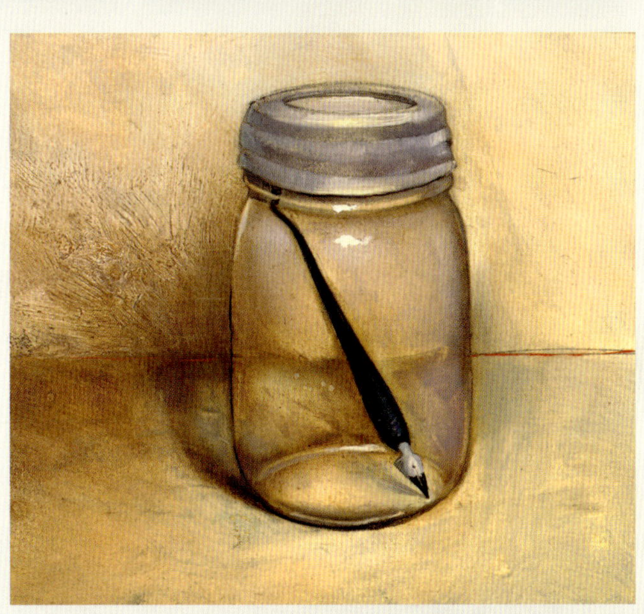

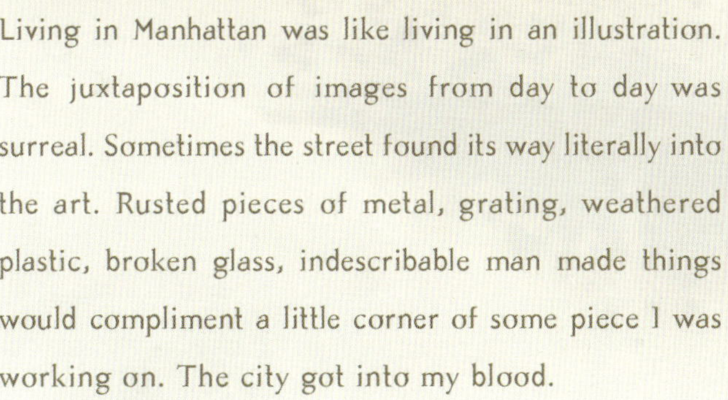

Living in Manhattan was like living in an illustration. The juxtaposition of images from day to day was surreal. Sometimes the street found its way literally into the art. Rusted pieces of metal, grating, weathered plastic, broken glass, indescribable man made things would compliment a little corner of some piece I was working on. The city got into my blood.

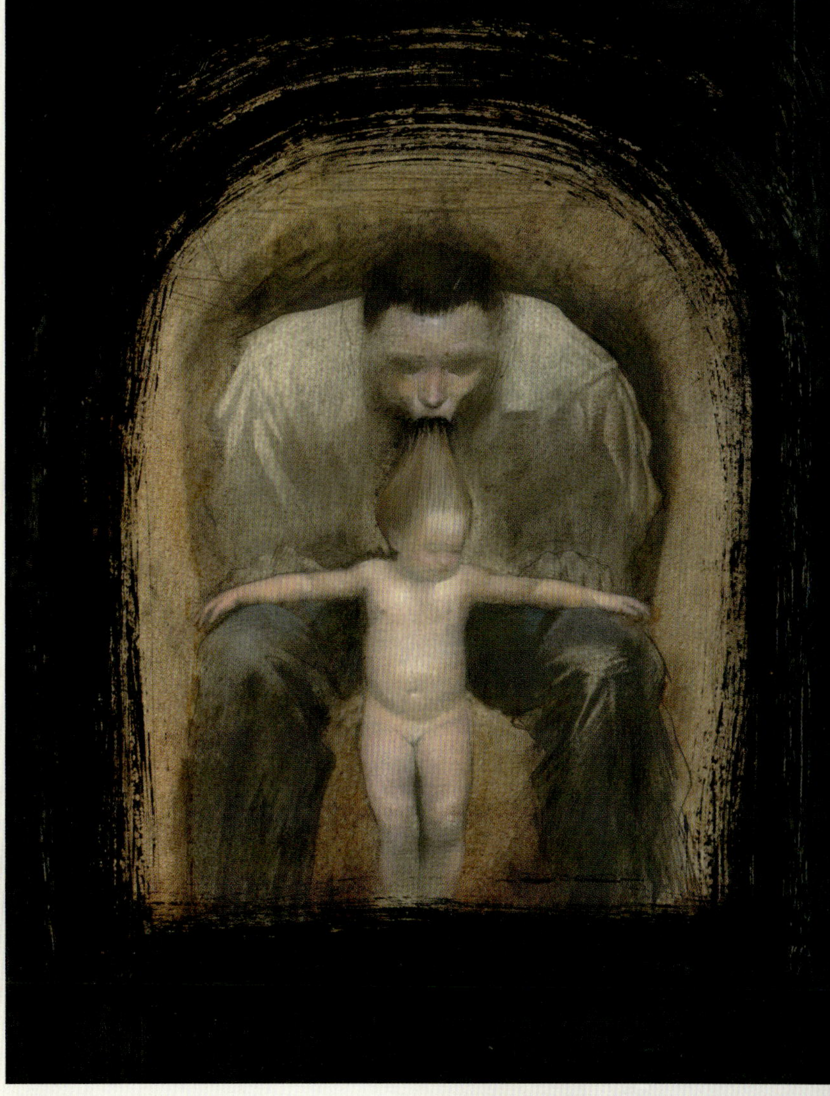

When I moved back to Los Angeles in 1990, Kent Williams suggested I check out the San Diego comic convention. It was here that I experienced new ways of perceiving what an art career could be. Pop culture was changing the face of commerce. Here were artists, writers, micro-publishers, filmmakers creating their own properties. Comic-Con was a think-tank of imagination, cross pollinating ideas and creative disciplines. Making a living from the support of your fans was a new paradigm of art career sustainability, which I embraced. Years later these principles would become the foundation of Artist As Brand®, to support artist entrepreneurs.

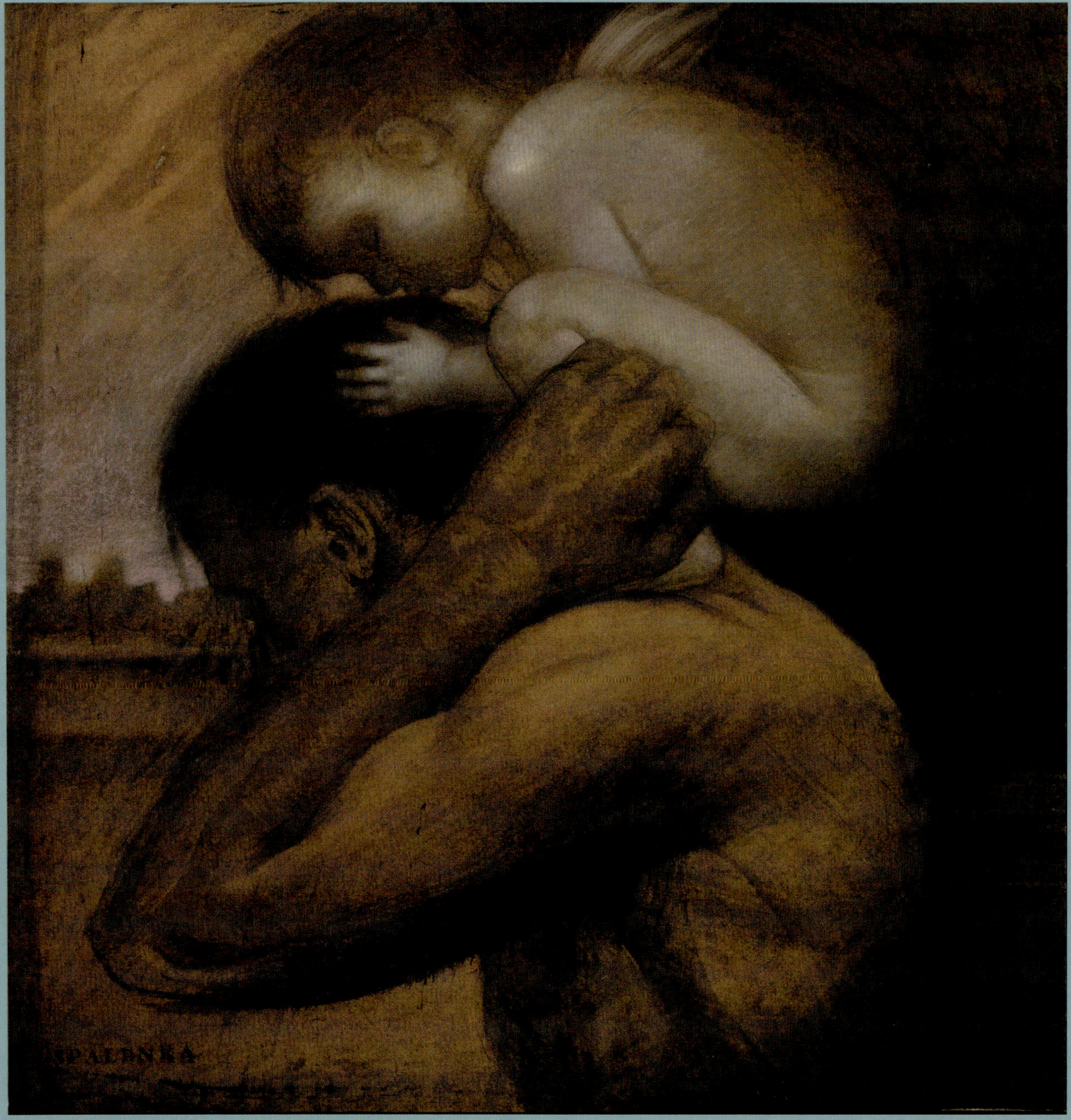

The computer became part of my tool kit and part of my art making process. This included scanning in drawings, working on them in Photoshop, then printing them out, painting on them with acrylics and oils, and then scanning them in again. My art began to lighten in tone, and I could feel a yearning to explore aspects of the ethereal, the sublime, and the divine. I became fascinated with unveiling the existence of our reality, revealing the devas, metaphysical sprites, and goddesses in our midst. The Divine Feminine is a facet found in much of my work today.

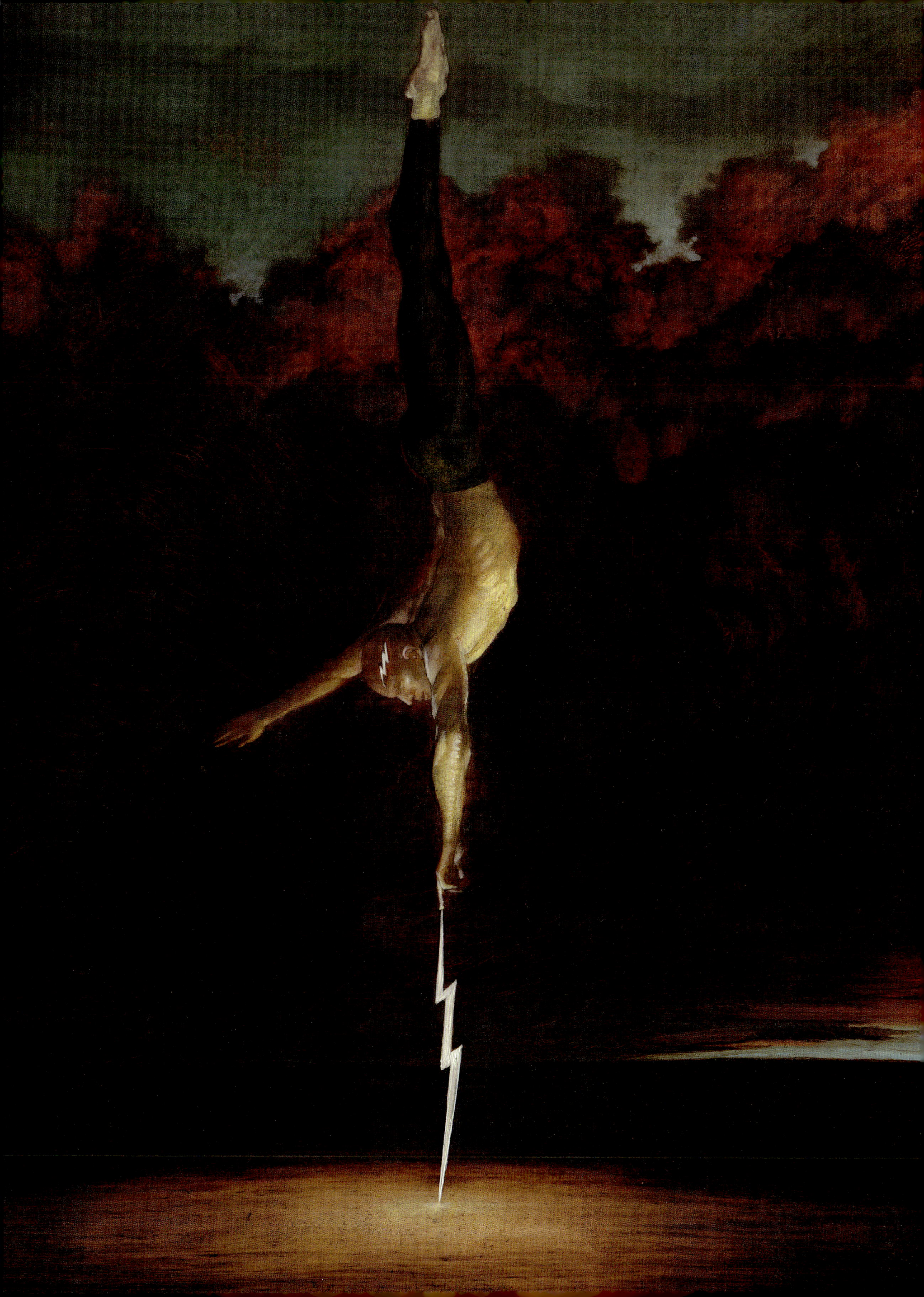

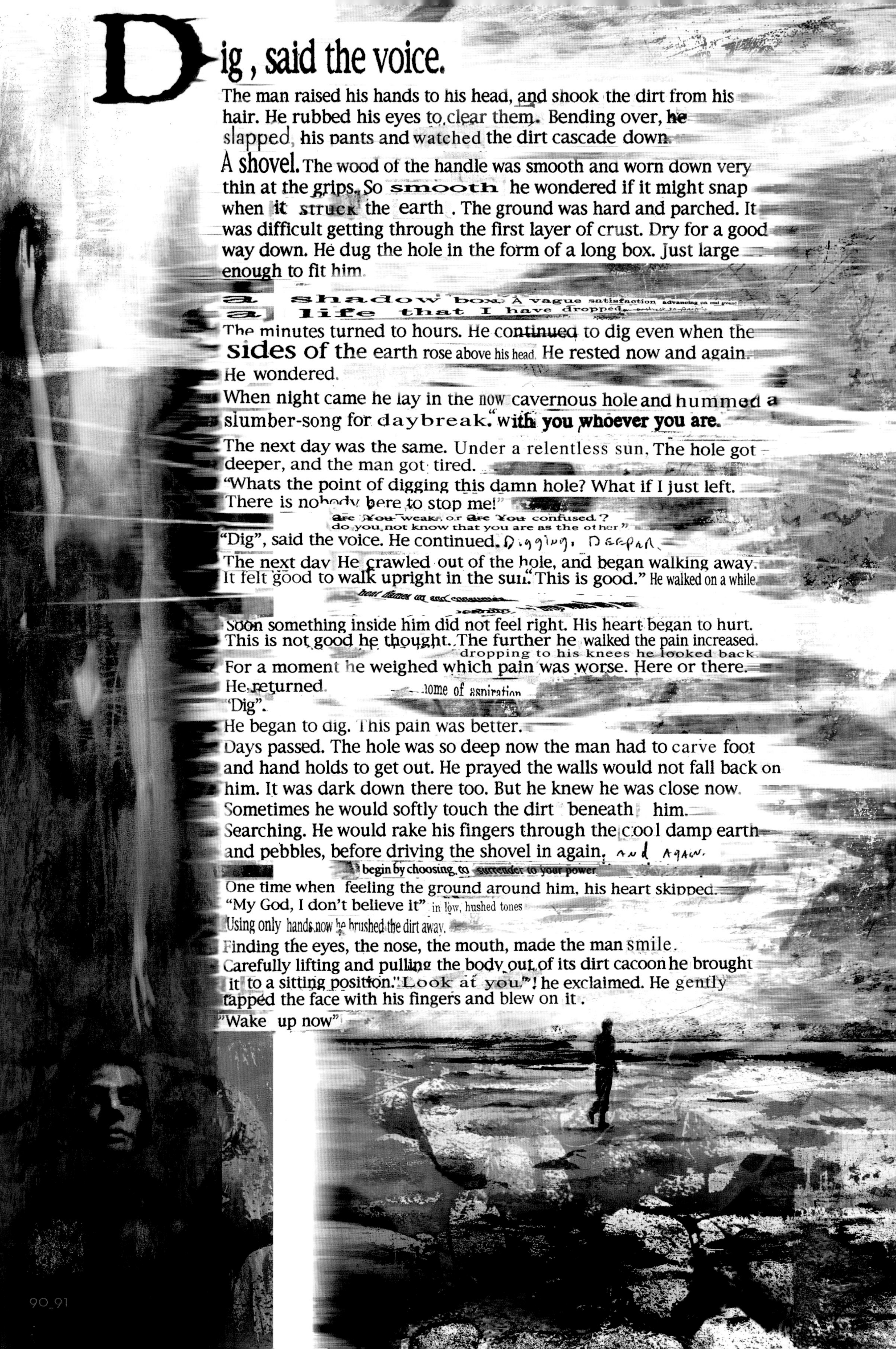

Dig, said the voice.

The man raised his hands to his head, and shook the dirt from his hair. He rubbed his eyes to clear them. Bending over, he slapped, his pants and watched the dirt cascade down.

A shovel. The wood of the handle was smooth and worn down very thin at the grips. So smooth he wondered if it might snap when it struck the earth . The ground was hard and parched. It was difficult getting through the first layer of crust. Dry for a good way down. He dug the hole in the form of a long box. Just large enough to fit him.

a shadow box. A vague satisfaction advancing on real ground
a life that I have dropped.

The minutes turned to hours. He continued to dig even when the sides of the earth rose above his head. He rested now and again. He wondered.

When night came he lay in the now cavernous hole and hummed a slumber-song for daybreak. "with you whoever you are.

The next day was the same. Under a relentless sun, The hole got deeper, and the man got tired.

"Whats the point of digging this damn hole? What if I just left. There is nobody here to stop me!"

are You weak, or are You confused ?
do you not know that you are as the other"

"Dig", said the voice. He continued. Digging. Deeper.

The next day He crawled out of the hole, and began walking away. It felt good to walk upright in the sun. "This is good." He walked on a while.

heat flames up and consumes

Soon something inside him did not feel right. His heart began to hurt. This is not good he thought. The further he walked the pain increased.

dropping to his knees he looked back.

For a moment he weighed which pain was worse. Here or there.

He returned — home of aspiration

"Dig".

He began to dig. This pain was better.

Days passed. The hole was so deep now the man had to carve foot and hand holds to get out. He prayed the walls would not fall back on him. It was dark down there too. But he knew he was close now. Sometimes he would softly touch the dirt beneath him. Searching. He would rake his fingers through the cool damp earth and pebbles, before driving the shovel in again. and again.

begin by choosing to surrender to your power

One time when feeling the ground around him, his heart skipped.

"My God, I don't believe it" in low, hushed tones

Using only hands now he brushed the dirt away.

Finding the eyes, the nose, the mouth, made the man smile.

Carefully lifting and pulling the body out of its dirt cacoon he brought it to a sitting position. "Look at you"! he exclaimed. He gently tapped the face with his fingers and blew on it .

"Wake up now"

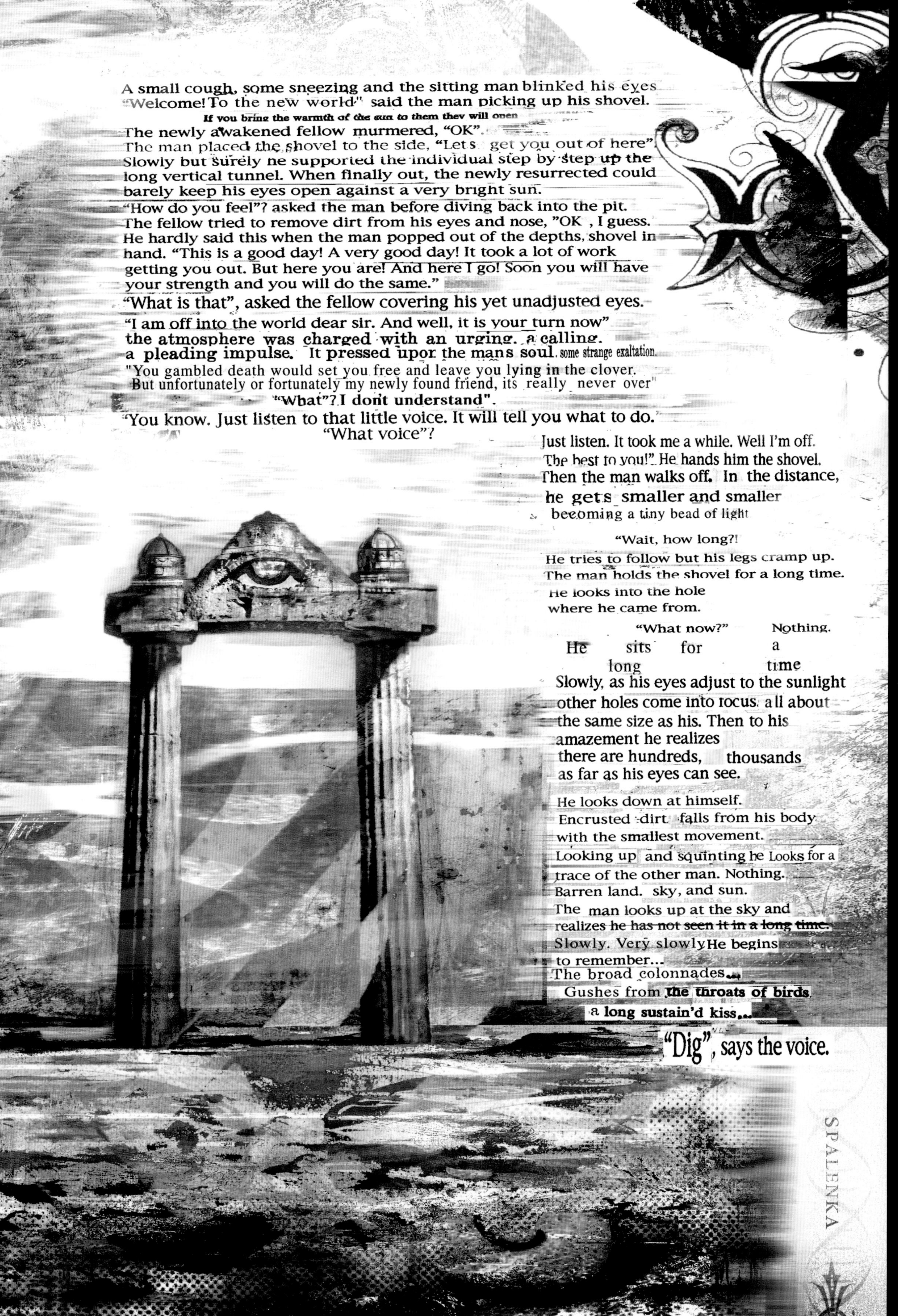

A small cough, some sneezing and the sitting man blinked his eyes
"Welcome! To the new world" said the man picking up his shovel.

If you bring the warmth of the sun to them they will open

The newly awakened fellow murmered, "OK".
The man placed the shovel to the side, "Lets get you out of here".
Slowly but surely he supported the individual step by step up the long vertical tunnel. When finally out, the newly resurrected could barely keep his eyes open against a very bright sun.
"How do you feel"? asked the man before diving back into the pit.
The fellow tried to remove dirt from his eyes and nose, "OK , I guess.
He hardly said this when the man popped out of the depths, shovel in hand. "This is a good day! A very good day! It took a lot of work getting you out. But here you are! And here I go! Soon you will have your strength and you will do the same."
"What is that", asked the fellow covering his yet unadjusted eyes.
"I am off into the world dear sir. And well, it is your turn now"
the atmosphere was charged with an urging, a calling, a pleading impulse. It pressed upon the mans soul. some strange exaltation.
"You gambled death would set you free and leave you lying in the clover.
But unfortunately or fortunately my newly found friend, its really never over"
"What"? I don't understand".
"You know. Just listen to that little voice. It will tell you what to do."
"What voice"?

Just listen. It took me a while. Well I'm off.
The best to you!". He hands him the shovel.
Then the man walks off. In the distance, he gets smaller and smaller becoming a tiny bead of light

"Wait, how long?!

He tries to follow but his legs cramp up.
The man holds the shovel for a long time.
He looks into the hole where he came from.

"What now?" Nothing.

He sits for a long time

Slowly, as his eyes adjust to the sunlight other holes come into focus, all about the same size as his. Then to his amazement he realizes there are hundreds, thousands as far as his eyes can see.

He looks down at himself.
Encrusted dirt falls from his body with the smallest movement.
Looking up and squinting he Looks for a trace of the other man. Nothing.
Barren land. sky, and sun.
The man looks up at the sky and realizes he has not seen it in a long time.
Slowly. Very slowly He begins to remember...
The broad colonnades...
Gushes from **the throats of birds**,
a **long sustain'd kiss...**

"Dig", says the voice.

SPALENKA

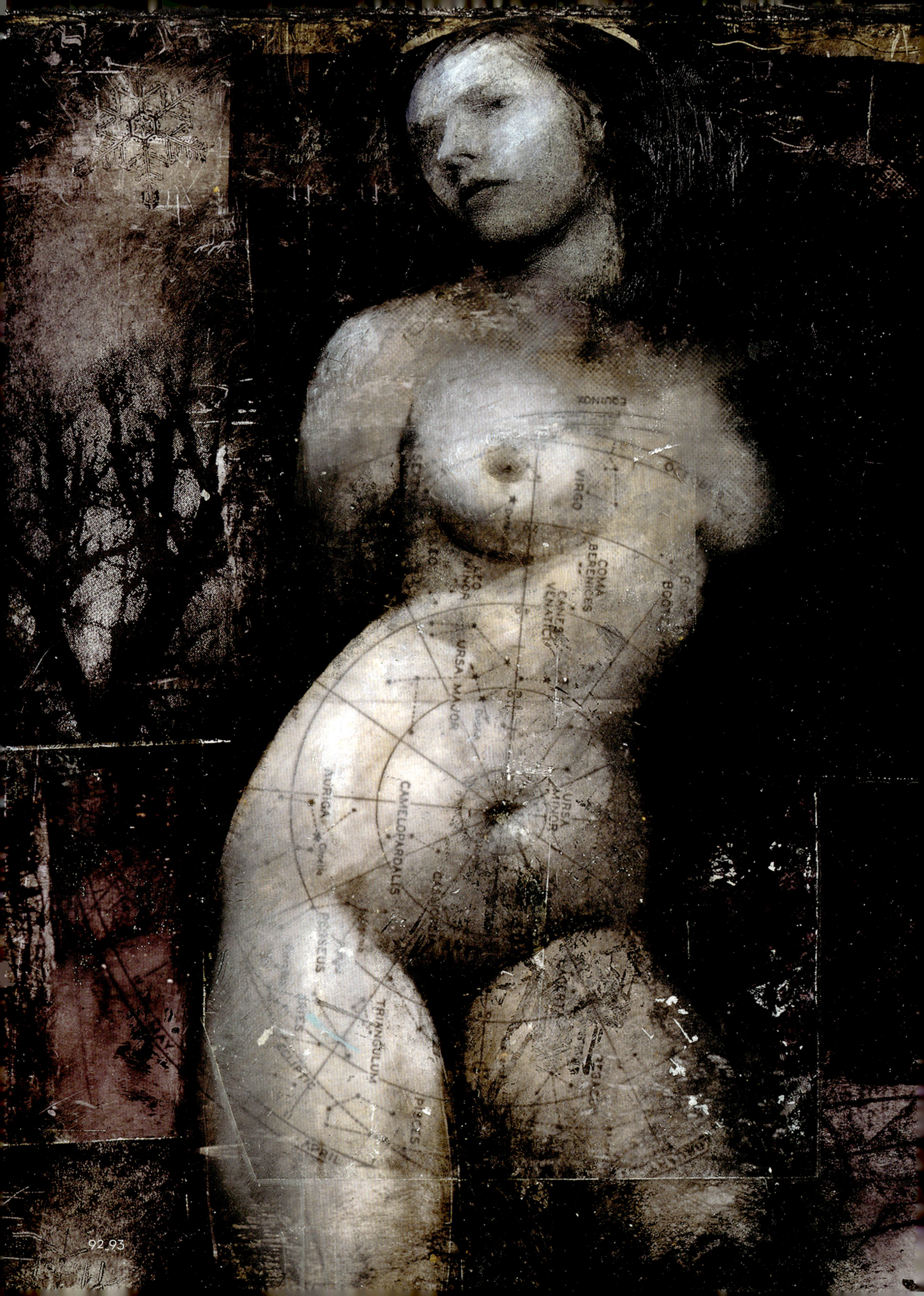
VIRGO
COMA BERENICES
CANES VENATICI
URSA MAJOR
AURIGA
CAMELOPARDALIS
URSA MINOR
PERSEUS
TRIANGULUM
PISCES

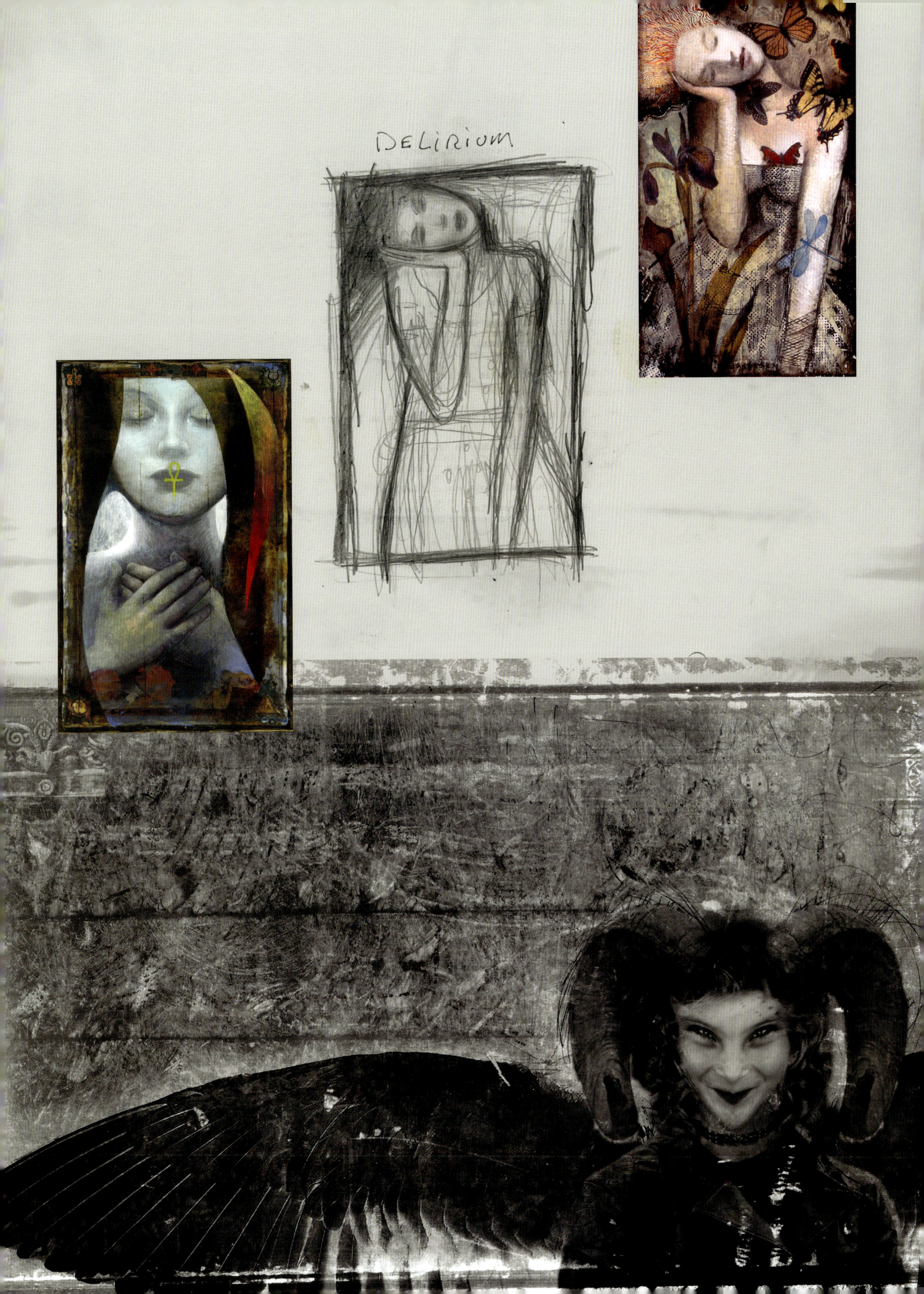
DELIRIUM

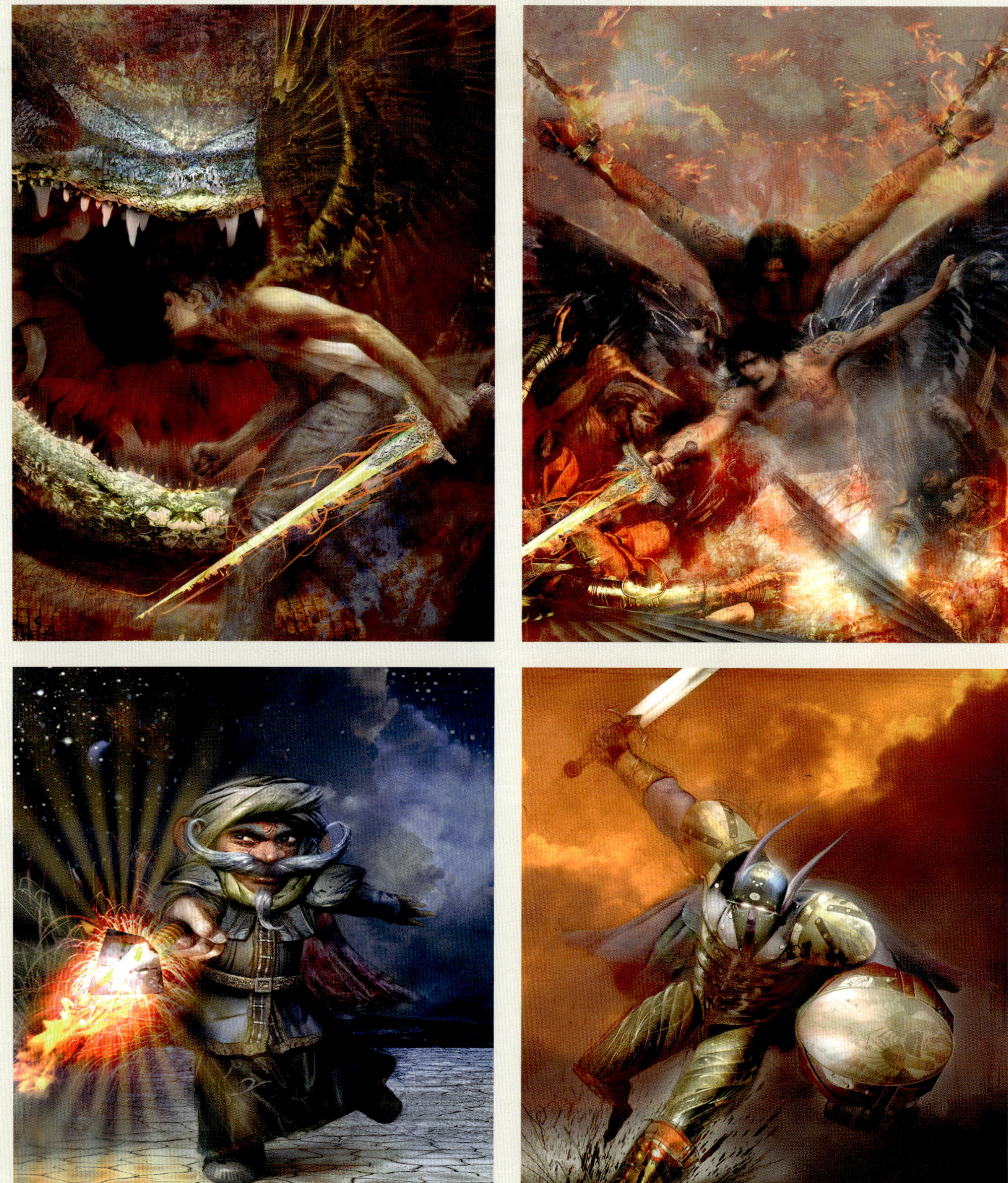

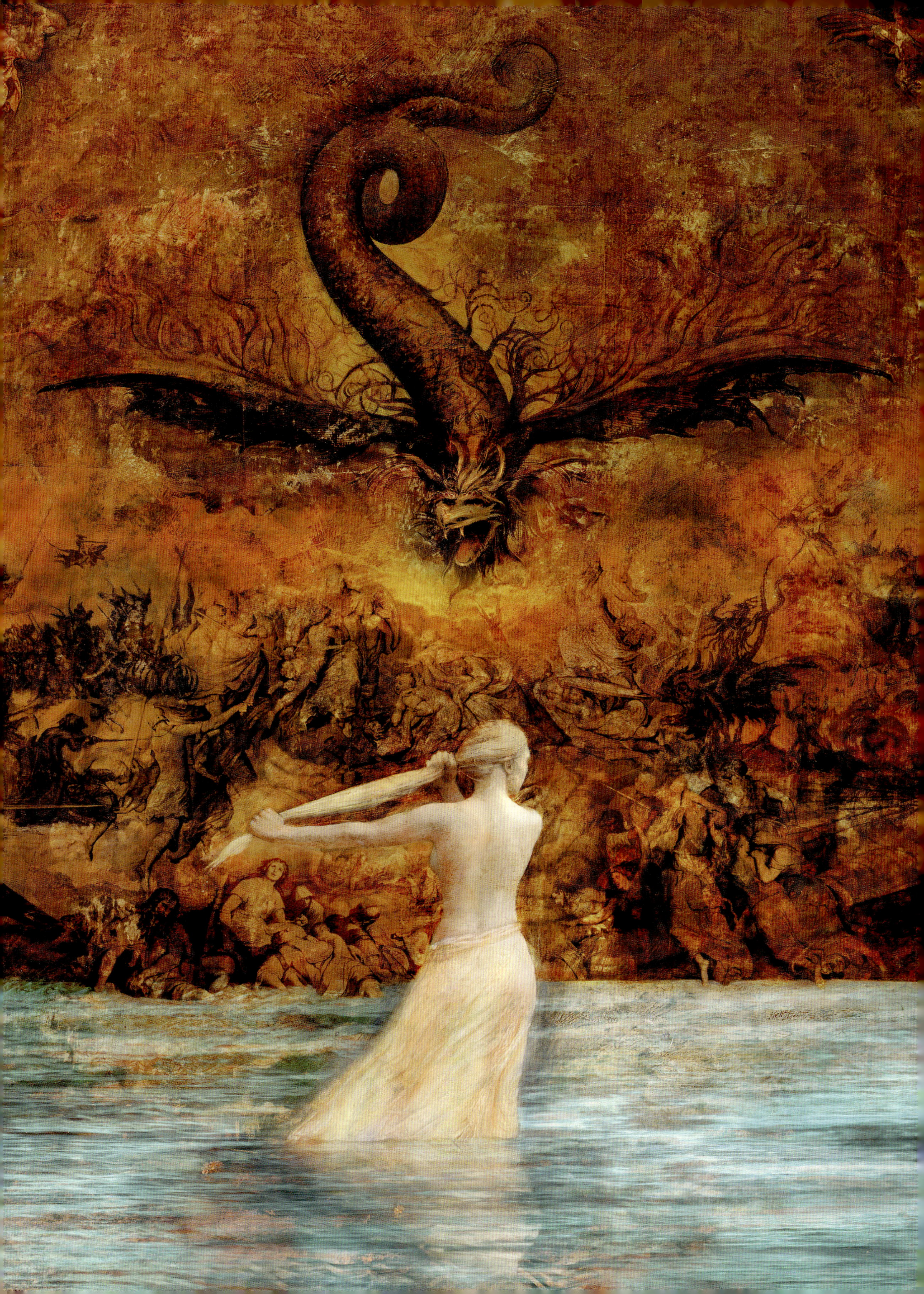

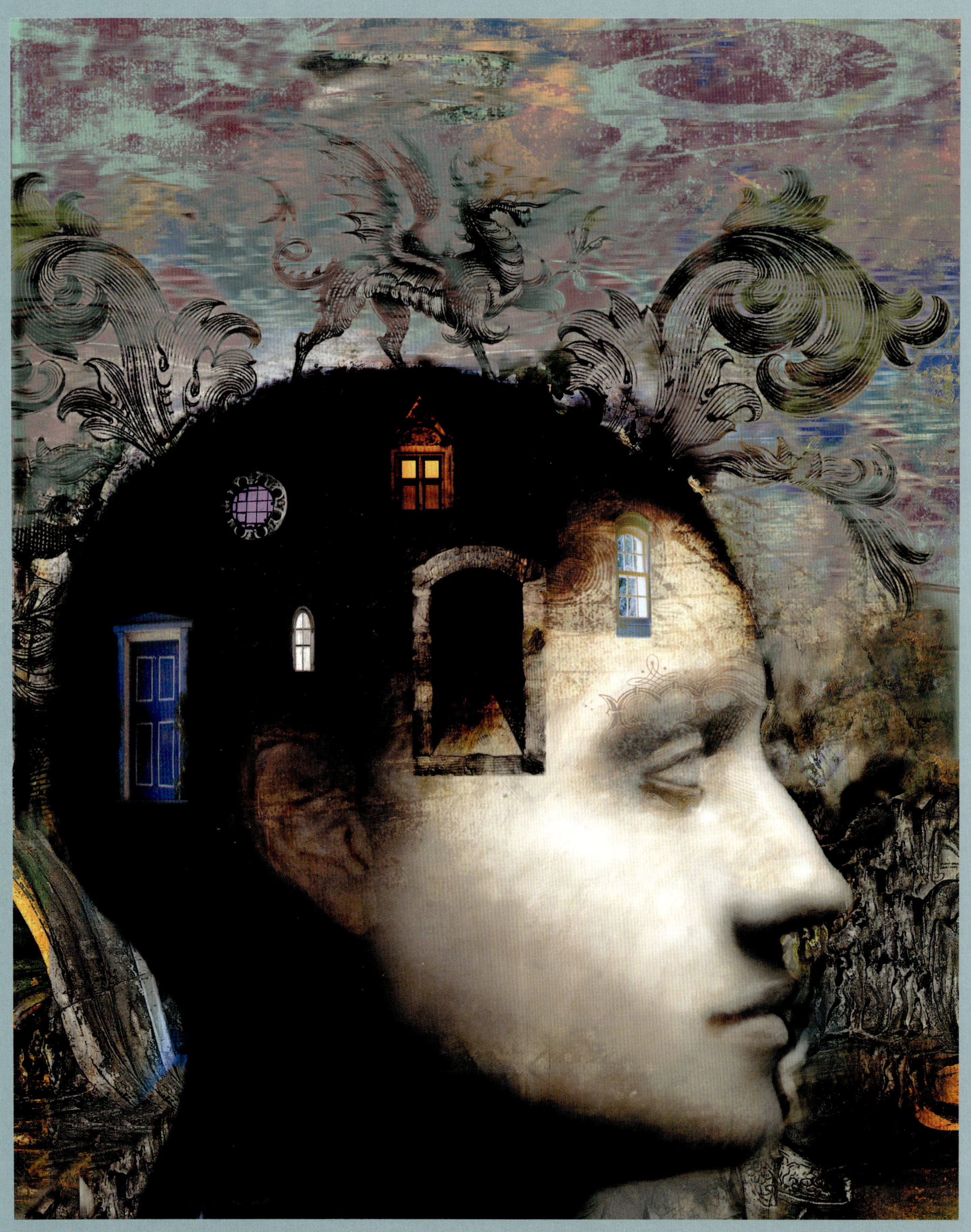

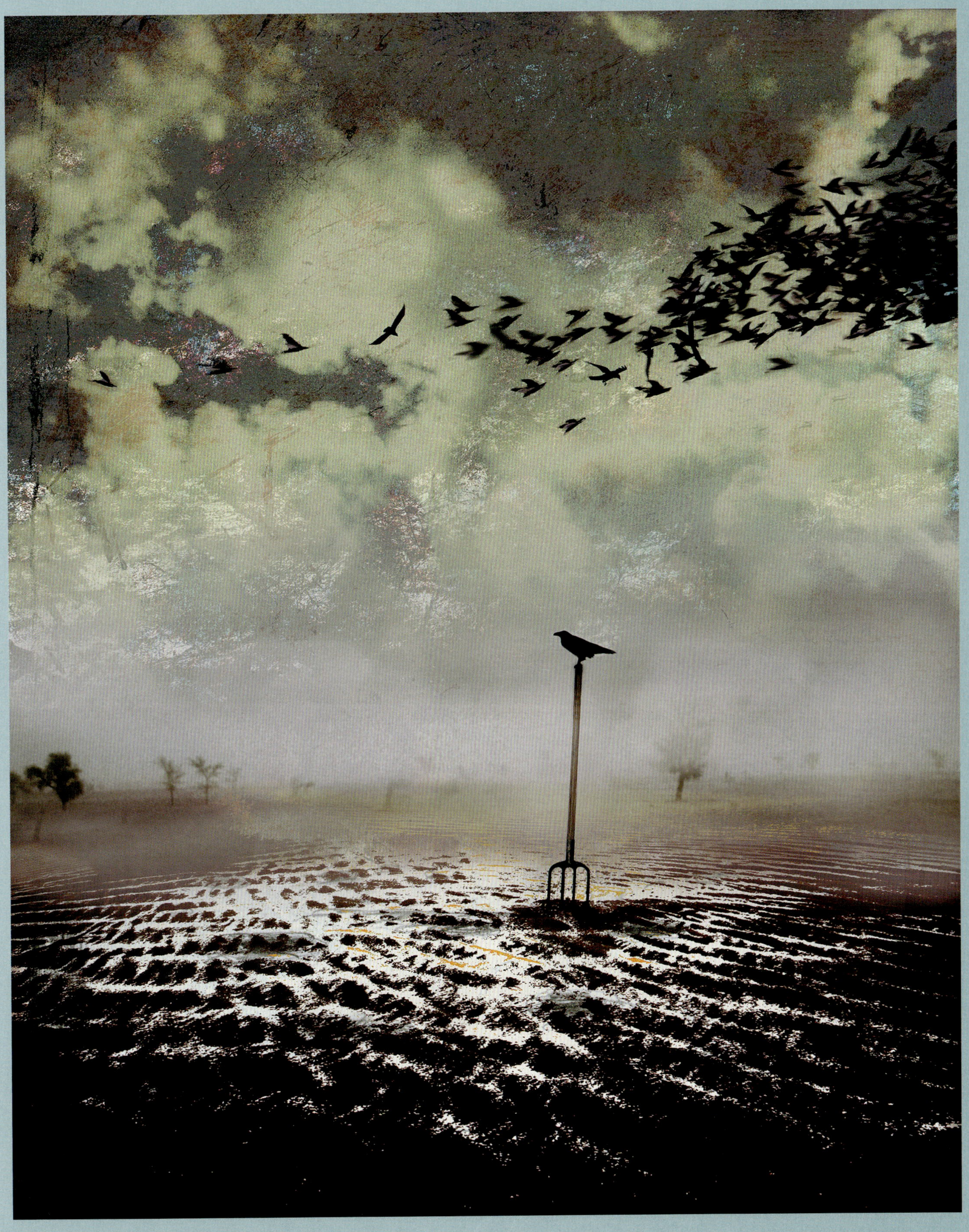

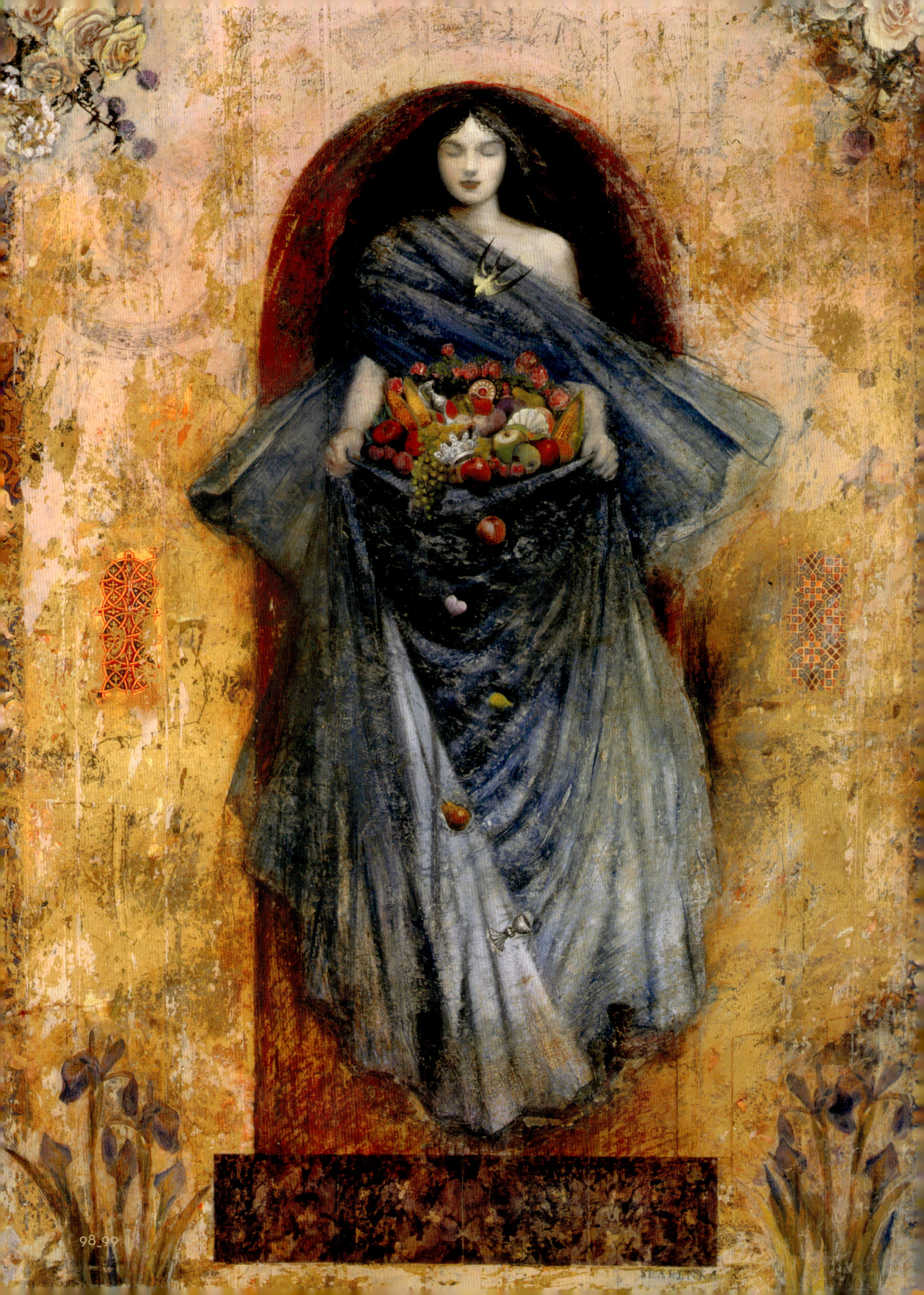
98_99

The Goddess heart a loving vine

weaving through my life entwined

within the flesh inside the mind

Sensual and Divine

G O D D E S S

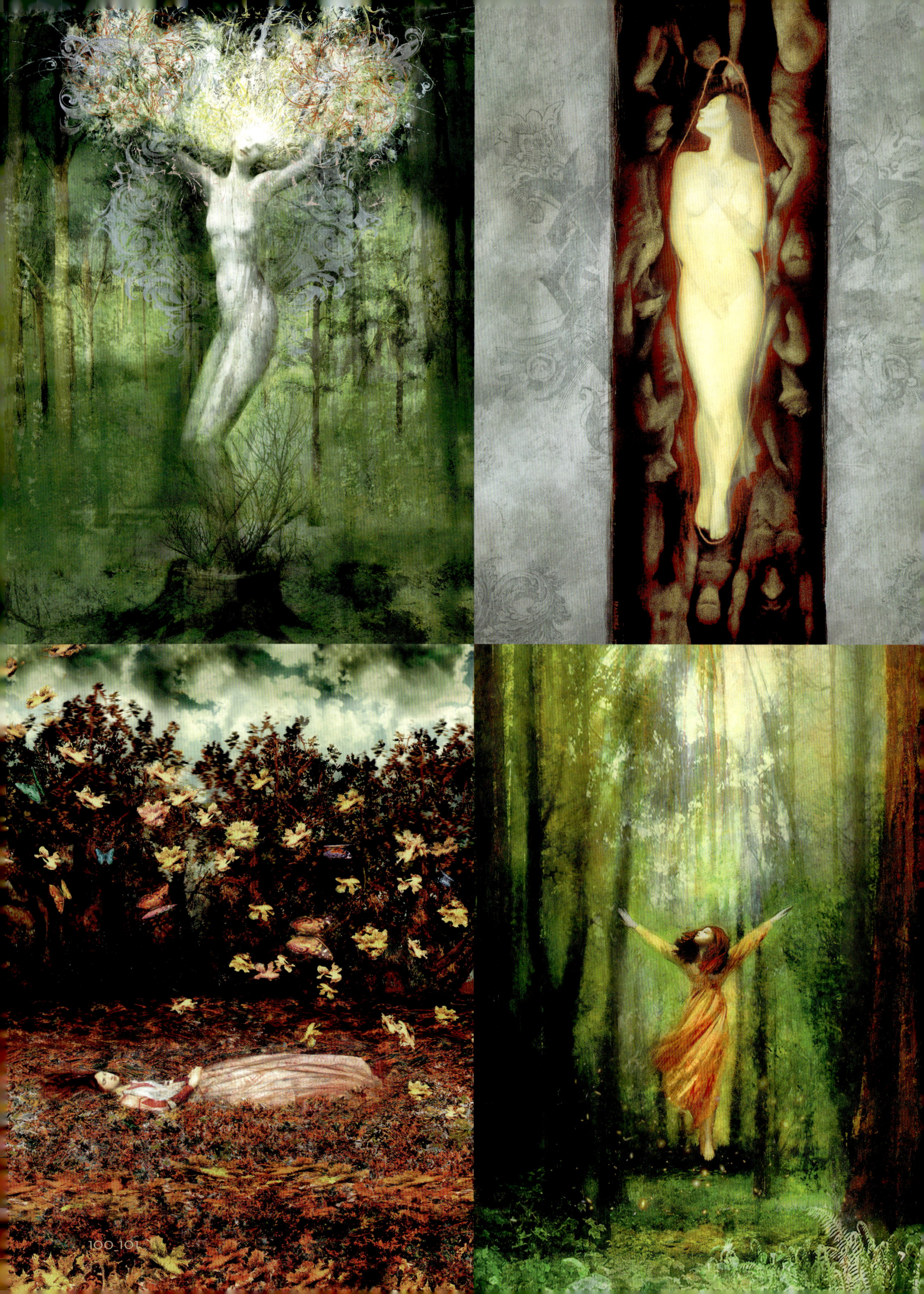

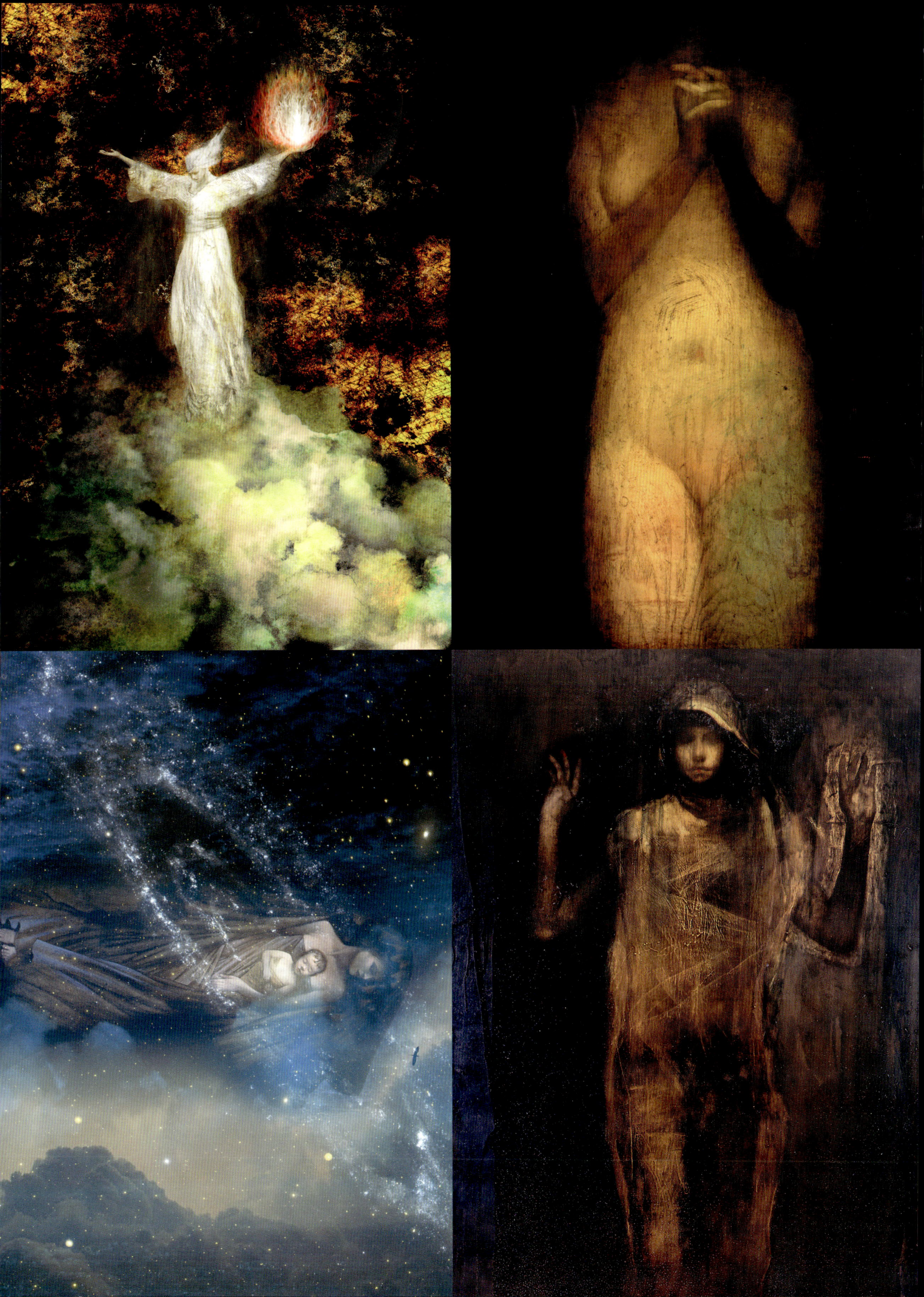

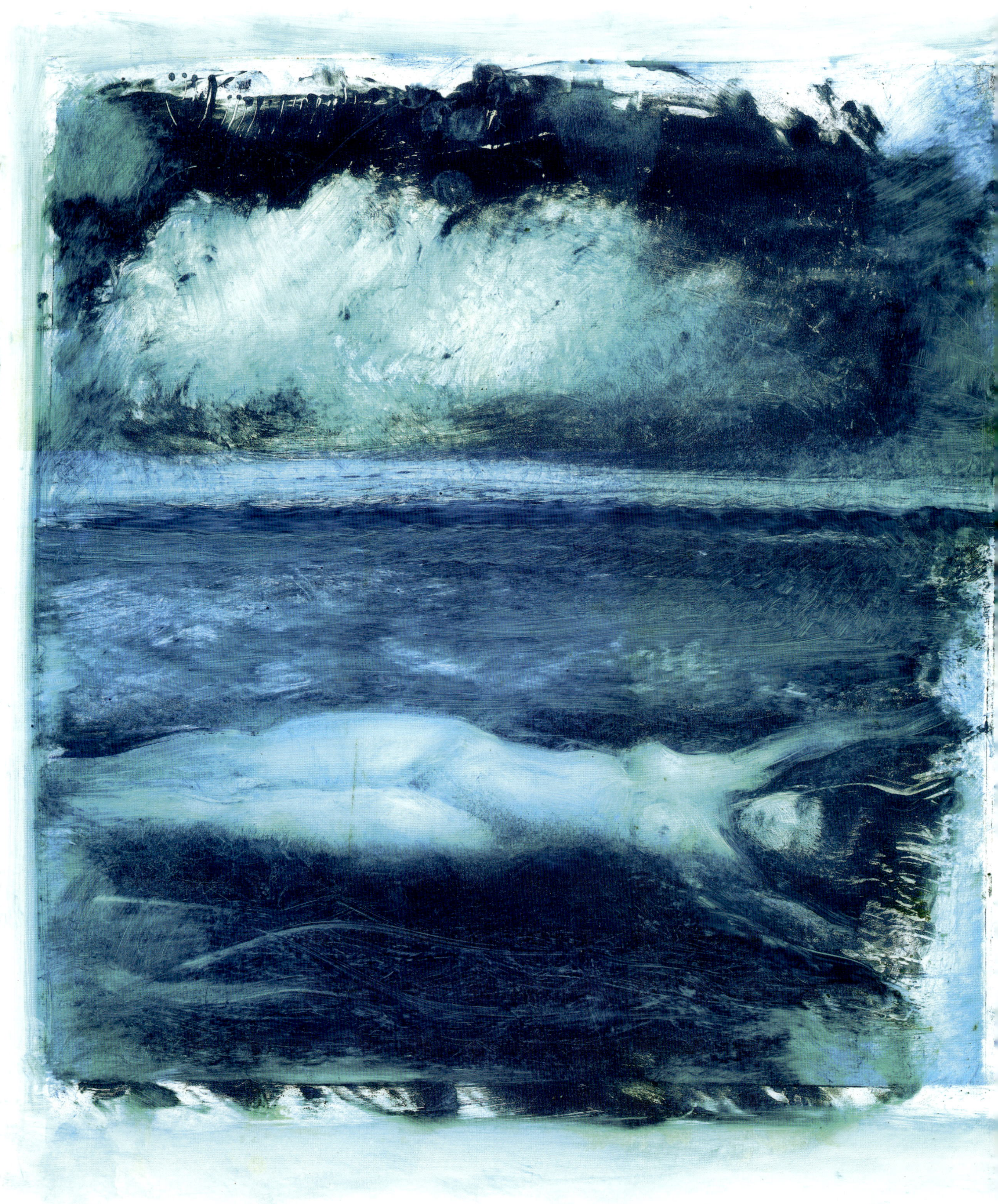

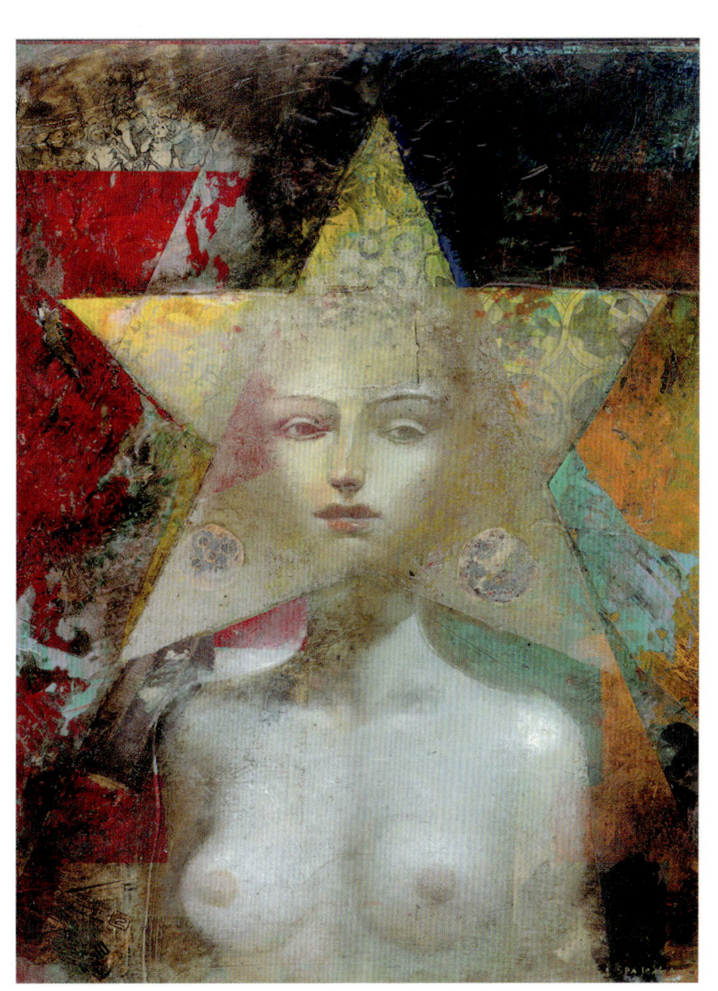

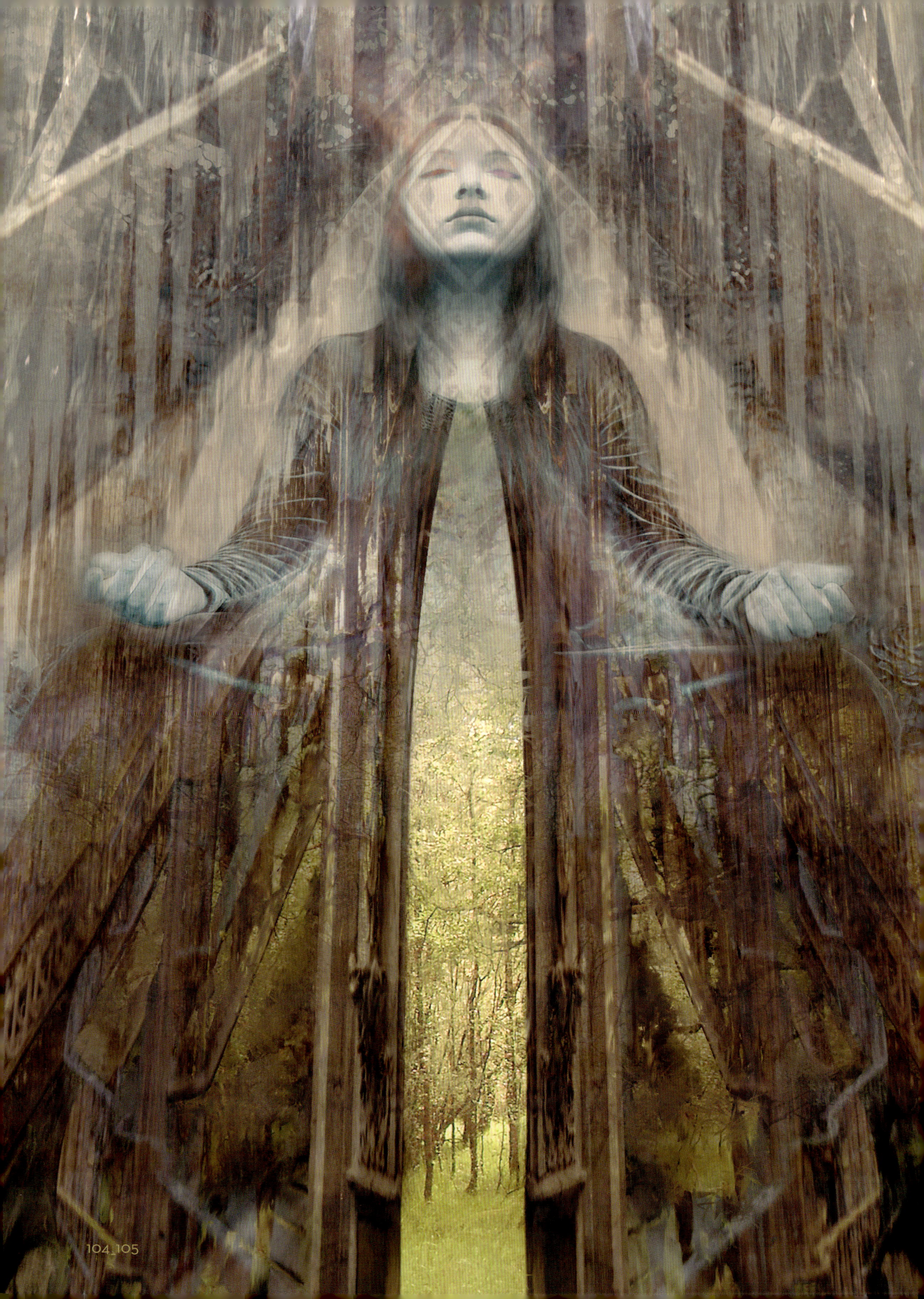

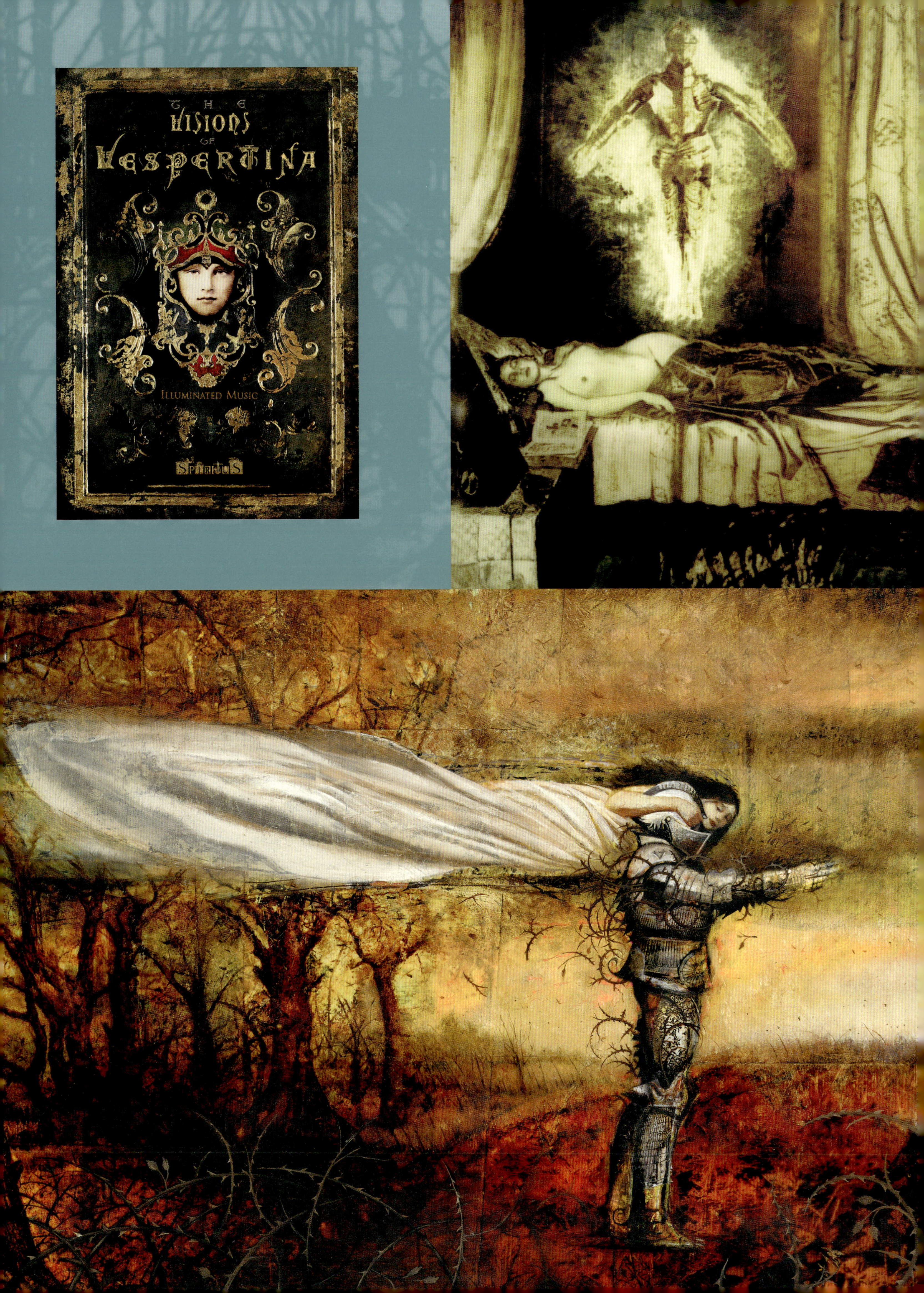
THE
VISIONS
OF
VESPERTINA
ILLUMINATED MUSIC
SPIRITUS

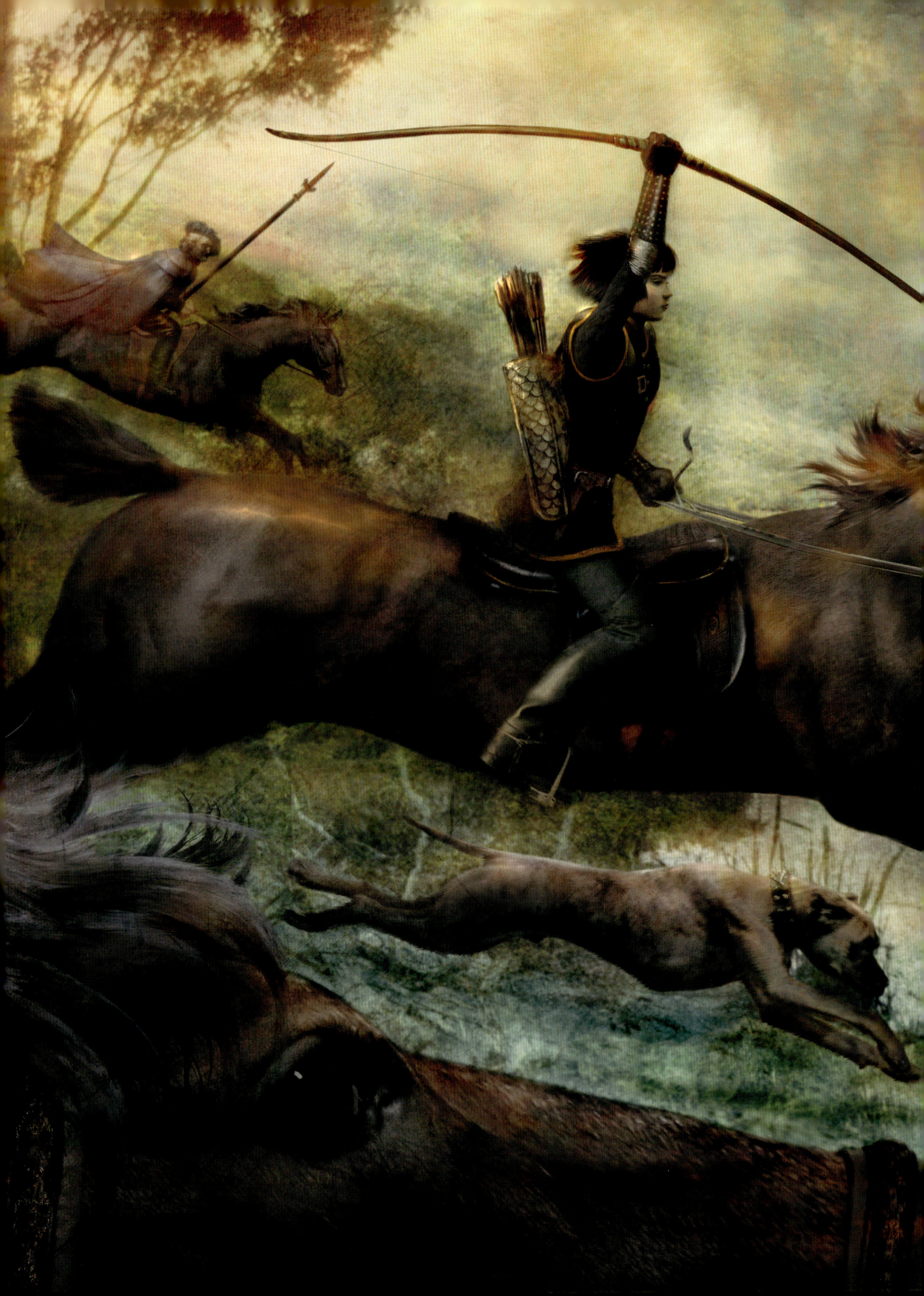

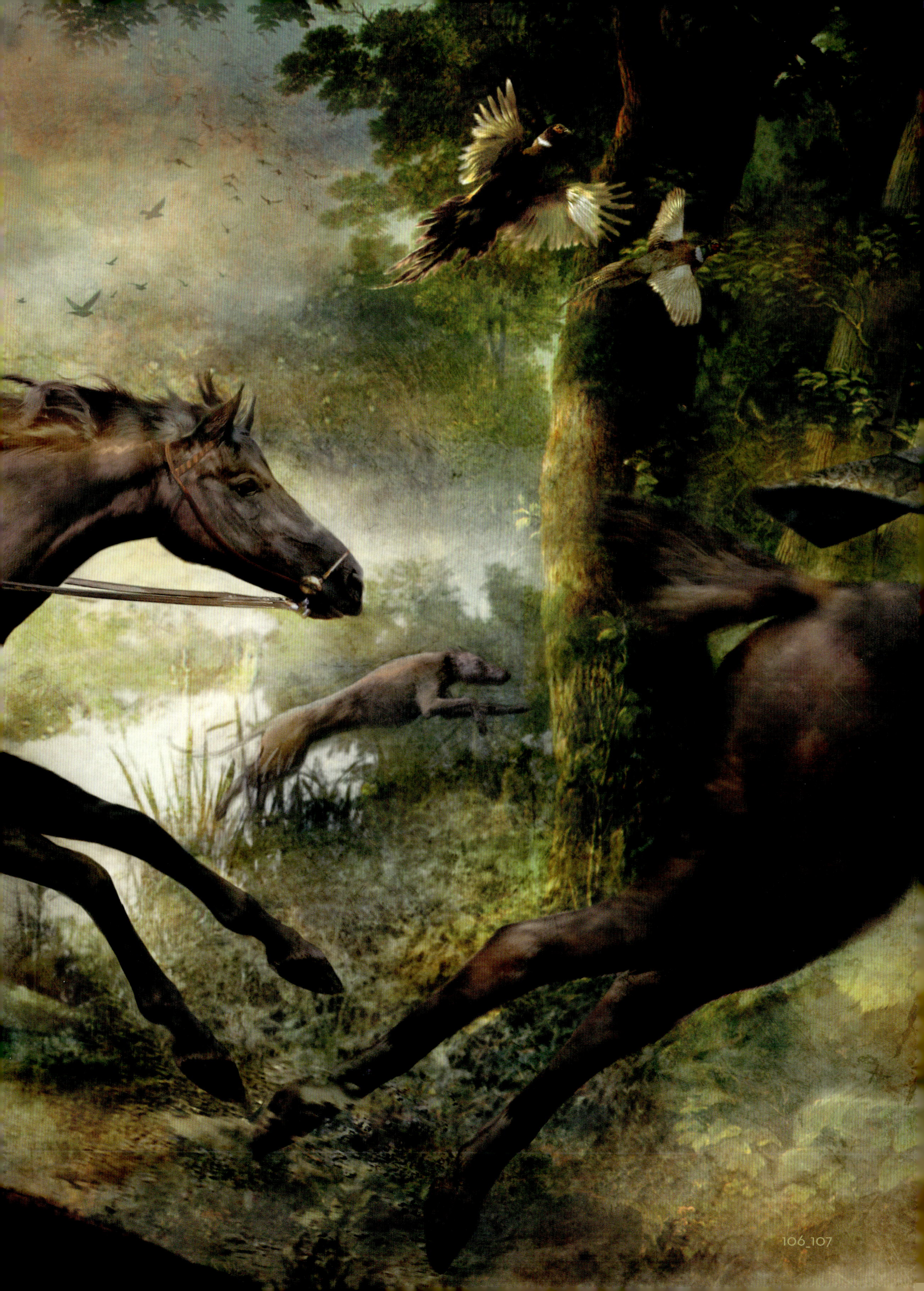

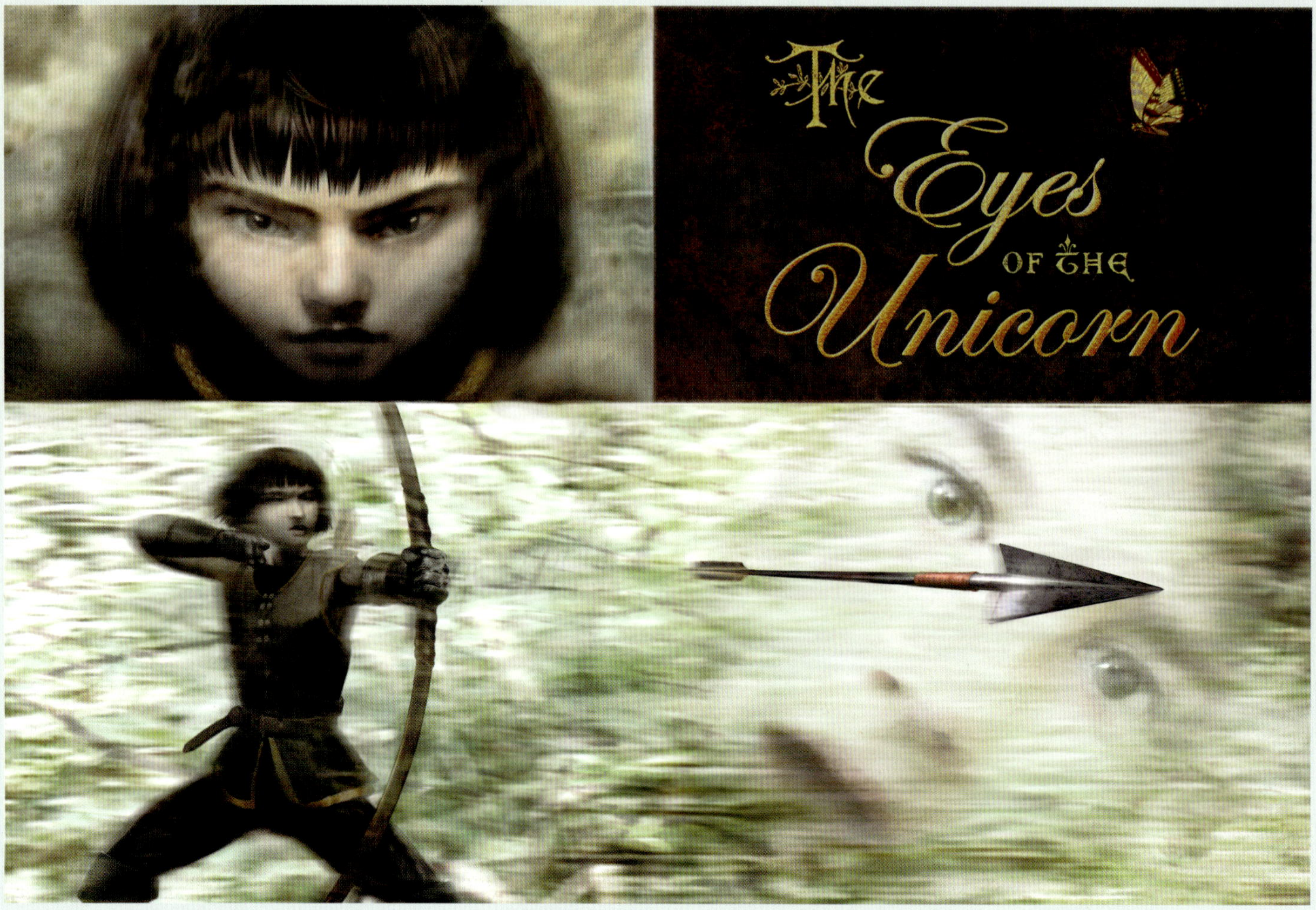

The Eyes of the Unicorn

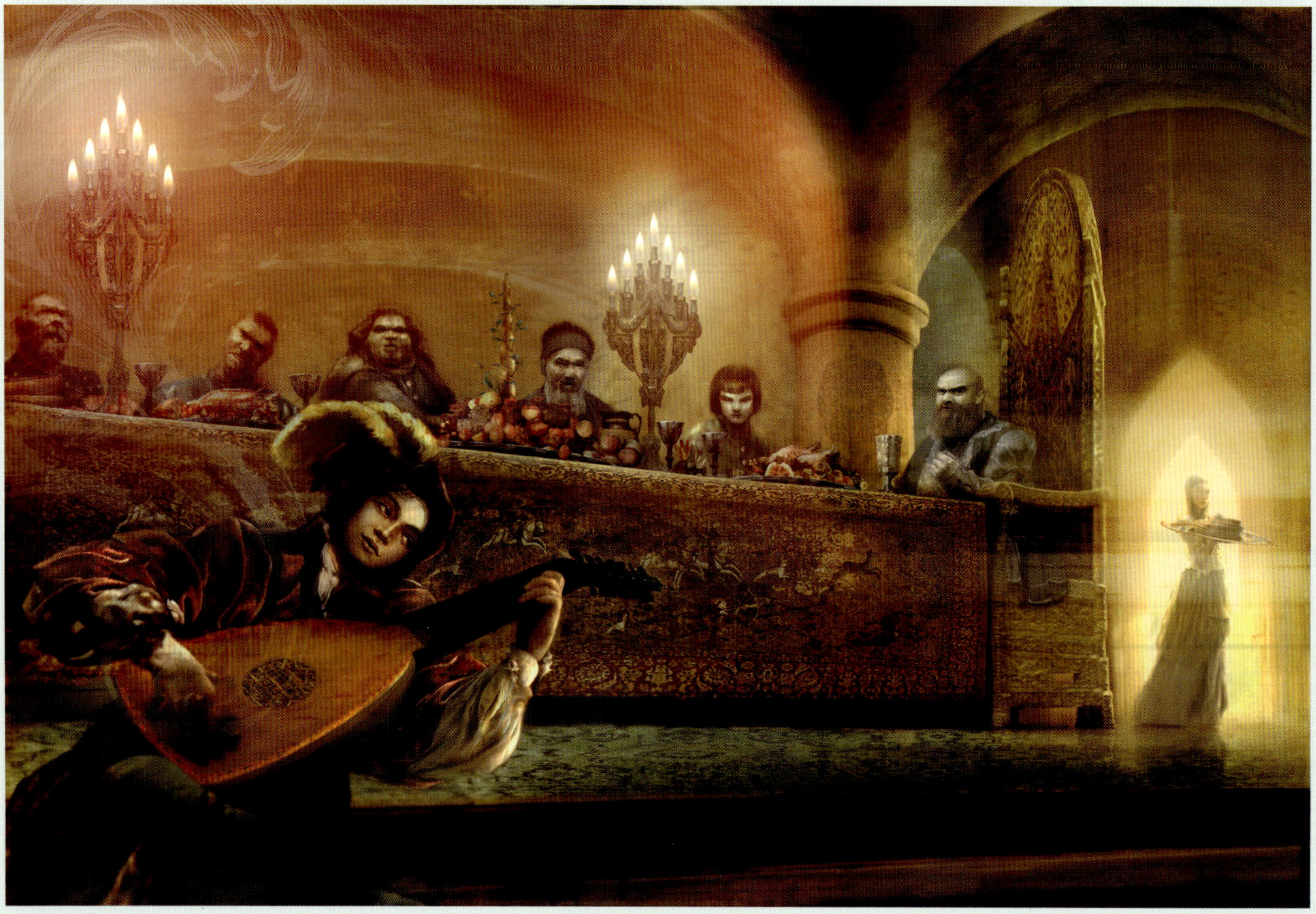

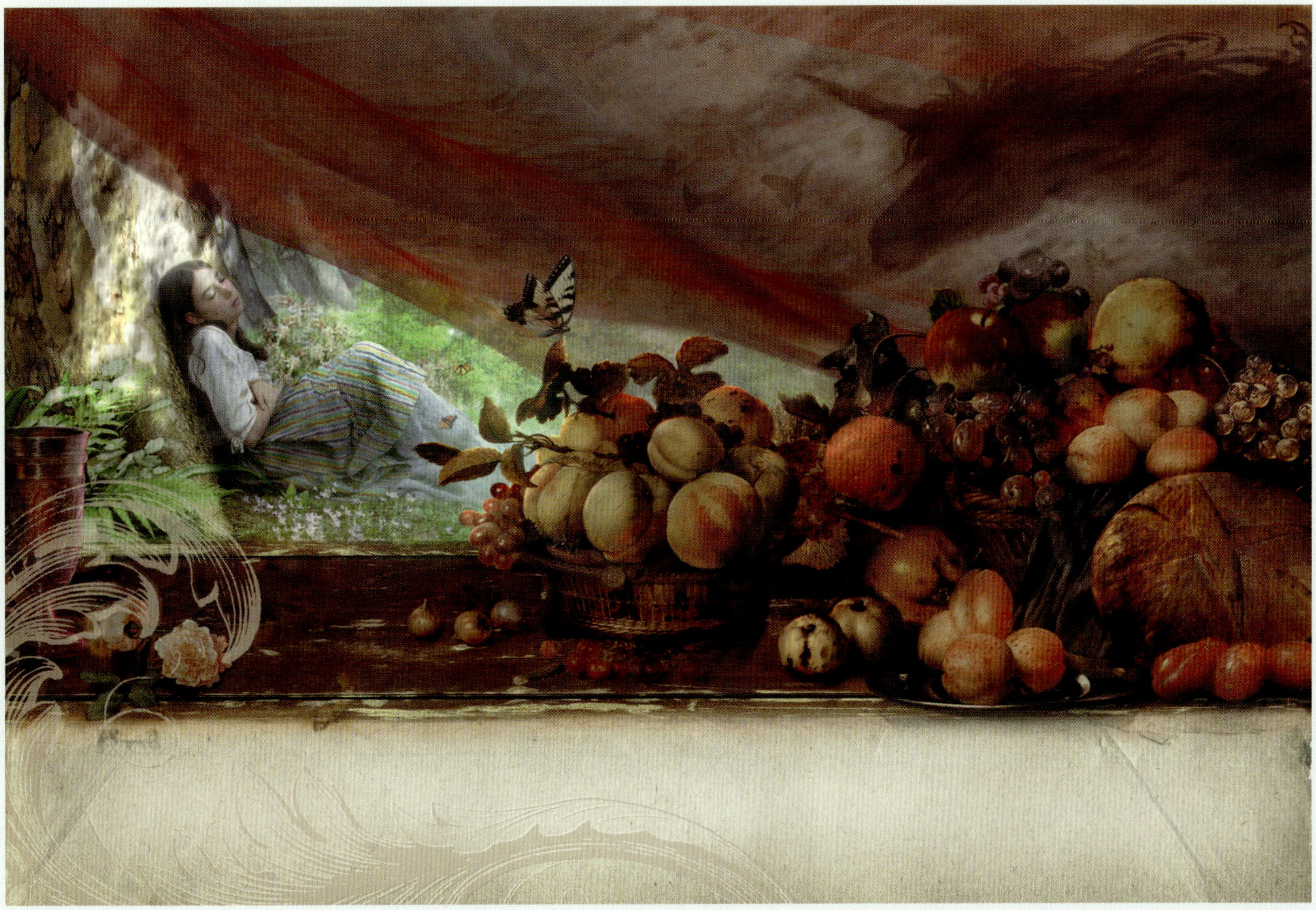

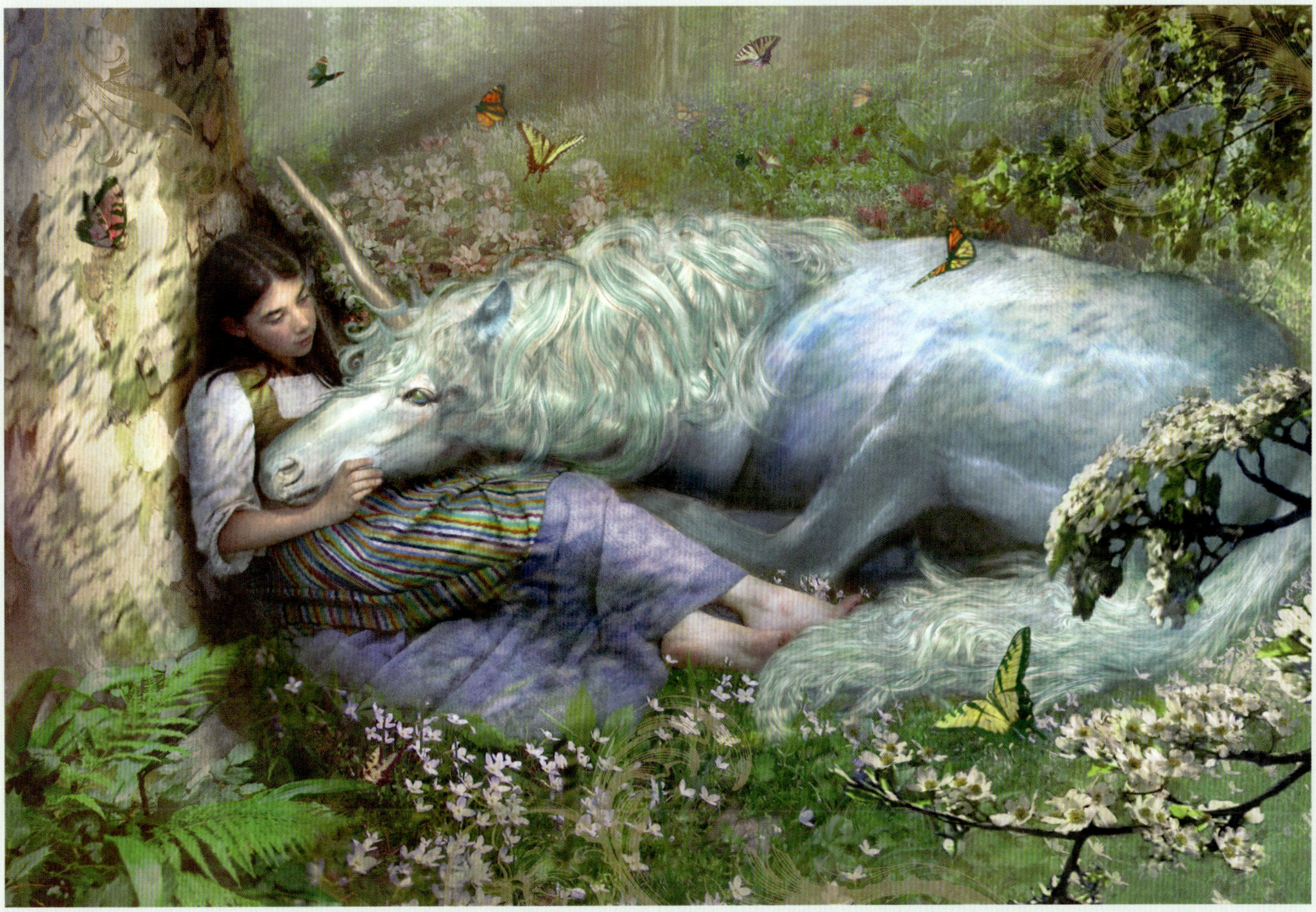

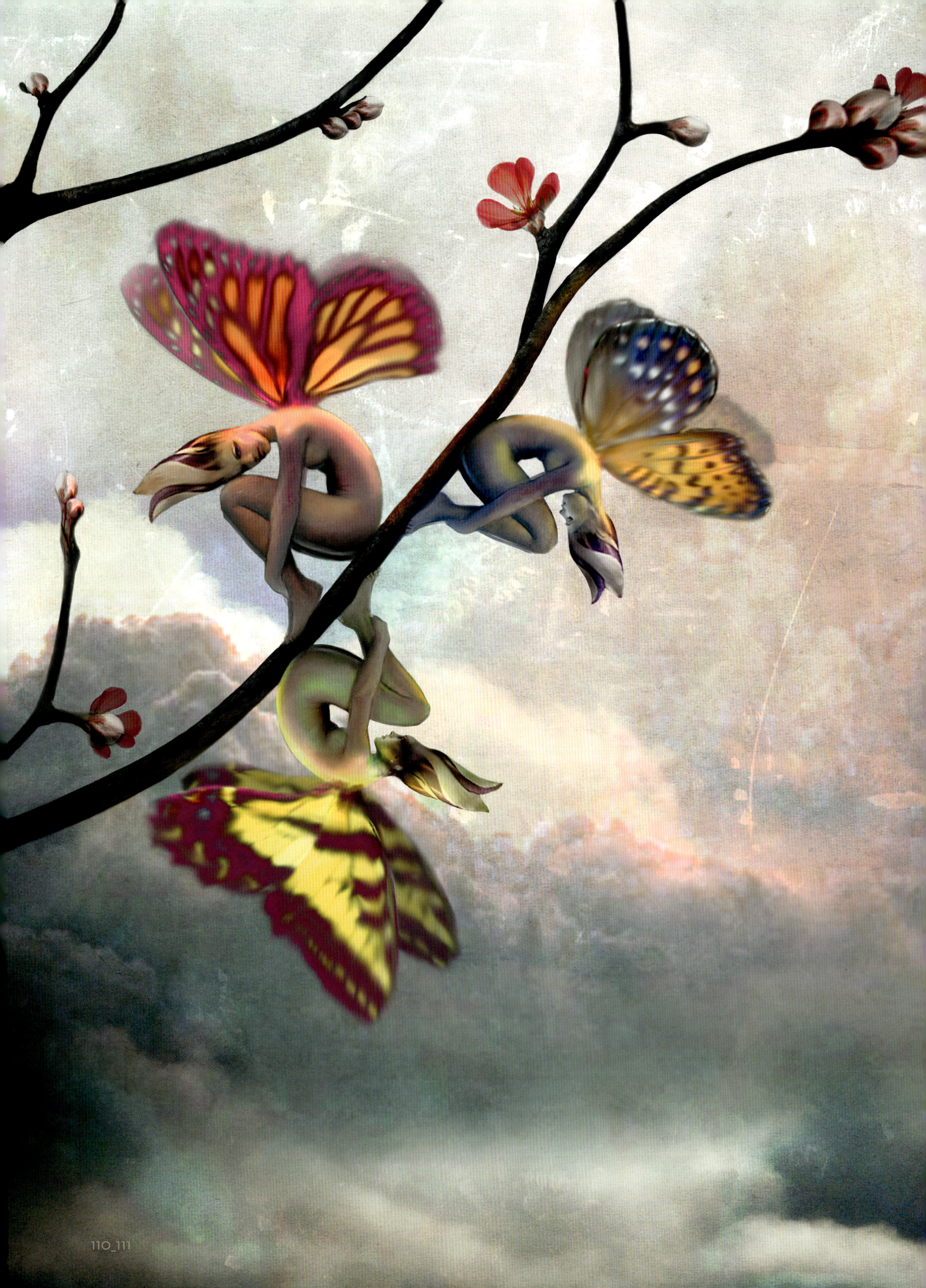

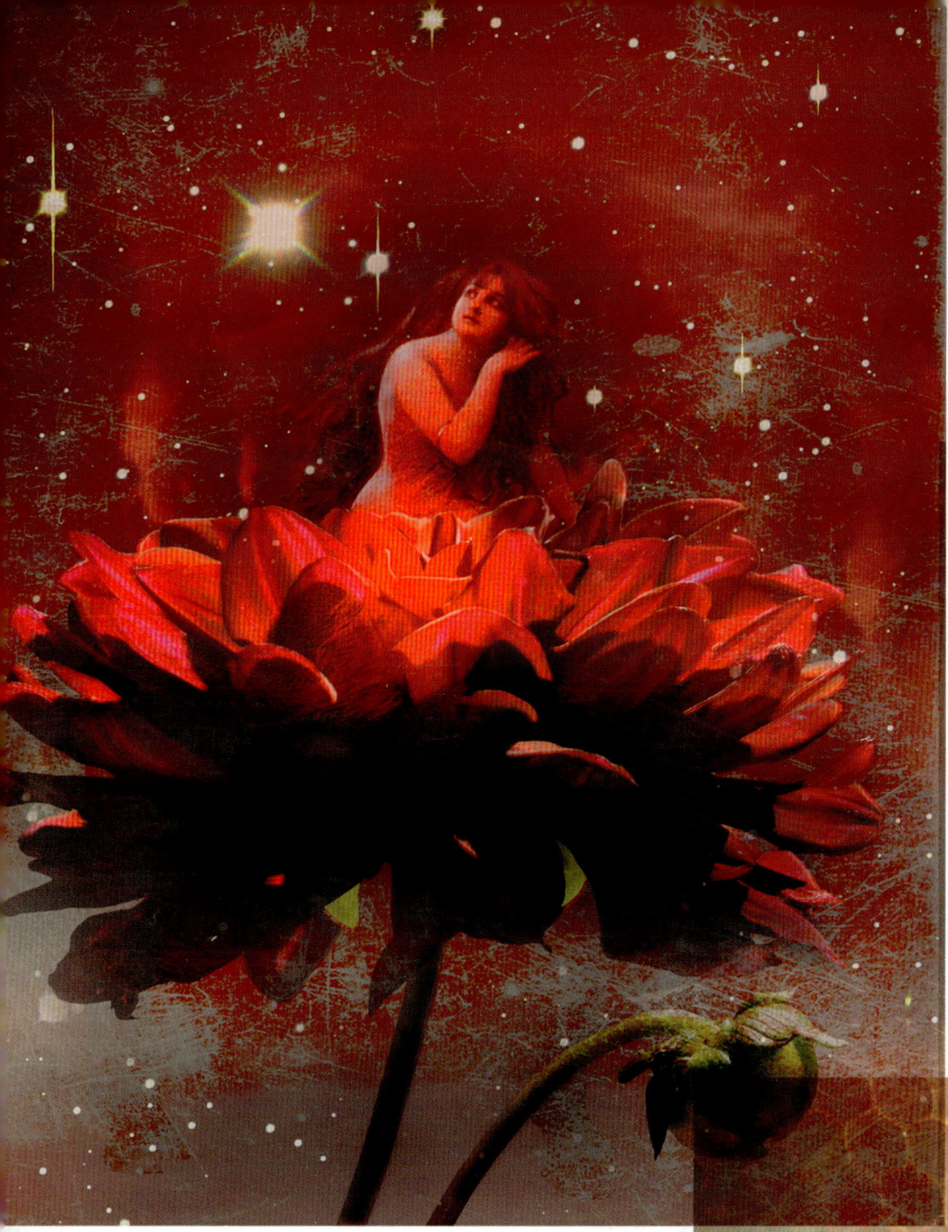

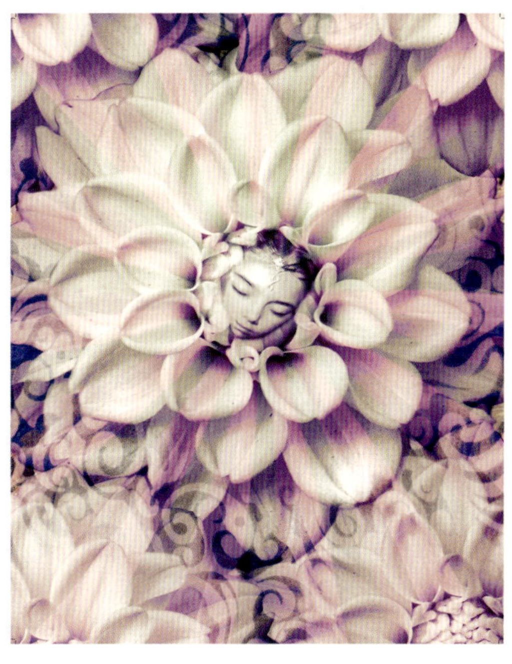

Flowers of Fortune

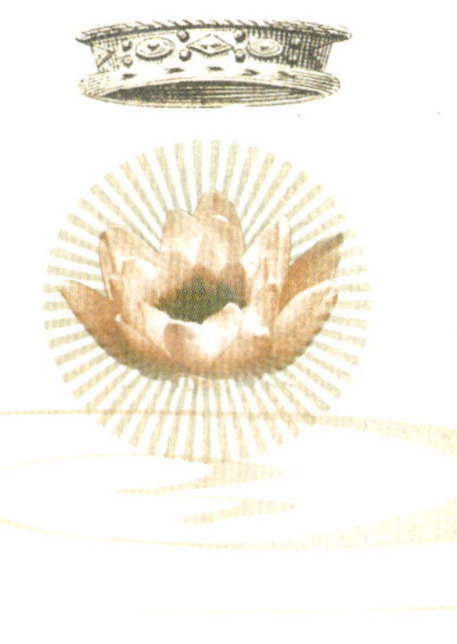

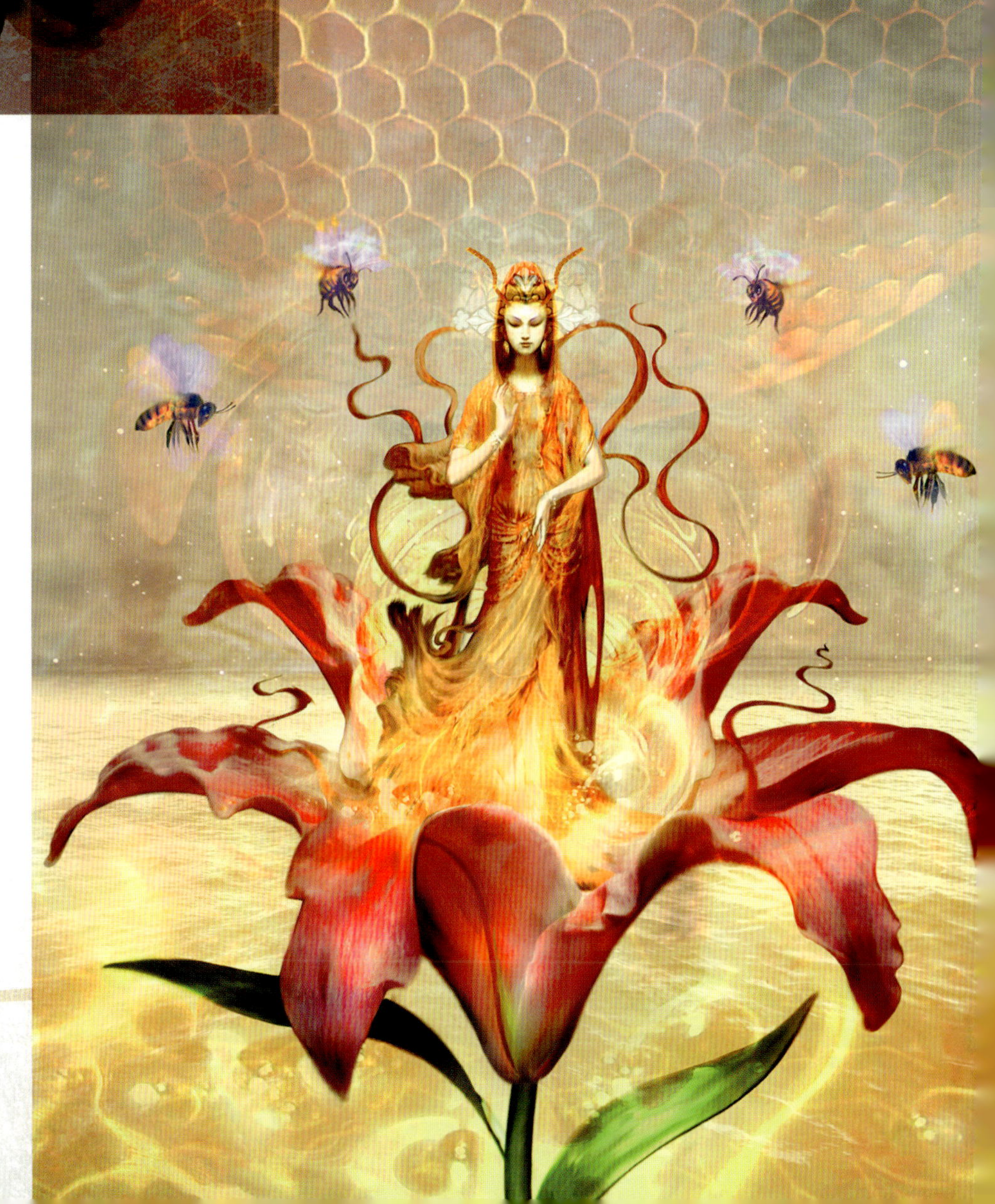

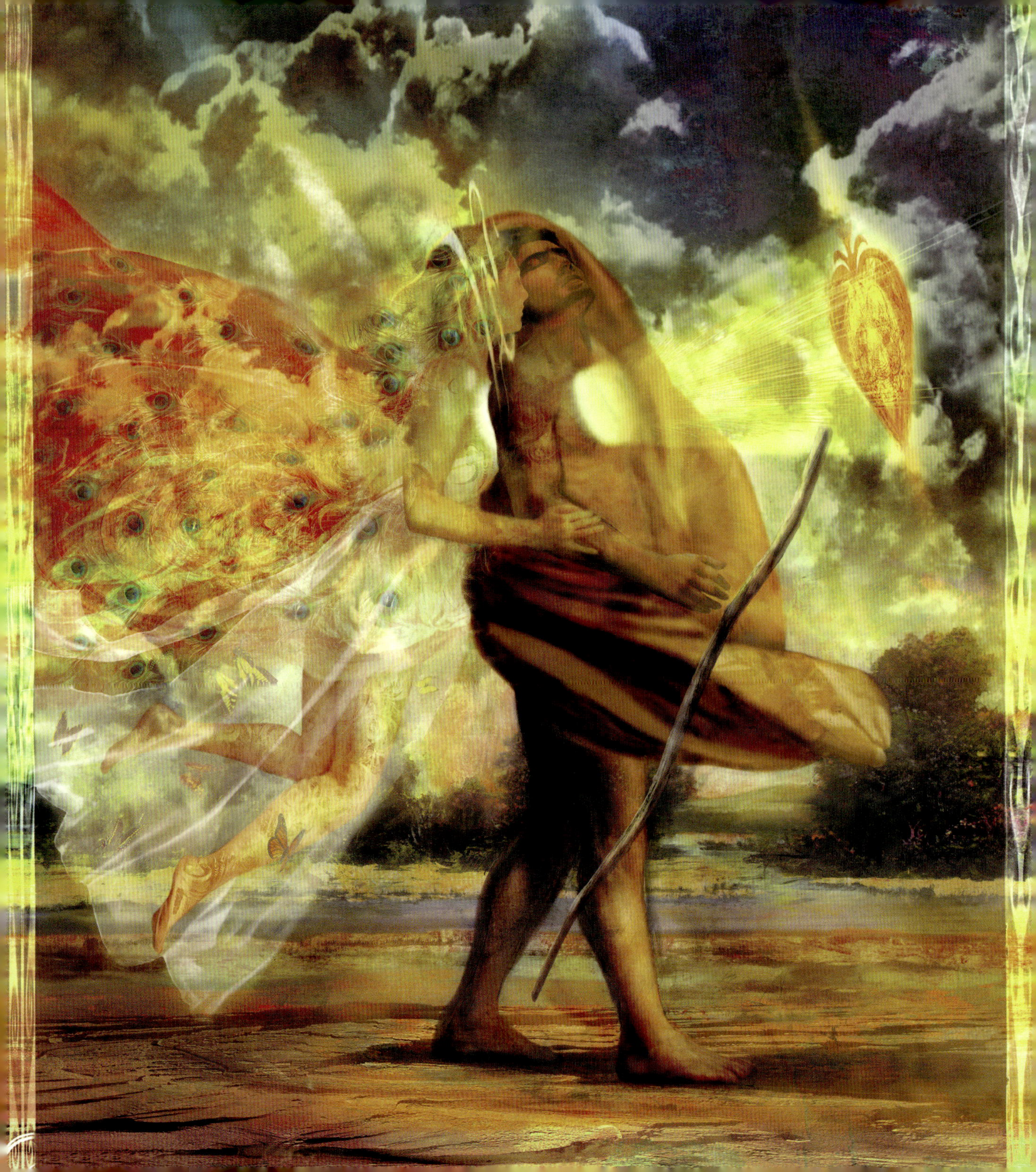

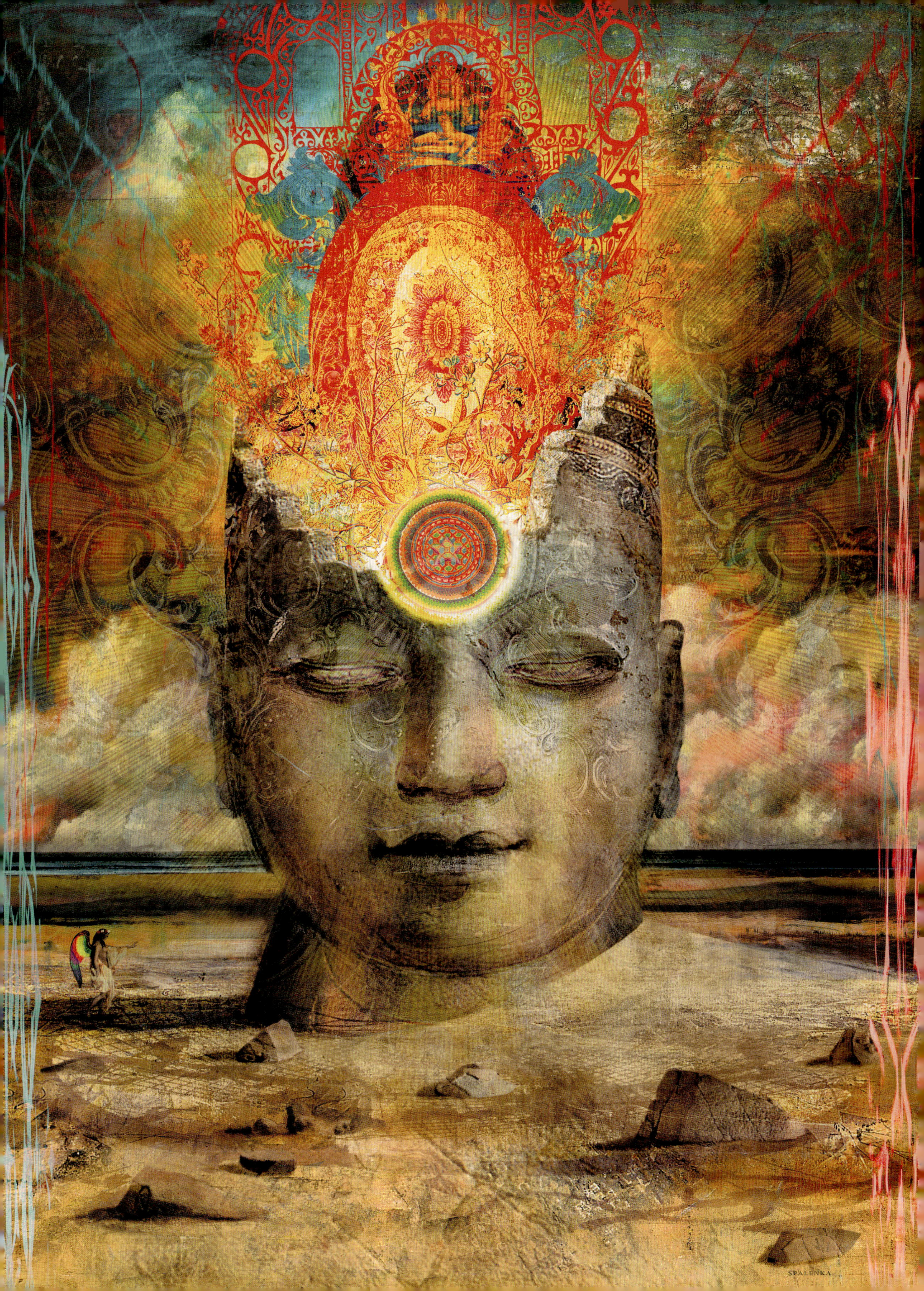
SPALENKA

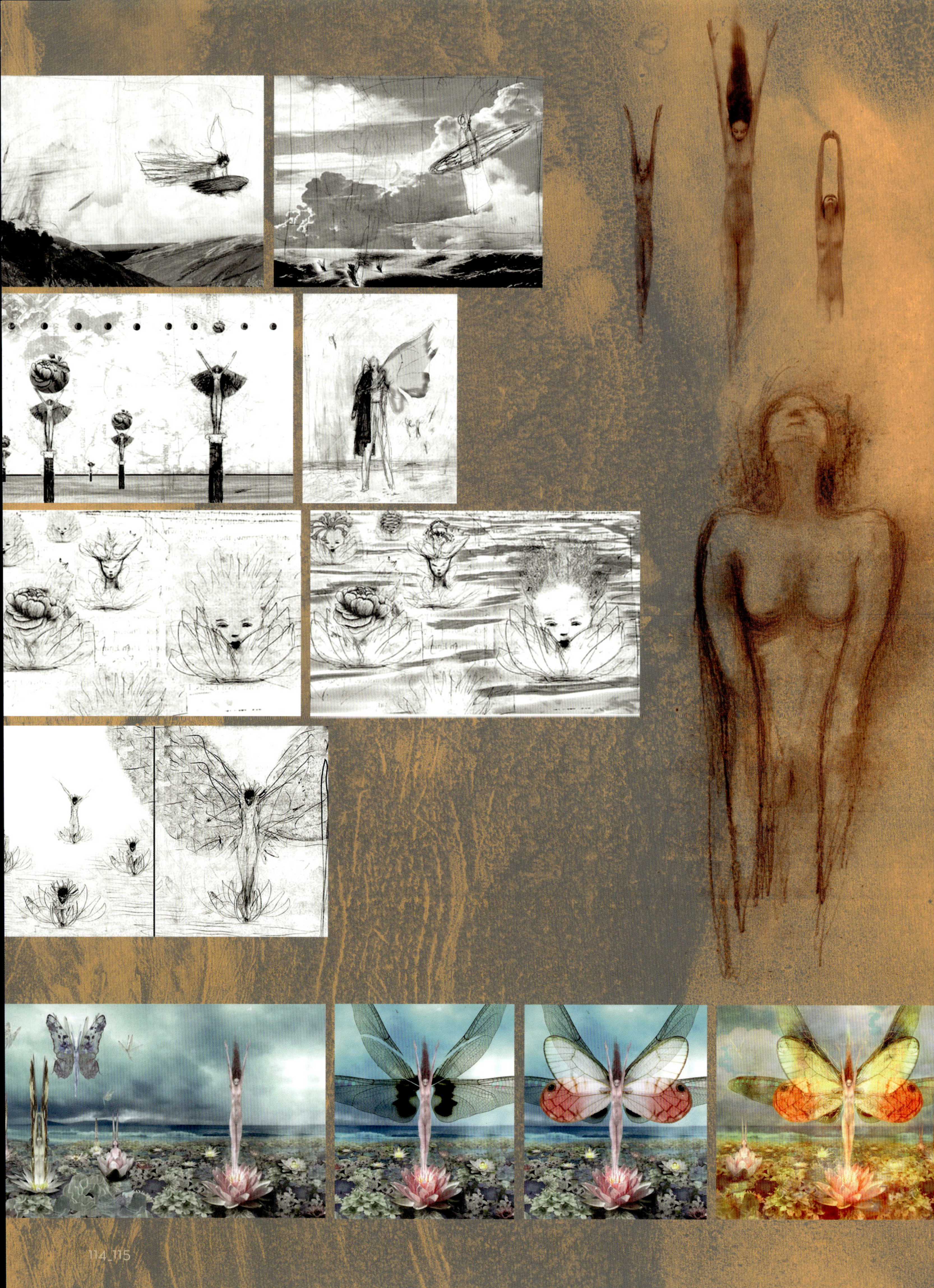

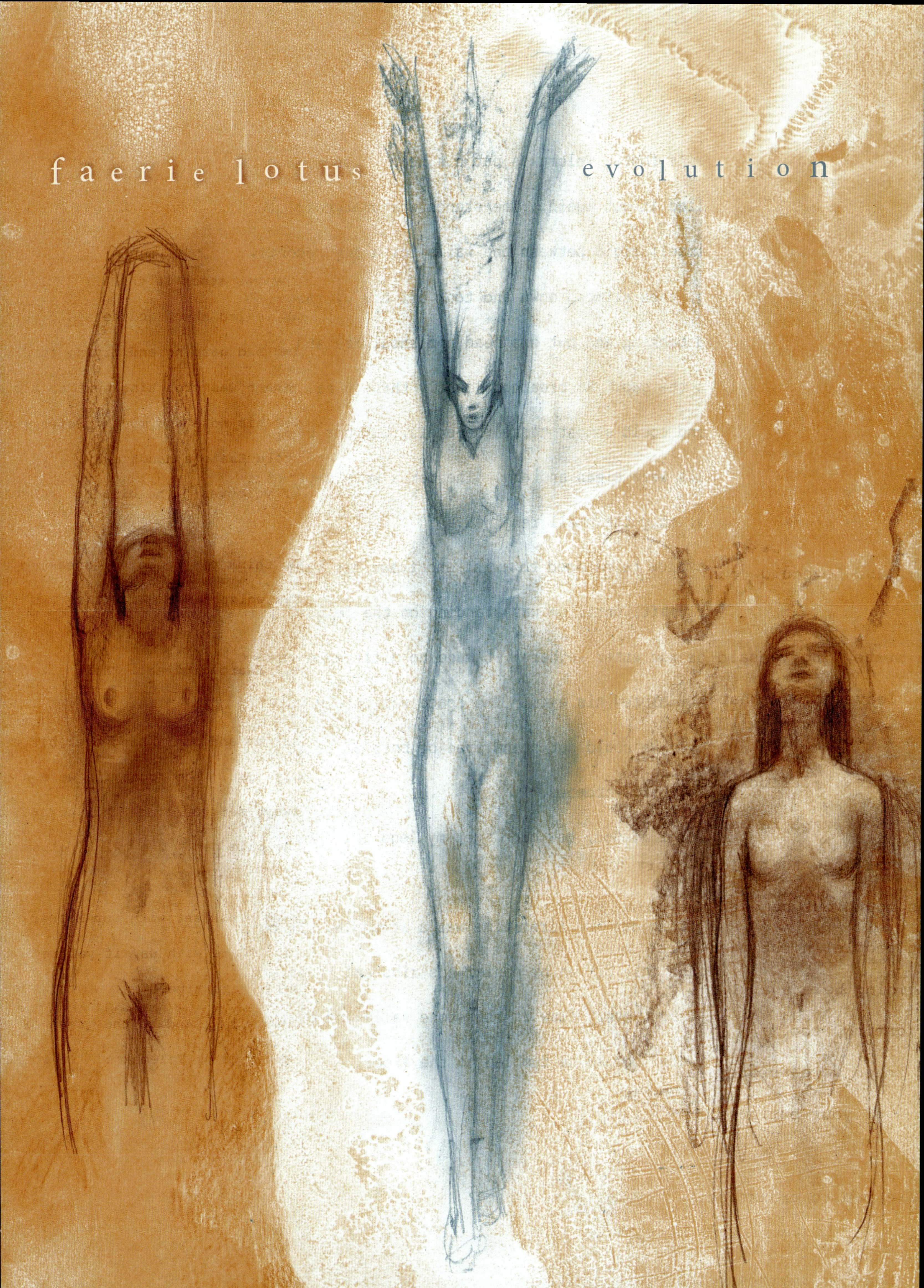
faerie lotus
evolution

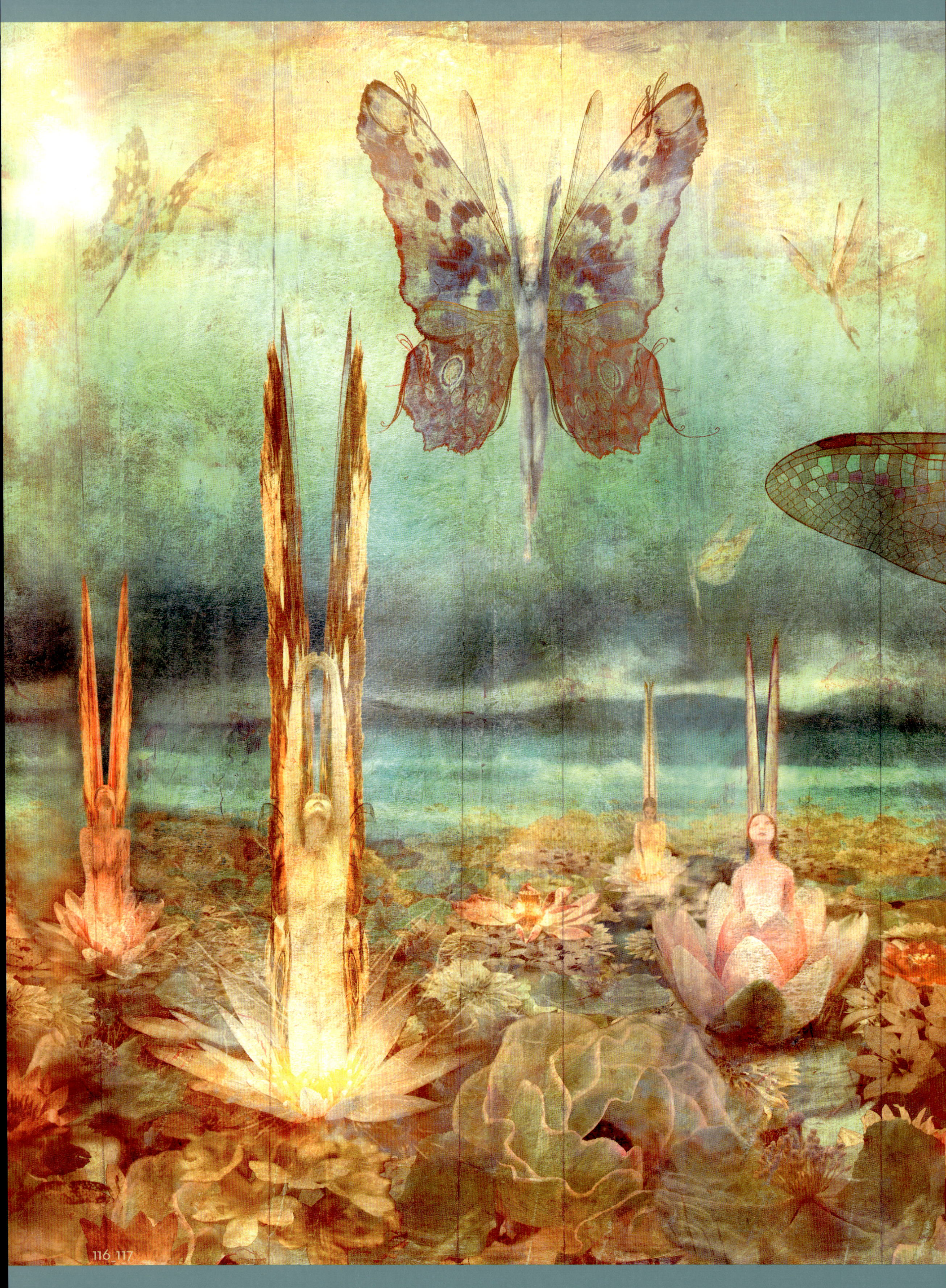

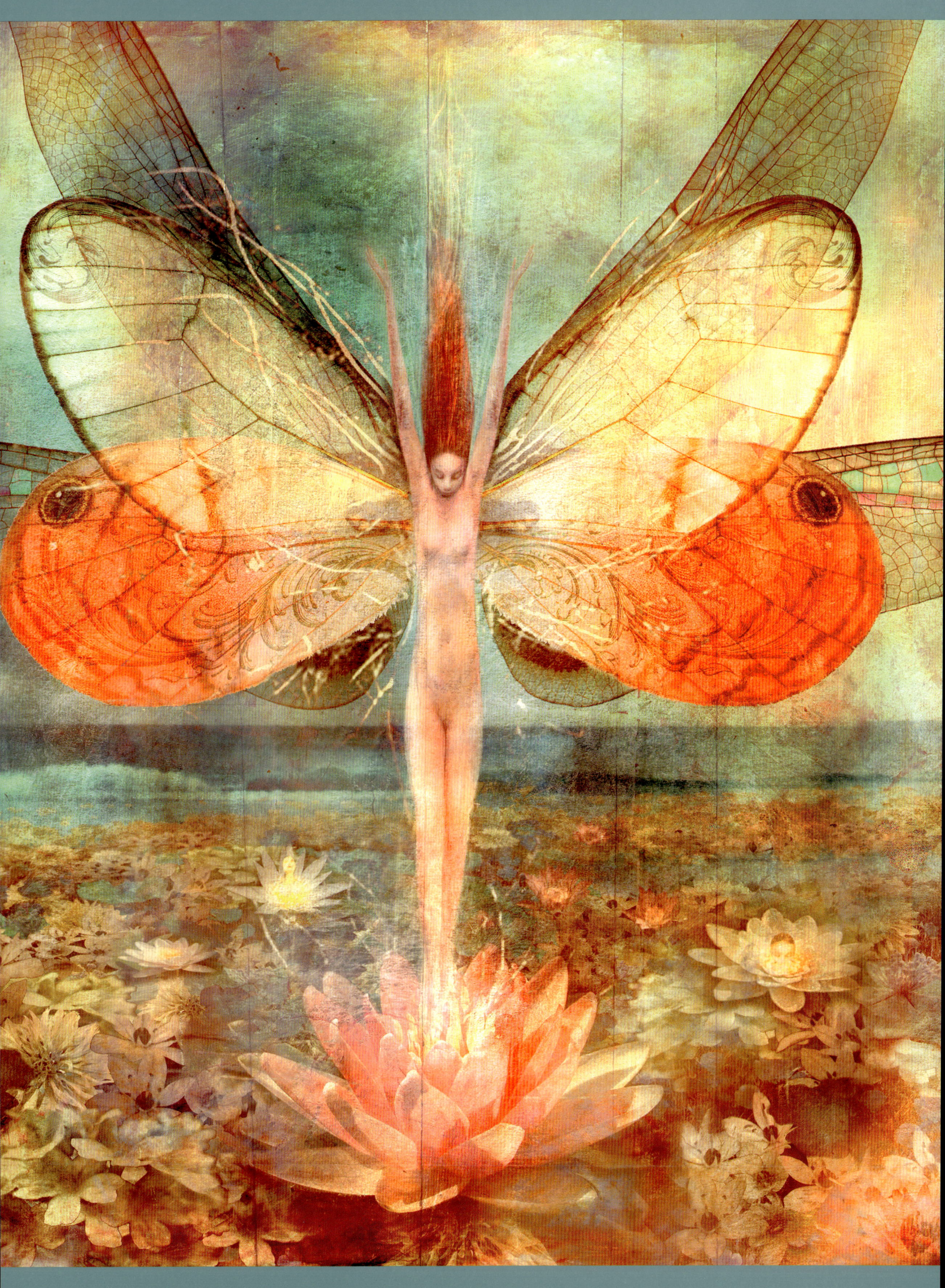

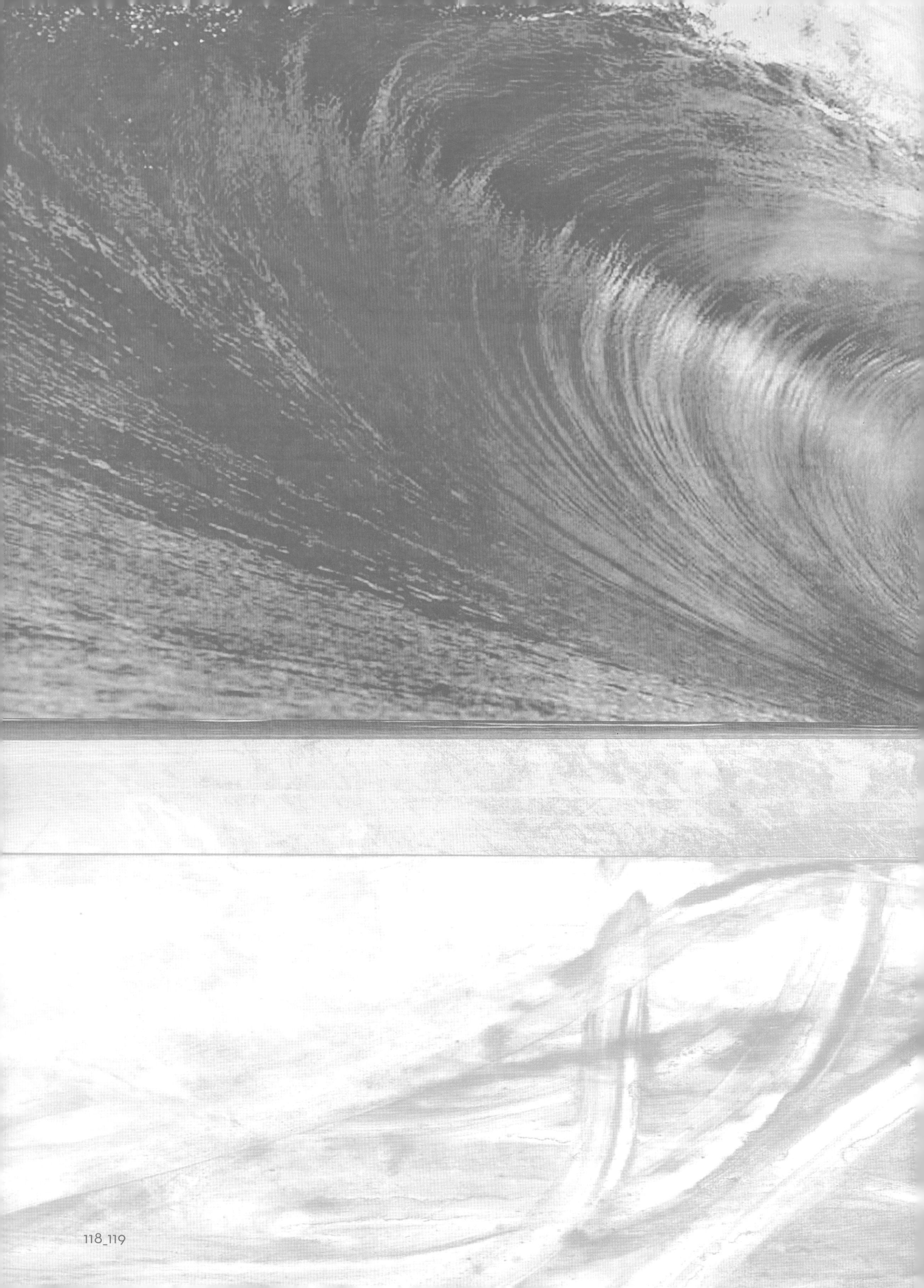

film work

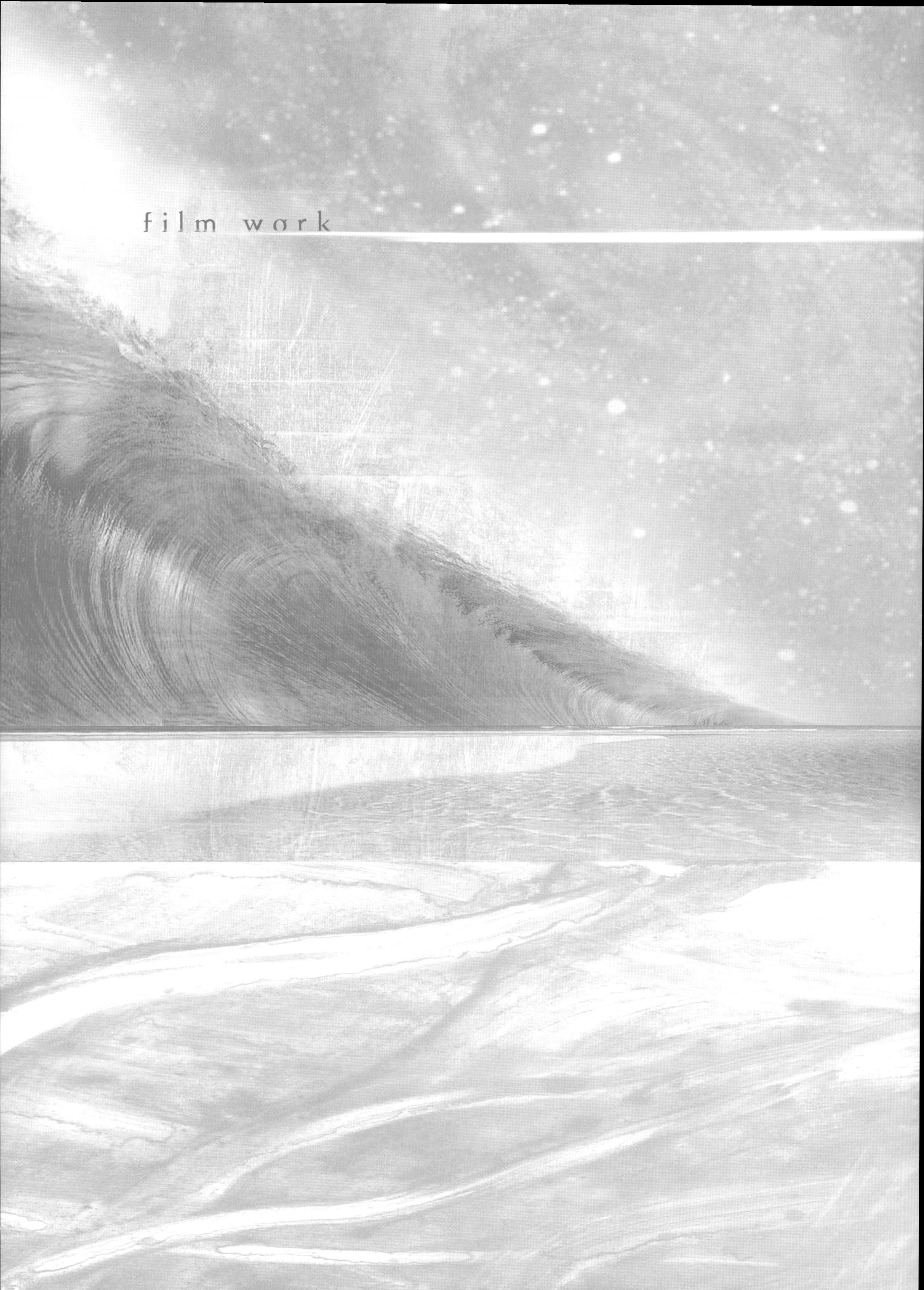

illuminated blueprints

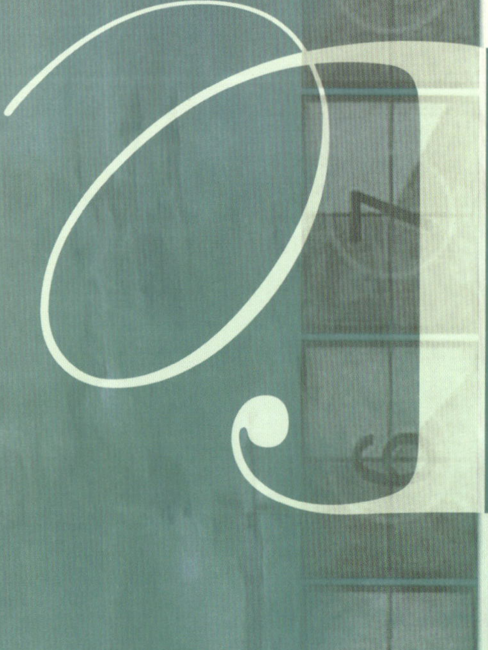

In 2004, production designer Barry Jackson asked me to join his team of talented concept designers to work on the Warner Brothers feature CG animated film *The Ant Bully*, directed by John Davis. Being part of this group was a tremendous education. I loved the camaraderie of working on something that was much bigger than myself. Films are complicated art forms, requiring many talents to piece them together, especially if they integrate computer generated imagery. Technology is the driver in this industry. The goal is to show the viewer something new, so pushing the limits of what is possible takes precedence. Artists must ride this evolving tech wave otherwise they can fall behind. It is a competitive and challenging business.

Concept design is mainly used at the beginning of the process, before the production becomes complicated. It is my job to produce the templates that will help everyone on that pipeline see what they are intending to create. Out of the hundreds of images I visualize for a production, only a very few ever make it to the screen, because of script changes, edits and the like. When they do it is very gratifying. What you will see here are some highlights from *The Golden Compass*, *The Ant Bully*, *Escape from Planet Earth* and *The Chronicles of Narnia: The Voyage of the Dawn Treader*.

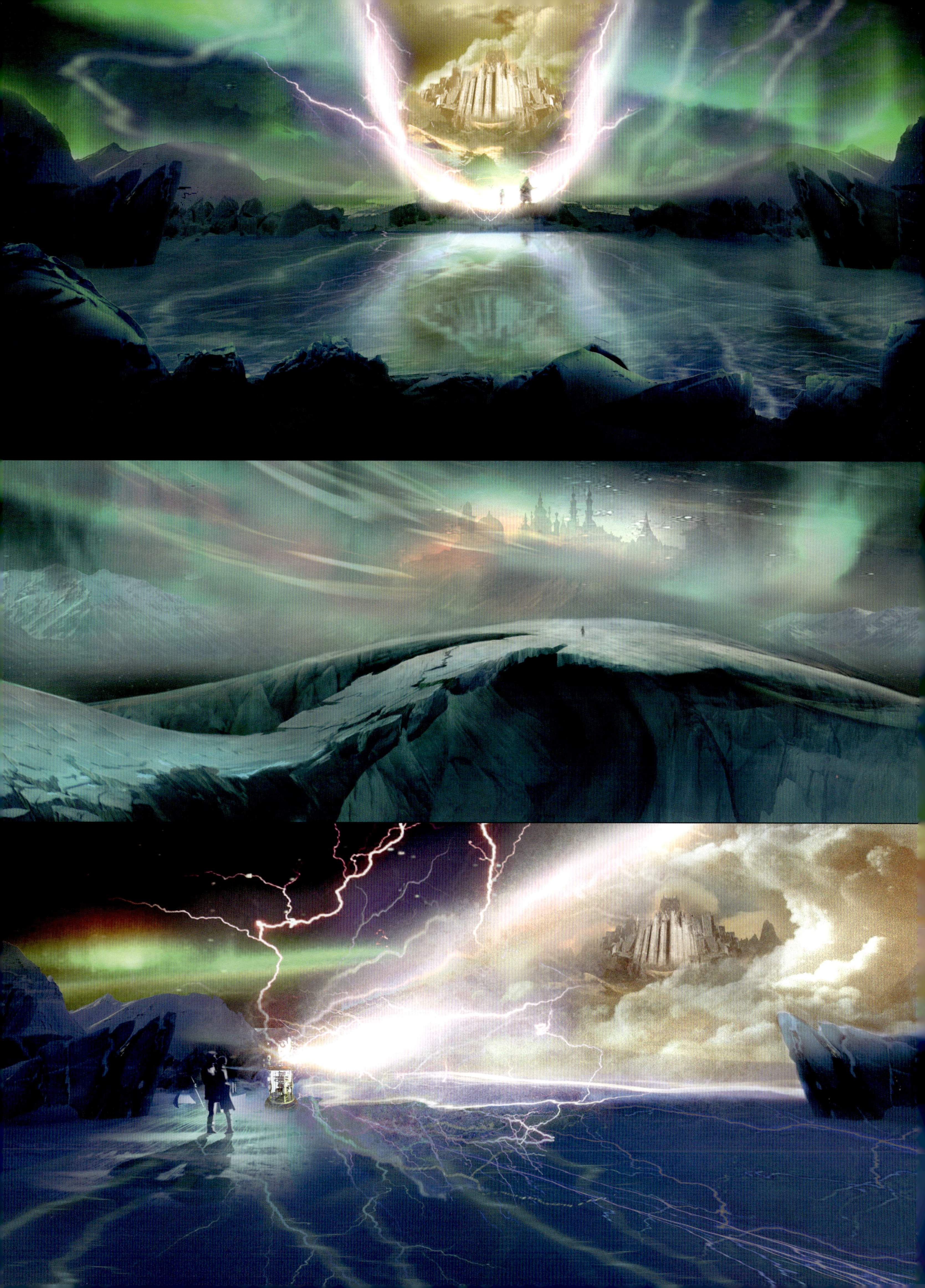

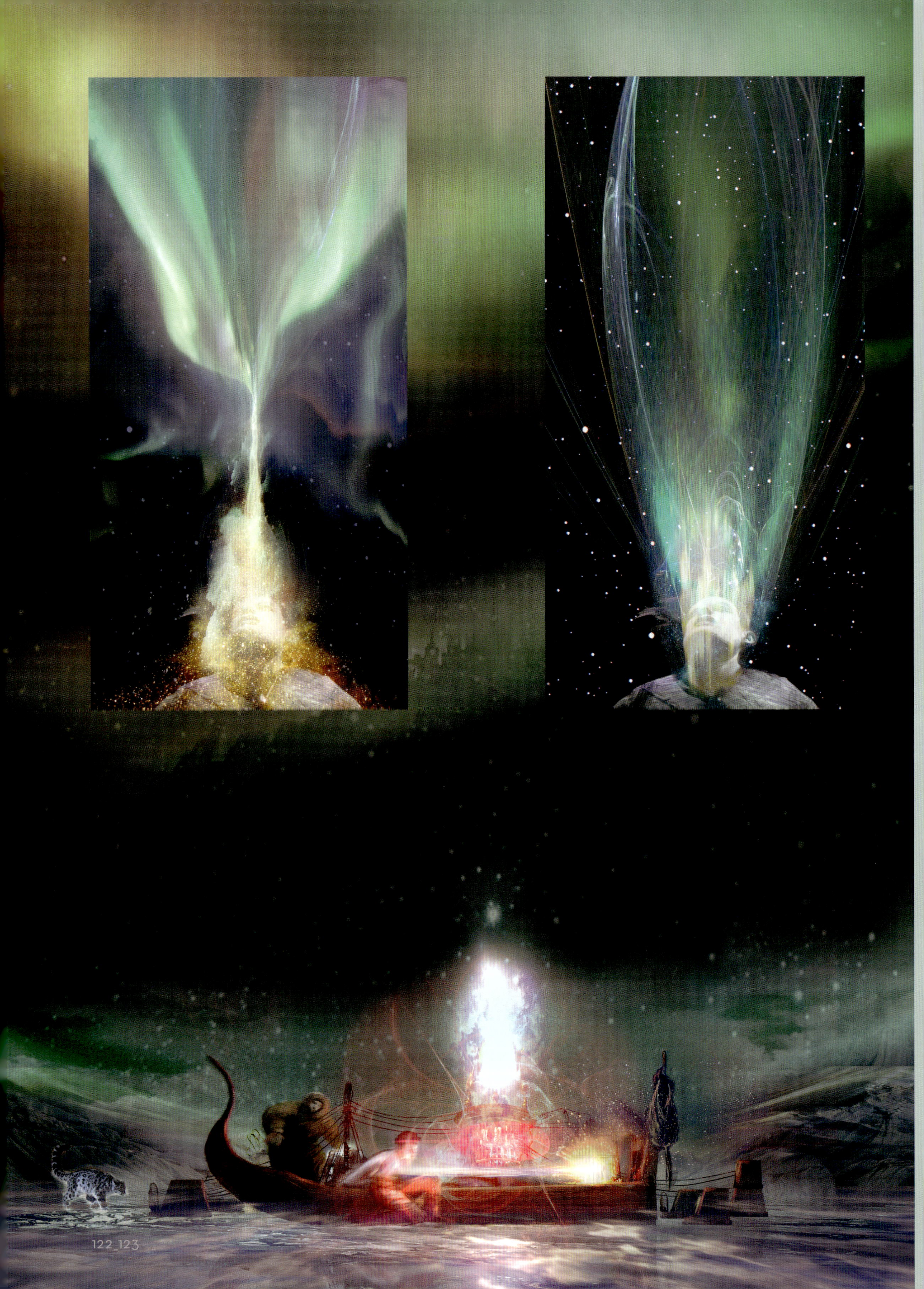

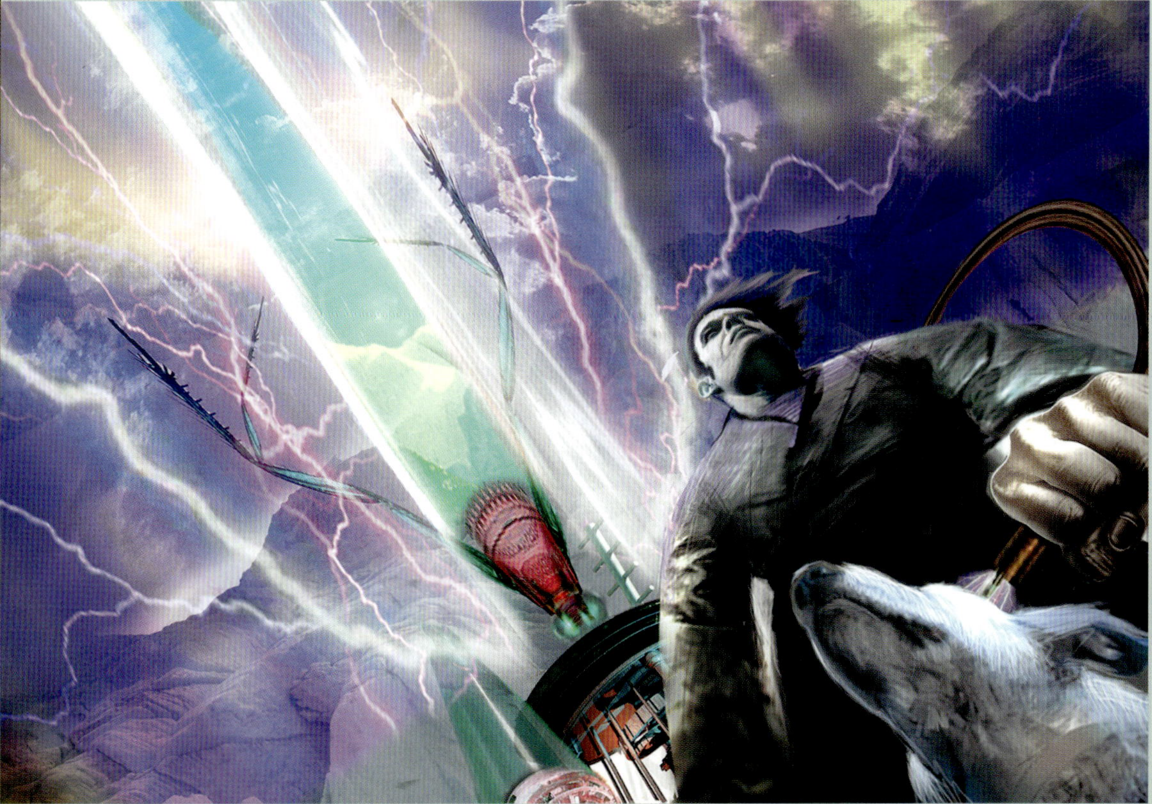

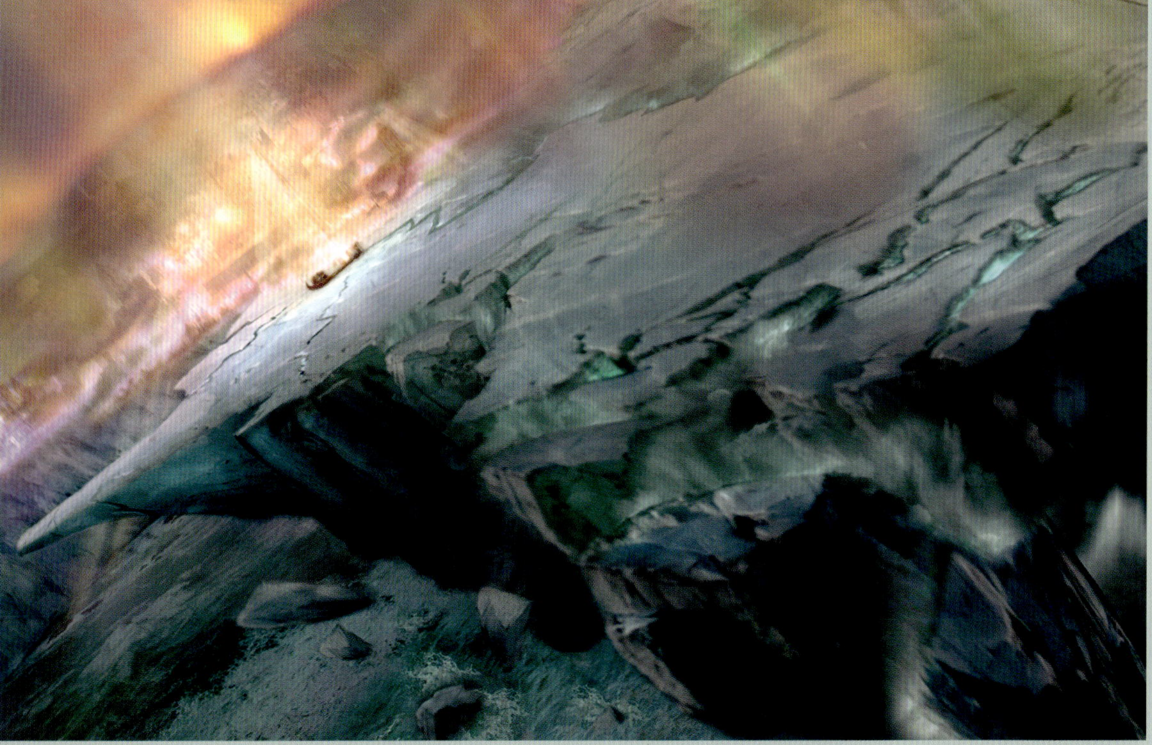

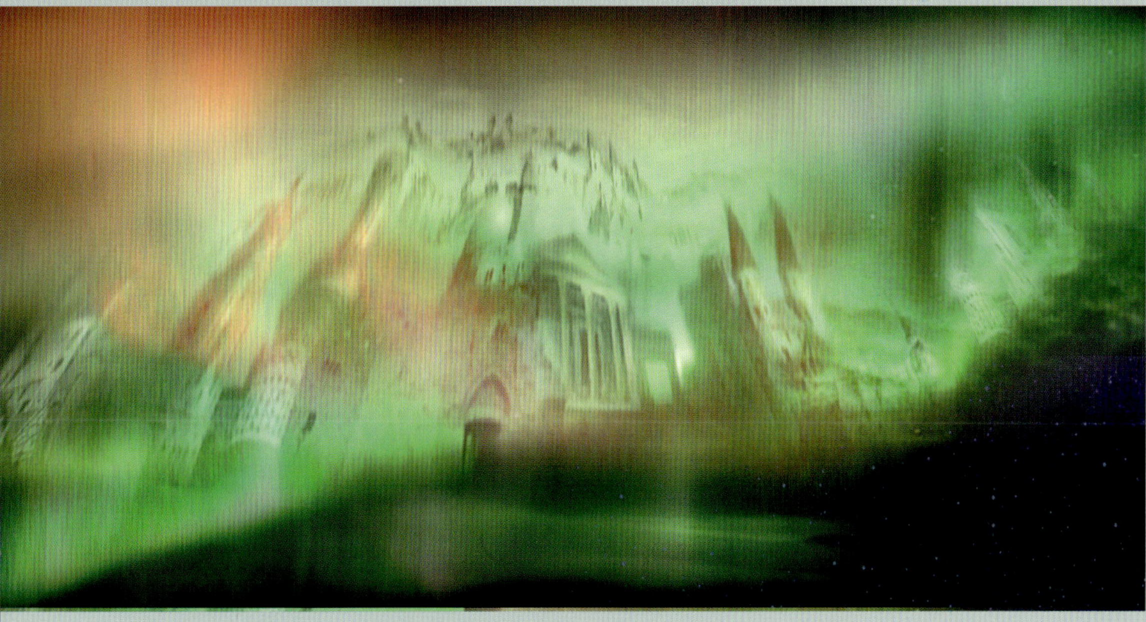

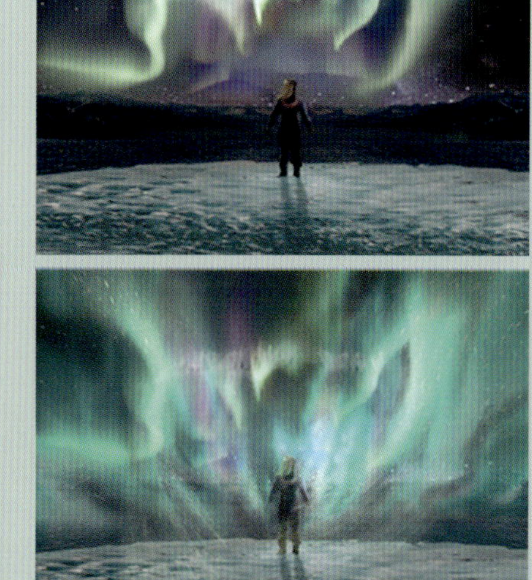

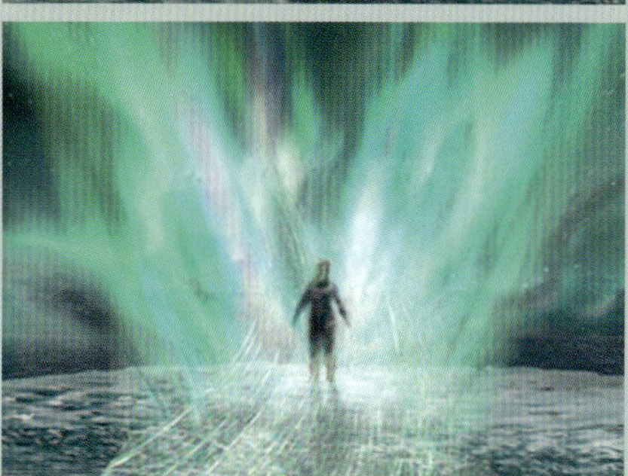

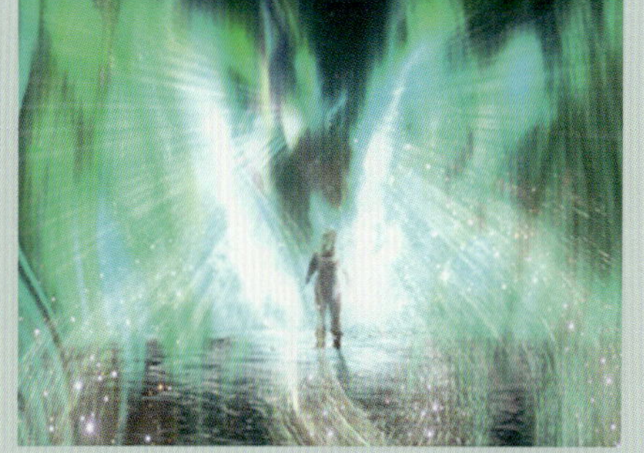

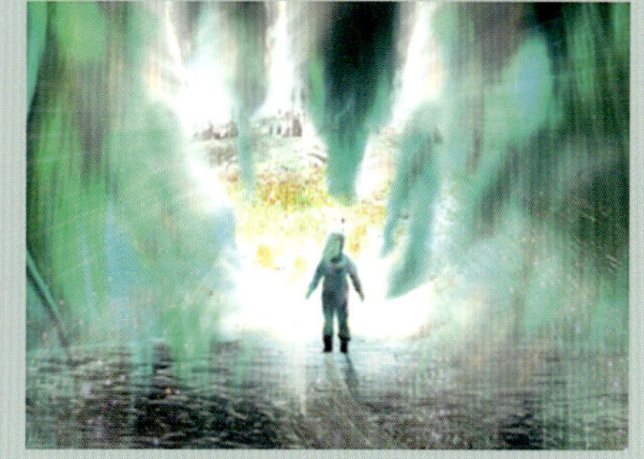

I worked with visual effects supervisor Bill Westenhofer on *The Golden Compass* (for which he received an Academy Award). All of my designs were for scenes at the end of the movie, but the script was changed, pushing my scenes to the beginning of the second film. Unfortunately there will not be a second film.

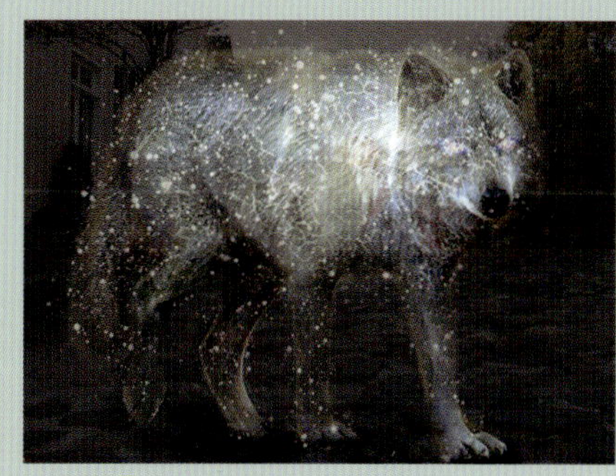

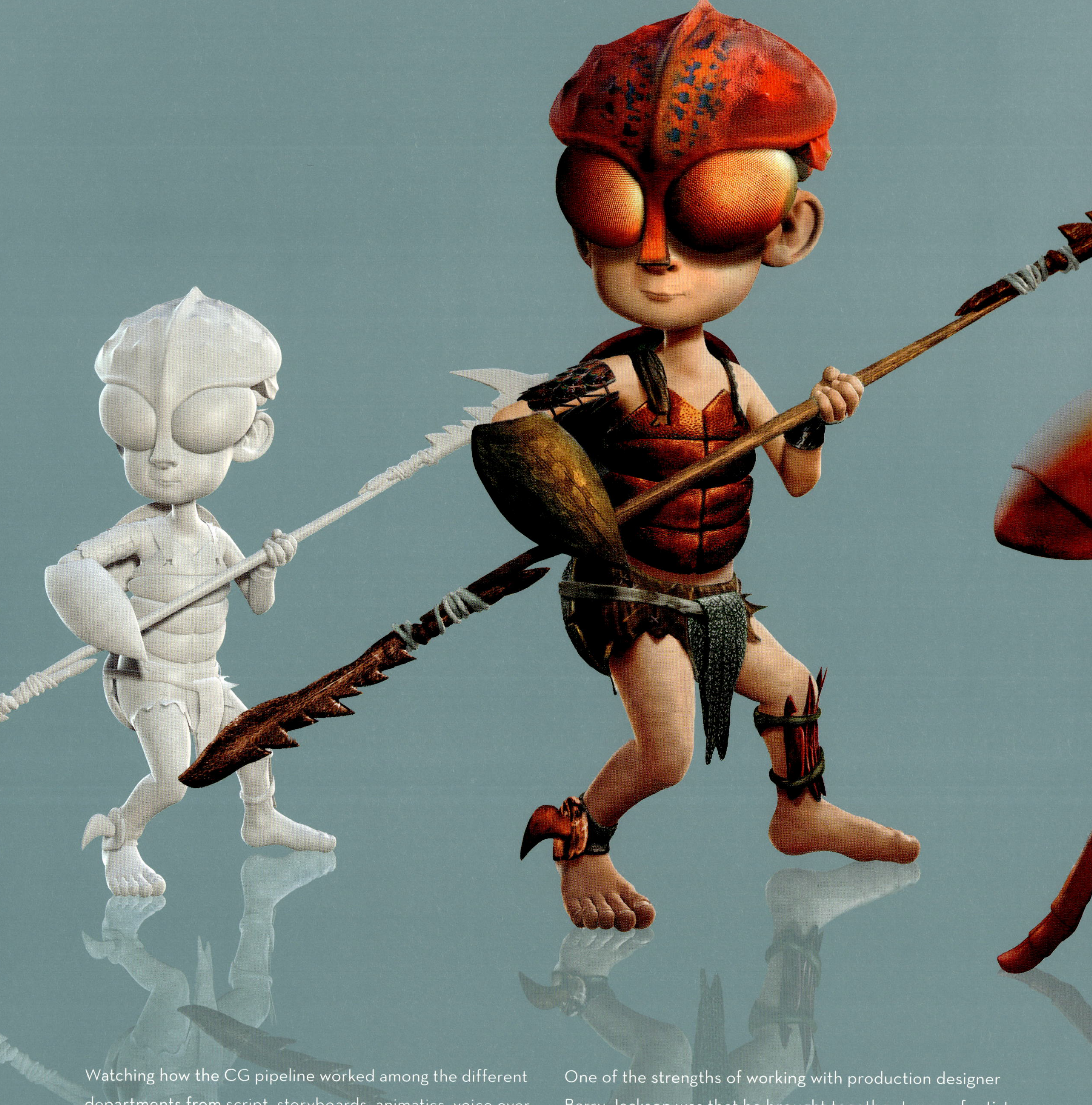

Watching how the CG pipeline worked among the different departments from script, storyboards, animatics, voice over, concept design, modeling, rigging, animation, environments, lighting, compositing, special effects, sound, music, to editing never ceased to amaze me. There can be a city of people working in one area of expertise. With so many decisions to be made, unending tech glitches and so much that can go wrong during a production, it's a wonder any movies get made at all. When a film production gets rolling we are essentially watching a controlled train wreck.

One of the strengths of working with production designer Barry Jackson was that he brought together teams of artists that worked well together, so well in fact that we even worked on each others art, experimenting and fusing our visions. It was an honor collaborating with Fred Gambino, David Krentz, Ian Miller, Chris Consani, Gary Glover, and others. I designed many of the interiors of the ant colony from tunnels to ant murals. I also textured existing character designs bringing them to life.

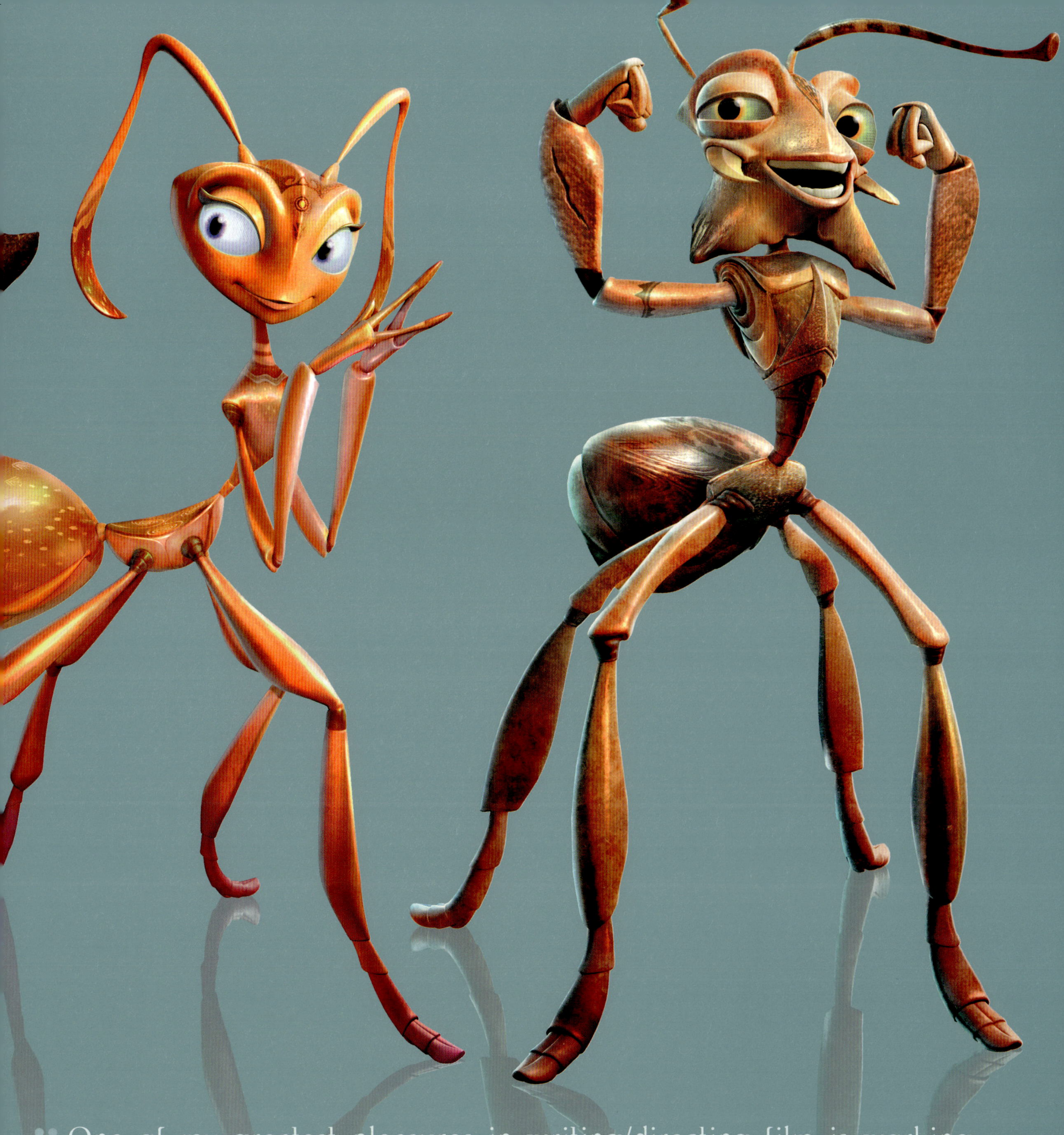

“One of my greatest pleasures in writing/directing film is working with the concept artists. The early stage of the project is a blank canvas which must be filled, and visualizing the look of the film universe is an exciting process. The concept artist’s visual ideas can have a direct effect on the script. It is a wonderful synergy.”

– JOHN A. DAVIS

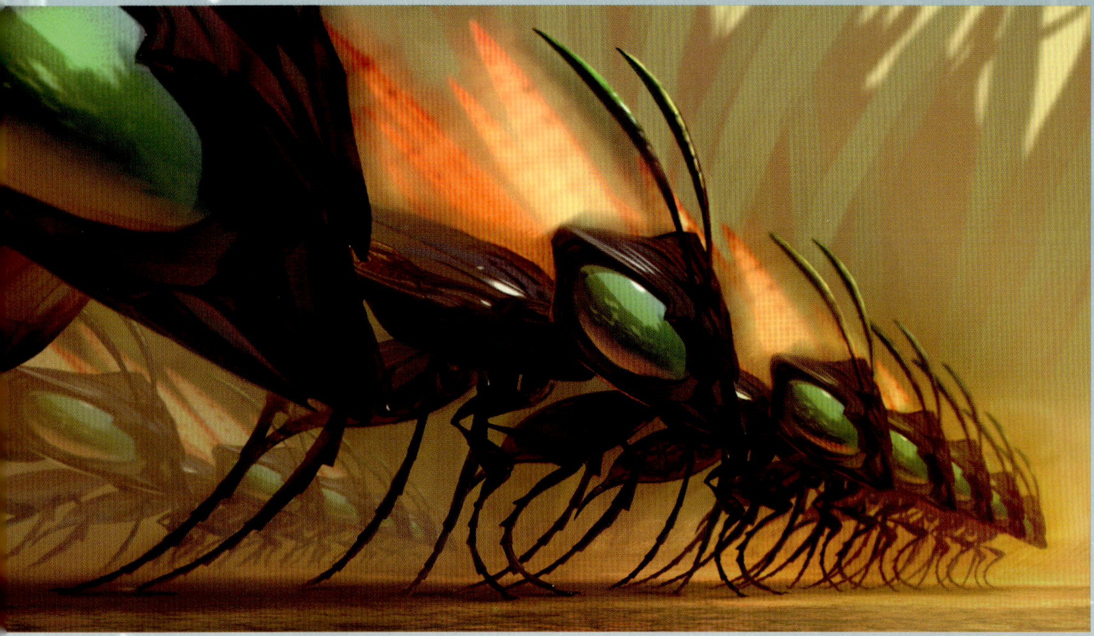

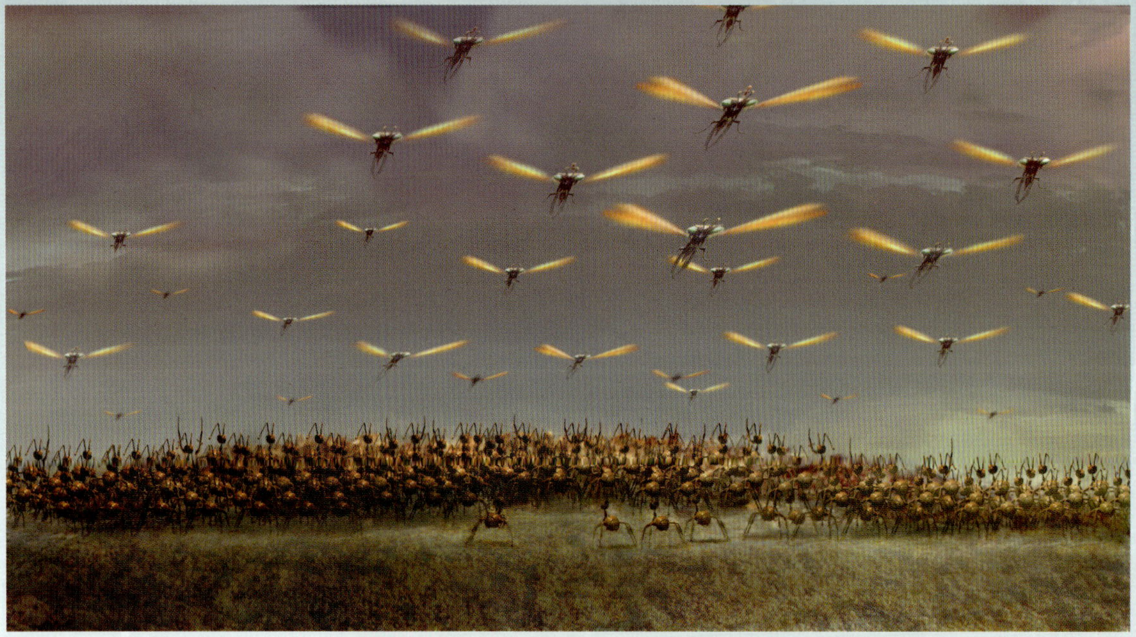

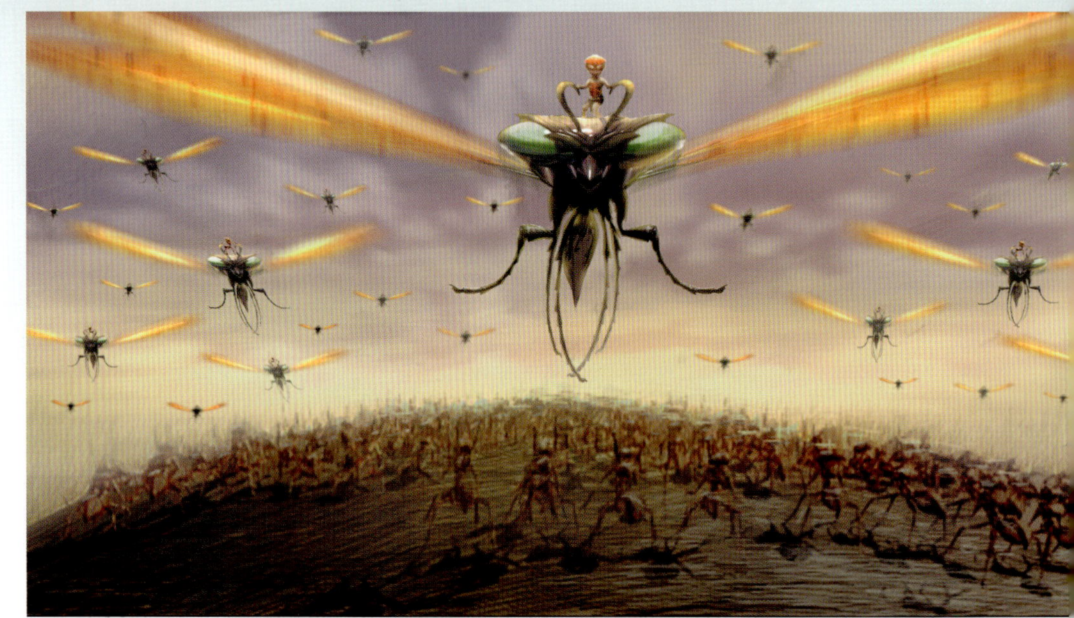

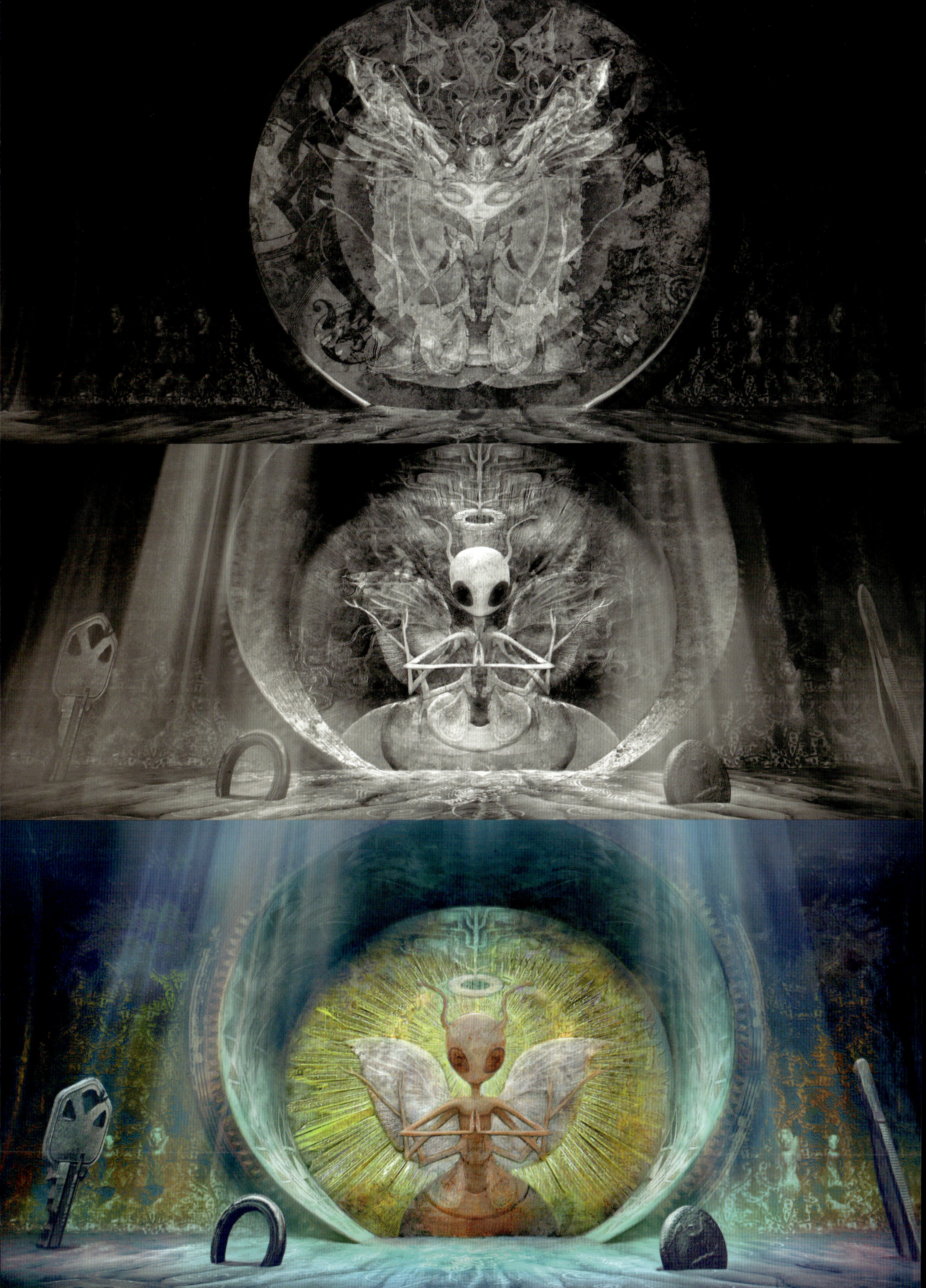

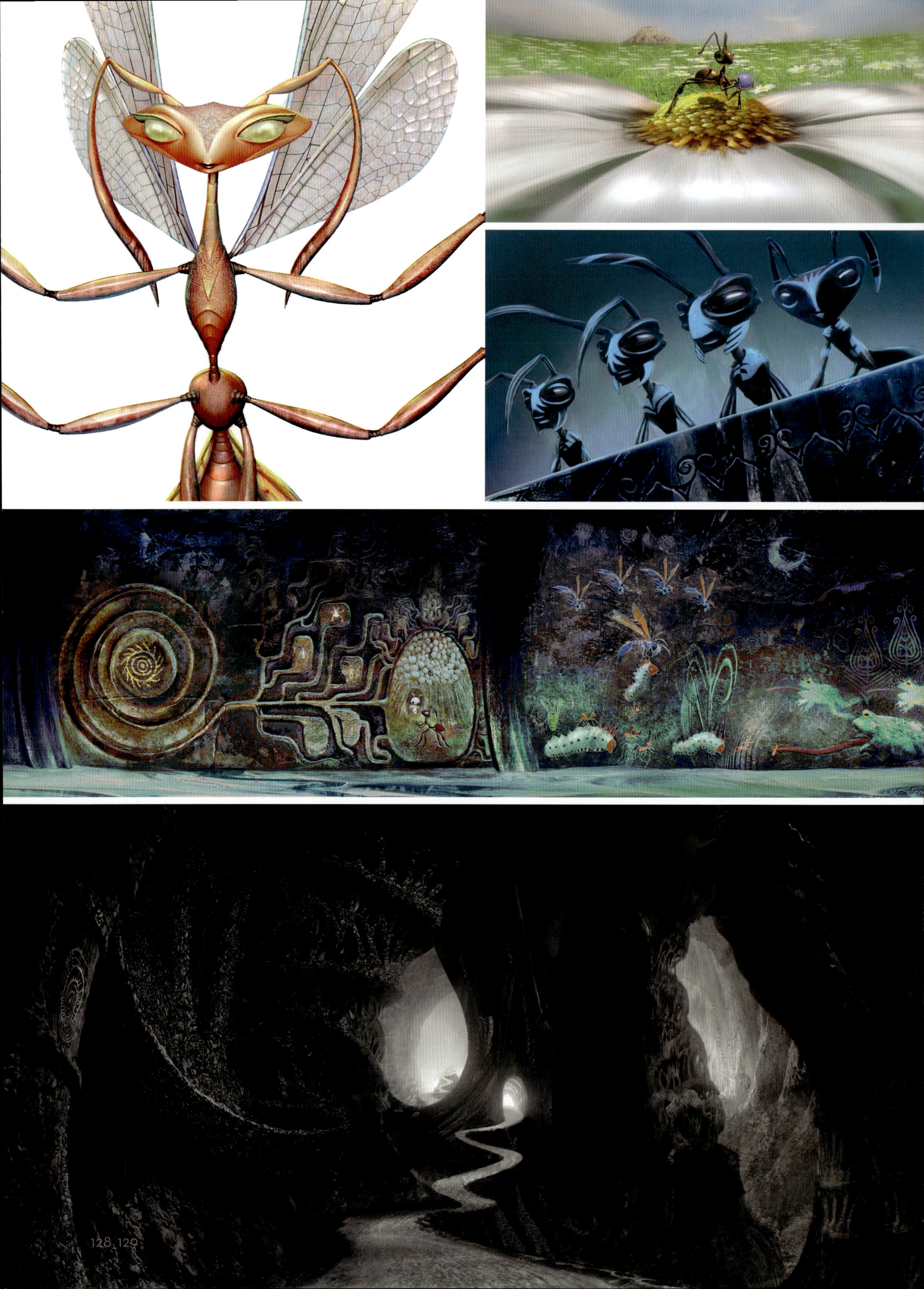

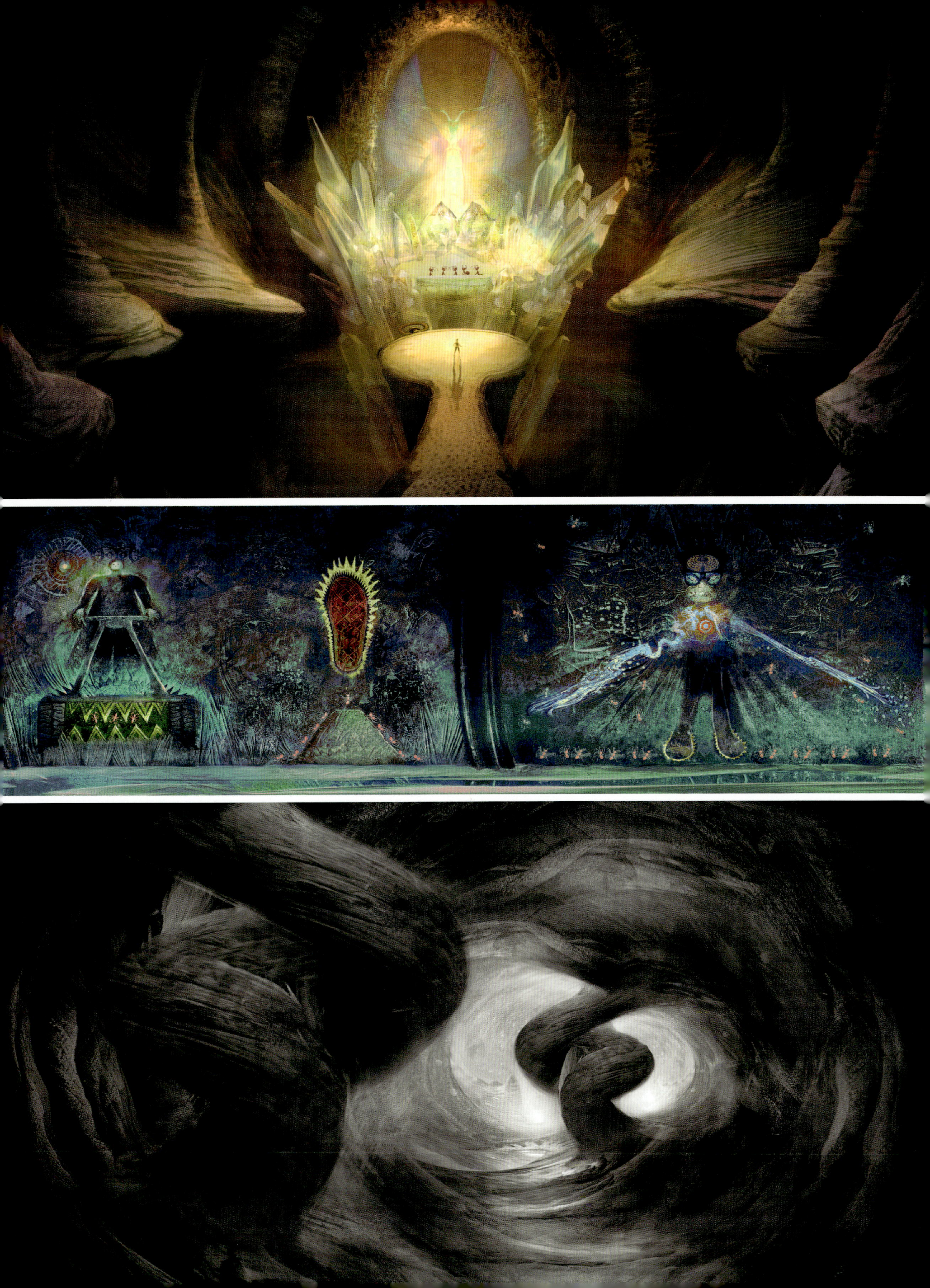

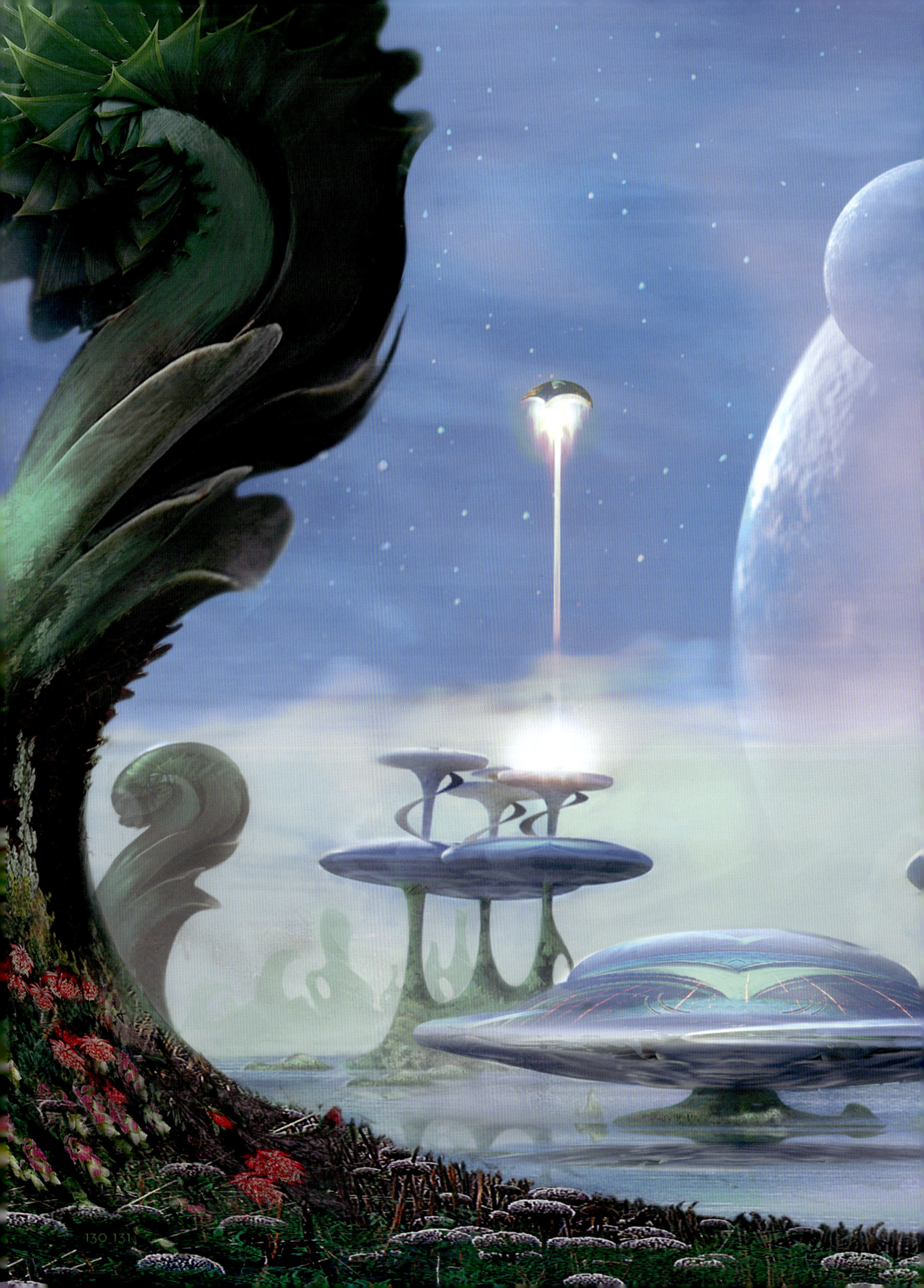

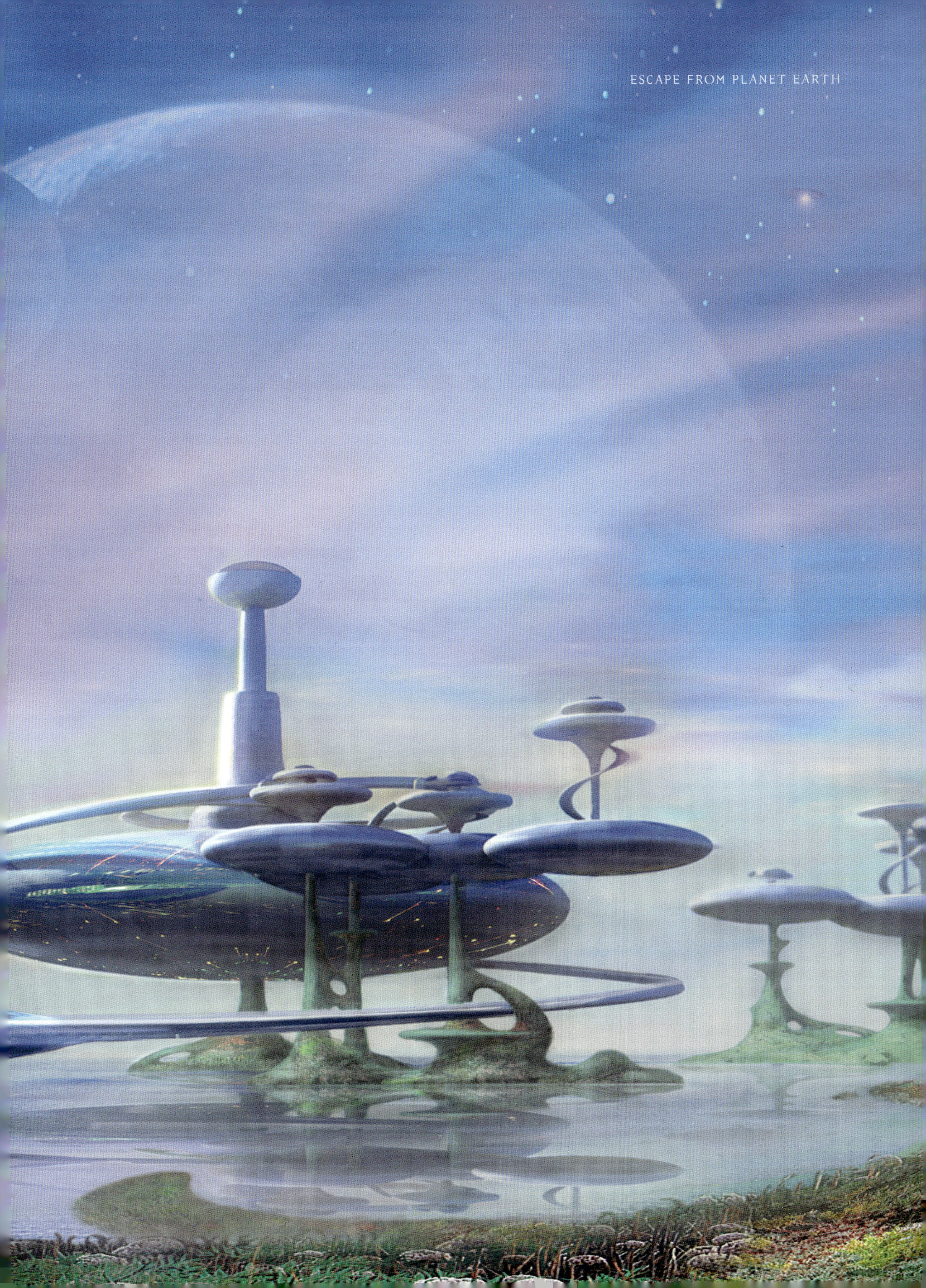

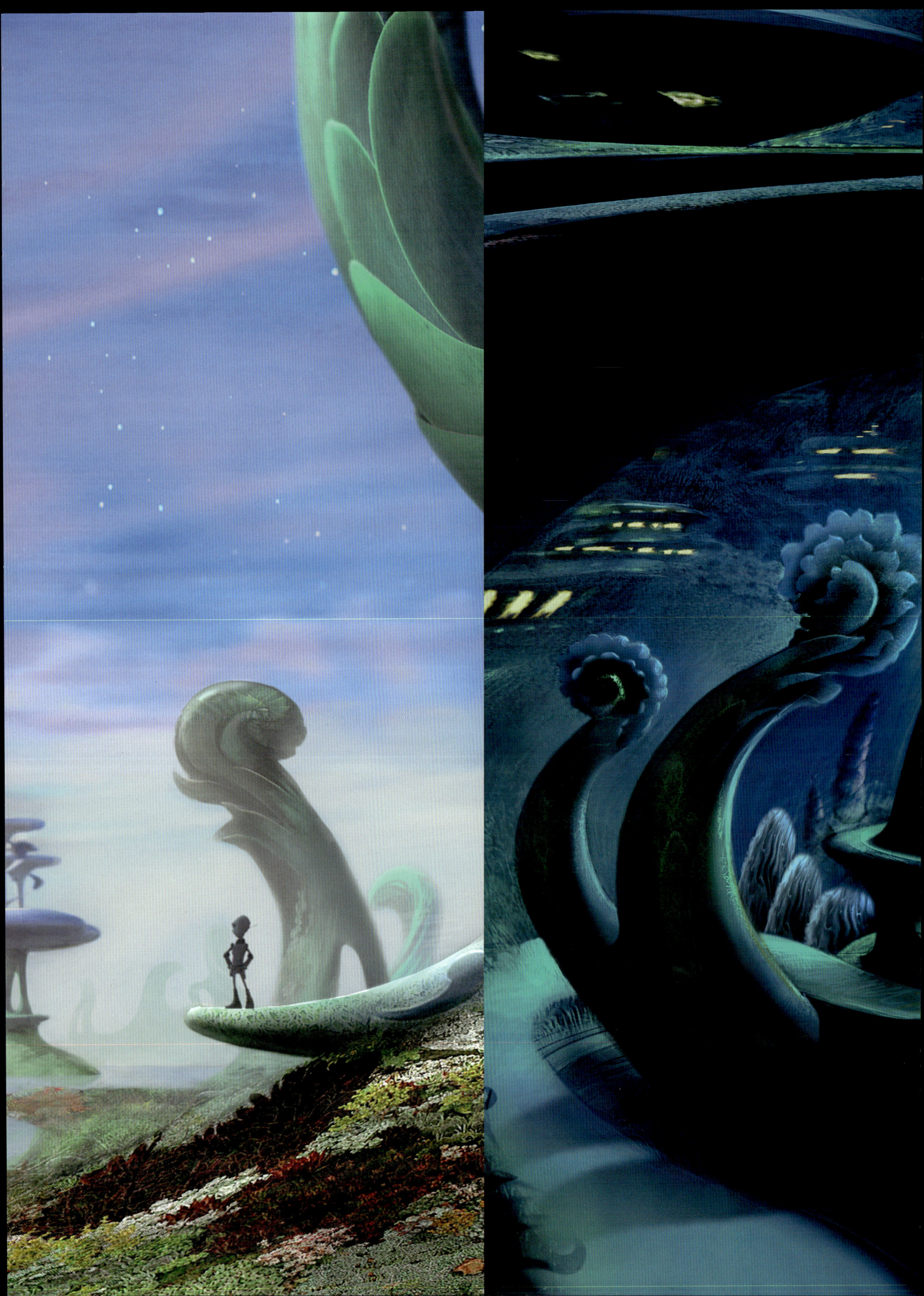

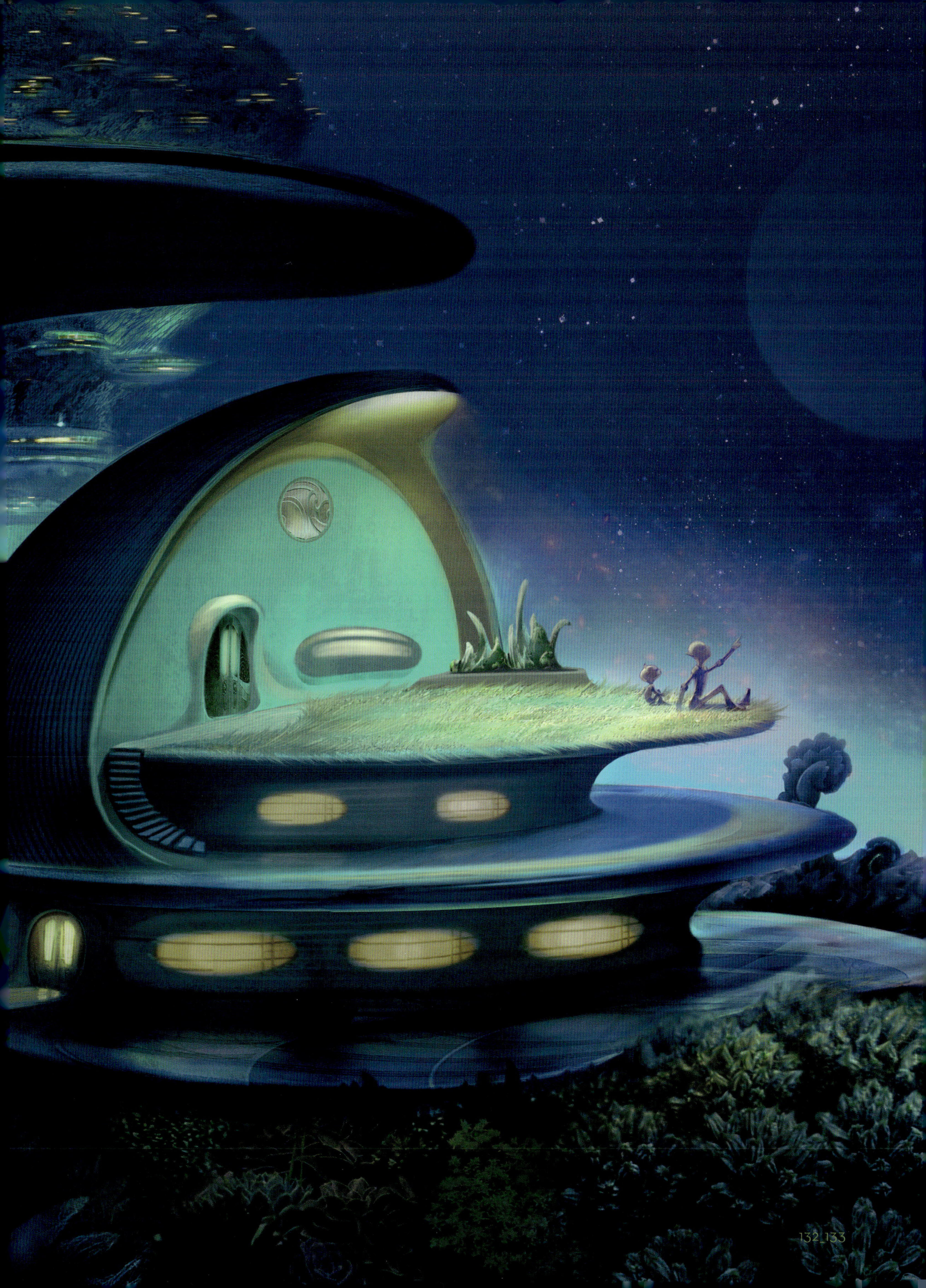

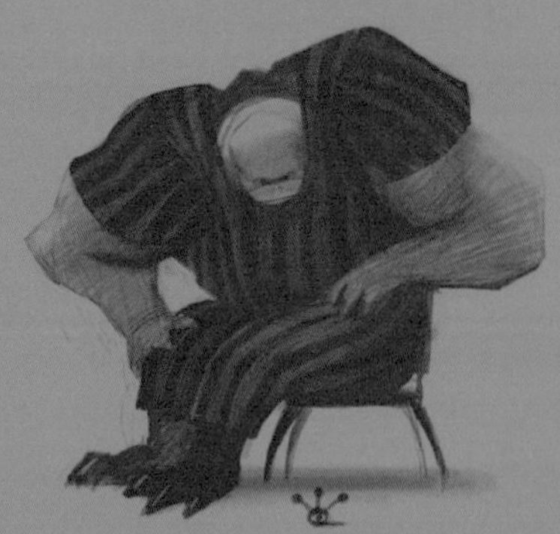

Escape From Planet Earth was a kid-friendly CG animated film about a bunch of captured aliens jailed in Area 51 and their attempt to break out. Jackson was the production designer on this film and again he pulled together a stellar team. Here I was creating environments for Area 51, the alien planet of Baab, the characters, and space craft.

I was also fusing elements of my ideas with those of the other artists. You can see two versions of these collaborative efforts in the Baabian space center spread with Fred Gambino and the large alien gun with Ian Miller.

This production was a difficult one. The first director did not work out and by the time the script was rewritten with a new director at the helm it would take seven years before this film was released.

The film industry is one of the most gratifying and difficult to be a part of because it is such a technically complicated medium, and also because it requires so much money is necessary to drive a production. Now with so many different people working together on projects in different parts of the world, it's even more of a challenge. However, when it all coalesces synergistically, film is one of the most powerful, heart opening story engines around.

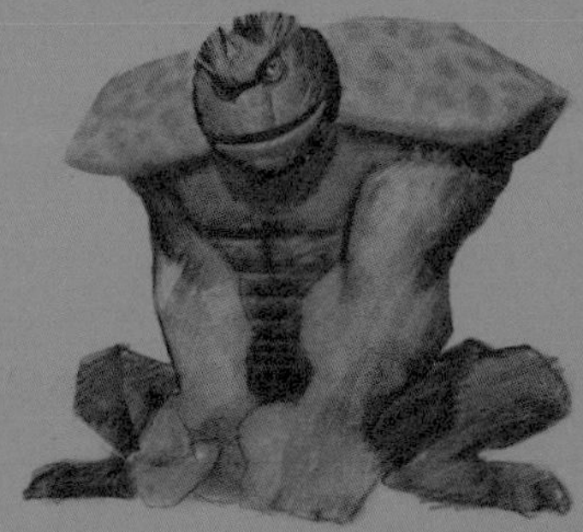

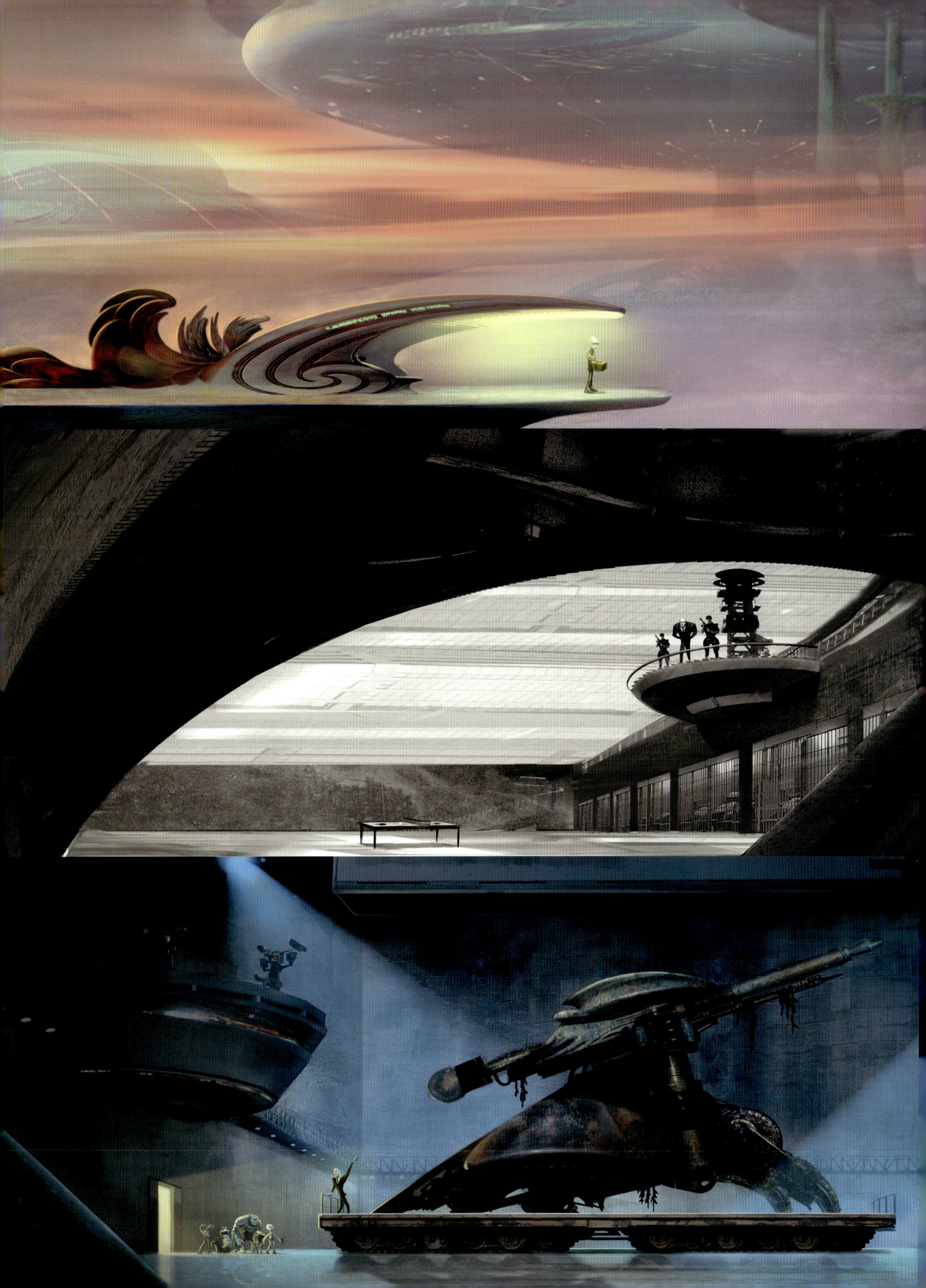

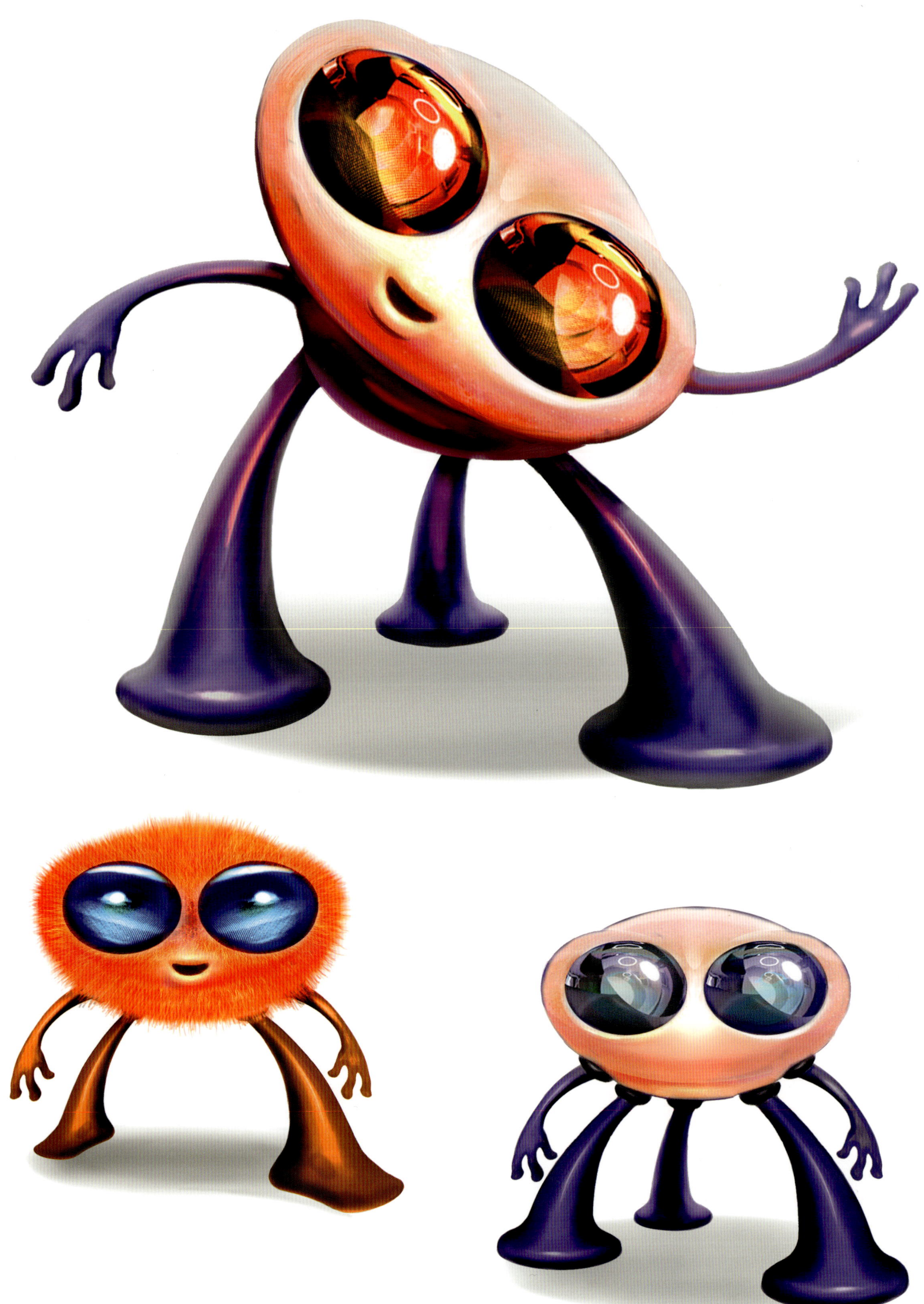

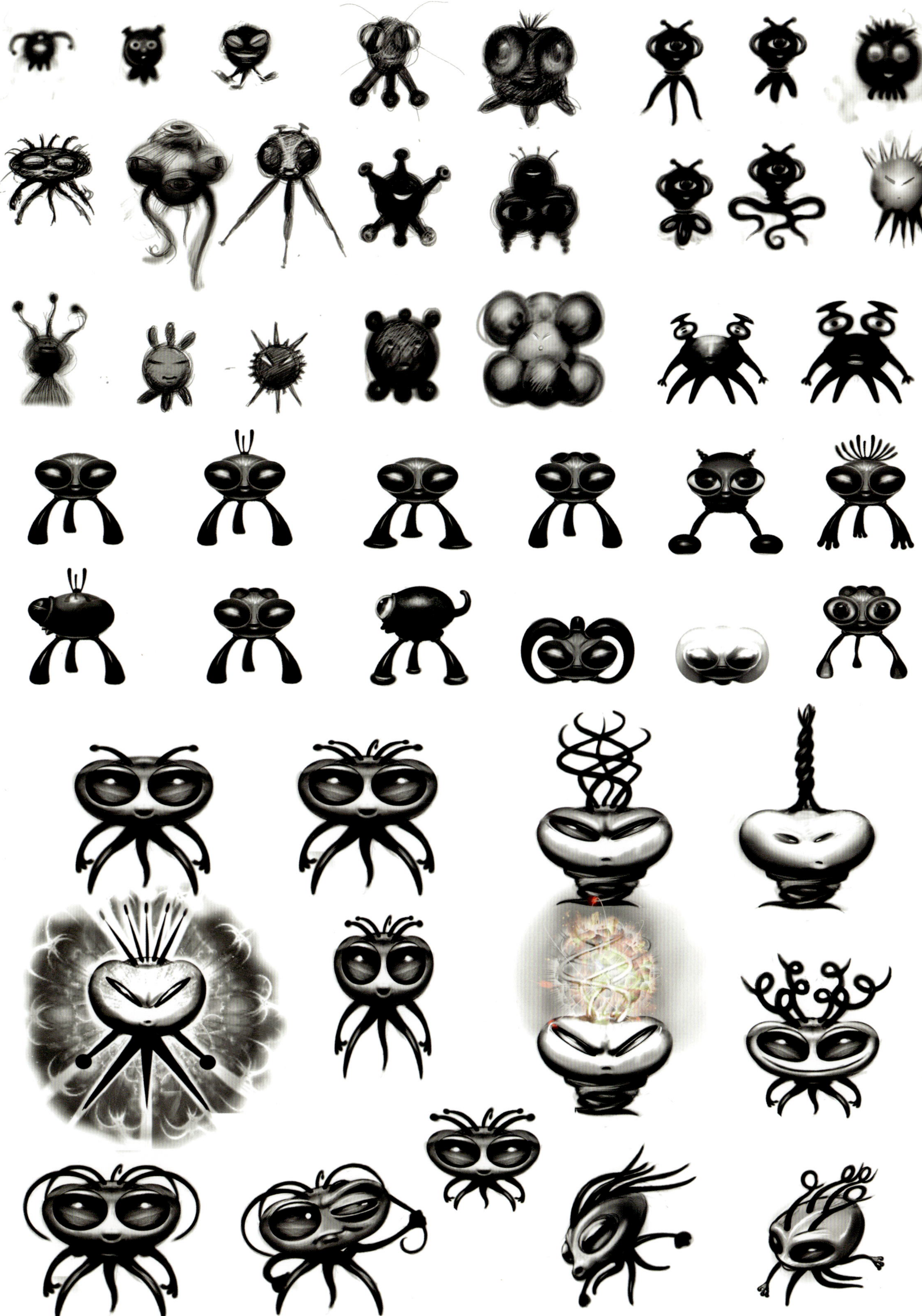

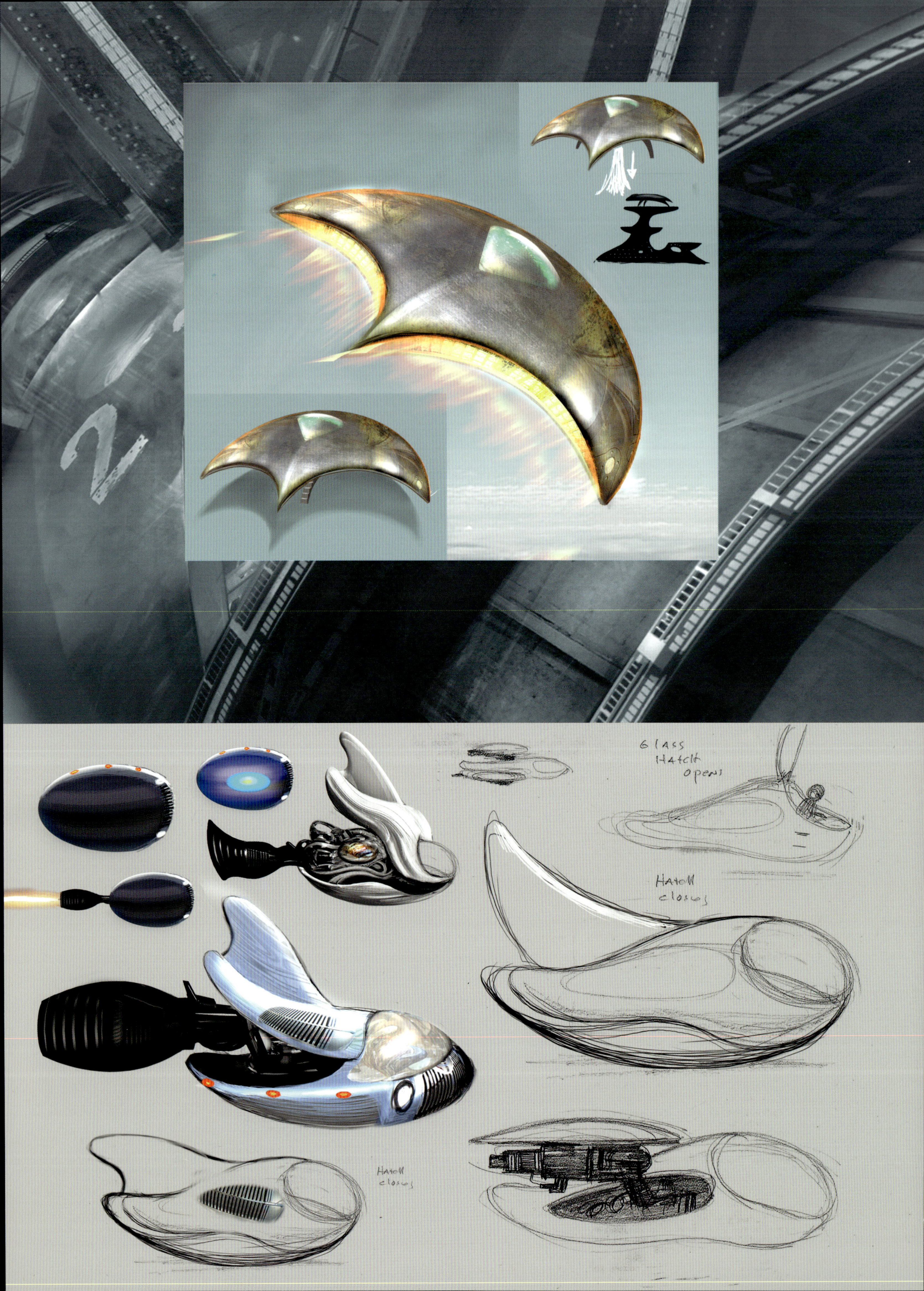
Glass Hatch opens
Hatch closes
Hatch closes

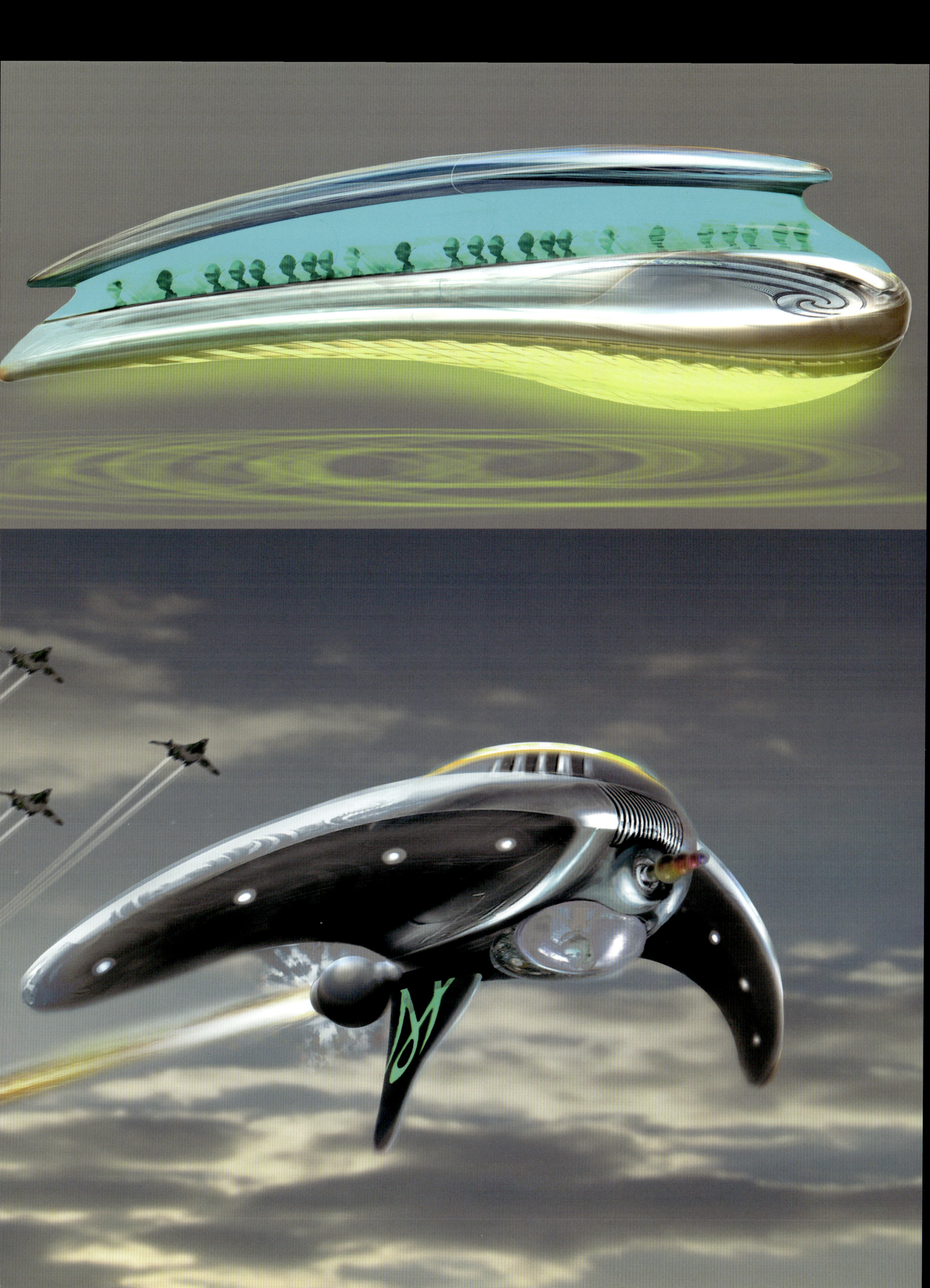

I really enjoyed working with director Michael Apted on the third Narnia film, *The Voyage of the Dawn Treader.* We connected right away with a visual direction. In the early script (which attempted to fuse two books, *TVODT* with *The Silver Chair*) a character called the Green Witch lived in a castle beneath the sea and was enslaving the Narnians by using a mystical serpent. Many of my concept designs were for these Green Witch scenes, which included different parts of the castle. I especially enjoyed imagining what her throne would look like. All this art was tossed when it was decided that fusing the two books was not such a good idea.

One of the skill sets I brought to this production was story boarding scenes with a near finished look. By providing the animators of the 3D CG animatics for this film with tight color scripted images, we helped Apted choreograph movement, camera angles, light, and shadow, etc. before principle photography was shot on location. I am very proud of my designs for the "infinite unbreaking wave" at the end of the film. Much brainstorming went into those scenes, some of which were very fantastical. Alas, they chose one of the more conservative versions for the film, but it still looks magnificent.

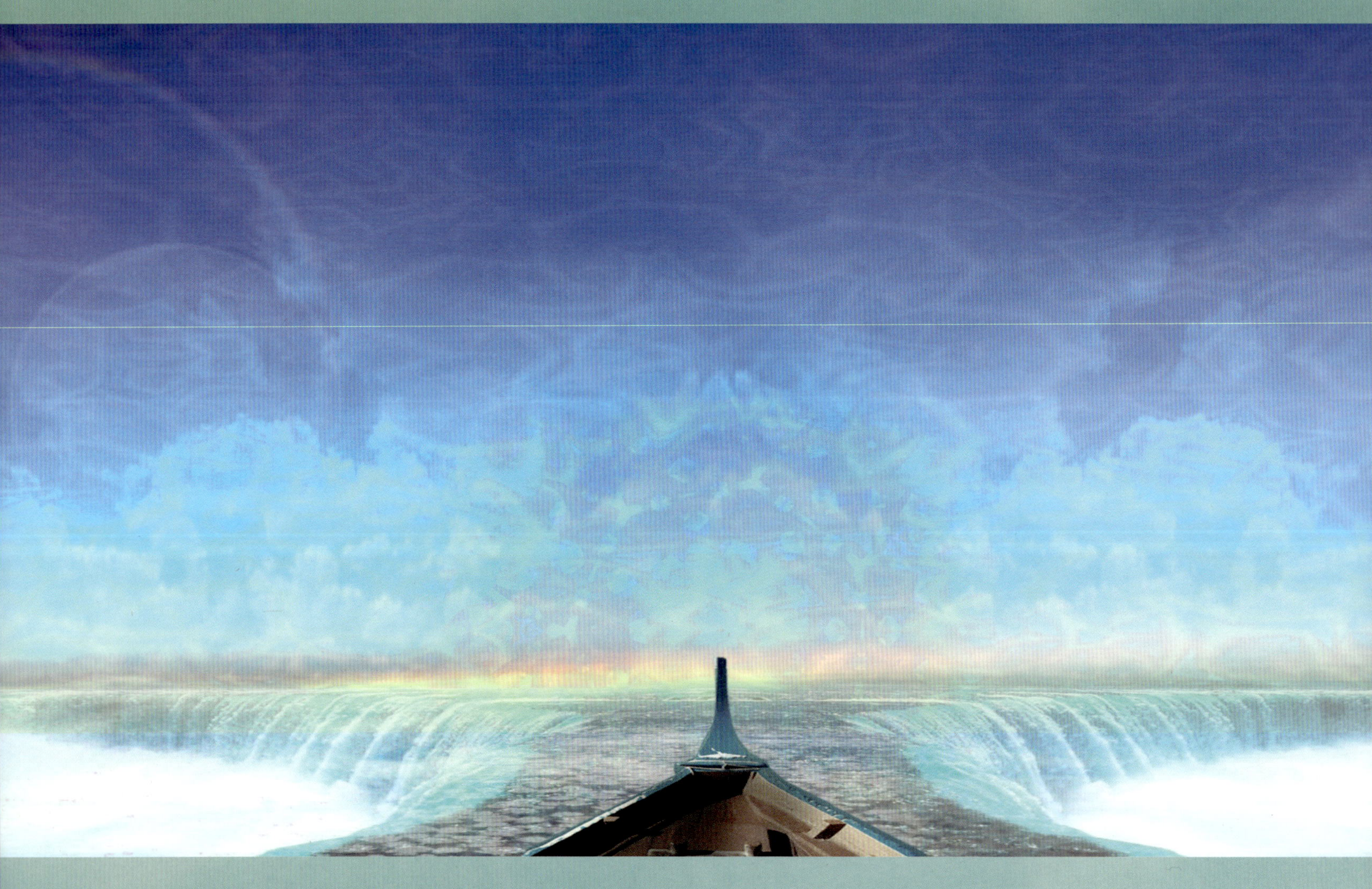

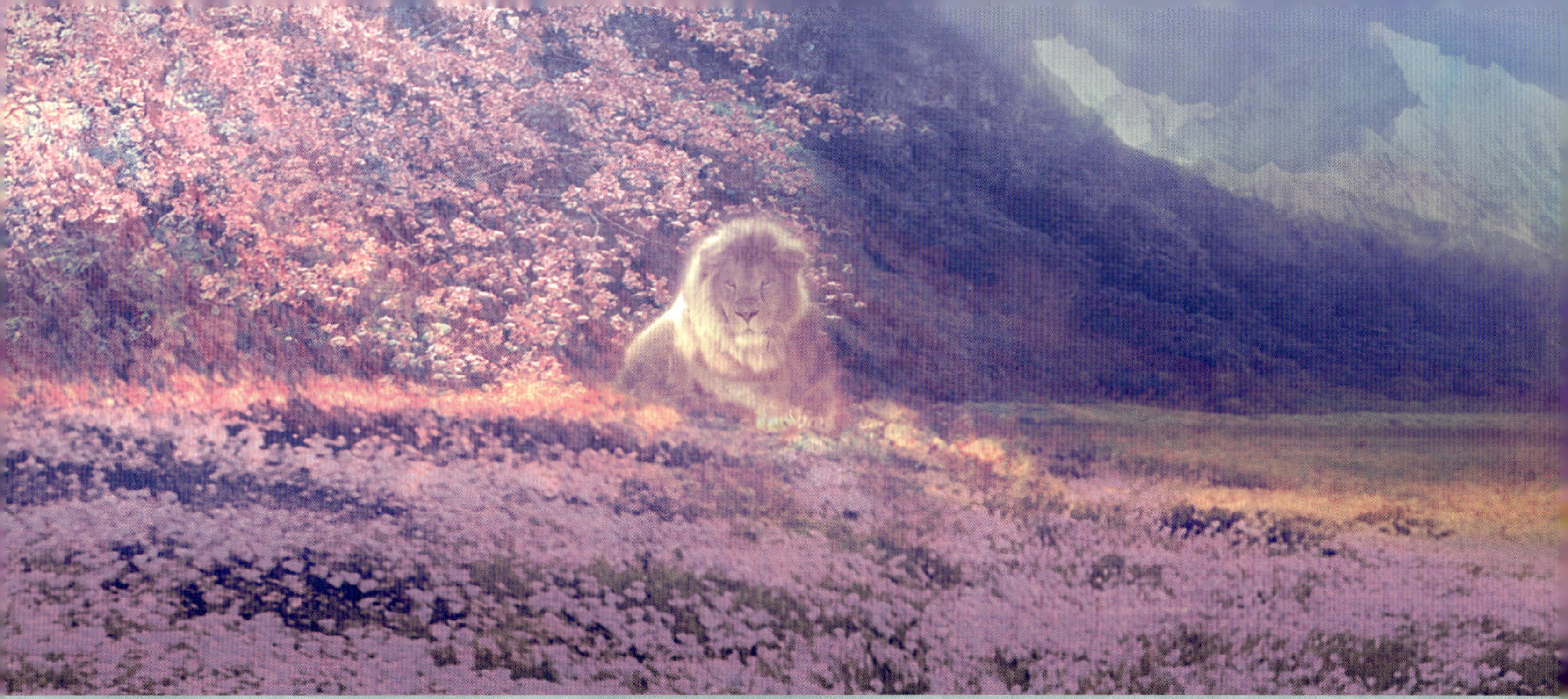

“Greg was a perfect fit for creating the tone and environment of the DAWN TREADER. He is highly imaginative with a real understanding of how to create magical images from the beauty of the natural world.”

– MICHAEL APTED
Director: *The Voyage of the Dawn Treader*

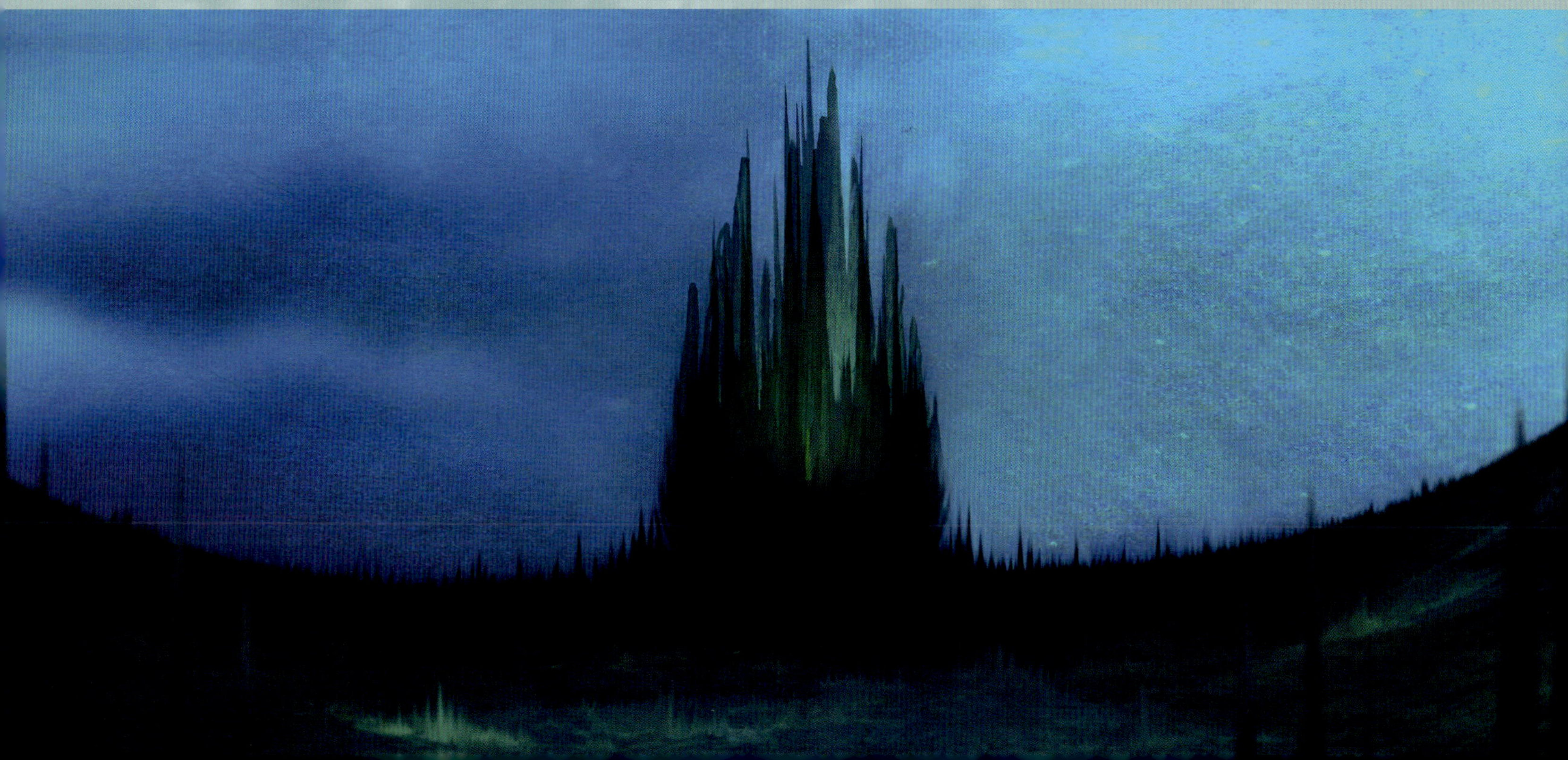

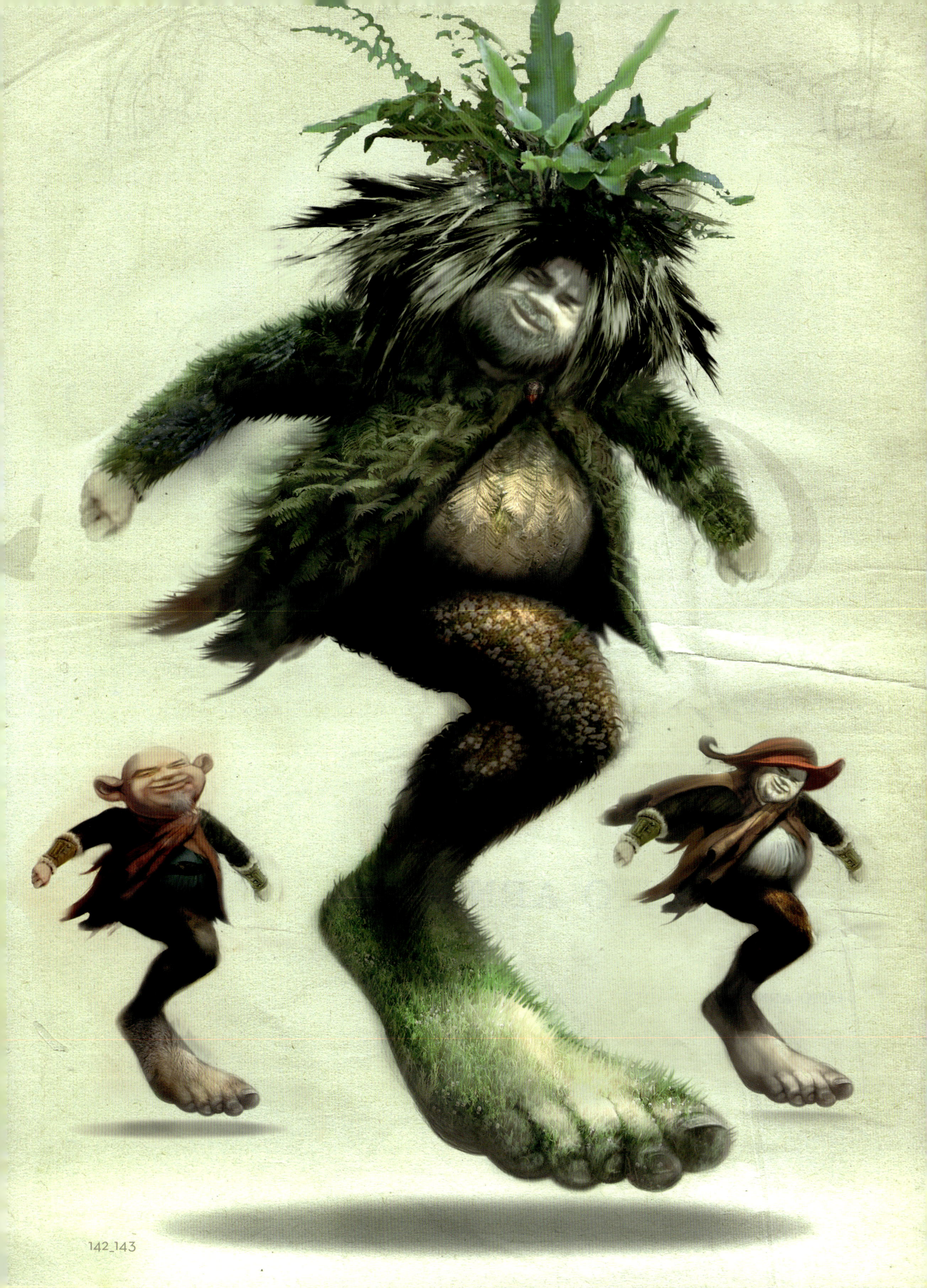

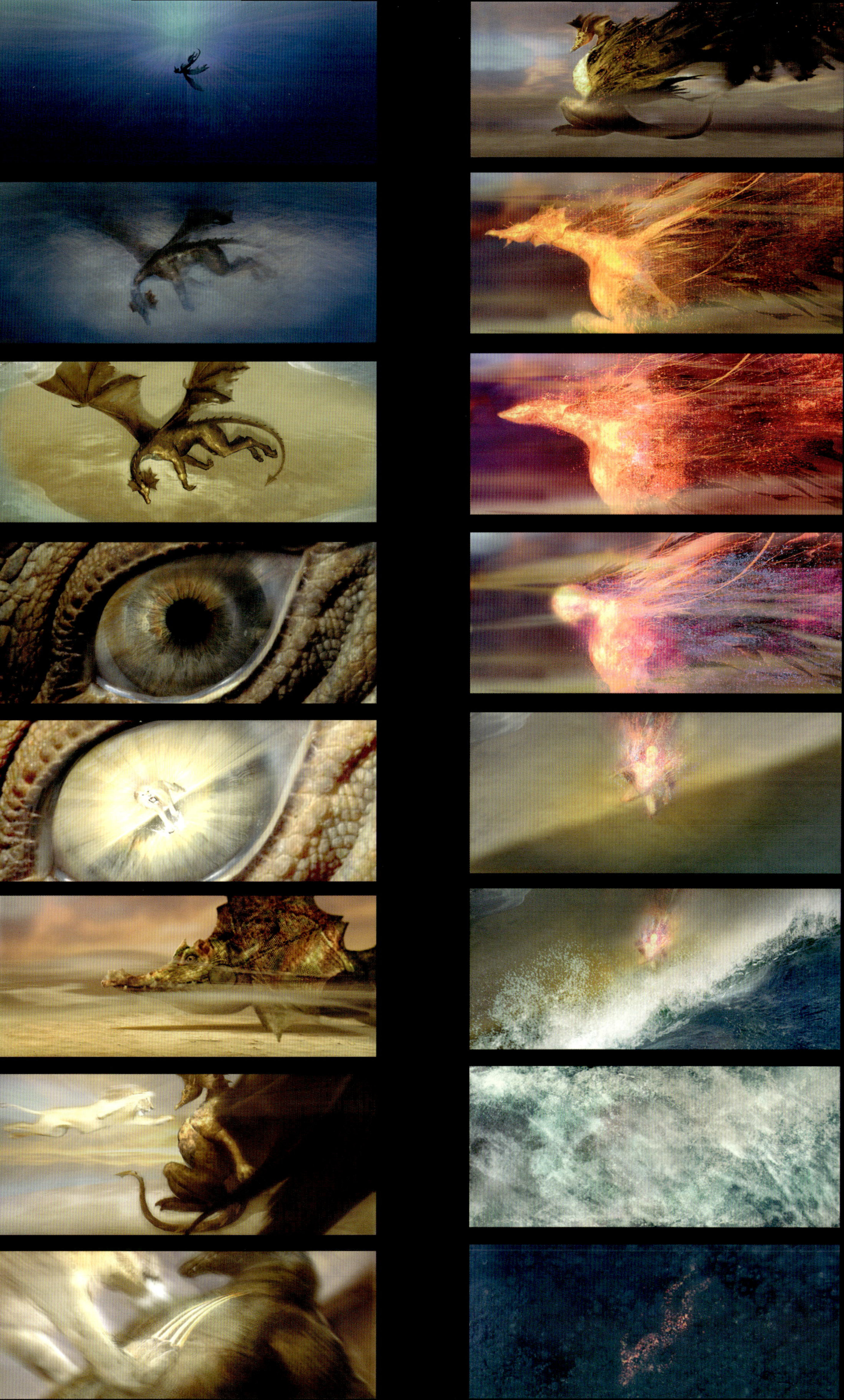

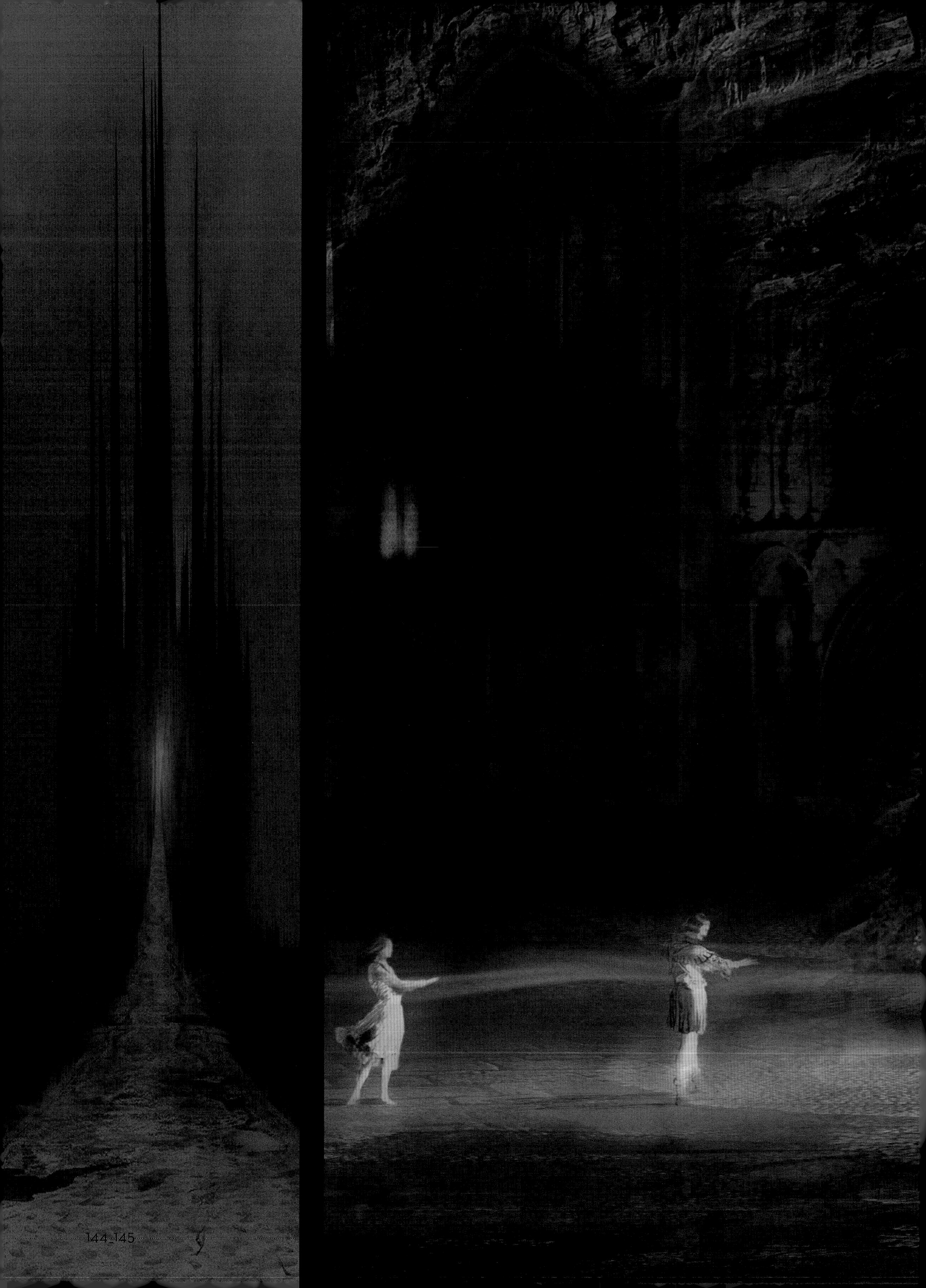

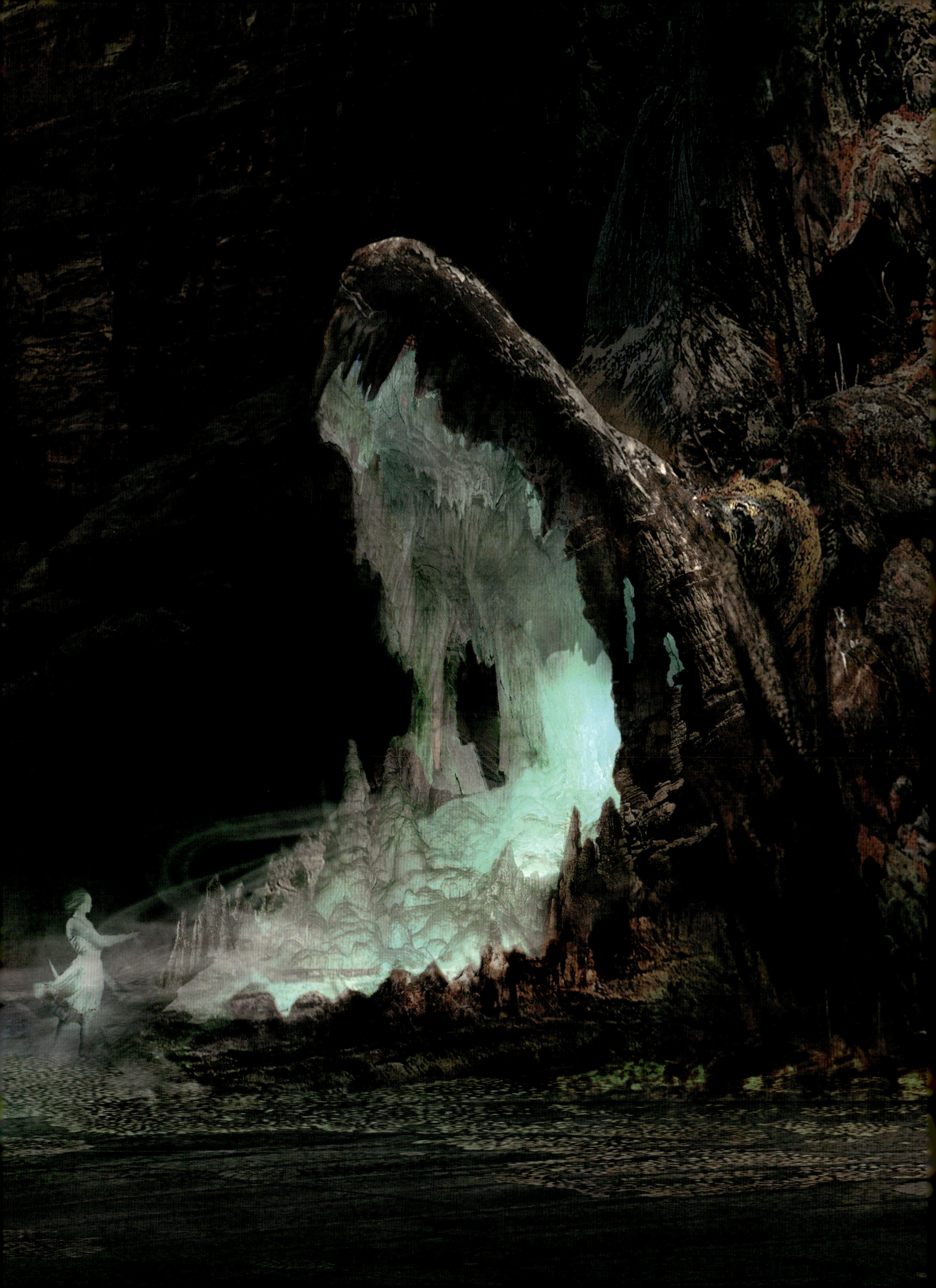

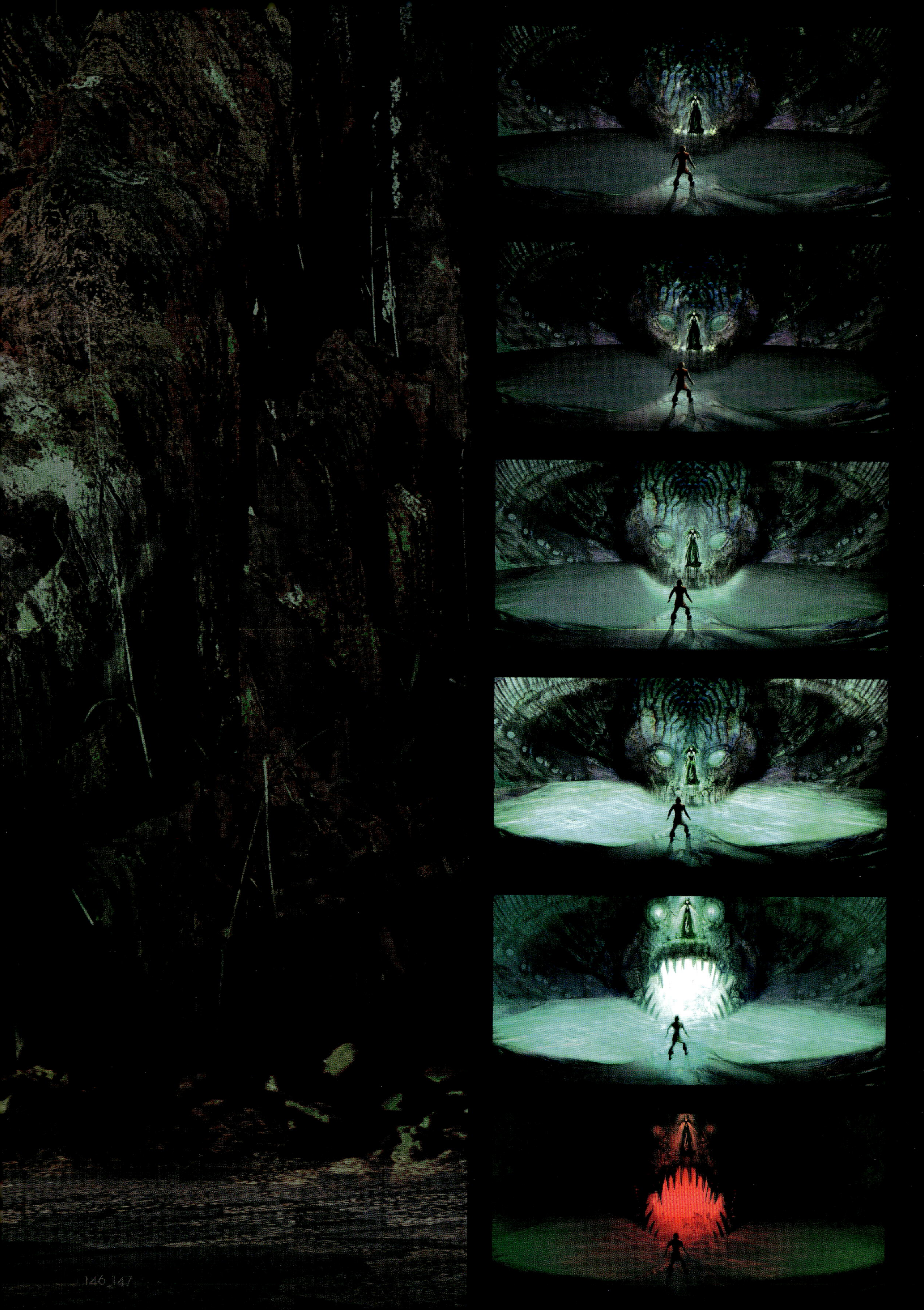

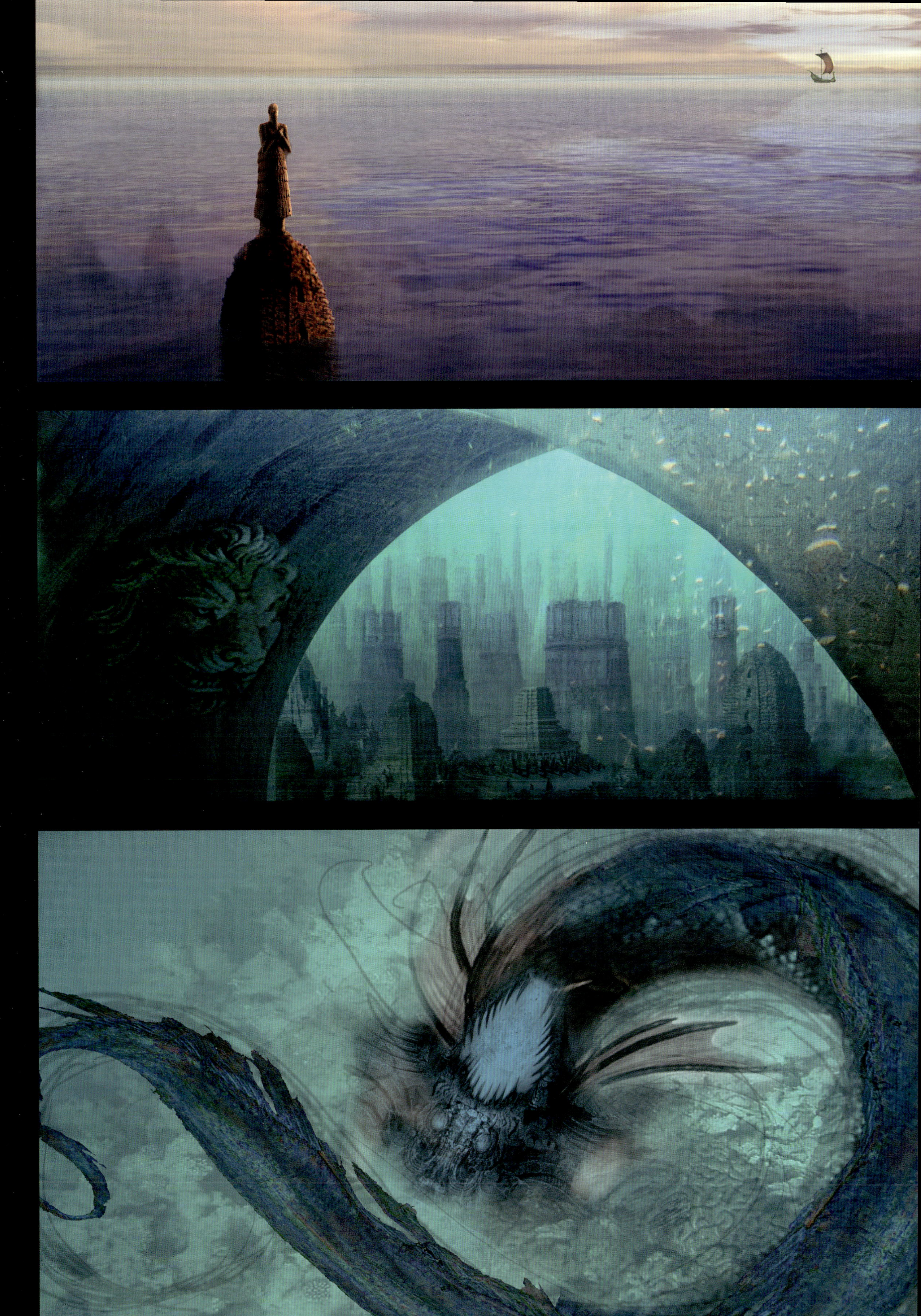

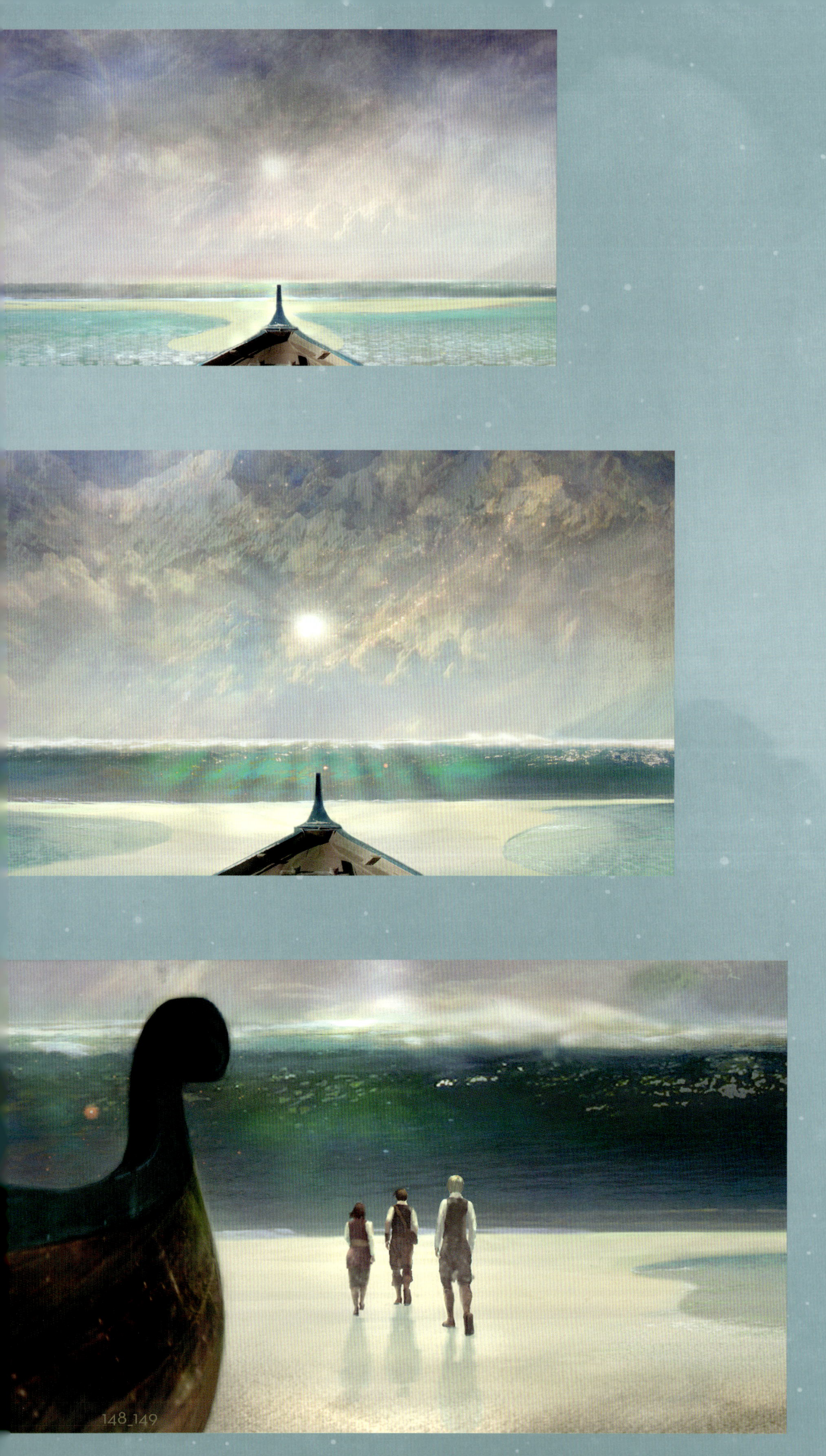

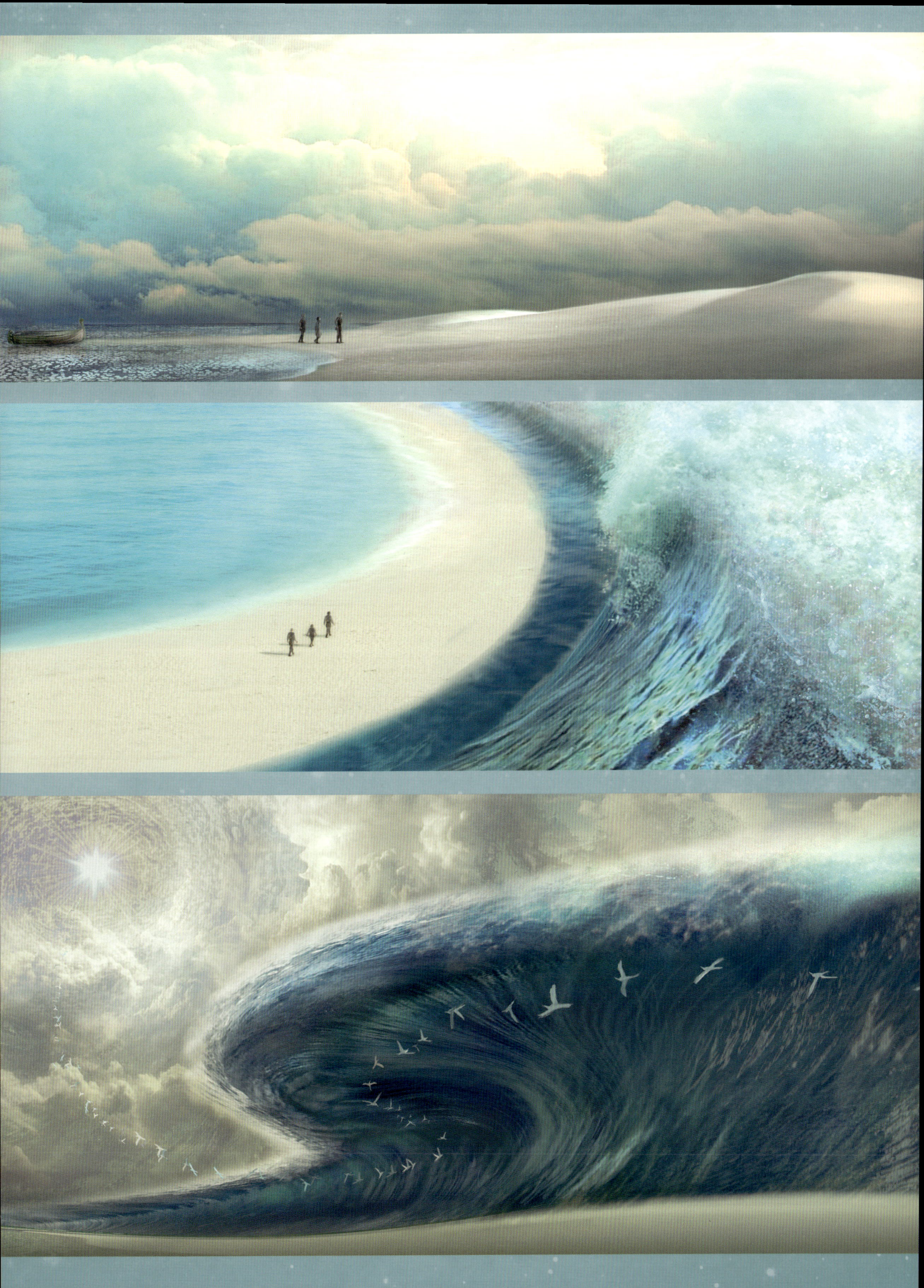

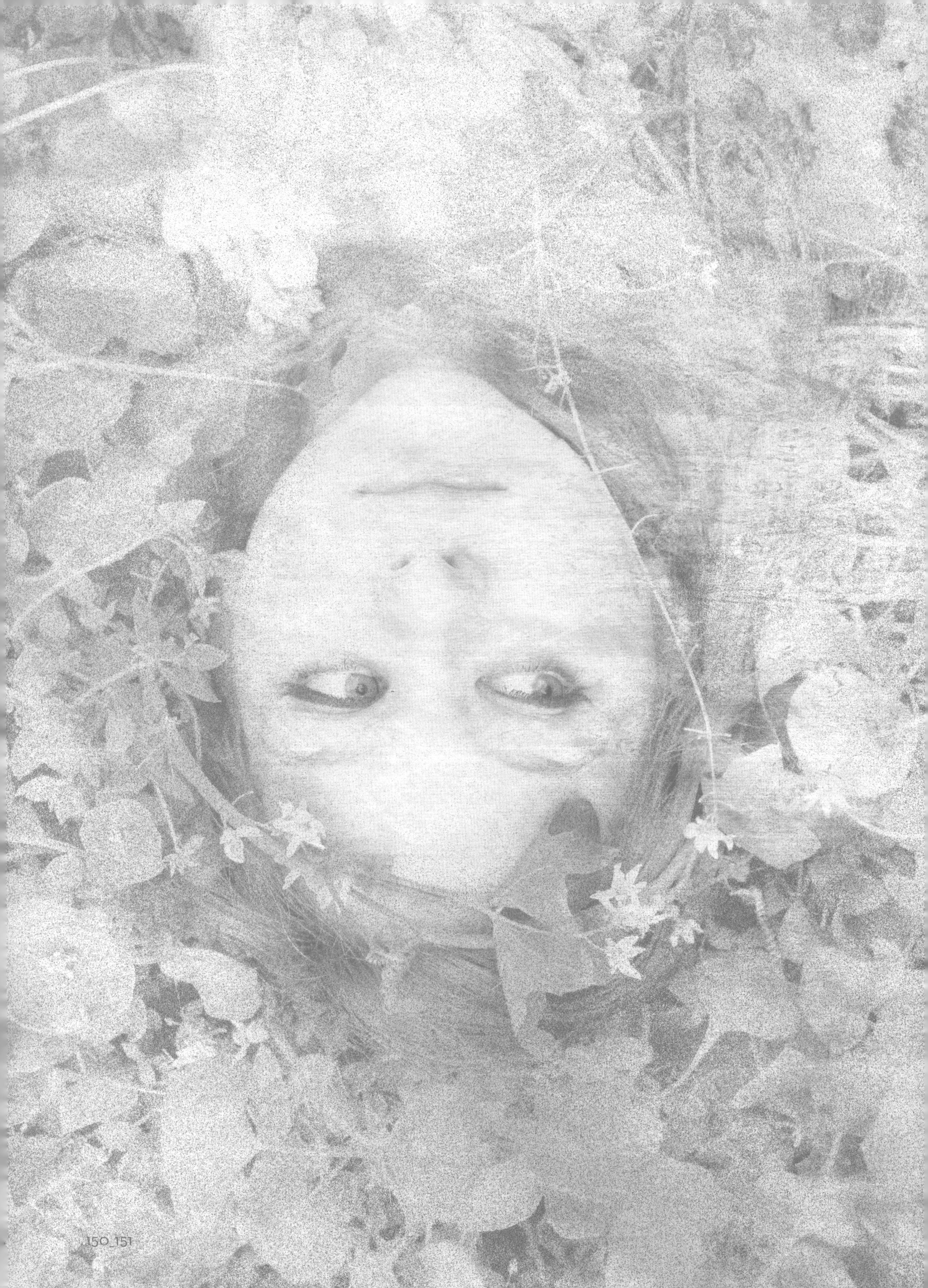

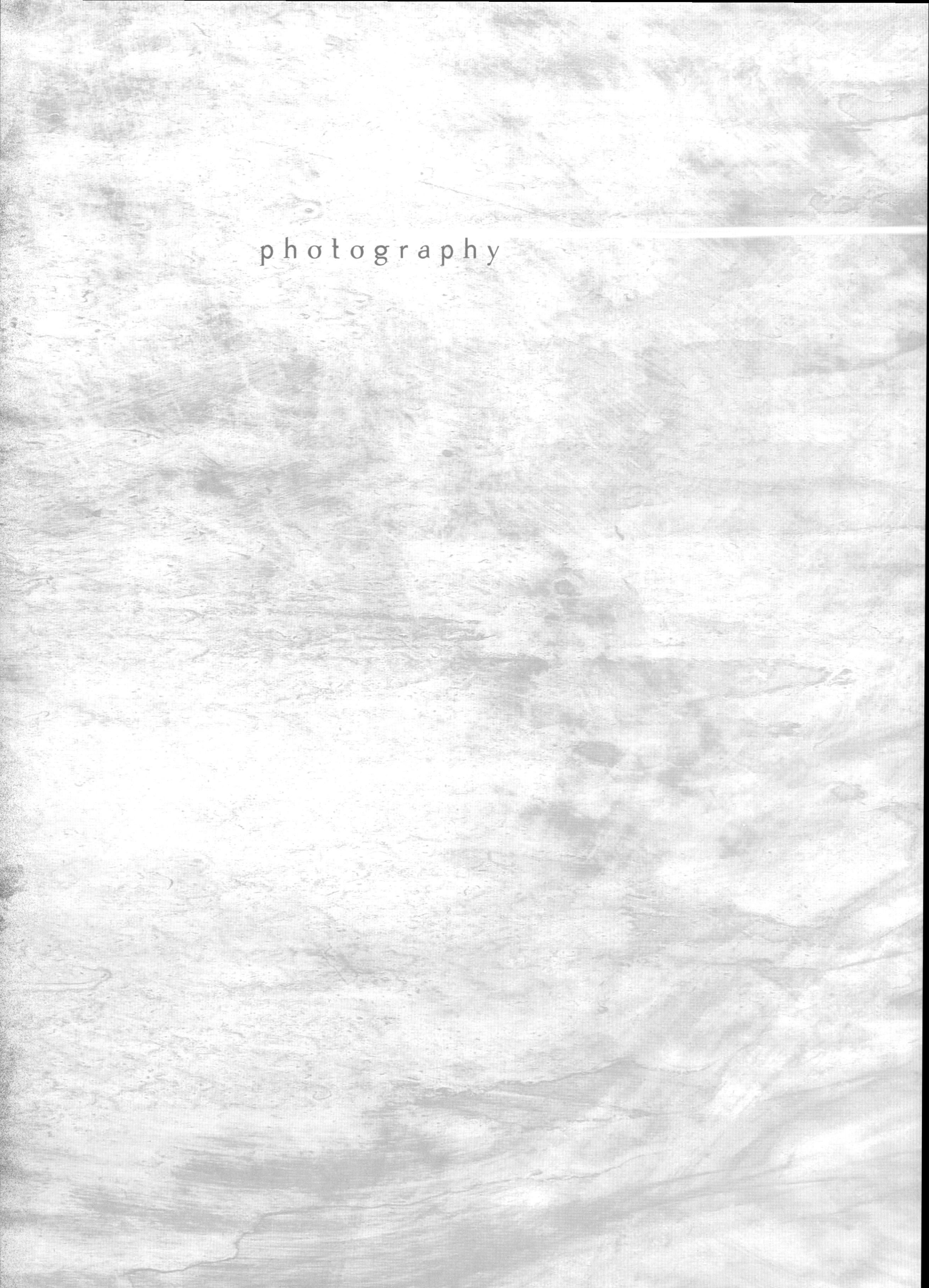

photography

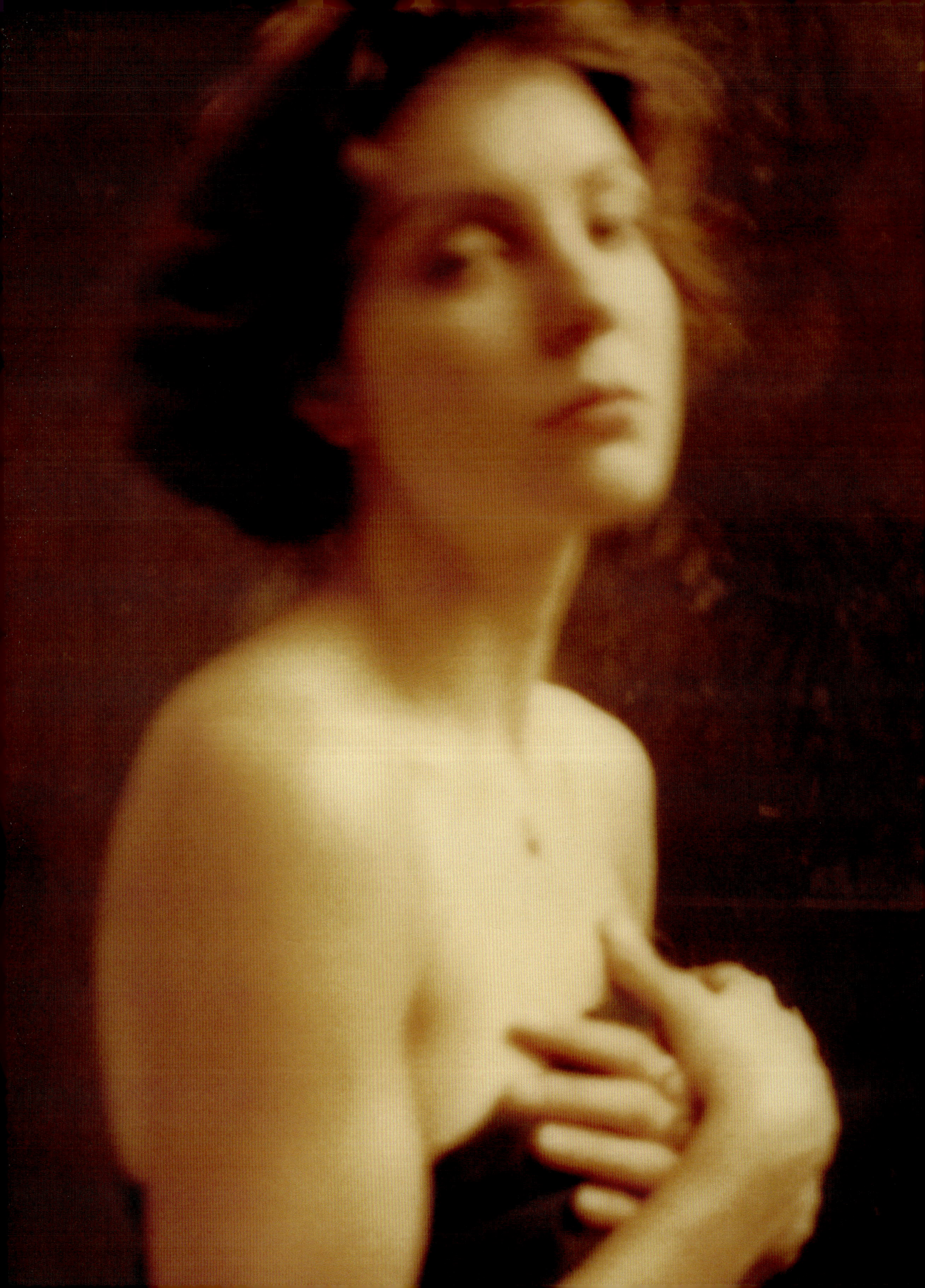

photography

light in a box

My love of process and happy accidents spills over into my fascination with photography. Using the camera as a journalistic device never really interested me. Setting up scenarios when I was younger with my brothers, sisters, friends, animals and various props was much more fun. I preferred to weave in some story or concept brewing in my imagination before I clicked the shutter.

Even when I was using the camera for reference pictures, I was looking for something more to say, always looking for the art in every moment.

I have used all sorts of cameras from a pin hole box to higher end digital SLRs. What strikes me most about photography is that, even though the technology keeps advancing, ultimately we are always in service to the image. Beautiful, timeless images have been produced from the beginning of this art form with only light sensitive chemicals adhered to metal. Even today, we have artists like Abelardo Morell who use camera obscura techniques, (pin hole), with eloquent mastery. Whether the camera is simple or sophisticated there are always moments of possibility to be found through its lens.

Photography helps manifest the ideas in my mind. It is part of my image making tool kit, and so usually this light in a box is merged into another piece of art. Though I am a process junkie, there is something to be said about knowing when to let it be. For instance, the Polaroid taken in St. Peter's cathedral, (pg 162), in the 80s reflected some magical optical energy that no amount of manipulation will improve. Sometimes the Gods and Goddesses of light and dark touch the lens of your camera catching the most magnificent moment. It is a mysterious and divine gift. Then I bow and back away.

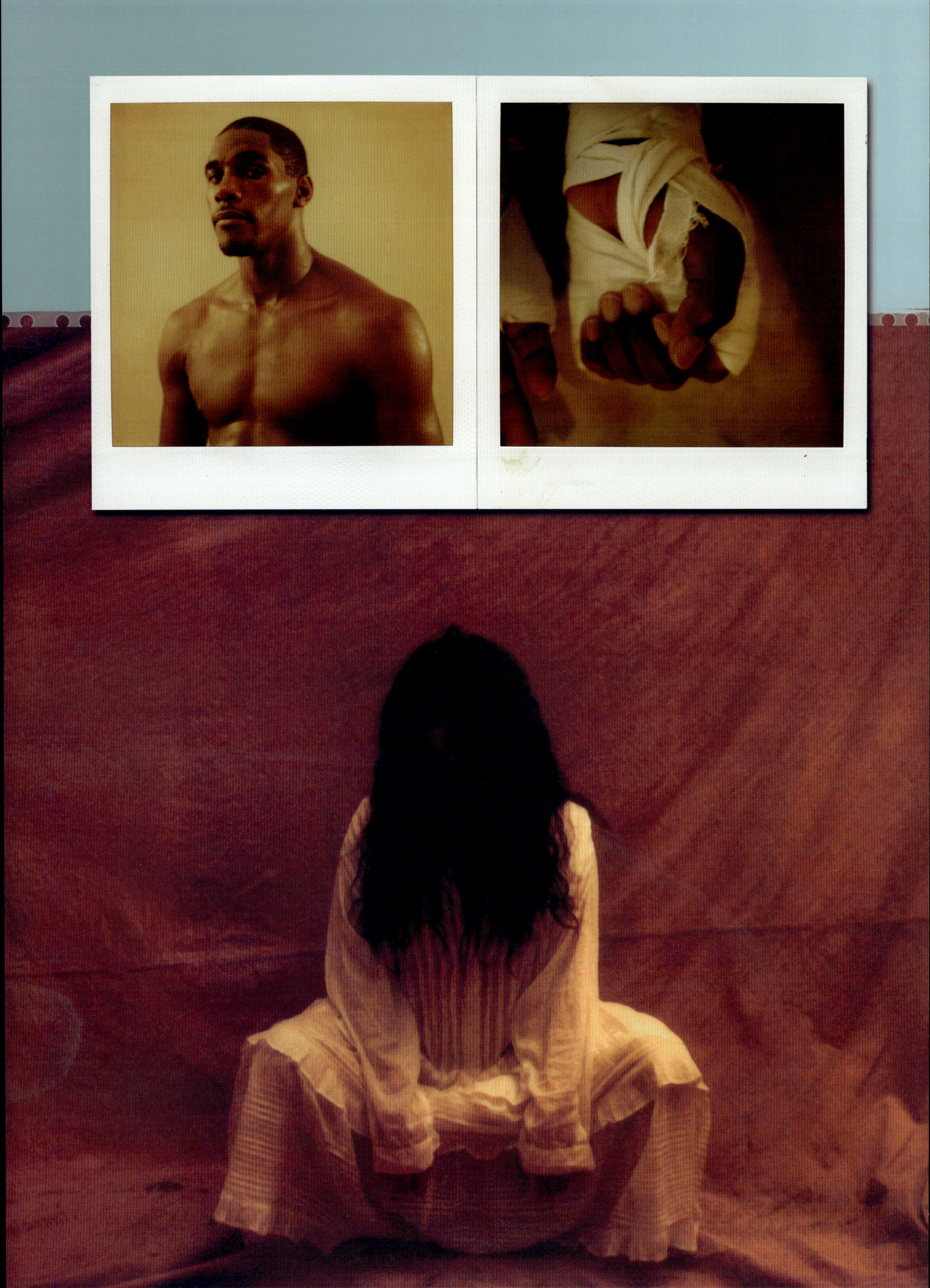

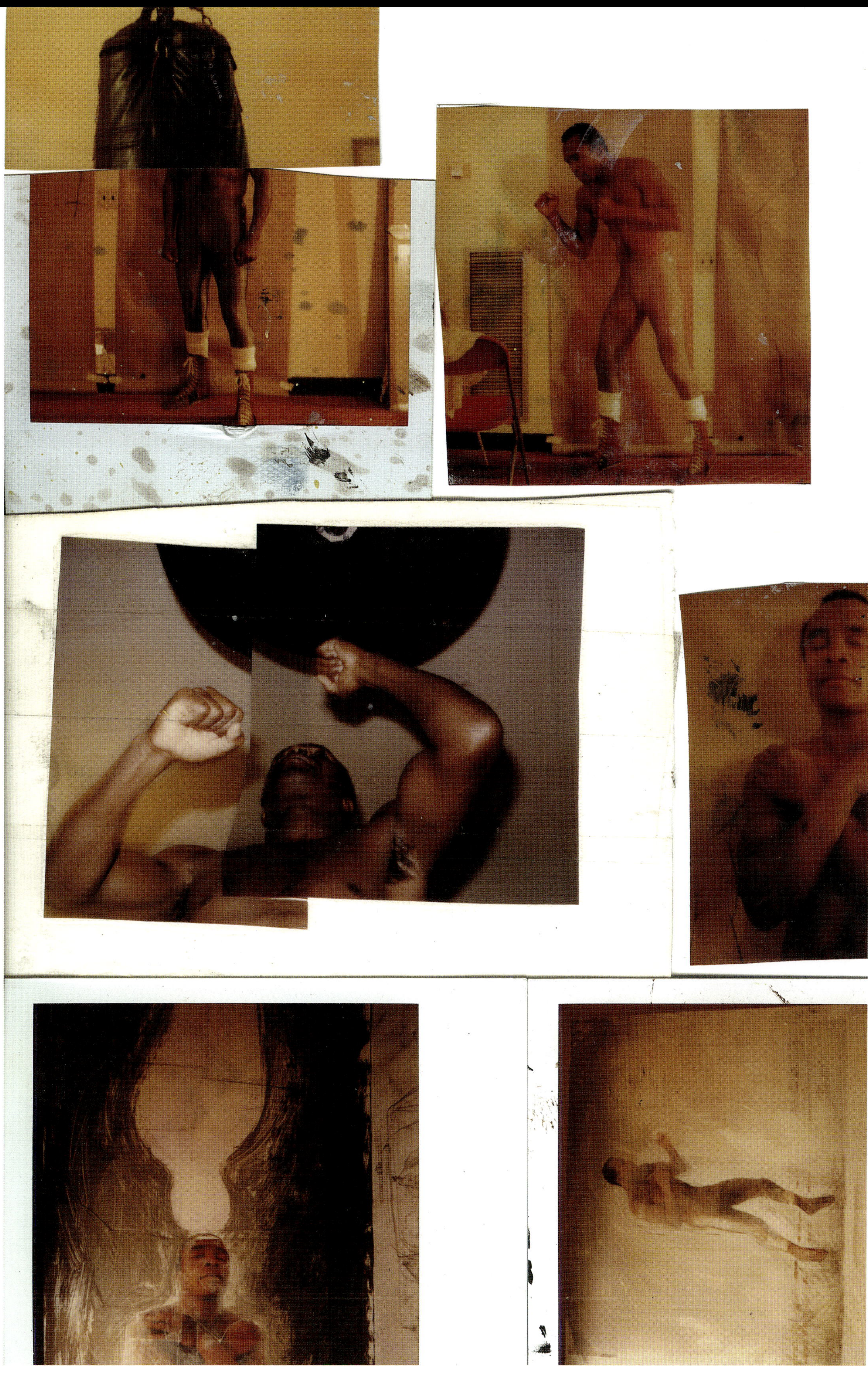

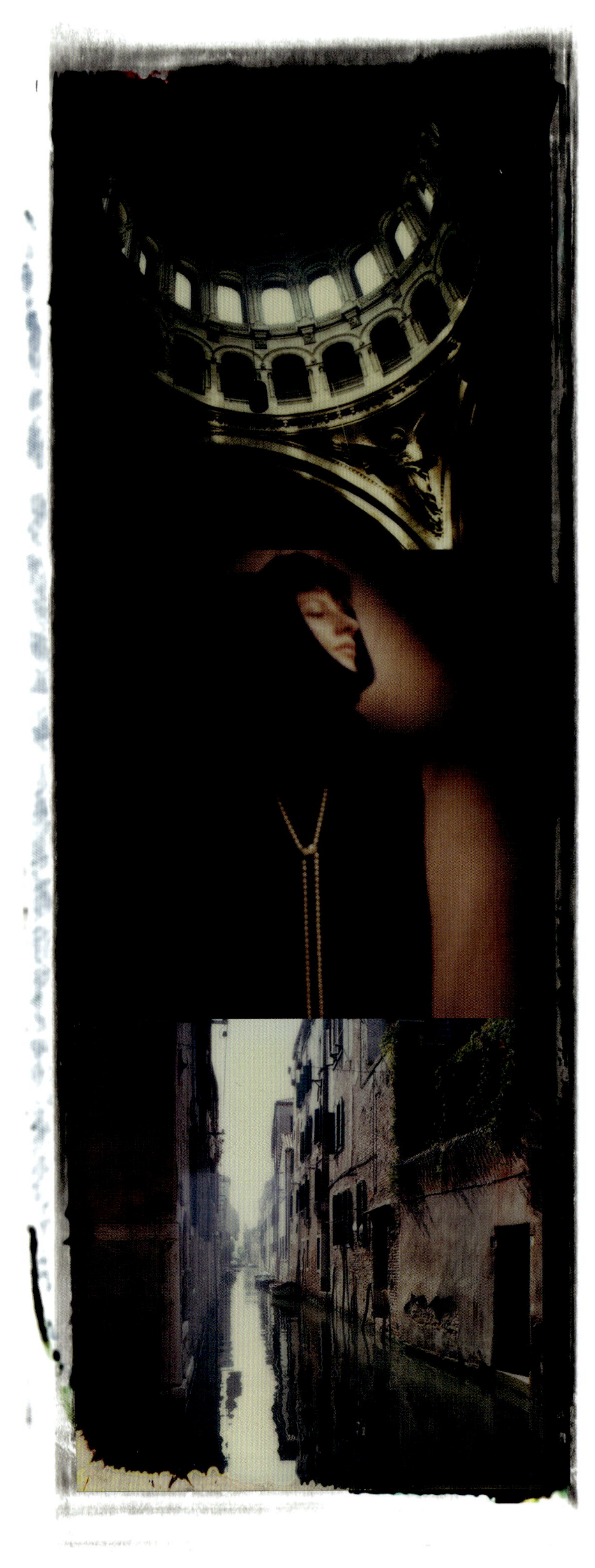

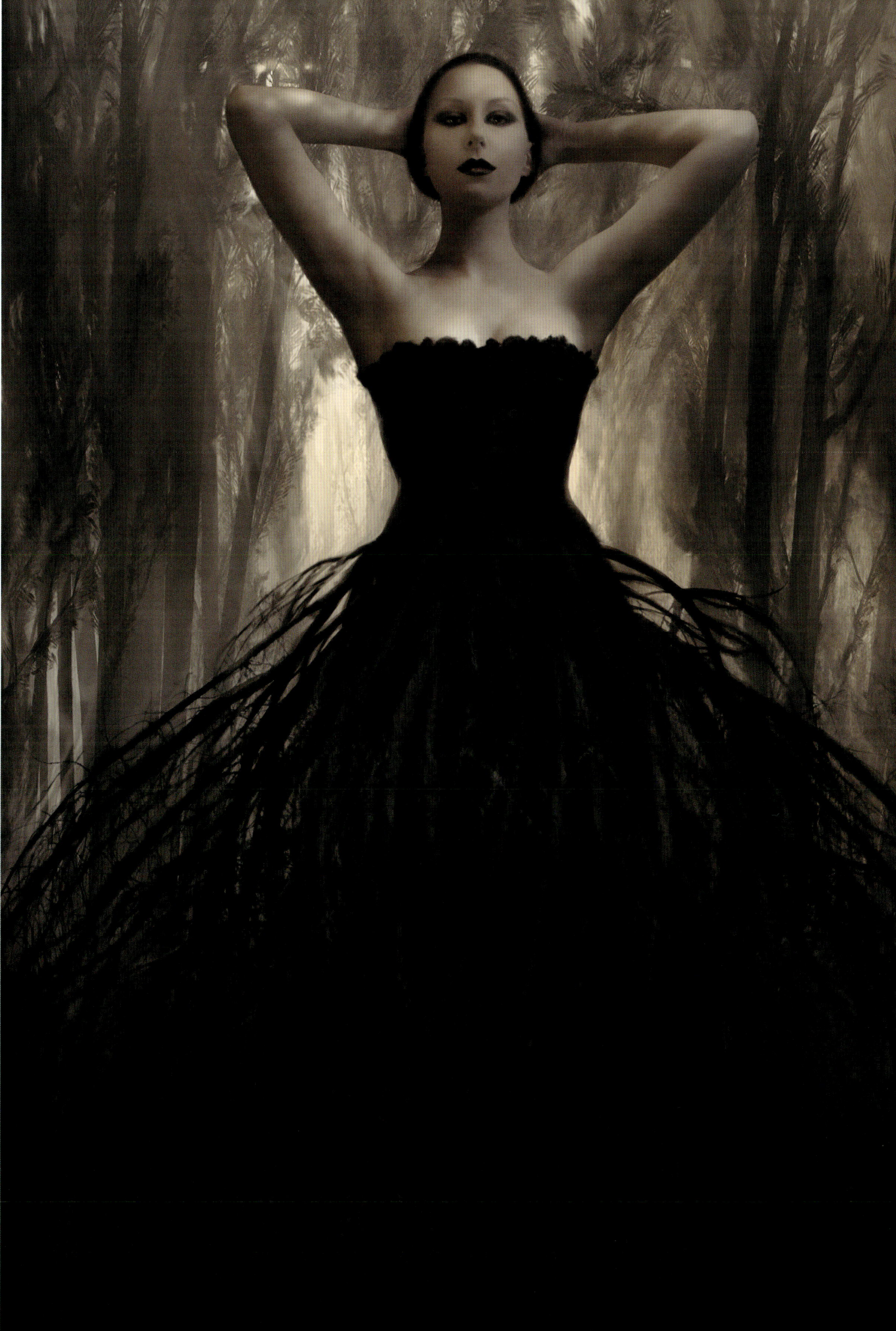

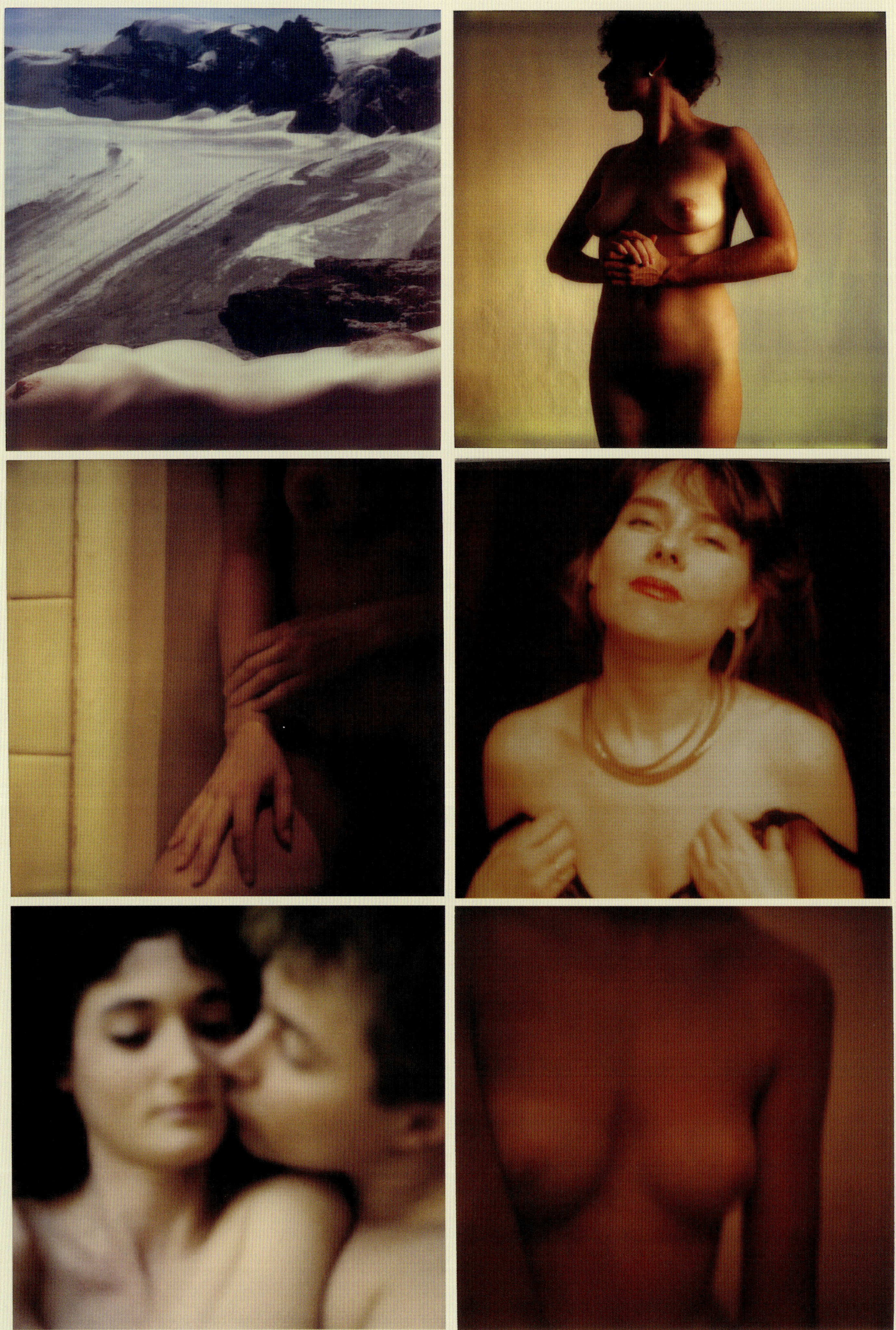

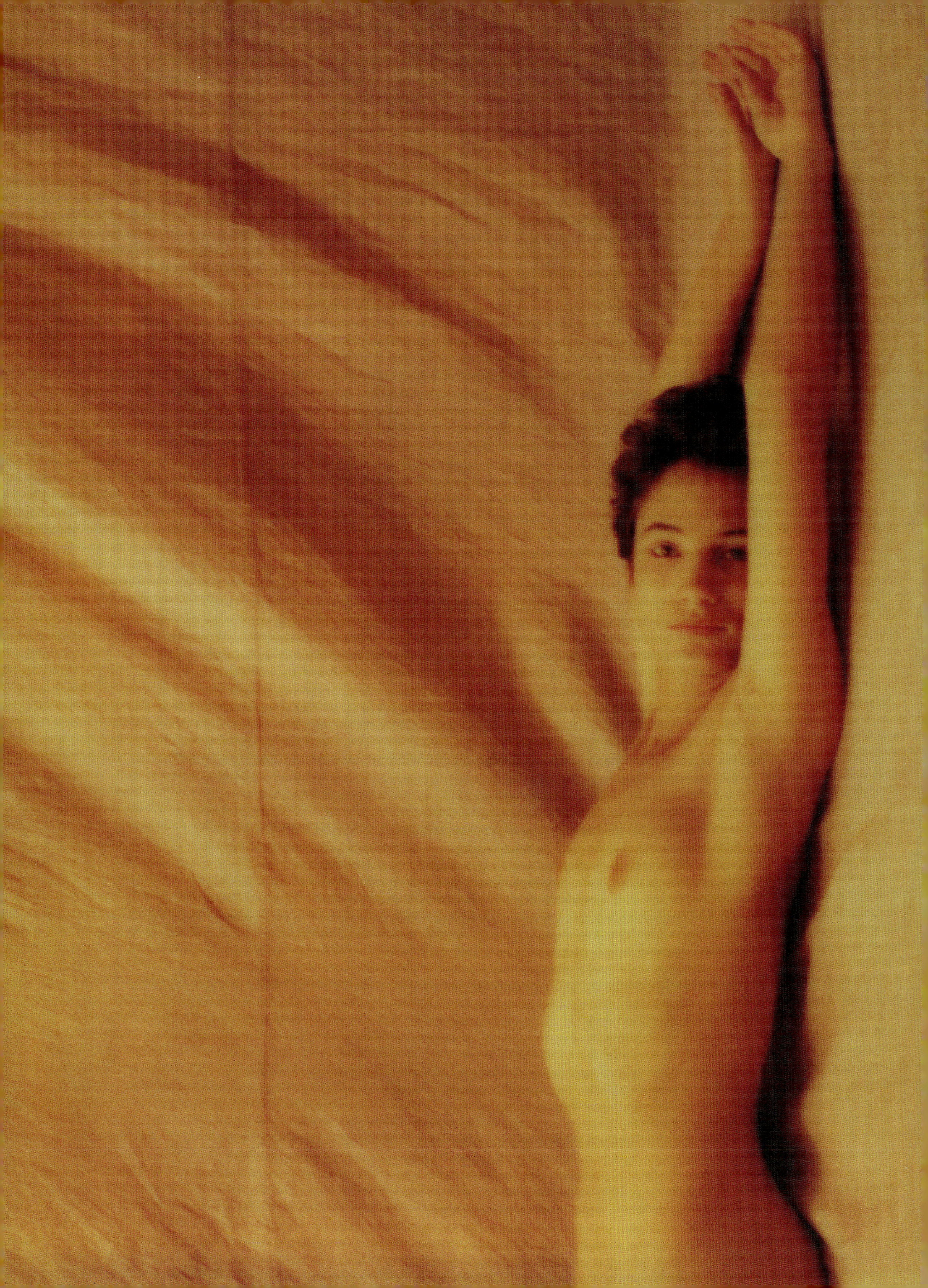

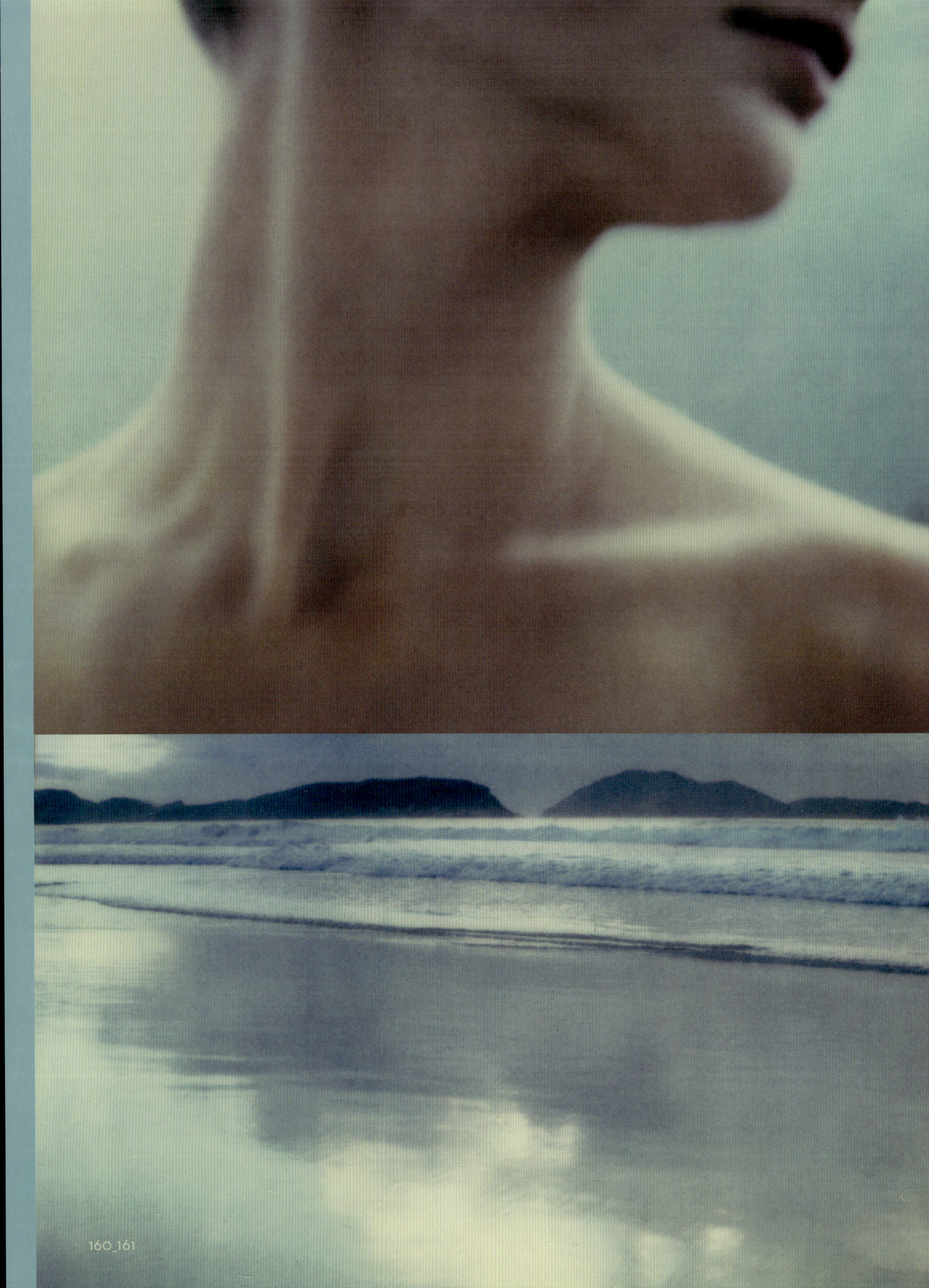

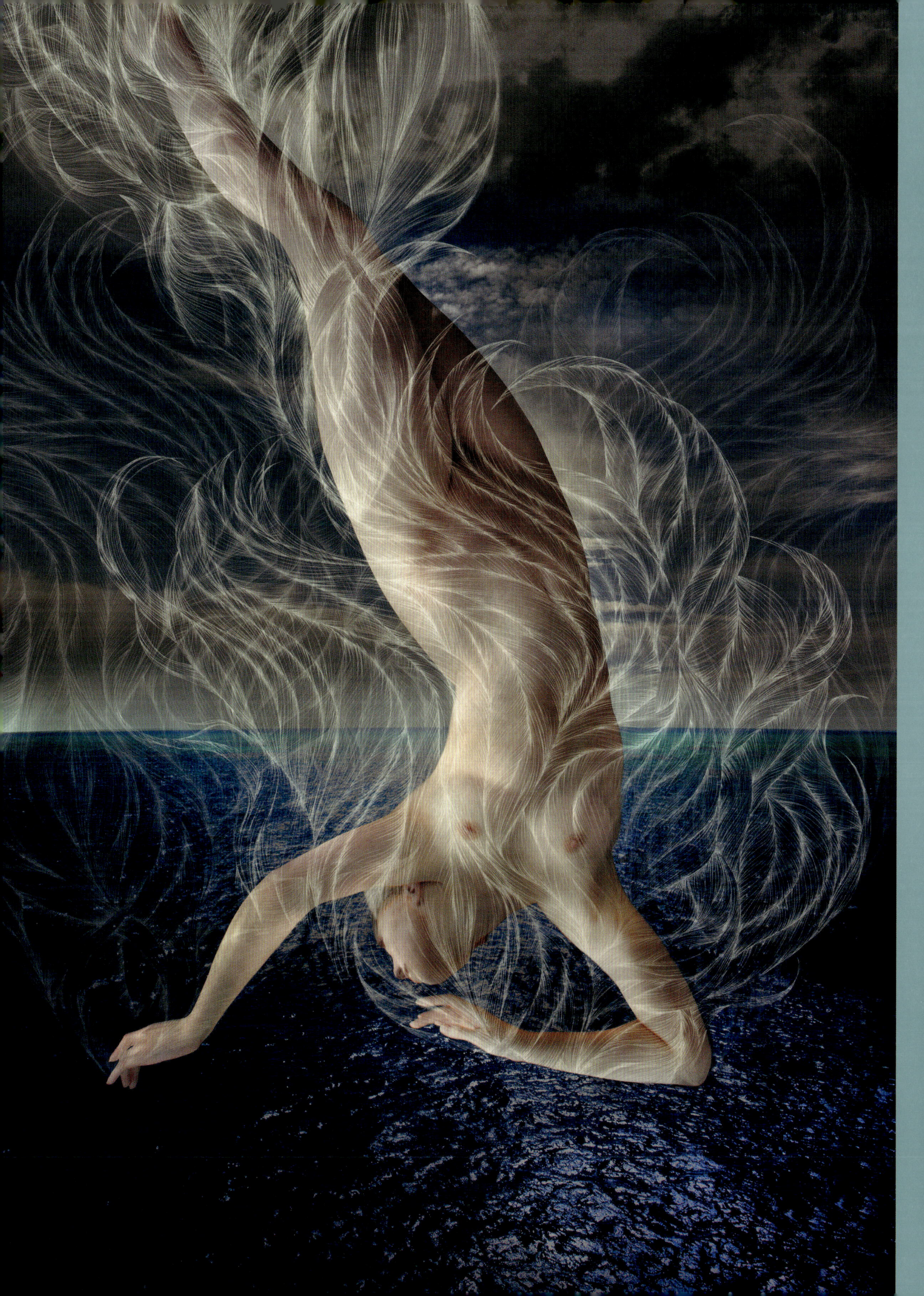

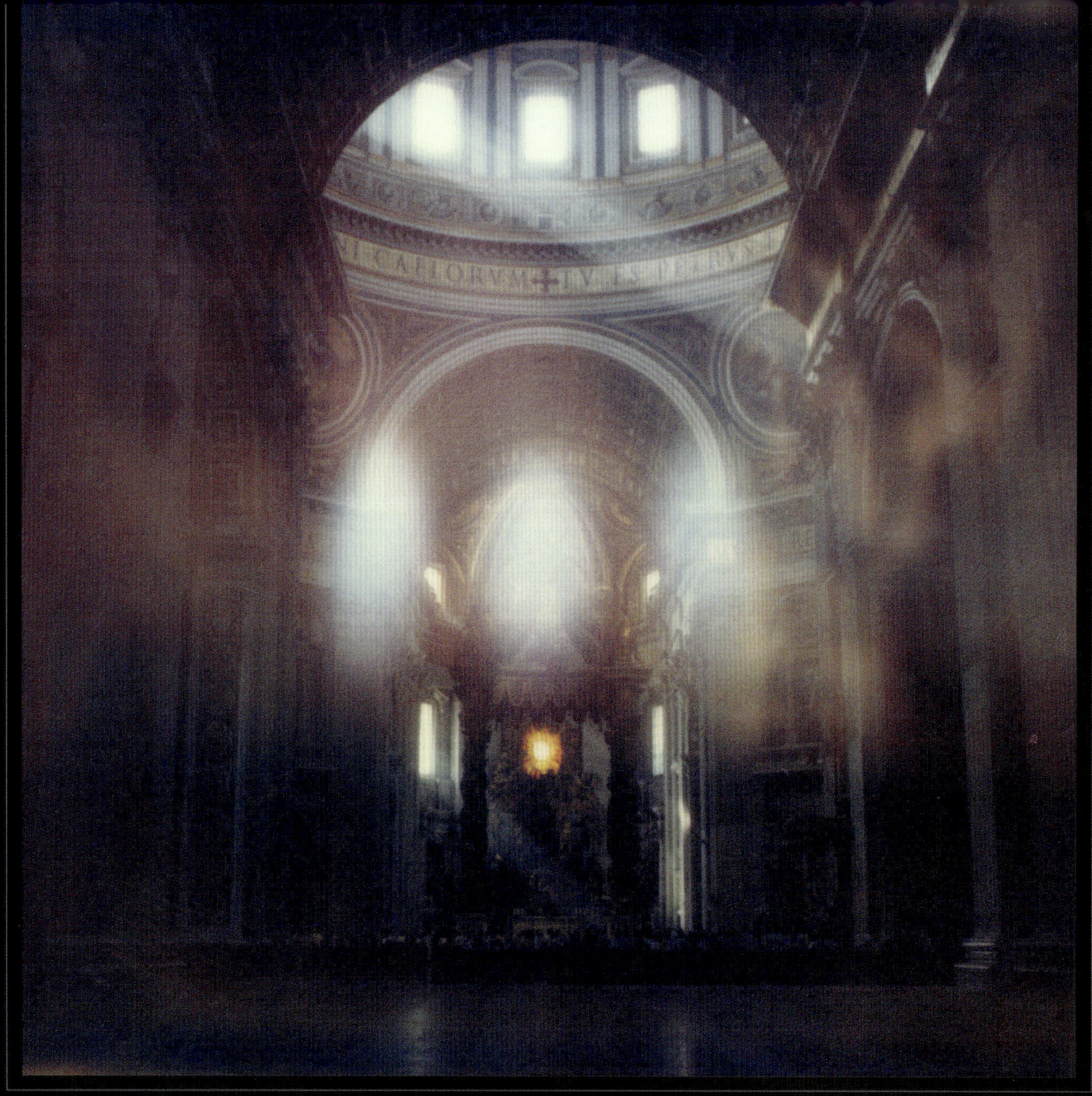

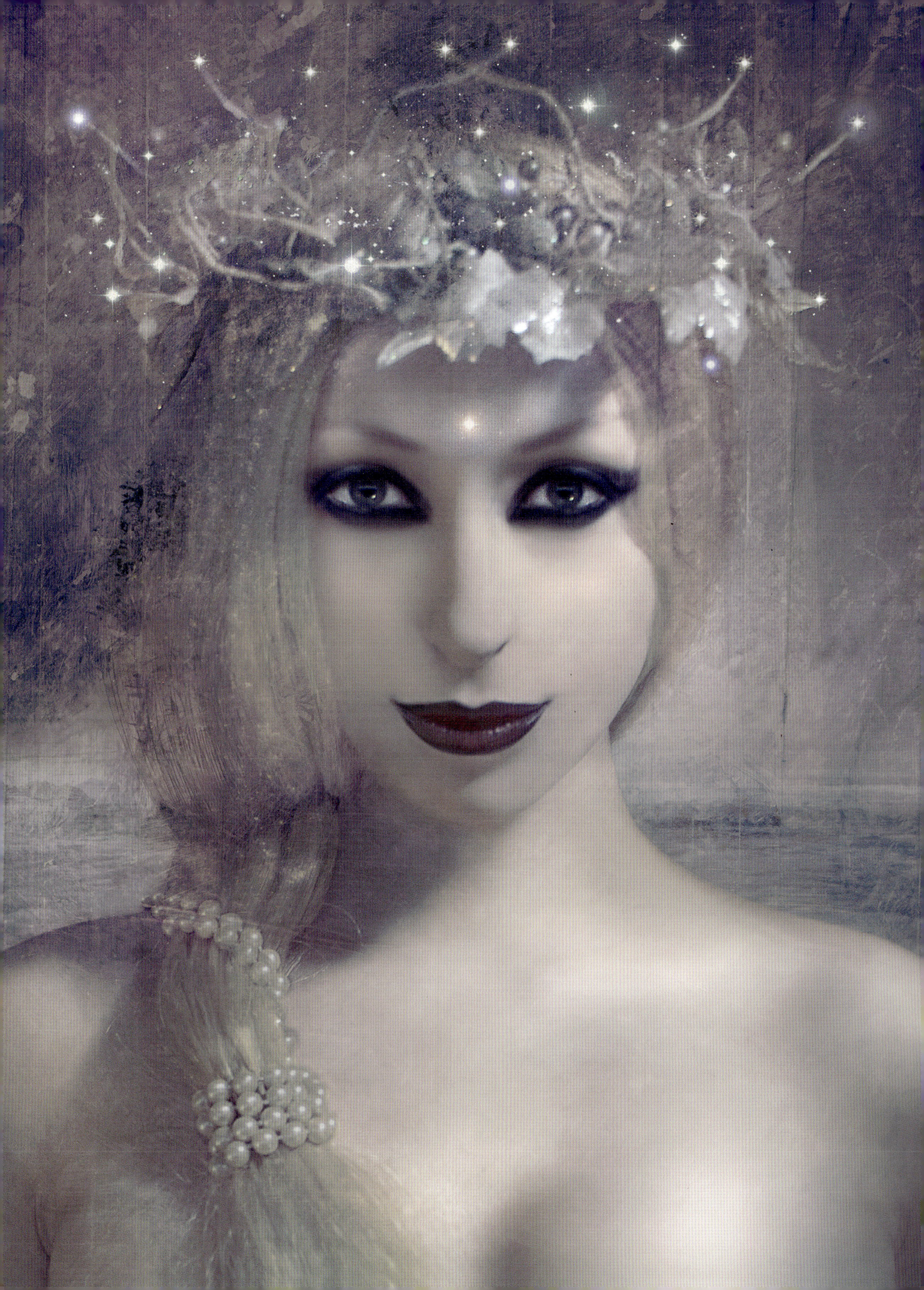

index

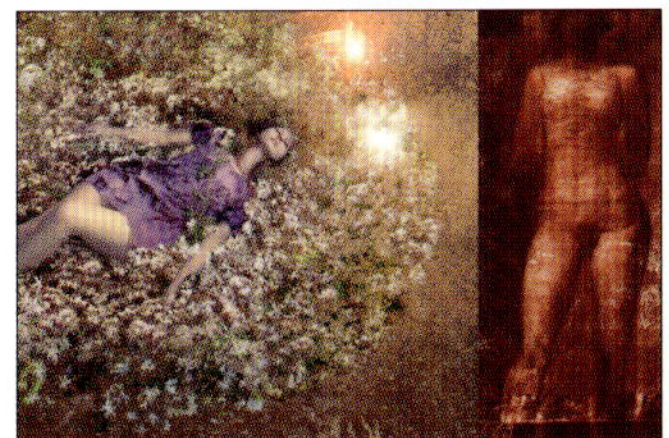

04

Summer

Roxana Illuminated Perfume: Blossom - 2013

digital

model: Gwen Cunningham

05

Red Blush

Life drawing study - 2003

charcoal, Xerox, imprimatura, on paper

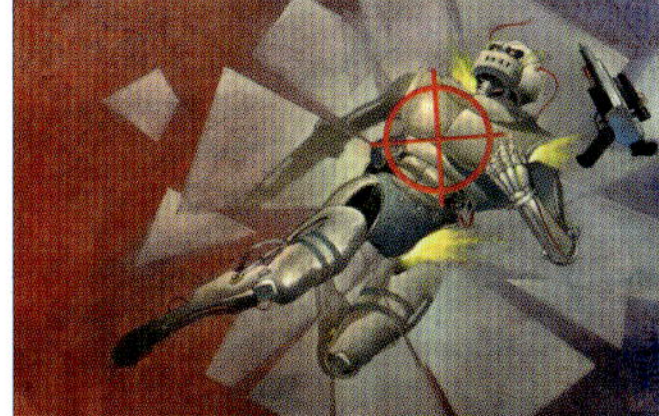

06-07

Bang!

Advertising art for Atari - 1983

graphite, acrylic & oil paint, crystal clear, on board

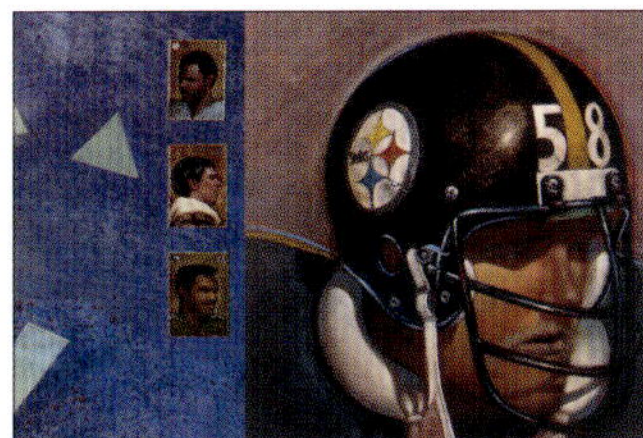

08

Warren Moon, Randall W. Cunningham, Jim Kelly

NFL Trading Cards - 1990s

graphite, acrylic & oil paint on board

09

Jack Lambert

1981

graphite, acrylic & oil paint, crystal clear, on board

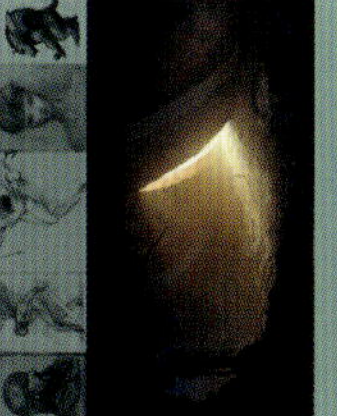

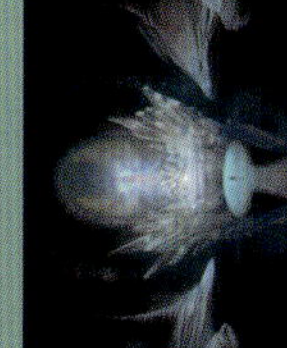

10

left to right

Book cover sketches for Faust - 1997

Book cover sketches for Fallen - 2003

The Loyal Heretic: Catholic Guilty and Gay for the *LA Weekly* - 1982

Meow! and Io character designs for *Escape From Planet Earth* - 2007

Concept design for The Ant Bully - 2005

digital

11

The Ant Mother Chamber

Concept design for *The Ant Bully* - 2005

digital

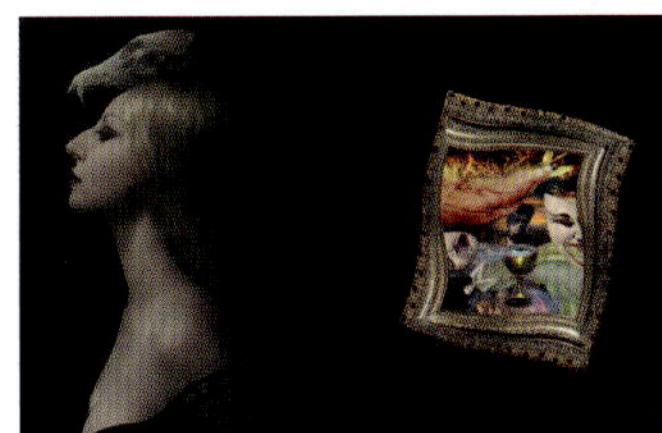

20

Noir

Roxana Illuminated Perfume: Noir - 2013

digital

model: Jessica Lough

21

Smoke and Mirrors

Book cover for *Smoke and Mirrors* by Neil Gaiman, Avon - 2005

digital

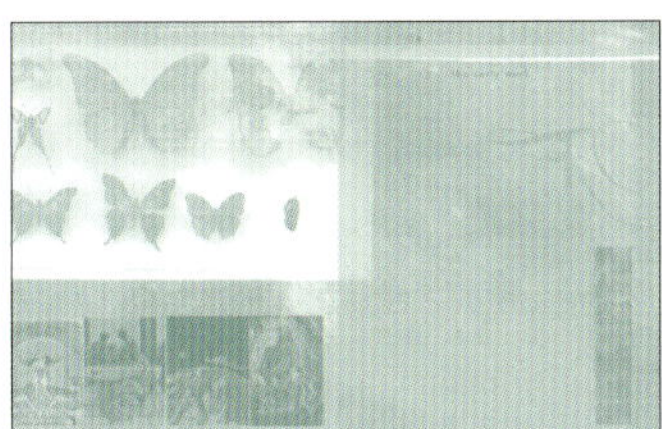

22

Orange Coast College Catalog Personal Paintings

1976-78

ink, rubylith, graphite, acrylic paint, on canvas

Popular art culture influences

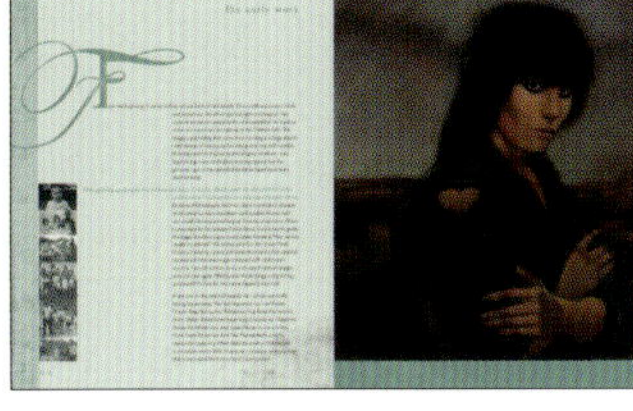

24

Family Polaroids and photos

1963-1973

25

Joan Jett

1982

graphite, acrylic, oil, crystal clear, on board

Popular art culture influences

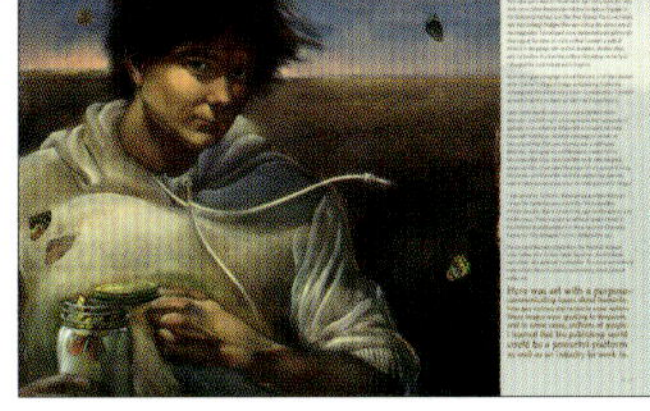

26-27

The Risk

Self portrait - 1990

graphite, butterfly wings, acrylic, oil, crystal clear, on board

Popular art culture influences

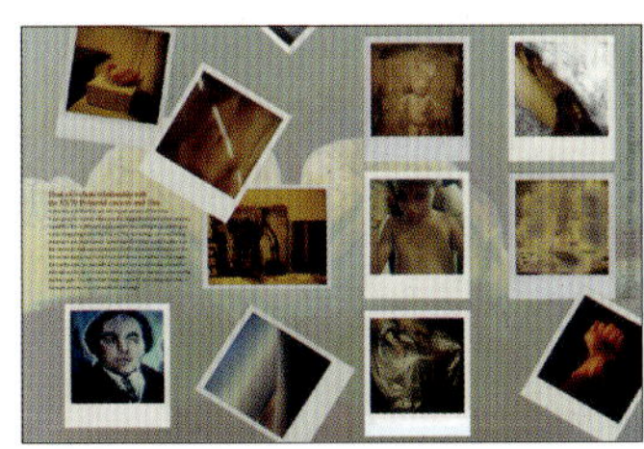

36-37

Polaroids

1979-1989

Reference and personal

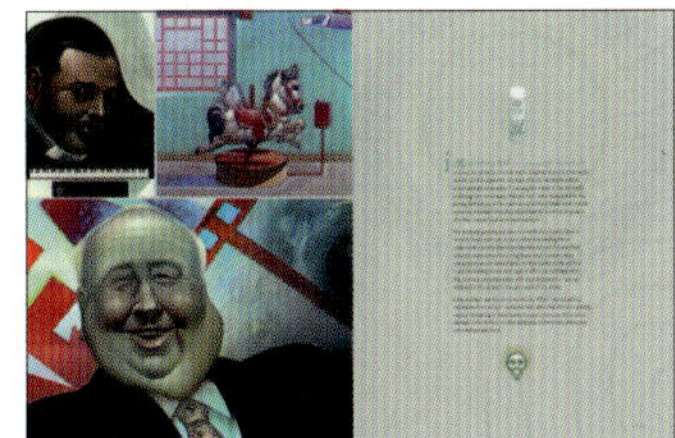

38

Duke

Art Center College of Design - 1979

graphite, prisma color pencils, acrylic, on board

East - West

Art Center College of Design - 1980

graphite, prisma color pencils, acrylic, on board

Alfred Hitchcock

Art Center College of Design - 1979

graphite, prisma color pencils, on board

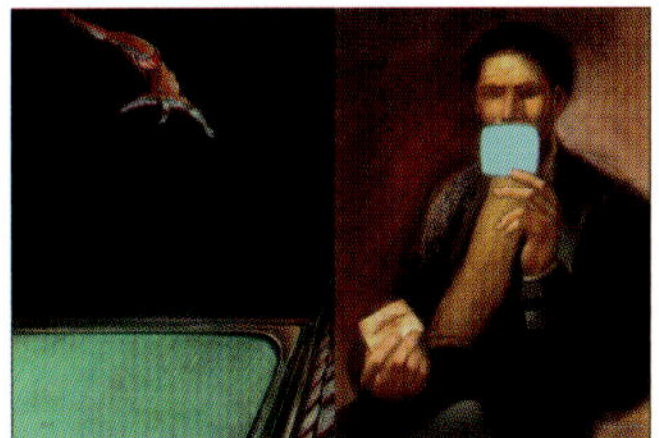

40

Tech Dive

PC World magazine - 1983

graphite, acrylic, oil, crystal clear, on board

41

Tech Hi!

PC World magazine - 1983

graphite, acrylic, oil, crystal clear, on board

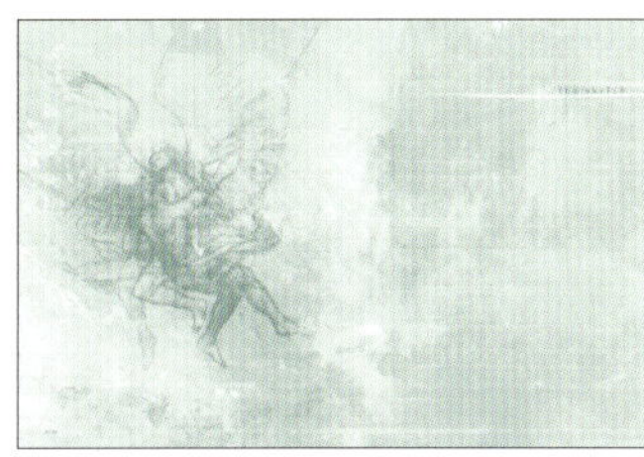

42

Sketch for Metaphysical Muscle

Graphite on paper - 2005

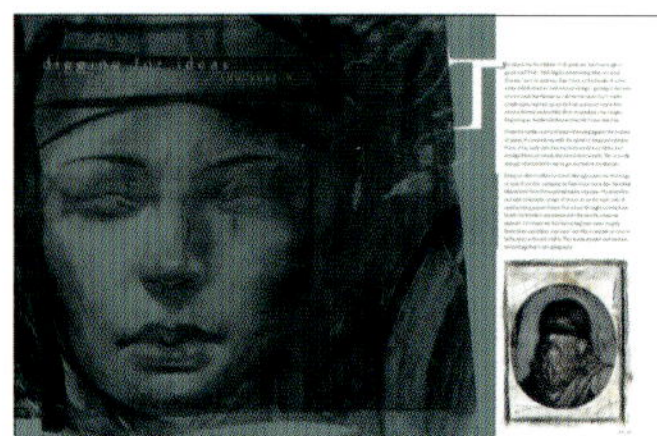

44
Head study
2003
charcoal, graphite, turpentine, on paper

45
Sketch for Faust book cover
1997
graphite, collage, on paper

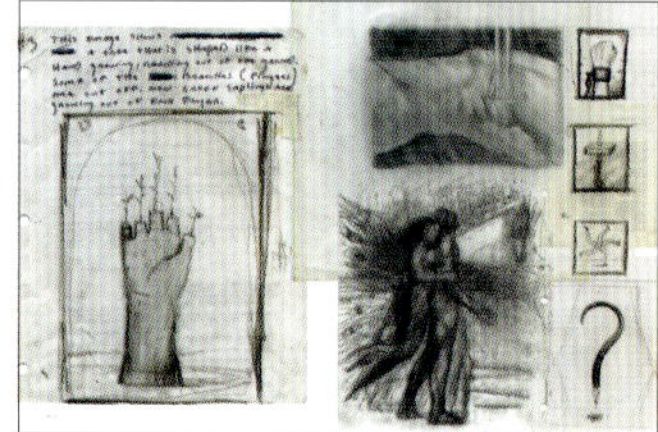

46-47
Various sketches
1997
graphite or charcoal, on paper

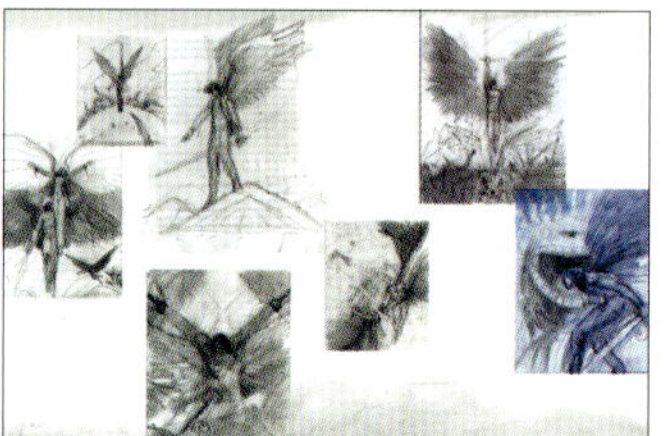

48-49
Sketches for The Fallen book covers
Simon and Schuster - 2000-2003
graphite or charcoal, on paper, digital

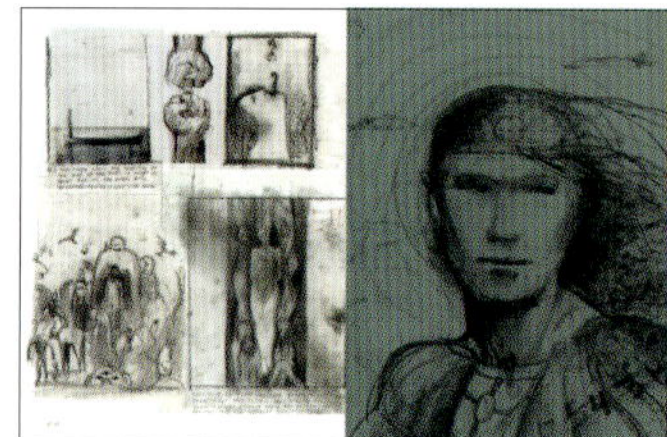

50-51
Sketches for:
Book cover, The Peace Alliance, Sandman (Desire), The Book of Magic, Lulu for the San Francisco Opera poster
1989-1999
graphite or charcoal, on paper

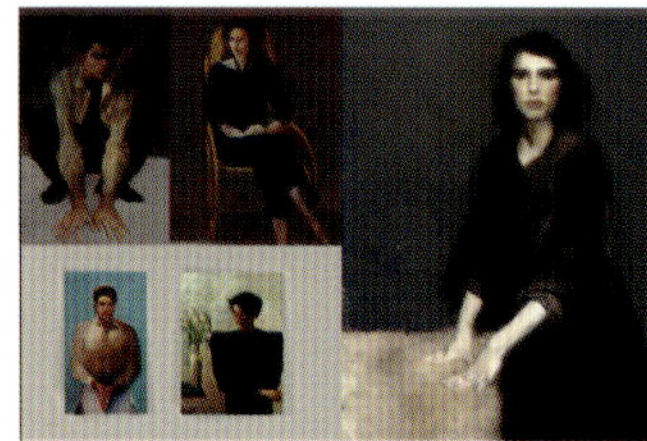

60-61
Philip Burke, Alexa Grace, Jeffrey Adams, Vivienne Flesher, Frances Jetter
Print magazine, Peer Portraits - 1985
graphite, acrylic, oil, on board

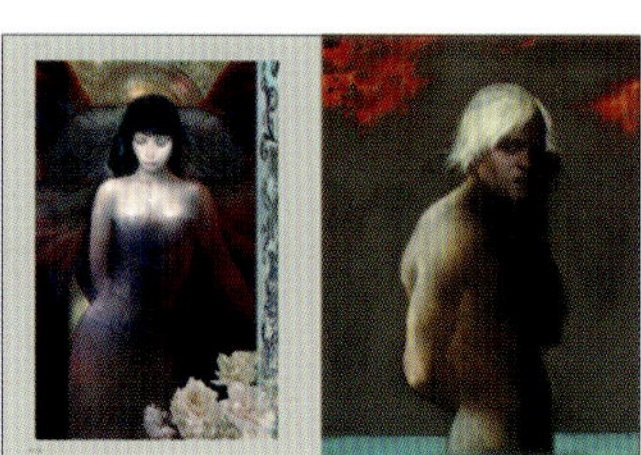

62-63
Danielle Polley
2008
digital

Klaus Kinski
Playboy - 1985
graphite, acrylic, oil, crystal clear, on board

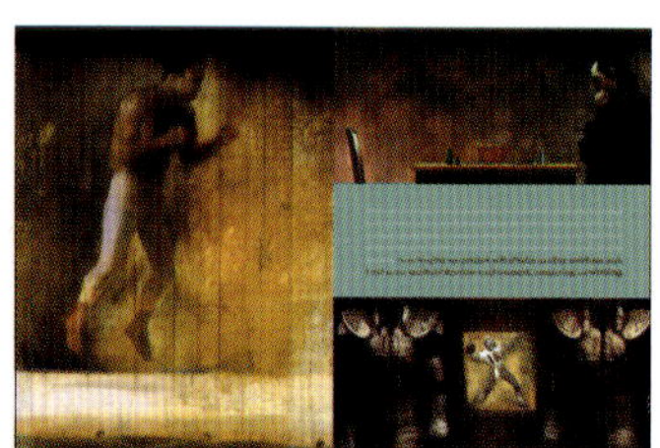

64
Sugar Ray Leonard
Sports Illustrated - 1989
graphite, Polaroids, acrylic, oil, tape, on board

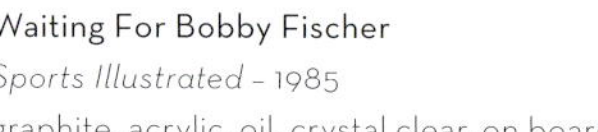

65
Waiting For Bobby Fischer
Sports Illustrated - 1985
graphite, acrylic, oil, crystal clear, on board

Joe Montana
NFL - 1997
graphite, Xerox, oil, glue, on board

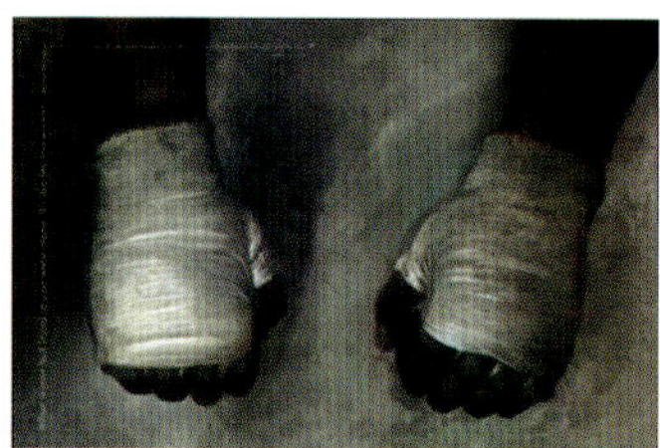

66-67
Mike Tyson's Fists
Print magazine - 1989
graphite, acrylic, oil, crystal clear, on board

More of the Mike Tyson project

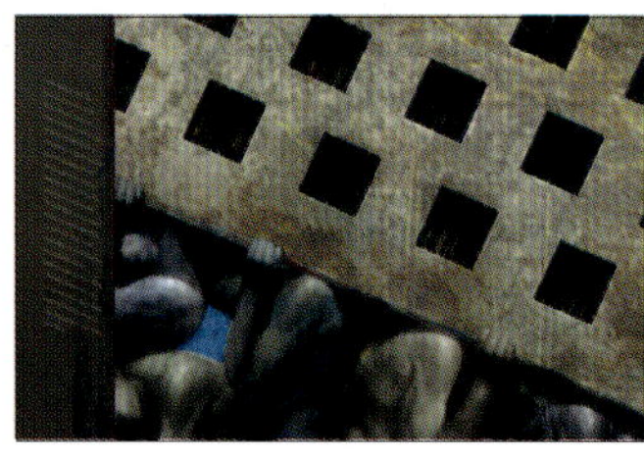

76-77
Prison Labor = Prison Profits
Labor Calendar - 1999
graphite, digital

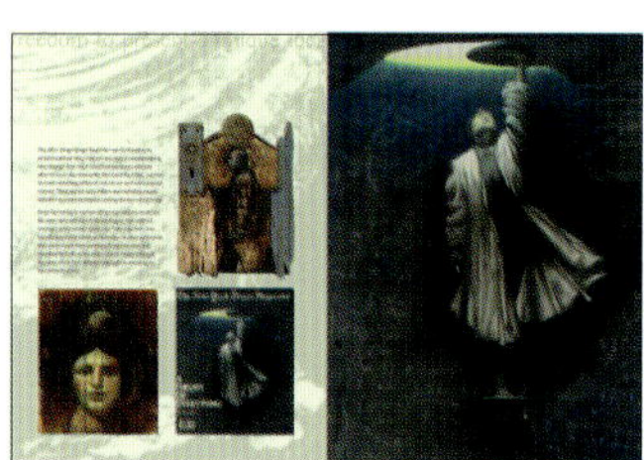

78-79
Ready to Write
Buzz magazine - 1995
graphite, acrylic, oil, tape, found objects, on board

Man & Rat
Psychology Today - 1991
graphite, acrylic, oil, polyurethane, on board

A Theory of Everything
New York Times Magazine - 1987
graphite, oil, crystal clear, on board

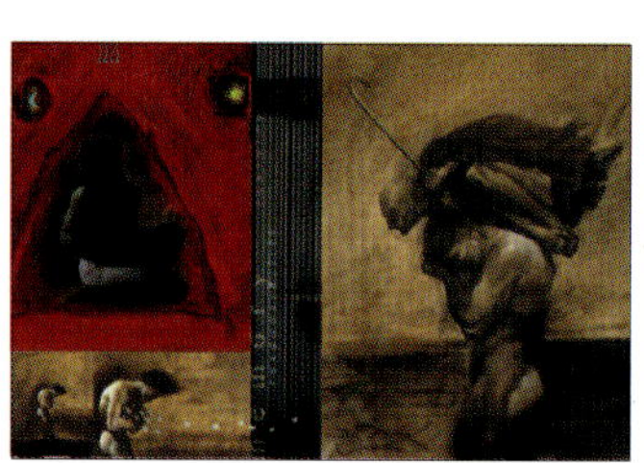

80
Yearning
10 year retrospective poster
Laguna College of Art and Design - 1992
graphite, acrylic, oil, crystal clear, on board

Holocaust Memories
Dimensions-A Journal of Holocaust Studies
1988
graphite, charcoal, conte, on paper

81
Karma
Cleveland magazine - 1988
graphite, charcoal, conte, on paper

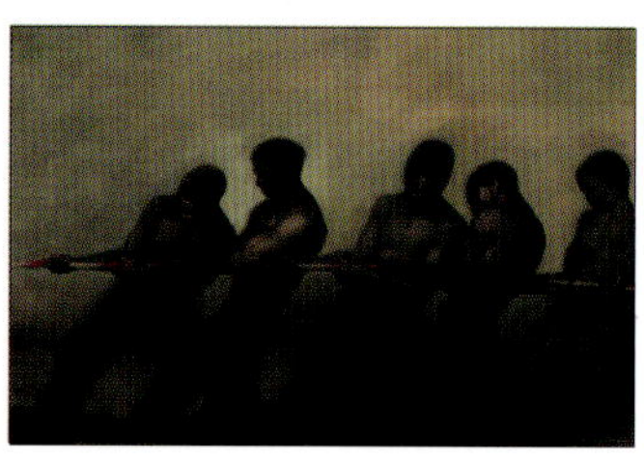

82-83
Racism in America
Playboy - 1987
graphite, oil, on board

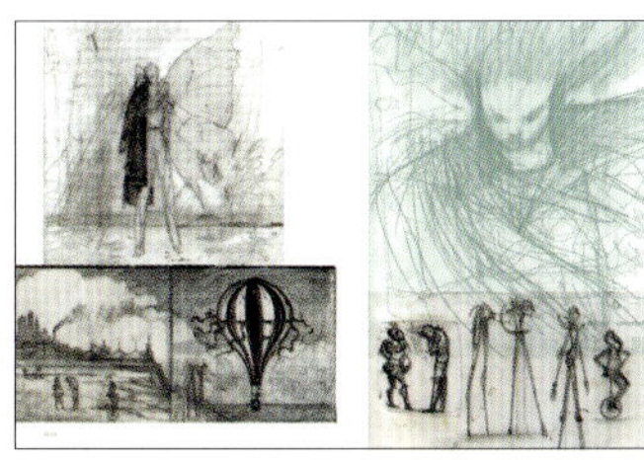

52-53
Sketches for:
Laguna College of Art and Design poster, Linda Perry, In Flight cd cover and character studies
1995-2003
graphite or charcoal, on paper

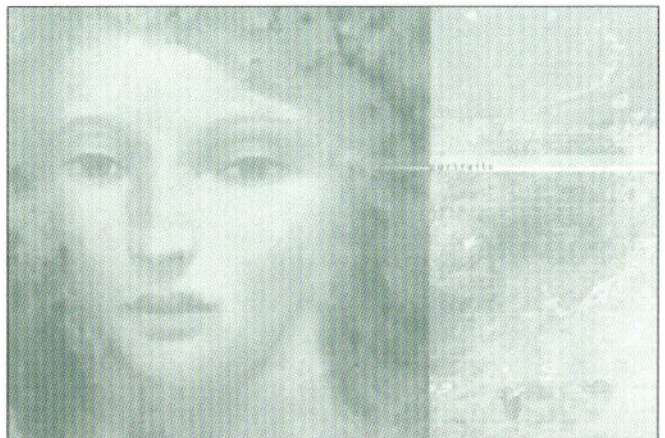

54
Head study
2000
graphite, coffee, on board

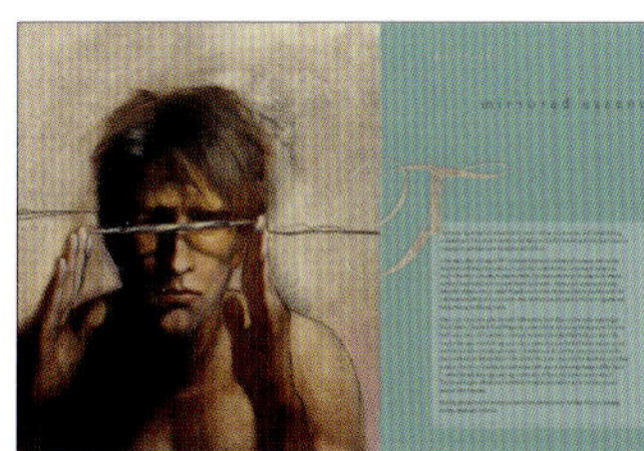

56
Matt Mahurin
Print magazine - 1985
graphite, oil, on board

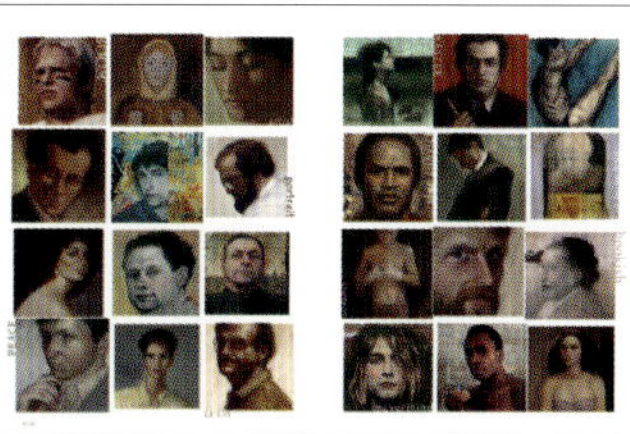

58
left to right-Row 1: "Boomer" Esiason (*NFL*), Nadia Hujtyn (*Print*), Vivienne Flesher (*Print*)R2: Elvis Costello (*Rolling Stone*), Bob Dylan (*Village Voice*), Steve Ciarcia (*BYTE*) R3: Elegant (commission), Dylan Thomas (*Paragon House*), Dominick Cirillo (*Village Voice*); R4: Dennis Kucinich (*Plain Dealer Magazine*), Sara Schwartz (*Print*), Jerry Pournelle (*BYTE*)

59
left to right-Row 1: Rodney Coronado (*West Magazine*), Ernest Hemingway (*New York Times Magazine*), Greg Louganis (personal project); R2: O.J. Simpson (*Time Magazine*), Bobby Fischer (*Sports Illustrated*), Robert Frost (*Vermont* magazine);R3: Boxer (*Print*), Architect (commission), Catherine Bowen (*Sports Illustrated*); R4: Kurt Cobain (*Grunge Comics*), Sugar Ray Leonard (*Sports Illustrated*), Classical (*Focus* magazine)

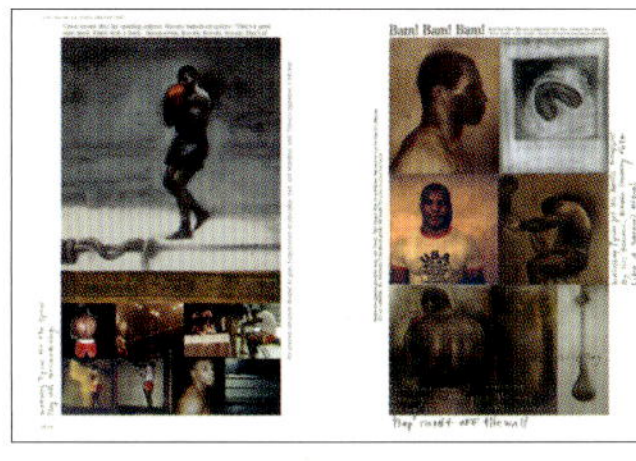

68
Iron Works - Mike Tyson
Print magazine - 1989
Iron Mike: graphite, acrylic, oil, crystal clear, on board
Polaroids

69
Iron Works - Mike Tyson
Print magazine - 1989
Profile: graphite, charcoal, oil, on butcher paper; Mouth Piece: graphite, acrylic, on paper, Polaroid; Taped Up: graphite, charcoal, oil, on butcher paper; The Back and the Bag: graphite, charcoal, oil, on butcher paper; Slip Bag: graphite, charcoal, acrylic, on paper

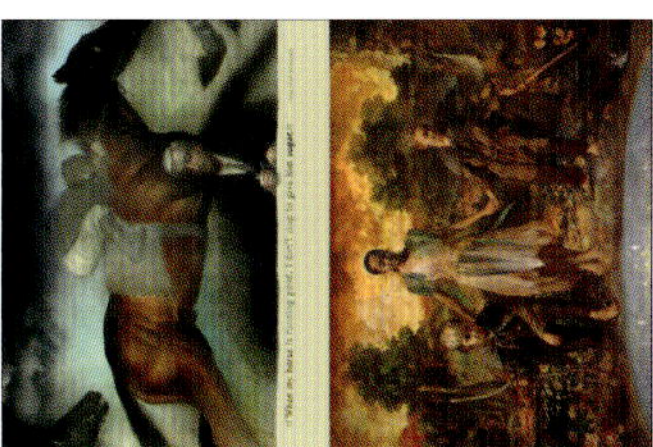

70
William Faulkner
Sports Illustrated - 1987
graphite, acrylic, oil, crystal clear, on board

71
Life is a Wonder
Portraits of Kelsey, Travis, Jake Berger
2004
graphite, collage, acrylic, oil, on board

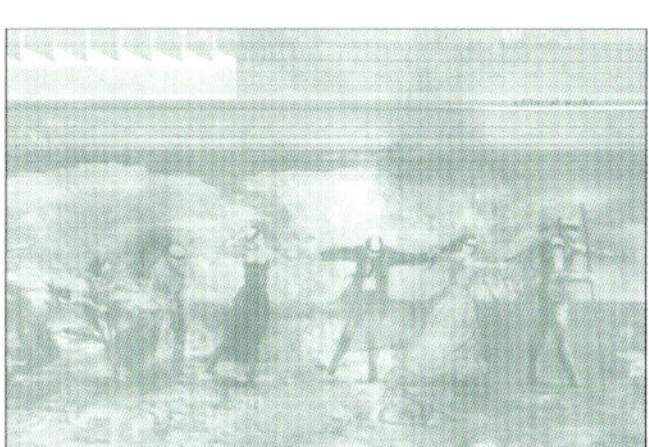

72-73
Blind Tech
Business Week - 2000
graphite, digital

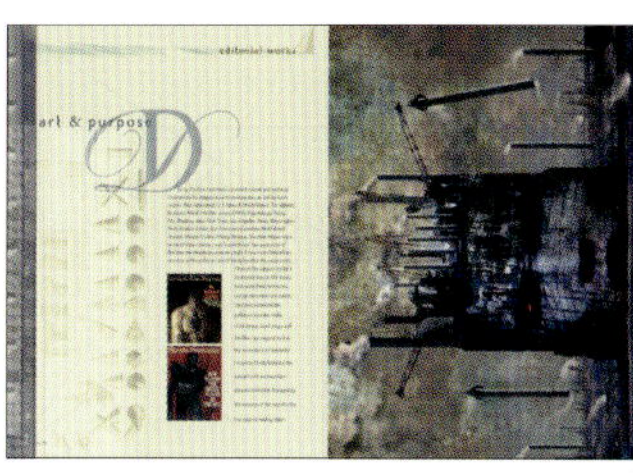

74
An American Contra
Cover: *Los Angeles Times Magazine* - 1987
graphite, acrylic, oil, crystal clear, on board

Plague of Injuries in the NFL
Cover: *Sports Illustrated* - 1986
graphite, acrylic, oil, crystal clear, on board

75
Monster
Labor Calendar - 1999
graphite, digital

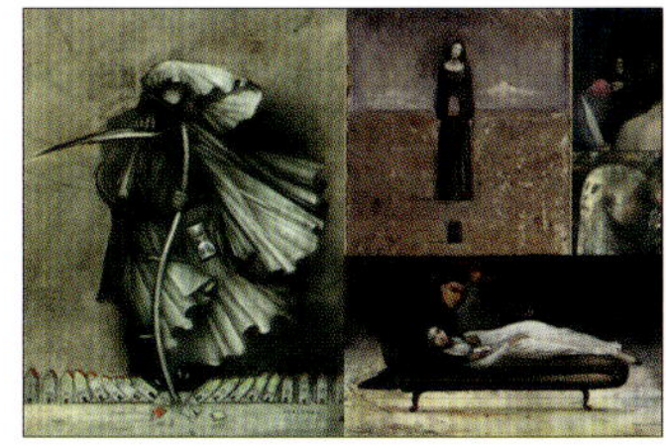

84
A Death Divides
Image magazine - 1988
graphite, oil, on board

85
clockwise from top: Womb to Tomb
Parenting magazine - 1996
graphite, collage, acrylic, oil, tape, on board

Kid Violence
Los Angeles Times - 1995
graphite, collage, acrylic, oil, tape, on board

Death Head
1994
graphite, collage, acrylic, oil, plexiglass, on board

The Psychologist's Bed
Psychology Today - 1991
graphite, acrylic, oil, tape, on board

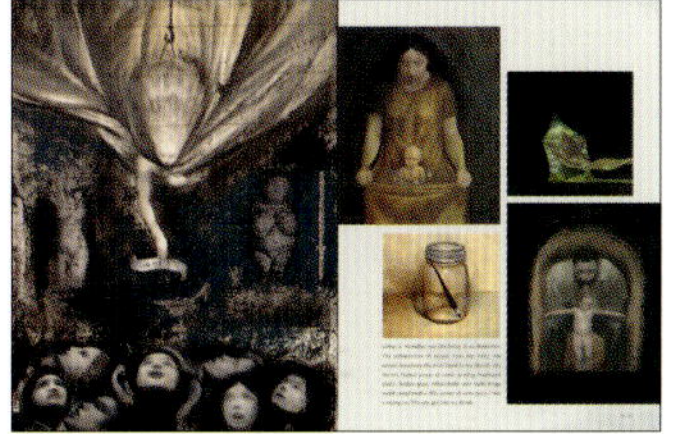

86
Facade
Los Angeles Times Magazine - 1993
graphite, collage, acrylic, oil, tape, on board

87
left to right: Postpartum Depression
Parenting magazine - 1996
graphite, egg tempera, oil, on board

Freedom
Health magazine - 1990
graphite, oil, on board

A Diary by Daisy Lee Donaldson
The Plain Dealer Magazine - 1984
graphite, acrylic, oil, crystal clear, on board

Child Abuse at the Presidio
West Magazine - 1988
graphite, acrylic, oil, crystal clear, on board

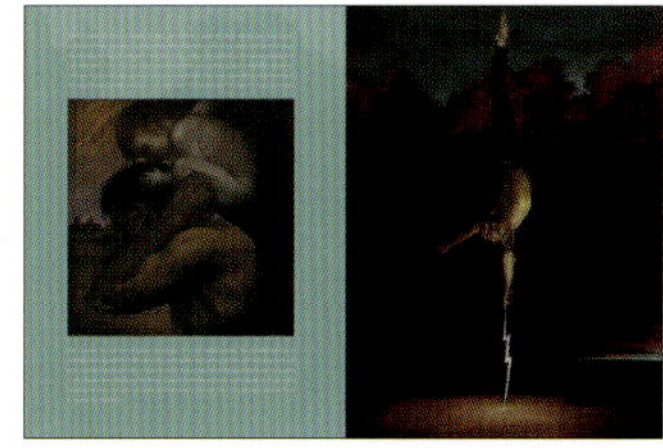

88
A Little Help
Personal - 1998
graphite, charcoal, conte, on paper

89
Mind Power
Managed Health Network - 1988
graphite, acrylic, oil, crystal clear, on board

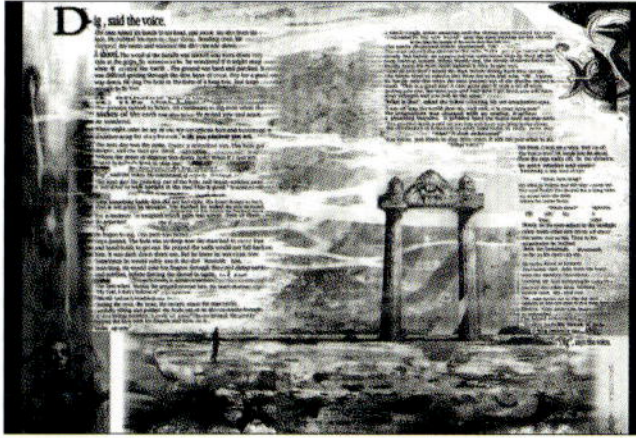

90-91
Dig
Tales from the Edge - 1995
graphite, collage, acrylic, on board, digital

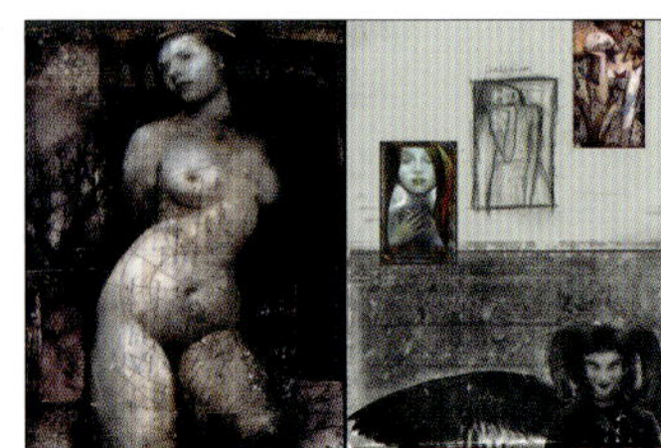

92
Beauty
Personal - 1997
graphite, Xerox, transparencies, acrylic, oil, crystal clear, on board

93
Death
DC Comics - 1998
graphite, collage, acrylic, oil, dried flowers, plexiglass, on board
Delirium sketch
DC Comics - 1999
graphite on paper
Delirium
DC Comics - 1999
graphite, collage, acrylic, oil, on board
A Little Devious
Personal - 2000
graphite, digital

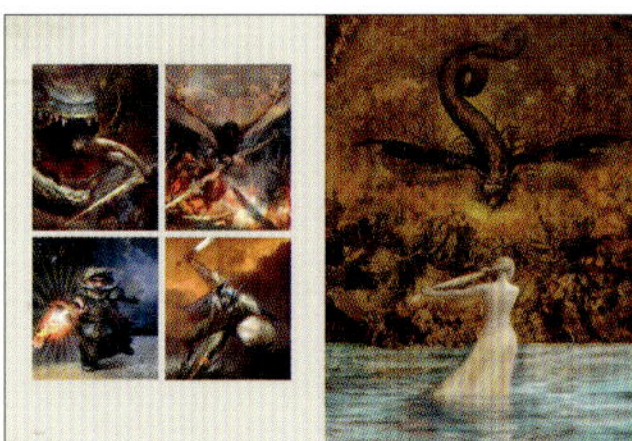

94
The Fallen (Leviathan)
Simon and Schuster - 2003
graphite, digital
The Fallen (Reckoning)
Simon and Schuster - 2004
graphite, digital
Blizzik Sparkcog
The World of Warcraft - 2006
graphite, digital
Milo the Unmerciful
The World of Warcraft - 2006
graphite, digital

95
Apocrypha
Philadelphia Opera Poster - 2003
graphite, collage, acrylic, oil, on board

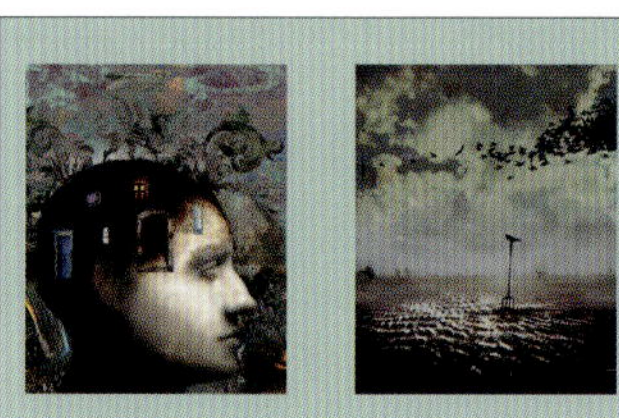

96
Thirteen Phantasms
Edgewood Press - 2000
graphite, digital

97
Winter Migration
Philadelphia Inquirer - 2002
graphite, digital

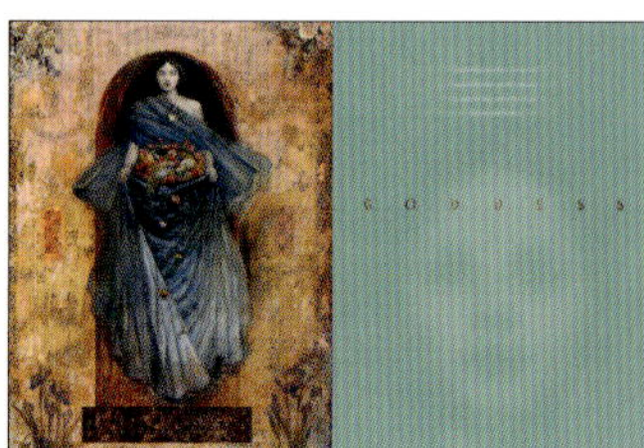

98
Blessings
Project Open Hand Poster - 1995
graphite, collage, acrylic, oil, on board

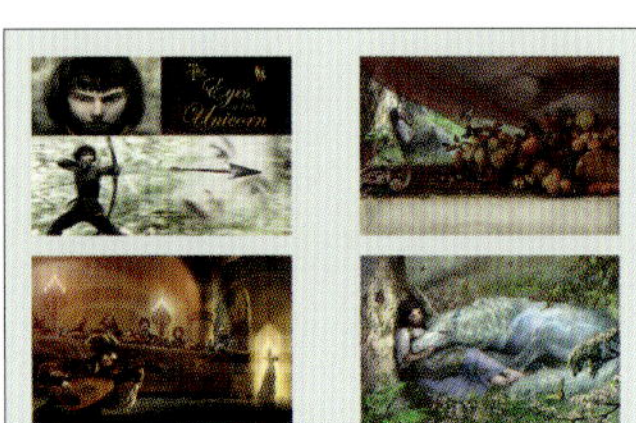

108-109
Spreads from The Eyes of the Unicorn
clockwise from upper left:
The Arrow Flies
The Apparition
Bliss
The Minstrel
The Eyes of the Unicorn
Holiday House - 2007
graphite, digital

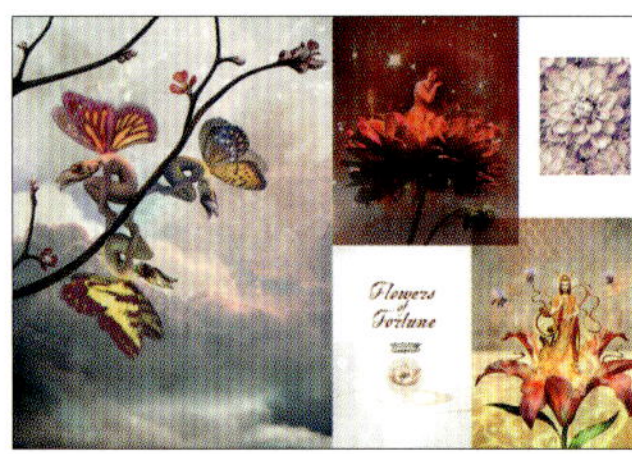

110-111
clockwise from left:
Gracing the Dawn
Red Star
Blooming Princess
Bee Prosperity
Flowers of Fortune Art Card Game - 2011
digital

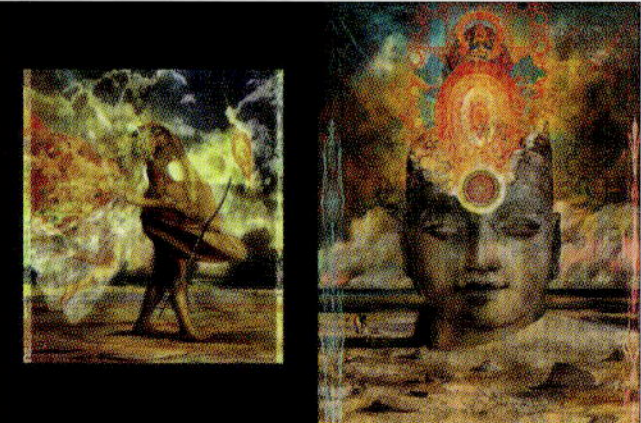

112-113
Laguna College of Art and Design Posters
Ignite Thy Passion
1999
graphite, digital
Expand Your Vision
1998
graphite, digital

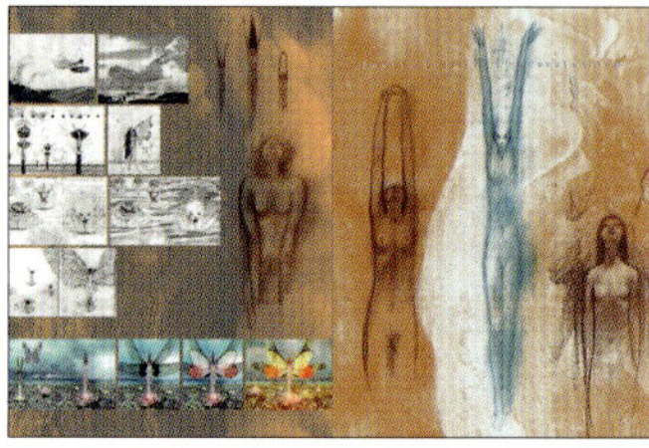

114-115
Sketches and art evolution for Faerie Lotus
2004
graphite, digital

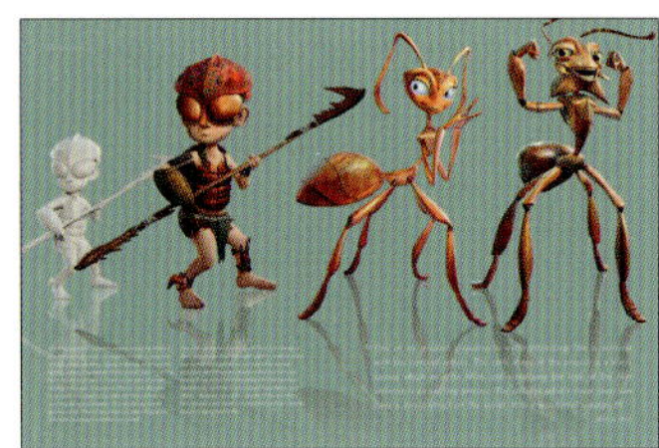

124-125
Texture and color designs for Buck Lewis characters on The Ant Bully
2004
digital
© Warner Bros.

126-127
Storyboards and Ant Mother shrine for The Ant Bully
2004
digital
© Warner Bros.

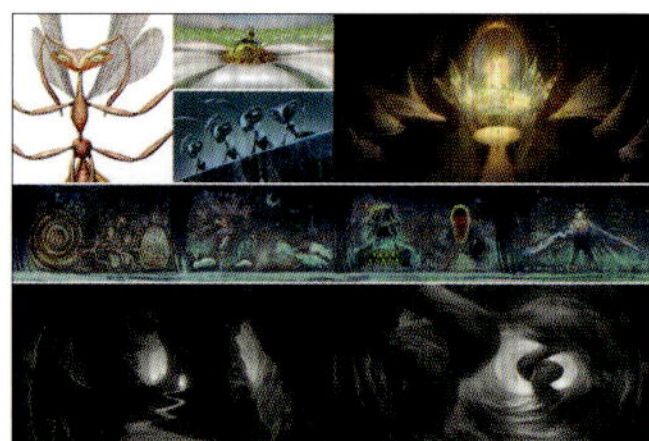

128-129
Texture and color designs, storyboards, color script, environments for The Ant Bully
2004
digital
© Warner Bros.

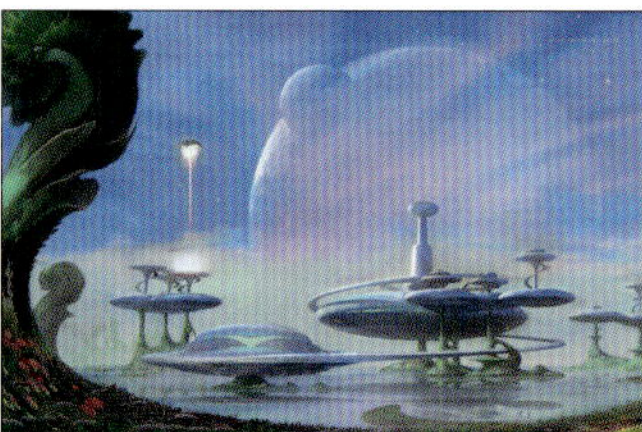

130-131
Concept Designs for Escape from Planet Earth
Co-designed with Fred Gambino
2007
digital
© Rainmaker Entertainment

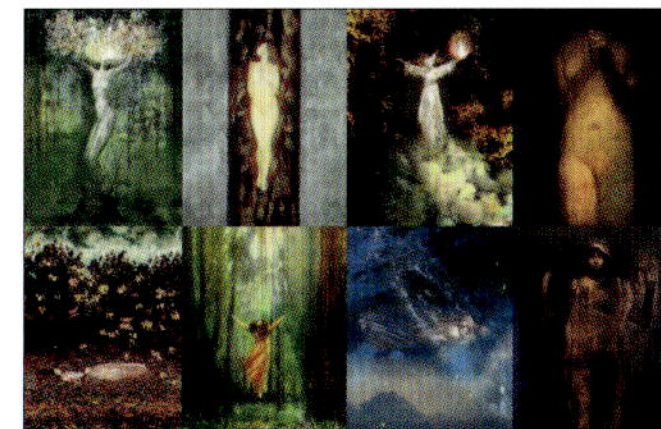

100
Divinus
Laguna College of Art and Design – 1995
LuLu
San Francisco Opera Poster - 1989
Enchantment
Del Ray Publisher – 2000
Messenger
Holiday House – 2005

101
The Visitor/Illuminare
HarperCollins – 2009
Grace
Personal – 1989
4'x4' graphite, acrylic, oil, polyurethane, wood
Cosmic Mother
Personal – 2009
Chastity
Personal – 1989
4'x7' graphite, acrylic, oil, polyurethane, wood

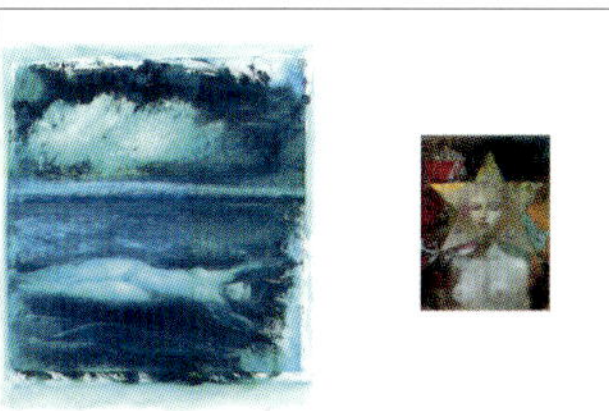

102
Blue Nude
Personal – 2009
monoprint, oil, on paper

103
Star Girl
Personal – 2001
graphite, digital

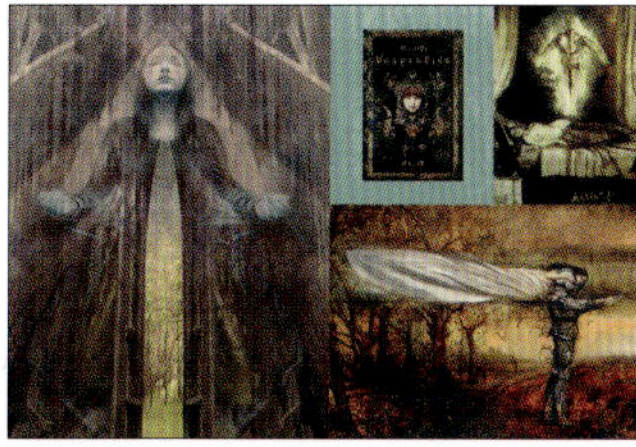

104
Astral Vespertina
Personal – 2012
graphite, digital

105
The Visions of Vespertina
CD cover and booklet for music/art project with Michelle Barnes – 1999
vintage book, oil, photograph, gold leaf, digital

Knight Dream
The Visions of Vespertina – 1999
Polaroid, collage, digital
model: Lisa Tate

Knightingale
The Visions of Vespertina – 1999
graphite, collage, acrylic, oil, tape, on board, digital
model: Lisa Tate

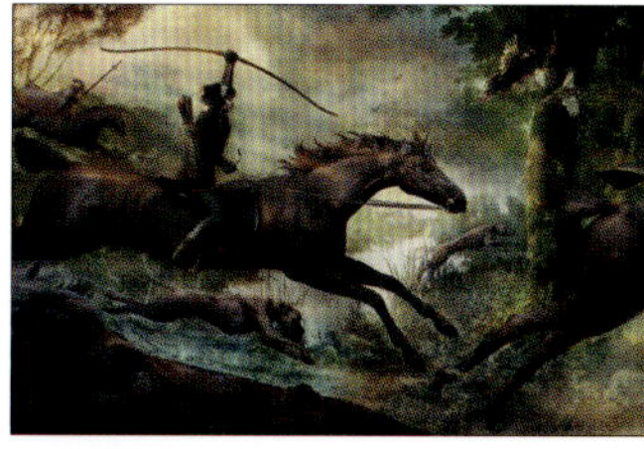

106-107
The Hunt
The Eyes of the Unicorn
Holiday House – 2007
graphite, digital

Vespertina

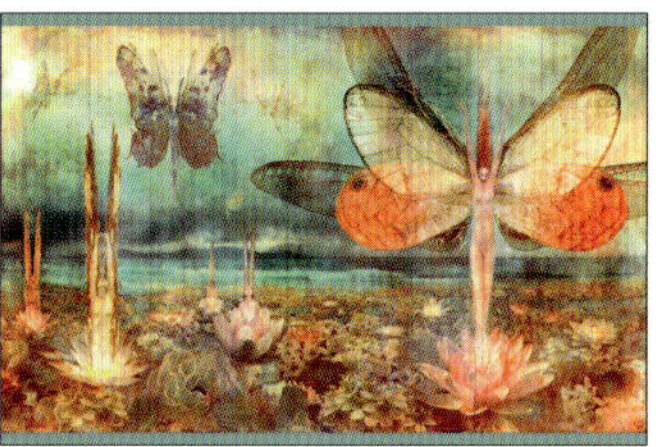

116-117
Faerie Lotus
Laguna College of Art and Design – 2004
graphite, digital

118-119
The Wave
Concept design for
The Voyage of the Dawn Treader – 2008
digital
© New Line Cinema

Greg Spalenka film reel

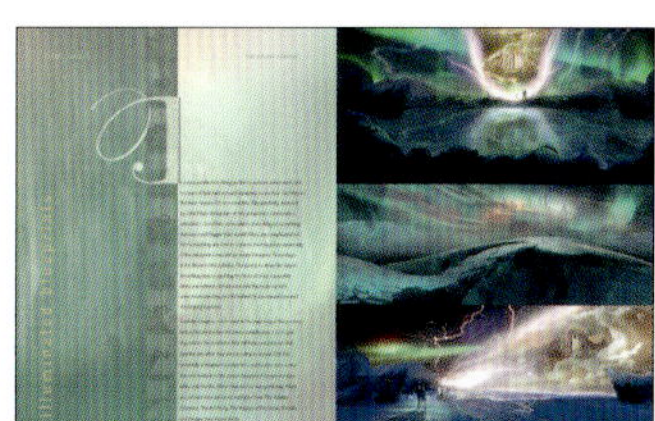

121
Concept designs for The Golden Compass
2006
digital
© New Line Cinema

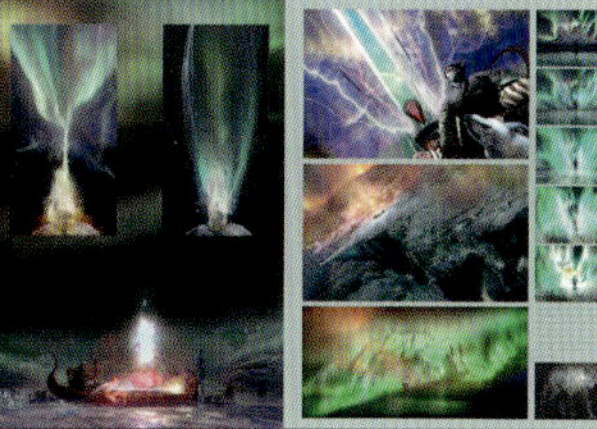

122-123
The Golden Compass
2006
digital
© New Line Cinema

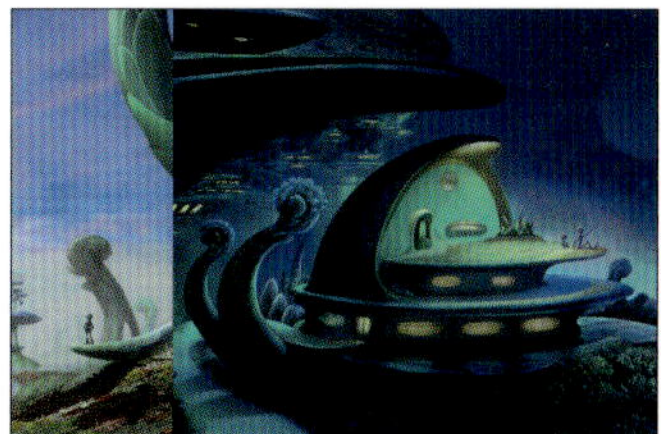

132-133
Concept designs for
Escape from Planet Earth
2007
digital
© Rainmaker Entertainment

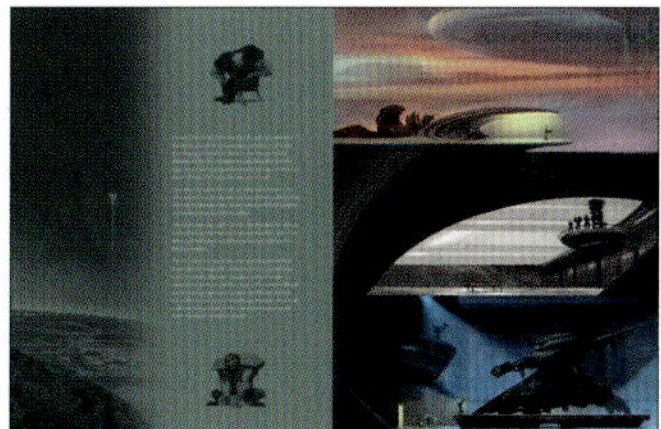

134-135
Concept designs for
Escape from Planet Earth
Alien gun design with Ian Miller
2007
digital
© Rainmaker Entertainment

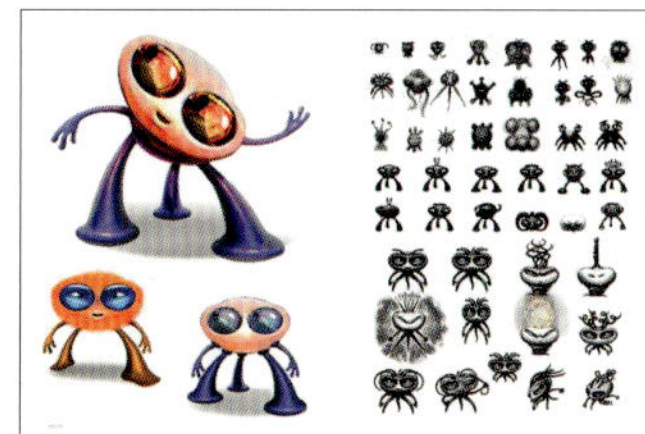

136-137
Character designs for
Escape from Planet Earth
2007
digital
© Rainmaker Entertainment

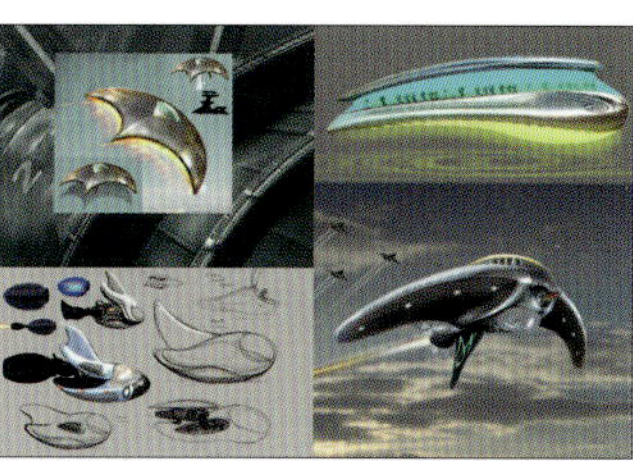

138-139
Concept designs for
Escape from Planet Earth
2007
digital
© Rainmaker Entertainment

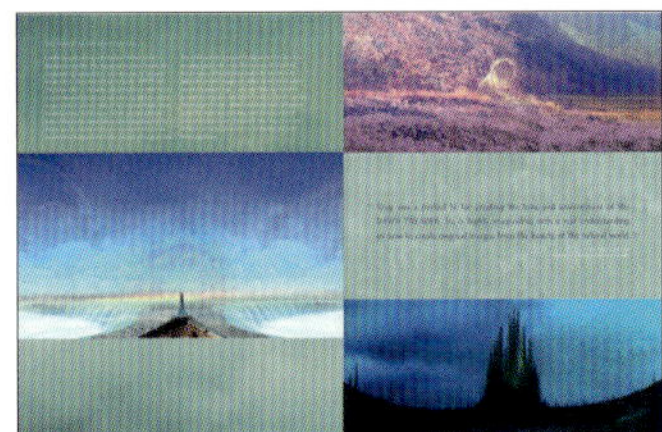

140-141
Concept designs for
The Voyage of the Dawn Treader
2006
digital
© Fox 2000 Pictures

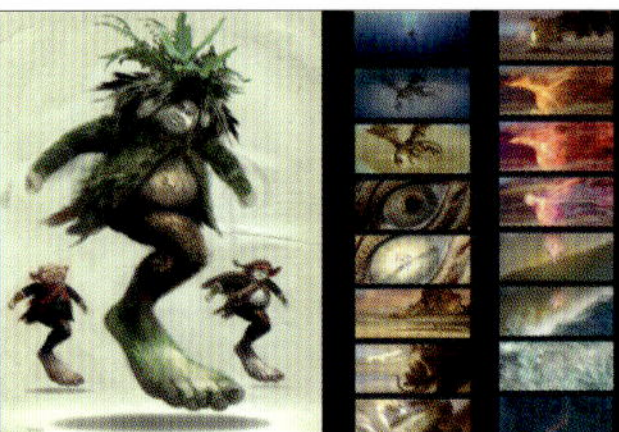

142-143
Dufflepod designs, storyboards for
The Voyage of the Dawn Treader
2006
digital
© Fox 2000 Pictures

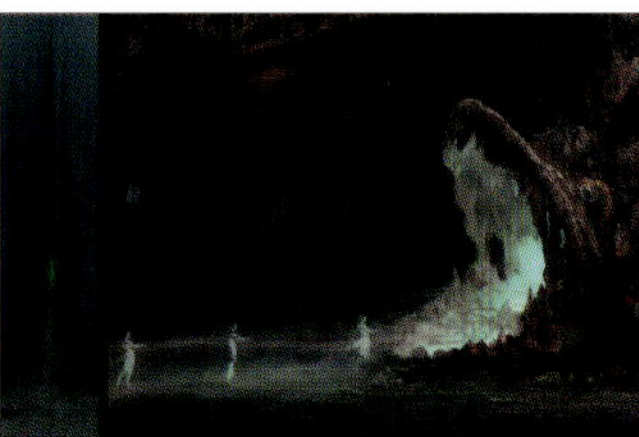

144-145
Concept designs for
The Voyage of the Dawn Treader
2006
digital
© Fox 2000 Pictures

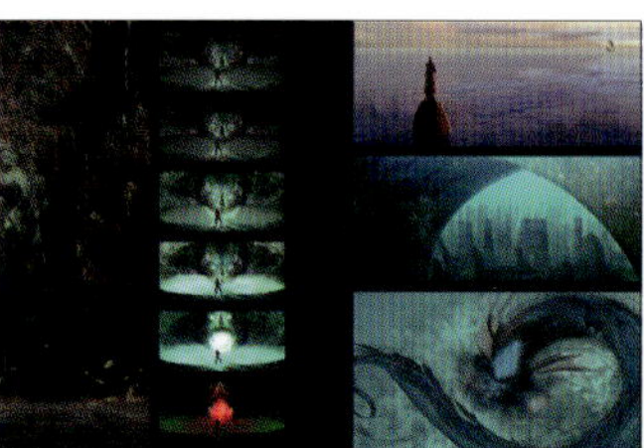

146-147
Storyboard and environment design for
The Voyage of the Dawn Treader
2006
digital
© Fox 2000 Pictures

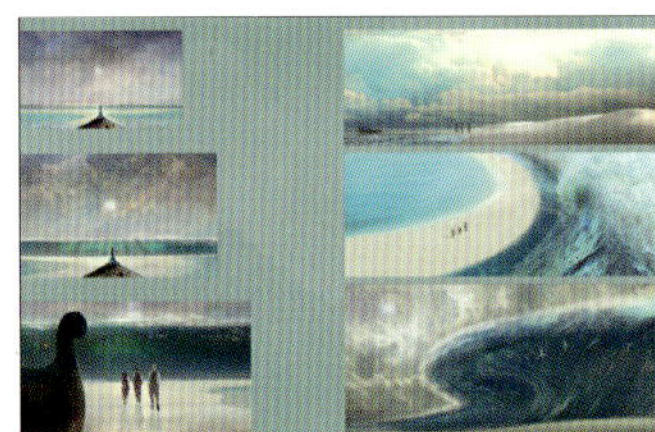

148-149
Concept Designs for
The Voyage of the Dawn Treader
2006
digital
© Fox 2000 Pictures

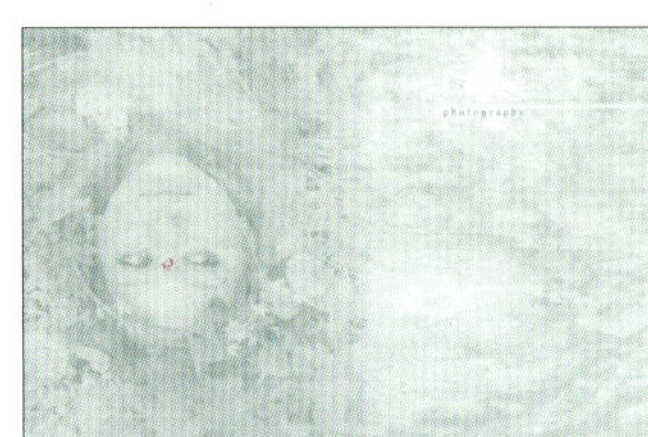

150-151
Gwen in Green
Roxana Illuminated Perfume - 2013
digital

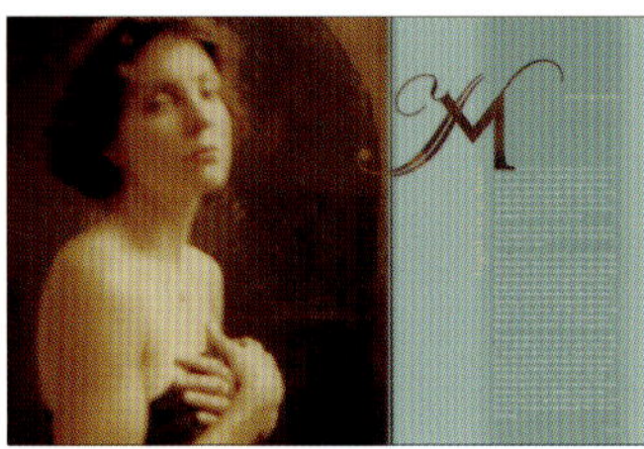

152-153
Victoria
Personal - 1989
Polaroid

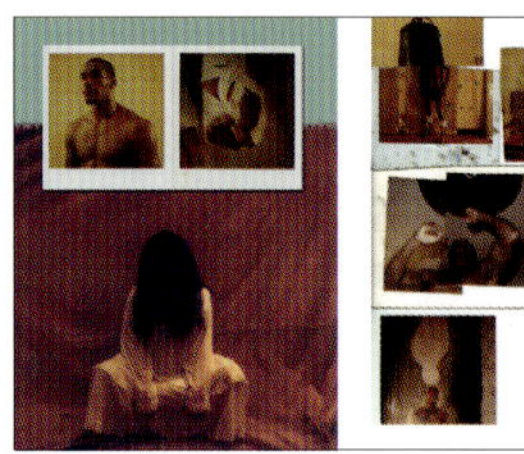

154
Contender
Personal - 1989
Polaroid

Wrapped
Personal - 1989
Polaroid

Dancer
Personal - 1988
Polaroid

155
Sugar Ray Leonard
Polaroid reference for
Sports Illustrated article - 1989

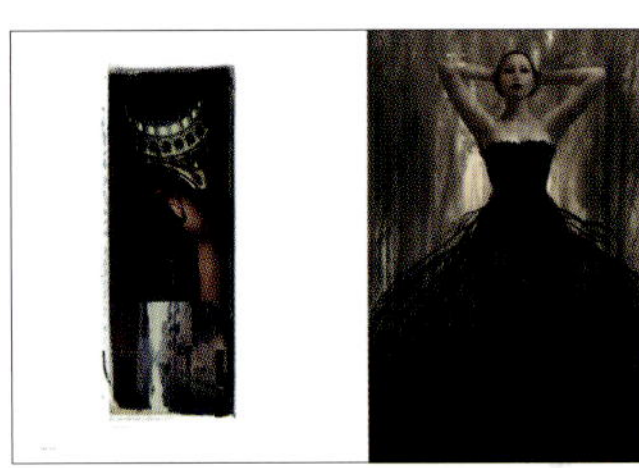

156
Dome Noir
Personal - 1983
Polaroid

Dark Madonna
Personal - 1984
Polaroid
model: The Q

Venice
Personal - 1983
Polaroid

157
Noir Woods
Roxana Illuminated Perfume - 2013
digital

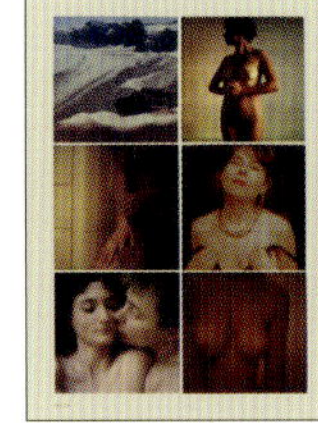

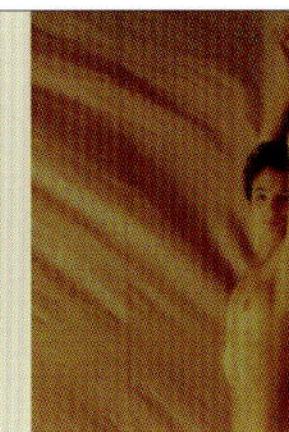

158
LEFT TO RIGHT
Zermot
Personal - 1984
Polaroid
model: The Q

Majorca
Personal - 1984
Polaroid
model: The Q

Feminine Touch
Personal - 1984
Polaroid
model: The Q

Exotic Muse
1989
Polaroid
model: Michelle Barnes

Lovers
Personal - 1988
Polaroid

Tender
Personal - 1988
Polaroid

159
Glowing Goddess
Personal - 1986
Polaroid

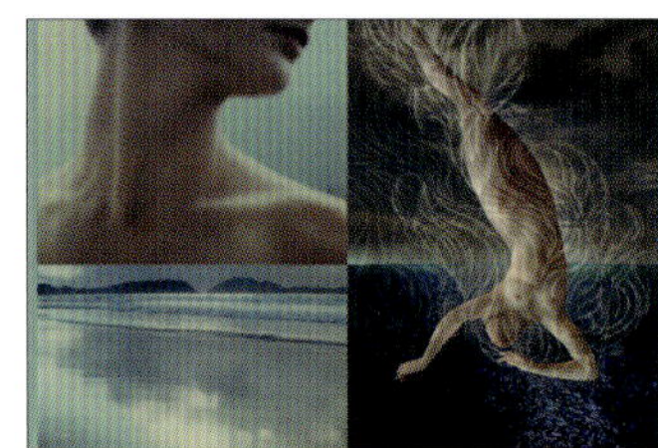

160
Morning Light
Personal - 1984
Polaroid

Morning Light, Cabo Frio
Personal - 1988
Polaroid

161
Mystic Current
Personal - 1986
digital
model: Jessica Lough

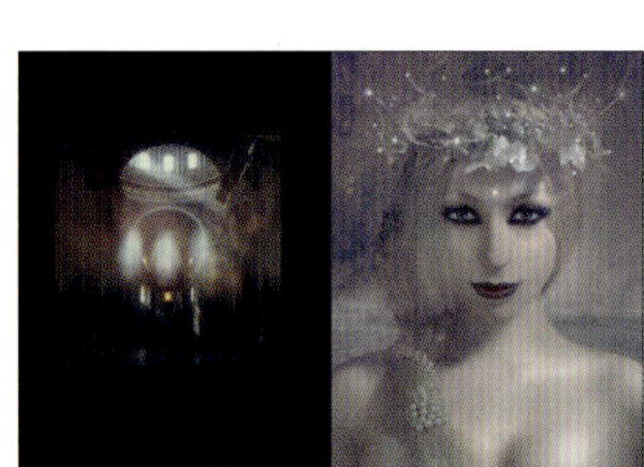

162
Divine Light
Personal - 1984
Polaroid

163
Stella Luna
Roxana Illuminated Perfume - 2014
digital

Alternative covers for
The Art of Greg Spalenka

THE ART OF GREG SPALENKA

ART & WORDS

Greg Spalenka

DESIGN

Jeff Burne & Greg Spalenka

SPECIAL ACKNOWLEDGEMENTS

I am blessed and grateful for the friendship of Jeff Burne and his awesome graphic design expertise with this book, Roxana Villa for her loving support and wisdom, Nick Landau, Vivian Cheung, Katy Wild, Jo Boylet, and everyone at Titan who helped make this project a reality. Thanks to Kevin Burne for his editing support. To all the artists that have filled me with inspiration, the art directors/editors/producers that believed in me, and the muses that are the art on these pages, I thank you. Hugs to David and Margie Spalenka, Dr. Paulette Shafranski, MaryAnn Pocapalia, Matt Mahurin, Lenny Scarola, Michelle Barnes. I am also grateful for the grace and guidance of Paramahansa Yogananda and bow to all who have accompanied me through this creative journey.

Spalenka.com ArtistAsBrand.com

The Art of Greg Spalenka
Standard ISBN 9781781168844
Limited ISBN 9781783294824

Published by
Titan Books
A division of Titan Publishing Group Ltd.
144 Southwark St, London SE1 0UP

First edition: June 2014
10 9 8 7 6 5 4 3 2 1

A CIP catalogue record for this title is available from the British Library.

Printed and bound in China.

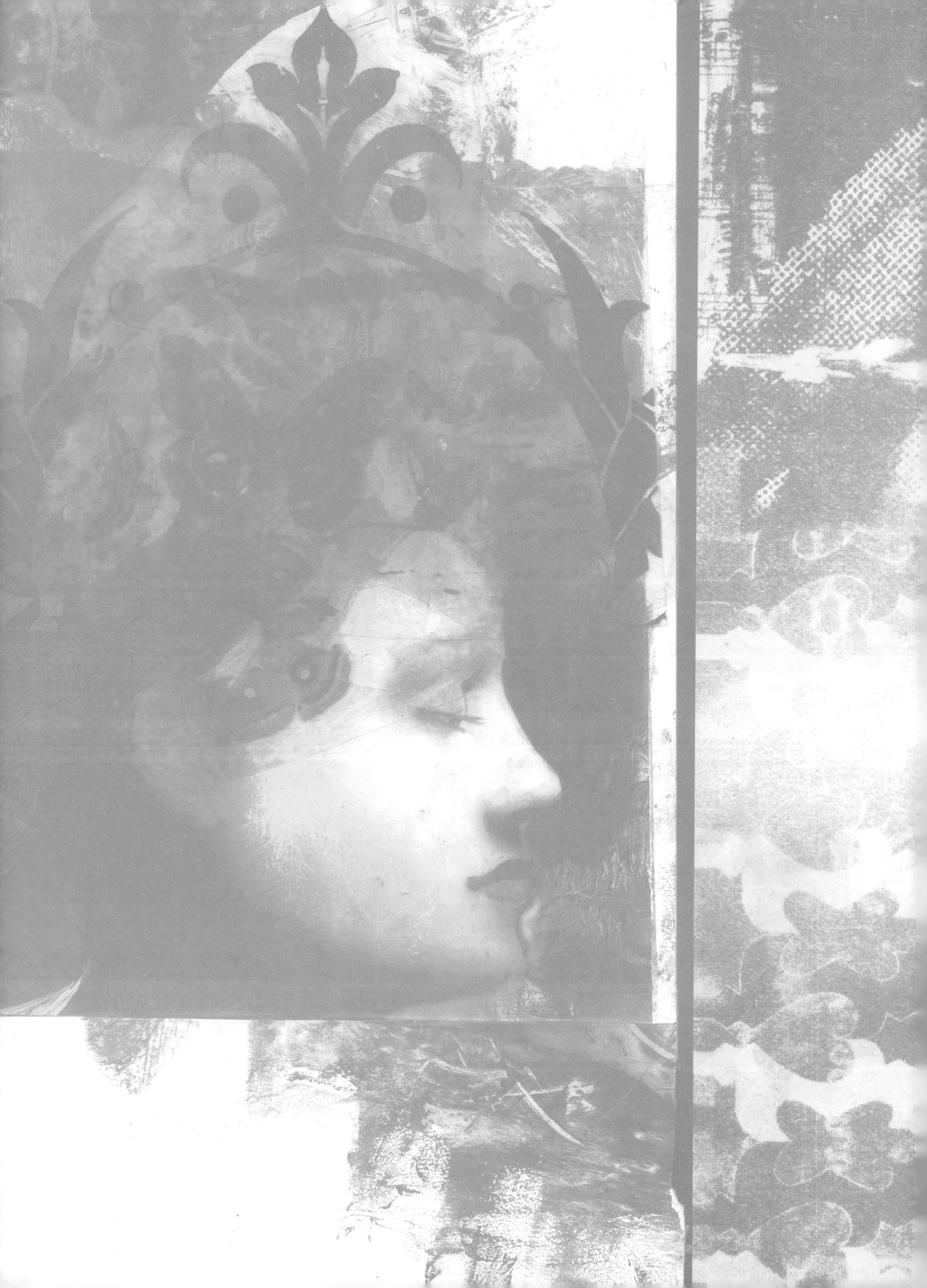